ADMINISTRATIVE LAW

Second Edition

Jack M. Beermann
Professor of Law, Boston University School of Law

The *Emanuel Law Outlines* Series

PUBLISHERS

76 Ninth Avenue, New York, NY 10011
http://lawschool.aspenpublishers.com

Aspen Publishers
Attn: Permissions Department
76 Ninth Avenue
New York, NY 10011

Printed in the United States of America.

1 2 3 4 5 6 7 8 9 0

ISBN 0-7355-5814-0

This book is intended as a general review of a legal subject. It is not intended as a source for advice for the solution of legal matters or problems. For advice on legal matters, the reader should consult an attorney.

Siegel's, Emanuel, the judge logo, Law in a Flash and design, Crunch Time and design, Strategies & Tactics and design, and The Professor Series are registered trademarks of Aspen Publishers.

About Aspen Publishers

Aspen Publishers, headquartered in New York City, is a leading information provider for attorneys, business professionals, and law students. Written by preeminent authorities, our products consist of analytical and practical information covering both U.S. and international topics. We publish in the full range of formats, including updated manuals, books, periodicals, CDs, and online products.

Our proprietary content is complemented by 2,500 legal databases, containing over 11 million documents, available through our Loislaw division. Aspen Publishers also offers a wide range of topical legal and business databases linked to Loislaw's primary material. Our mission is to provide accurate, timely, and authoritative content in easily accessible formats, supported by unmatched customer care.

To order any Aspen Publishers title, go to *http://lawschool.aspenpublishers.com* or call 1-800-638-8437.

To reinstate your manual update service, call 1-800-638-8437.

For more information on Loislaw products, go to *www.loislaw.com* or call 1-800-364-2512.

For Customer Care issues, e-mail *CustomerCare@aspenpublishers.com*; call 1-800-234-1660; or fax 1-800-901-9075.

Aspen Publishers
a Wolters Kluwer business

To the memory of Arthur H. Beermann, the senior partner in the family firm

Abbreviations Used in Text

FEDERAL STATUTES

APA	Administrative Procedure Act
CAA	Clean Air Act
CEA	Commodity Exchange Act
FACA	Federal Advisory Committee Act
FCA	Federal Communications Act
FIFRA	Federal Insecticide, Fungicide, and Rodenticide Act
FOIA	Freedom of Information Act
FTC Act	Federal Trade Commission Act of 1914
FTCA	Federal Torts Claims Act
ICA	Interstate Commerce Act
NEPA	National Environmental Policy Act
NIRA	National Industrial Recovery Act
OSH Act	Occupational Safety and Health Act
PRA	Paperwork Reduction Act of 1980

FEDERAL AGENCIES

BIA	Bureau of Indian Affairs
CFTC	Commodity Futures Trading Commission
CAB	Civil Aeronautics Board
CIA	Central Intelligence Agency
EPA	Environmental Protection Agency
FAA	Federal Aviation Administration
FBI	Federal Bureau of Investigation
FCC	Federal Communications Commission
FDA	Food and Drug Administration
FDIC	Federal Deposit Insurance Corporation
FEC	Federal Election Commission
FPC	Federal Power Commission
FTC	Federal Trade Commission
HHS	Department of Health and Human Services
ICC	Interstate Commerce Commission
INS	Immigration and Naturalization Service
IRS	Internal Revenue Service
ITC	International Trade Commission
NHTSA	National Highway Transportation and Safety Administration
NLRB	National Labor Relations Board
NRC	Nuclear Regulatory Commission
OIRA	Office of Information and Regulatory Affairs
OMB	Office of Management and Budget
OSHA	Occupational Safety and Health Administration

SEC	Securities and Exchange Commission
SSA	Social Security Administration
USDA	United States Department of Agriculture

TERMS, NONGOVERNMENTAL GROUPS, AND AGENCY PROGRAMS

AFDC	Aid to Families with Dependent Children
ALJ	Administrative Law Judge
AMA	American Medical Association
ATA	American Trucking Association
CMA	Chocolate Manufacturers Association
EDF	Environmental Defense Fund
EIS	Environmental Impact Statement
INPO	Institute for Nuclear Power Operations
NAAQS	National Ambient Air Quality Standards
NPRM	Notice of Proposed Rulemaking
WIC	Women, Infants, and Children

Summary of Contents

Table of Contents

CHAPTER 1

INTRODUCTION TO STUDYING ADMINISTRATIVE LAW

CHAPTER 2

SEPARATION OF POWERS AND DISTRIBUTION OF ADMINISTRATIVE POWER

CHAPTER 3
THE AVAILABILITY OF JUDICIAL REVIEW OF ADMINISTRATIVE DECISIONS

CHAPTER 4

JUDICIAL REVIEW OF ADMINISTRATIVE DECISIONS

CHAPTER 5

AGENCY CHOICE OF POLICYMAKING MODE

CHAPTER 6
APA RULEMAKING PROCEDURES

CHAPTER **7**

AGENCY ADJUDICATION AND DUE PROCESS

CHAPTER 8

SUBSTANTIVE POLICYMAKING IN AGENCIES

CHAPTER 9

AGENCY ENFORCEMENT AND LICENSING

Chapter 10
AGENCY INFORMATION GATHERING

CHAPTER 11

PRIVATE ENFORCEMENT OF REGULATORY NORMS AND PREEMPTION

CHAPTER 12
LIABILITY OF AGENCIES AND OFFICIALS

Preface

Thank you very much for choosing this *Emanuel Law Outline*. I hope it will be of great help in your study of Administrative Law.

The growth of government regulation has made Administrative Law one of the central elements in the law school curriculum. Many students worry about taking Administrative Law because they have heard it is complex and challenging. This book is designed to present Administrative Law as an interesting, relevant, and accessible subject matter that will enrich your studies and make you more aware of the importance of administrative agencies to our government and our daily lives.

This *Emanuel Law Outline* is not intended to substitute either for your class materials or for careful attention to class discussion. However, it can serve as a useful supplement to clarify areas of uncertainty and to deepen understanding of important issues. Whether you are pondering the nagging separation of powers issues lurking behind almost every issue in Administrative Law or searching for the meaning of the applicable provision of the APA, I believe you will find this book a useful tool.

Here are some of the book's special features:

- **Casebook Correlation Chart**: This chart, following this Preface, correlates each section of the outline with the pages covering the same topic in the five leading Administrative Law casebooks.

- **Capsule Summary**: This is a 29-page summary of the key concepts of Administrative Law, specially designed for use in the week or so before your final exam.

- **Quiz Yourself**: At the end of each chapter are short-answer questions that allow you to test yourself on the key concepts and issues in Administrative Law.

- **Exam Tips**: These tips, at the end of every chapter, alert you to what issues tend to come up on Administrative Law exams. The tips also suggest how you should approach the questions from the perspective of a long-time teacher of Administrative Law—me!

- **Glossary**: A glossary of important Administrative Law terms located near the end of this book will help ensure that you get the most out of Administrative Law and this book.

This book is intended for use throughout the semester and for exam preparation. Here are some suggestions about how to use it as a valuable supplement to reviewing your casebook, class notes, and other course materials.

1. You can use this book to prepare in advance for the next day's class. After you read the assignment in your casebook, look for the corresponding pages in the *Casebook Correlation Chart* and then read the pages to help strengthen your grasp of the material.

2. If you just want to read up on a particular case, look for the case name in the table of cases at the back of this book and focus on the sections of this book that discuss that case. This book contains extended discussions of major cases.

3. If you are going to make your own outline for the course, this book can help provide a structure for that outline, and you may use parts of the book to supplement what you have put into your outline from your notes and the casebook.

4. At the end of each unit in your course, you may want to use the *Quiz Yourself* questions in the appropriate chapters to be sure that you have a good grasp of the important parts of the unit. At the end of the course, you may use the sample exam questions and answers at the end of the book to

make sure you have a good understanding of the course as a whole. It often helps to take at least one sample exam under exam-like conditions and exchange papers with a classmate to critique and help each other prepare for the exam.

5. When you begin studying for the exam, you might want to read through the *Capsule Summary*. This will help structure your studying and give you an idea of where you feel you need to focus in preparing for the exam.

6. On the day before the exam, you may want to read through the *Exam Tips* in each chapter and also do some of the *Quiz Yourself* questions to get ready for writing the exam.

I want to acknowledge some people who helped me complete this book. Thanks to Dean Ronald Cass of Boston University School of Law for supporting this project; Dean Teree Foster of DePaul University College of Law for supporting this project while I was a visitor there; Ronald Cass and Colin Diver, my co-authors on our Administrative Law casebook; Boston University and DePaul University research assistants including Melissa Lopes, John Mercer, Lisa Bebchick, Payam Moradian, Caroline Hoen, Judith Terek, Kristen Josefek, Melissa Connell, Courtney Worcester, and Amy Olson; Boston University students Jennifer Schweiger and Kelly Honohan for allowing me to use their exam answers in the sample exam section of this book; and most of all my students at Boston University and DePaul University whose input is present on every page of this book.

Good luck and enjoy Administrative Law! If you'd like any other publication of Aspen Publishers, you can find it at your bookstore or at http://lawschool.aspenpublishers.com.

Jack M. Beermann
Professor of Law
Boston University School of Law
beermann@bu.edu

P.S. I'd welcome your suggestions for making this book even more useful. Please email me at the above address with any suggestions or comments.

Casebook Correlation Chart

(**Note:** general sections of the outline are omitted for this chart. **NC** = not directly covered by this casebook.)

Emanuel's Administrative Law Outline *(by chapter and section heading)*	Breyer, Stewart, Sunstein, & Vermeule: *Administrative Law and Regulatory Policy: Problems, Text, and Cases* (6th Ed., 2006)	Cass, Diver, & Beermann: *Administrative Law: Cases and Materials* (5th Ed., 2006)	Funk, Shapiro, & Weaver: *Administrative Procedure and Practice: Problems and Cases* (3d Ed., 2006)	Schwartz, Corrada, & Brown: *Administrative Law: A Casebook* (6th Ed., 2006)	Strauss, Rakoff, & Farina: *Gellhon and Byse's Administrative Law* (10th Ed., 2003)
CHAPTER 1 **INTRODUCTION TO STUDYING ADMINISTRATIVE LAW**					
I. What Is Administrative Law?	2-3	1-6	5-12	1-5	7-13
II. The Origins and Roles of Administrative Agencies	16-30	6-14	5-12	5-18, 36-51	13-26
III. The Functions of Administrative Agencies	11-13	1-6	12-22	12-32	NC
IV. Public Interest and Public Choice Explanations of Regulation and the Structure of Administrative Agencies	3-11	6-10	56-61	56-60	20, 25-26, 31-32, 466
CHAPTER 2 **SEPARATION OF POWERS AND DISTRIBUTION OF ADMINISTRATIVE POWER**					
I. The Nondelegation Doctrine	36-75	16-38, 53, 125-126, 829	522-539	54-73	38-45, 60, 66-83
II. Congressional Control of Administrative Agencies	83-102	15-64	552-561	53-89	176-237
III. Executive Control of Administrative Agencies	102-121	65-103	552-561	28-36	138-176
IV. Adjudication within Administrative Agencies	122-140	503-513	194-283	89-126	118-138
CHAPTER 3 **THE AVAILABILITY OF JUDICIAL REVIEW OF ADMINISTRATIVE DECISIONS**					
I. Jurisdiction	747-756, 934-944	206-209	407-408	171-176, 616-627	NC
II. Reviewability	769-812	209-267	26-28, 388-389, 407-519	663-752	1181-1228
III. Standing to Secure Judicial Review	813-886	267-303	407, 411-436	596-616	1118-1181
IV. The Timing of Judicial Review: Ripeness, Exhaustion, and Mootness	887-933	303-323	409-410, 492-519	648-652	1229-1256

Emanuel's Administrative Law Outline (by chapter and section heading)	Breyer, Stewart, Sunstein, & Vermeule: *Administrative Law and Regulatory Policy: Problems, Text, and Cases* (6th Ed., 2006)	Cass, Diver, & Beermann: *Administrative Law: Cases and Materials* (5th Ed., 2006)	Funk, Shapiro, & Weaver: *Administrative Procedure and Practice: Problems and Cases* (3d Ed., 2006)	Schwartz, Corrada, & Brown: *Administrative Law: A Casebook* (6th Ed., 2006)	Strauss, Rakoff, & Farina: *Gellhon and Byse's Administrative Law* (10th Ed., 2003)
CHAPTER 4 **JUDICIAL REVIEW OF ADMINISTRATIVE DECISIONS**					
I. Standards of Judicial Review under the APA	191	109-119	282-285	575-595	902-908
II. Review of Questions of Fact after Agency Adjudication: The Substantial Evidence Test	192-221	160-187	282-297	670-671	936-978
III. De Novo Review of Questions of Fact	NC	159-198	297, 308	NC	735
IV. Review of Questions of Law	228-301	124-158	298-308	670-671	978-1098
V. Review of Questions of Policy	347-403	159-198	308-318	663-737	1014-1015, 1037-1040
VI. Remedies on Judicial Review	NC	201-204	409-410, 492-503	111-119, 628-648	496-497, 602, 606, 608, 884-901, 1099-1100, 1107-1117
CHAPTER 5 **AGENCY CHOICE OF POLICYMAKING MODE**					
I. Constitutional Constraints on Choice of Policymaking Mode	136-137, 480-487	335-336	250-283	347-411	238-276, 837-838
II. Choice of Policymaking Procedure	488-514	333-376	319-401	262-296	493-497, 565-574
III. Informal Policymaking	591-604	377-378	351-352	296-303	484-556, 834-835
CHAPTER 6 **APA RULEMAKING PROCEDURES**					
I. APA §553 Informal ("Notice and Comment") Rulemaking Procedures	488-513, 520-573	174-188, 379-386, 421-435, 455, 797-798	96-126	262-266	484-485, 498-540, 666-678
II. Formal Rulemaking Procedures: The Additional Requirements of APA §§556 and 557	514-520	377-379	90-95, 126-134	287-289, 463, 480, 502, 521-522, 526, 554, 564, 532-533	269-271, 329-331, 401
III. The Negotiated Rulemaking Act	570-574	455-467	135-143	313-319	627-638
IV. Direct Final Rulemaking	NC	454-455	NC	NC	NC

Emanuel's Administrative Law Outline *(by chapter and section heading)*	**Breyer, Stewart, Sunstein, & Vermeule:** *Administrative Law and Regulatory Policy: Problems, Text, and Cases* (6th Ed., 2006)	Cass, Diver, & Beermann: *Administrative Law: Cases and Materials* (5th Ed., 2006)	**Funk, Shapiro, & Weaver:** *Administrative Procedure and Practice: Problems and Cases* (3d Ed., 2006)	**Schwartz, Corrada, & Brown:** *Administrative Law: A Casebook* (6th Ed., 2006)	**Strauss, Rakoff, & Farina:** *Gellhon and Byse's Administrative Law* (10th Ed., 2003)
CHAPTER 7 AGENCY ADJUDICATION AND DUE PROCESS					
I. Constitutional Authority for Agency Adjudication	122-140	503-513	522-533	89-100	118-138
II. Due Process and the Adjudicatory Hearing	605-680	514-582	250-283	347-432	414-417, 420-421, 429, 783-791, 800-823, 839-851
III. Statutory Hearing Rights	633-634	583-615	334-336	578-590	592-594, 802, 1232
CHAPTER 8 SUBSTANTIVE POLICYMAKING IN AGENCIES					
I. Permissible Considerations in Agency Policymaking	495-513	375-376	349-355	NC	690-691
II. Cost-Benefit Analysis	168-176, 307-314	469-487	NC	242-249	645-647
III. Impact Statements	160-190	488-500	NC	NC	638-645
IV. Consistency and Clarity Requirements	405-478	377-378	313-314, 339-344	250-252	446-447, 556-566, 832-834, 908-936, 1088-1089
CHAPTER 9 AGENCY ENFORCEMENT AND LICENSING					
I. Prosecutorial Discretion	NC	648-658	214	NC	920-921
II. Licensing and Ratemaking	128, 222-227, 495, 591-592, 607-608, 817-818	745-826	337-338	341-347	252, 393-401, 421-422, 435, 486
CHAPTER 10 AGENCY INFORMATION GATHERING					
I. Inspections	NC	621-647	582-608	136-162	281-294, 308-312
II. Production of Information and Documents	681	647-650	599-609	127-206	294-308
III. The Paperwork Reduction Act	116-117	102	612-616	NC	292-294

Emanuel's Administrative Law Outline *(by chapter and section heading)*	**Breyer, Stewart, Sunstein, & Vermeule:** *Administrative Law and Regulatory Policy: Problems, Text, and Cases* (6th Ed., 2006)	Cass, Diver, & Beermann: *Administrative Law: Cases and Materials* (5th Ed., 2006)	**Funk, Shapiro, & Weaver:** *Administrative Procedure and Practice: Problems and Cases* (3d Ed., 2006)	**Schwartz, Corrada, & Brown:** *Administrative Law: A Casebook* (6th Ed., 2006)	**Strauss, Rakoff, & Farina:** *Gellhon and Byse's Administrative Law* (10th Ed., 2003)
CHAPTER 11 **PRIVATE ENFORCEMENT OF REGULATORY NORMS AND PREEMPTION**					
I. The Citizens' Suit	934	659-662	411-436, 444-445	656-662	1142-1144
II. The Implied Private Right of Action	NC	665-682	NC	NC	757-758
III. Alternative State Remedies and Regulatory Preemption	NC	684-697	NC	677-691	717-719, 1243-1245
CHAPTER 12 **LIABILITY OF AGENCIES AND OFFICIALS**					
I. Sovereign Immunity and Suits against Federal Agents and Agencies	747-757	703-720	NC	661-662	1107-1015, 1278-1297
II. Liability of Individual Federal Officials	766-769	725-744	449-453	661-662	1258-1275
III. Liability of State and Local Government Officials	766-769	725-744	NC	661-662	1258-1275, 1297-1302
CHAPTER 13 **FREEDOM OF INFORMATION AND OPEN MEETINGS**					
I. The Freedom of Information Act	681-689	831-867	649-690	187-189	733-766
II. Discovery from the Government in Litigation	NC	841-852	NC	202-205	739-753
III. Open Meetings Requirements	690-692	873-886	710-715	177-189, 451	762-766

Introduction: Overview of the Organization of the United States Government

The United States government has three branches:

The *legislative branch* is Congress, which is composed of the Senate and the House of Representatives. Each state has two senators. The House has 435 members who represent districts of roughly equal populations. Each house of Congress is divided into committees and subcommittees. Congress also has numerous employees who work for members, committees, or Congress as a whole, and who perform functions in aid of legislation and constituent services.

The *legislative branch* interacts with federal agencies in a large variety of ways. Committees monitor agency performance and hold hearings when an issue that concerns the committee arises. Such monitoring can result in redefining legislation, limiting or expanding agency power, or adjusting the agency's budget to register approval or disapproval with agency performance: Congressional employees, such as the comptroller general, also research and report on agency performance and can influence congressional action vis-à-vis the agencies.

The *executive branch* is headed by the President and includes departments of the government such as the departments of Labor, State, Defense, and Energy. Most agencies of the federal government are within a department. Departments are headed by secretaries who answer to the President. Some agencies, such as the Environmental Protection Agency, are not within a department and are headed by administrators who answer directly to the President. The executive branch also includes the so-called independent agencies, which are typically headed by commissioners appointed by the President with the advice and consent of the Senate. These agencies are designated by Congress as independent of the executive branch and are not within any department of the government. The President also has a large staff and many agencies exist largely to advise the President and help the President run the executive branch. These include the Office of Management and Budget (OMB), which has important regulatory supervision responsibilities:

A great deal of adjudication occurs within the executive branch, presided over by administrative law judges (ALJs). Usually, decisions of ALJs are appealable to higher agency officials — sometimes the head or heads of the agency. There are also adjudicatory bodies that function like courts of law but are actually executive branch courts whose judges do not have the protections of Article III judges.

The *judicial branch* includes the Supreme Court, which is created by Article III of the Constitution, and the lower courts that Congress has created. The principal lower courts are the United States district courts (which are trial courts) and the United States courts of appeals (which are intermediate appellate courts). The United States is divided into twelve judicial circuits, each with its own court of appeals that hears appeals from the district courts within the circuit. The courts of appeals also have original jurisdiction over many petitions for judicial review. All Article III federal judges have life tenure and compensation that cannot be reduced. There are also specialized courts such as the Tax Court and the Court of Appeals for the Federal Circuit, which hear a narrow range of cases. There are some federal courts, like the Bankruptcy Court, that are staffed by judges without Article III protections and function as adjuncts to the lower federal courts.

Figure 1 depicts the organization of the government of the United States, downloaded from *The United States Government Manual 2005/2006*, which is the official handbook of the federal governement.

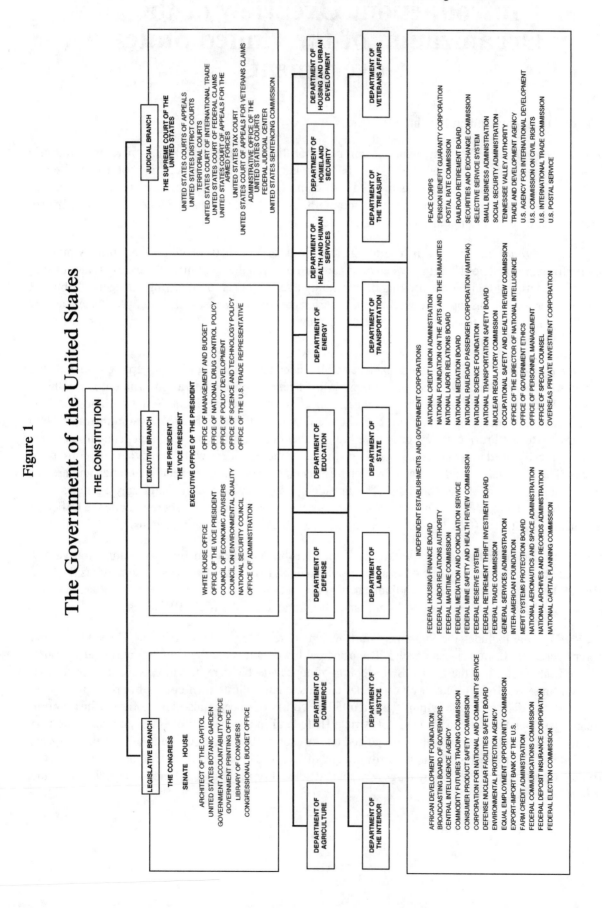

Figure 1

Capsule Summary

To maximize the usefulness of this Capsule Summary, the focus of discussion reflects the importance of material that is especially helpful for exam preparation. Thus, some levels of the outline that are discussed in the main text are not discussed here, since—while they provide important background material—they are less significant once the reader begins to prepare for the exam.

CHAPTER 1

INTRODUCTION TO STUDYING ADMINISTRATIVE LAW

I. OVERVIEW OF ADMINISTRATIVE LAW

Administrative law regulates the exercise of authority by executive officials including officials of independent agencies. [1]

A. Administrative Law Derives Mainly From Four Sources

1. The Constitution

2. The Administrative Procedure Act

3. Particular agency enabling acts

4. Administrative common law [1-2]

B. The Study of Administrative Law

In studying administrative law, the focus is on the source and limits of agency power, potential constitutional limitations on agency power, and the procedural requirements placed on the agency by the Constitution, the APA, the agency's enabling act, and any other administrative law doctrine. [2]

C. Judicial Review

Judicial review is the mechanism for enforcing procedural and substantive constraints on agency action. Thus, it is vital to be aware of whether judicial review is available, and if so, what standard of judicial review governs. [2]

D. Enforcement

Regulatory norms are enforceable by agencies and sometimes also by private parties affected by alleged violations of regulatory norms. It is important to be aware of the enforcement tools available to both sets of potential enforcers. [2]

II. THE ORIGINS AND ROLES OF ADMINISTRATIVE AGENCIES

The administrative state, as we know it, began in 1887 with the creation of the Interstate Commerce Commission, although the antecedents to the administrative state go back to the beginning of the republic. [3]

A. Structure of the Administrative State

While most federal administrative agencies are within a department of the executive branch, Congress has designated some agencies as "independent"—not within any department of the federal government and not under the supervision of the President or any cabinet officer. [3]

B. The Roles of Administrative Agencies

Administrative agencies, as the name implies, administer government programs established by Congress. [3]

III. THE FUNCTIONS OF ADMINISTRATIVE AGENCIES

Administrative agencies perform a wide variety of functions in the United States at the local, state, and federal levels. These functions include distribution of government benefits, granting of licenses and permits, and policymaking in a wide variety of regulated areas. Agencies employ a wide array of policymaking methods including rulemaking, adjudication and informal policymaking. [3]

IV. PUBLIC INTEREST AND PUBLIC CHOICE UNDERSTANDINGS OF ADMINISTRATIVE LAW

Public interest theory explains administrative policymaking and the structure of administrative agencies based on the traditional notion that agencies act to further the public good and are structured to maximize their ability to further the public good. Public choice theory, by contrast, explains regulation and the structure of agencies as products of the political process in which parties with political power enlist government coercion to achieve goals that they could not achieve in a free market. Public choice theory explains agency structure as maximizing the ability of parties with power to influence government action, rather than as structures created because of views about good policy. [4-6]

CHAPTER 2

SEPARATION OF POWERS AND DISTRIBUTION OF ADMINISTRATIVE POWER

I. THE NONDELEGATION DOCTRINE

The nondelegation doctrine prohibits Congress from delegating excessive legislative discretion to the executive branch. [9]

A. Historical Origins of the Nondelegation Doctrine

Early cases stated that the Constitution absolutely prohibited the delegation of legislative authority from Congress to the executive branch. Delegations of discretionary authority to the executive branch were permissible so long as Congress made the legislative decisions and the executive branch merely "filled up the details." The discretion exercised by executive officials was not legislative but rather was discretion inherent in execution of the laws. [9]

B. The Intelligible Principle Test

In *J.W. Hampton, Jr. & Co. v. United States*, 276 U.S. 394 (1928), the Court stated that a delegation is permissible when Congress "lay[s] down by legislative act an intelligible principle to which the person or body authorized to fix such rates is directed to conform." The "intelligible principle" standard remains the test for determining whether Congress has delegated too much legislative discretion to the executive branch. [9-10]

C. Delegation During the New Deal

The Supreme Court greeted New Deal legislation with a great deal of skepticism, and in addition to many decisions invalidating state and federal legislation on other grounds, it struck down three federal statutory provisions on two nondelegation grounds. First, the legislation granted broad enforcement powers without specifying when enforcement was required. *See Panama Refining Co. v. Ryan*, 293 U.S. 388 (1935). Second, power was sometimes delegated to private groups, such as trade associations. *See Carter v. Carter Coal Co.*, 298 U.S. 238 (1936). Each of these features was held unconstitutional. [10]

D. The Return to a Lenient Nondelegation Doctrine

Beginning in the 1940s and continuing to the present time, the Court has been very lenient in nondelegation cases, requiring only a minimally intelligible principle for a statute to withstand nondelegation attack. Even though the Court continues to evaluate challenges to delegations on the "intelligible principle" standard, the Court always manages to find sufficient legislative guidance to withstand attack, even in very general legislative instructions and goals. [10-11]

E. *Benzene* and Nondelegation

A recent hint of a strict nondelegation doctrine was in the Benzene case, in which both the plurality and concurring opinions argued that standardless prosecutorial discretion under the Occupational Safety and Health Act (OSH Act) created nondelegation problems. *See Industrial Union Department, AFL-CIO v. American Petroleum Institute (The Benzene Cases)*, 448 U.S. 607 (1980). Justice Stevens's plurality opinion relied upon the nondelegation doctrine to limit the Occupational Safety and Health Administration's (OSHA) authority to prescribe occupational health and safety standards to situations in which a substantial health or safety risk has rendered a workplace "unsafe." Justice Rehnquist's *Benzene* concurrence went further, arguing that the statute violated the nondelegation doctrine because it failed to specify when the agency was required to pursue the goal of a virtually risk-free workplace. Justice Rehnquist's opinion argued that the Court should reinvigorate the nondelegation doctrine because it serves the three related goals of (1) forcing Congress, the representative branch of government, to make important policy choices; (2) increasing the guidance under which agencies act;, and (3) facilitating judicial review by requiring more definite statutory standards against which courts can measure administrative decisions. [11]

F. Attempted Revival of the Nondelegation Doctrine: *Whitman v. American Trucking Associations, Inc.*

Since the *Benzene* case, the Court has rejected several delegation challenges. In *American Trucking Associations, Inc. v. U.S. Environmental Protection Agency*, 175 F.3d 1027 (D.C. Cir. 1999), the D.C. Circuit found a violation of the nondelegation doctrine not so much because the statute lacked an intelligible principle but rather because EPA had not adopted an intelligible principle to confine its own discretion. The Supreme Court reversed, reaffirming the intelligible principle test and rejecting the idea that an agency can cure a delegation violation with its own limiting construction. The Court observed that under the D.C. Circuit's analysis, leaving it to the agency to decide on a limiting construction should itself be a nondelegation violation. *See Whitman v. American Trucking Associations, Inc.*, 531 U.S. 457 (2001). [12-13]

II. CONGRESSIONAL CONTROL OF ADMINISTRATIVE AGENCIES

A. Congressional Influence

Members of Congress attempt to influence agencies through formal and informal means. These include numerous informal contacts, influence over appointments to agencies, and, more formally, controlling agency funding, statutorily restricting agency action, and statutorily overruling regulations. Congress also attempts to increase its influence on agency action by creating independent agencies that are less subject to presidential control. [13]

B. The Legislative Veto and Review of Regulations

Until the Supreme Court held it unconstitutional, the legislative veto was an important device used by Congress to control agency action. Under legislative veto provisions of many enabling acts, Congress could, without presentment to the President, reject agency action (usually regulations). This could be done, depending on the particular provision, by a vote of both houses of Congress, by one house of Congress, or in some cases, even by a single congressional committee. In *Immigration and Naturalization Service v. Chadha*, 462 U.S. 919 (1983), the Supreme Court held a one-house legislative veto unconstitutional on the grounds that the one-house veto violated the bicameralism and presentment requirements of the Constitution. Bicameralism and presentment apply to all congressional actions that affect the legal rights and duties of persons outside the legislative branch. Two-house vetoes are also unconstitutional because they violate the requirement that legislation be presented to the President. [13-14]

C. Congressional Involvement in Appointment and Removal of Executive Officials

1. **Appointments:** The Appointments Clause of the Constitution provides for presidential appointment, with Senate confirmation, of officers of the United States. The clause allows Congress to specify that inferior officers may be appointed by the President alone, by heads of departments, or the courts of law. In *Buckley v. Valeo*, 424 U.S. 1 (1976), the Court held that officials appointed under a procedure not provided for in the Appointments Clause may not exercise authority under the laws of the United States. Congress, especially the Senate through its advice and consent power, exercises significant political influence over presidential appointments. [14]

2. **Removal:** Officers of the United States may not be subject to removal by congressional action, except by impeachment by the House and conviction by the Senate. Congress statutorily restricts the removal of administrative officials and Congress may delegate the removal power to an official under presidential control. For example, in *Morrison v. Olson*, 487 U.S. 654 (1988), the Court upheld the Independent Counsel Act under which a prosecutor appointed to investigate alleged wrongdoing by executive officials could be removed only by the Attorney General, and only for cause. [15]

3. **Members of Congress may not serve as administrative officials:** The Incompatibility Clause, Article I, Section 6, Clause 2 of the Constitution, forbids members of Congress from holding an executive appointment during their term in Congress. In addition to violating the In compatibility Clause, it would violate separation of powers for members of Congress to serve as administrators. [15]

III. EXECUTIVE CONTROL OF ADMINISTRATIVE AGENCIES

A. Inherent Executive Power

In *Youngstown Sheet & Tube Co. v. Sawyer*, 343 U.S. 579 (1952), the Supreme Court held that President Truman lacked inherent power, without congressional authorization, to order seizure of the nation's steel mills when they were threatened with a strike during the Korean War. In a famous concurring opinion, Justice Jackson argued that the President's power is at its greatest when acting pursuant to express or implied congressional authorization and at its weakest when acting contrary to Congress's will. Jackson argued that when the President acts with neither support nor disapproval from Congress, the President's power to act may be concurrent with Congress's, and the lack of congressional authorization does not necessarily mean that the President is going beyond executive authority. [16]

B. The Unitary Executive Theory

The unitary executive theory holds that the Constitution vests all executive power in the President, and thus any attempt by Congress to insulate officials and agencies from complete presidential control is suspect and probably unconstitutional. [16]

C. Presidential Appointment and Removal of Executive Officials

1. **Appointment:** The President, with the advice and consent of the Senate, appoints officers of the United States. Congress may specify that inferior officers are appointed by the President alone, by the heads of departments, or by the courts of law. [16]

   a. **Principal officers:** While there is no clear line between principal officers and inferior officers, principal officers are high-level officials in the executive branch, such as department heads and heads of independent agencies. [16-17]

   b. **Inferior officers:** Inferior officers are lower-level executive officials who are under the supervision of other executive officials beneath the President. In *Morrison v. Olson*, the Court held that an independent counsel investigating wrongdoing by executive branch officials was an inferior officer because of the limited scope and duration of the independent prosecutor's appointment and the Attorney General's removal power. [17]

c. Employees: Employees are low-level officials who are employed by the federal government but exercise no discretion or authority to administer federal law. They are neither principal nor inferior officers and thus may be appointed pursuant to procedures other than those provided for in the appointments clause, such as a civil-service-type appointments process.

2. **Removal:** The Constitution does not mention the removal of officials except through impeachment and conviction. In the absence of statutory restrictions, the President has the power to remove executive officials at will. Congress may, under most circumstances, restrict the President's power to remove executive officials, but Congress itself may not retain advice and consent power over removal of officials or participate in the removal of officials except through impeachment. [17-18]

D. **Direct Presidential Supervision of Administrative Agencies**

The degree to which the President has inherent authority to supervise administrative agencies is an unsettled and controversial area of law. Today, all but the highest government positions are filled with civil service employees with statutory job security. Further, the First Amendment limits the President's right to replace government officials for political reasons. [19-20]

E. **The Line Item Veto:**

The Line Item Veto Act is unconstitutional since in effect it grants the President unilateral power to amend or repeal legislation. *See Clinton v. City of New York*, 524 U.S. 417 (1998). The Act gave the President the power to cancel items in bills after signing the bills. The problem with this is that once the President signed the bill passed by Congress, the entire bill became law, and only further legislation by both Houses of Congress could amend or repeal it. [20]

IV. ADJUDICATION WITHIN ADMINISTRATIVE AGENCIES

Agency adjudication raises a separation of powers problem because Article III vests the judicial power of the United States in the Article III courts, and it has been argued that administrative agencies usurp that power when they adjudicate cases. However, the Supreme Court has approved of a great deal of agency adjudication as long as administrative agencies adjudicate in areas closely connected to federal regulatory programs and do not seize the central attributes of judicial power. Limited jurisdiction, limited powers, and judicial review and enforcement of judgments in Article III courts are factors that support the constitutionality of administrative adjudication. [20-22]

CHAPTER 3

THE AVAILABILITY OF JUDICIAL REVIEW OF ADMINISTRATIVE DECISIONS

I. JURISDICTION

The petition for judicial review must be brought in a court that has jurisdiction over the claim, normally either the district court or court of appeals. In most cases, the choice between the court of appeals and the district court is simple because the agency's governing statute identifies the proper forum for judicial review. Most of these statutes provide for review of administrative action in the court of appeals. If no statute states otherwise, review must be sought in the district court under that court's original jurisdiction. For reasons of judicial economy, courts interpret specific statutes, whenever possible, to direct review to the court of appeals—even in cases of informal agency action where there is no formal agency record. [26-27]

II. REVIEWABILITY

A. Presumption in Favor of Judicial Review

There is a longstanding presumption that judicial review of agency action is available. The Administrative Procedure Act (APA) provisions granting judicial review in favor of persons adversely affected or aggrieved by final agency action reinforce this presumption, subject to APA created exceptions. [28]

B. Exceptions to Reviewability

APA §701 specifies two situations in which APA judicial review is not available: when "statutes preclude judicial review," §701(a)(l), and when "agency action is committed to agency discretion by law."§701(a)(2). [28]

1. **Agency Action:** Review under the APA is available only for "agency action." The President is not an agency within the meaning of the APA. Further, the Supreme Court has required that the petitioner identify a particular agency action that is being challenged, holding that APA review is not available to challenge the general manner in which an agency regulates. *See Norton v. Southern Utah Wilderness Alliance*, 542 U.S. 55 (2004).

2. **Statutory preclusion:** For a statute to preclude judicial review it should explicitly mention judicial review and either preclude it completely or provide for a particular form of judicial review and preclude all others. [28-29]

3. **"Committed to agency discretion by law":** The traditional understanding of "committed to agency discretion by law" is that judicial review is not available when the governing statutes are drawn in such broad terms that in a given case there is no law to apply. Review may also be "committed to agency discretion by law" when the statute suggests that Congress intended for the agency to have final authority over a decision or when the agency action is in a category of administrative decisions that have traditionally been held to be committed to agency discretion. [30-32]

4. **Reviewability of prosecutorial discretion:** The Supreme Court has created, under APA §701(a)(2), a strong presumption that agency prosecutorial decisions, such as choosing targets for administrative enforcement or areas in which to regulate, are unreviewable as "committed to agency discretion by law." The presumption exists because few enabling acts contain precise instructions about when an agency must act, and because the decision of when to act and against whom often involves balancing multiple factors such as available resources and effective enforcement policy. The presumption against review of prosecutorial discretion may be rebutted if the agency's enabling act requires the agency to act under certain specified circumstances or within a certain time period. [32-33]

C. Preclusion of Review of Constitutional Questions

Because precluding judicial review of constitutional challenges itself raises a serious constitutional question, courts have interpreted statutes precluding judicial review to preclude review only of nonconstitutional questions, while preserving review of constitutional issues. It is unsettled whether and to what degree Congress may bar review of constitutional questions. [33]

III. STANDING TO SECURE JUDICIAL REVIEW

A party seeking judicial review must have standing. Constitutional standing doctrine requires that the plaintiff must be injured by the challenged conduct and must stand to gain from a favorable ruling (redressability). In addition to the constitutional injury and redressability requirements, the federal courts have imposed prudential standing limitations that bar plaintiffs from asserting the rights of third parties and from seeking redress for generalized grievances, which affect society as a whole. [34]

There are exceptions to the prudential limitations such as the doctrine that allows third parties to assert the constitutional rights of those who are unable to assert their own rights. The party asserting the rights must still meet the constitutional injury and redressability requirements. Further, because the prudential limitations on standing are judge made and not constitutionally compelled, Congress has the power to overrule them. [34, 38-40]

A. Standing: The Old "Legal Right" Test

Early administrative law standing cases allowed review only on behalf of parties whose own legal rights had been allegedly violated by agency action. Parties injured by agency treatment of others, for example, when an agency loosens regulation on a competitor, lacked standing to seek judicial review of the agency's treatment of the third party or parties. [34-35]

B. Standing: The "Injury-in-Fact Fairly Traceable" Test

In reaction to criticism of the legal right test, the Court has replaced it with the requirement that the plaintiff have suffered an injury-in-fact that is fairly traceable to the challenged conduct and is redressable by a favorable judgment. Further, the plaintiff must be in the zone of interests of the statute under which relief is sought. [35]

1. **Abstract injury not sufficient:** Persons or groups with an abstract interest in a regulatory scheme do not have standing without an actual injury. For example, an environmental group does not have standing to challenge the treatment of a wilderness area unless members of the group actually use the area in question. [35]

2. **The injury must be "fairly traceable" to the challenged conduct:** The injury must be "fairly traceable" to the challenged conduct, or in other words, the conduct challenged must have actually caused the injury. While the concept of causation is not particularly difficult to understand, it is often not clear why the Supreme Court finds causation present in some cases and absent in others. [36]

3. **Redressability:** To have standing, the plaintiff must show that the remedy sought will redress the injury. A plaintiff seeking relief against past harm may lack standing on **redressability** grounds if the harm is not continuing and the plaintiff is not entitled to damages or any other form of compensation for the past harm. [36-37]

C. APA Standing and the Zone of Interests Test

The Supreme Court has held that to have standing the plaintiff must establish that "the interest sought to be protected by the complainant is arguably within the zone of interests to be protected or regulated by the statute or constitutional guarantee in question." The zone of interests test applies to cases in which the plaintiff seeks to challenge agency treatment of someone else (such as a competitor) and asks whether the plaintiff's interests were considered by Congress or the regulatory body in the decision to regulate the third party. [37-38]

D. Associational Standing

Associations (such as interest groups and trade associations) have standing to litigate their own claims and also the claims of their members as long as the members themselves would have standing to sue, the interests the association is suing over are within the association's purpose, and the litigation will not be adversely affected by the absence of individual plaintiffs. [40-41]

IV. THE TIMING OF JUDICIAL REVIEW: RIPENESS, EXHAUSTION, AND MOOTNESS

Judicial review may not be sought too early (ripeness), too late (mootness), and in some cases, without exhausting administrative remedies.

A. Ripeness and the APA's Grant of Review of "Final Agency Action"

APA §704's grants of judicial review of "final agency action for which there is no other adequate remedy in a court" is essentially a ripeness requirement, which excludes from review agency action that is not yet complete. Even though a rule is "final" upon promulgation, the Supreme Court has held that a rule is ripe for review upon promulgation (before enforcement) only if the issues are fit for judicial review and the party seeking review would suffer substantial hardship if review were delayed until after enforcement. *Abbott Laboratories v. Gardner*, 387 U.S. 136, 148 (1967). [41-42]

B. Ripeness of Informal Agency Action

When informal agency action has the effect of granting or denying permission to take a requested course of action, a court might consider it final agency action even though the decision was made without any formal procedures. [42-43]

C. Ripeness of Agency Inaction or Refusal to Act

If the agency formally declines to take action, that decision can be a "final agency action" subject to judicial review. If an agency fails to answer a request to act, the failure to act is ripe for review only in the rare circumstance that agency inaction is the equivalent of a decision not to act or appears from the circumstances to amount to a decision not to act. If an agency is statutorily required to act in an emergency, agency inaction in response to a petition alleging an emergency may amount to a decision that no emergency exists that requires agency action. [43-44]

D. Exhaustion of Administrative Remedies Prior to Seeking Judicial Review

One of the oldest, most established doctrines in administrative law is that challengers must exhaust remedies within the agency before seeking judicial review. [44]

1. **Exceptions to the exhaustion requirement:** A party is not required to exhaust administrative remedies when (1) exhaustion would cause undue prejudice to the protection of the rights at issue; (2) the administrative agency lacks power to grant effective relief; or (3) the exhaustion would be futile because the administrative body is biased. [44]

2. **APA exhaustion doctrine:** The Supreme Court has held that if agency action is final under §704, no further exhaustion is required and review is available immediately. Under §704, exhaustion is required only of those remedies expressly required by statute or agency rule. [44-45]

E. Mootness

A case is moot if there is no longer a live controversy between the parties. For example, if a party is no longer subject to an agency rule or if the agency repeals the rule, a claim for judicial review of the rule may be moot. There are exceptions to mootness: a claim may be heard despite mootness if the claim is "capable of repetition yet evading review" or when the defendant voluntarily ceases the challenged conduct but remains free to resume it. [45]

CHAPTER 4

JUDICIAL REVIEW OF ADMINISTRATIVE DECISIONS

I. STANDARDS OF JUDICIAL REVIEW UNDER THE APA

APA standards of judicial review govern unless the agency's enabling act contains a provision establishing a standard of review that differs from the applicable APA standard. [51]

A. APA §706 and Standards of Review

APA §706(2)(D) applies the substantial evidence test to formal adjudication and formal rulemaking. [51]

APA §706(2)(E) applies de novo review when (1) "the [agency] action is adjudicatory in nature and the agency factfinding procedures are inadequate" or (2) "issues that were not before the agency are raised in a proceeding to enforce nonadjudicatory agency action." [52]

APA §706(2)(A) provides that any agency action should be set aside if it is "arbitrary, capricious, an abuse of discretion, or otherwise not in accordance with law." The arbitrary and capricious test contains no limitation on its applicability, and thus it applies to all reviewable administrative actions. Because it is the most deferential standard of review, parties challenging administrative action prefer de novo or substantial evidence review. [52]

B. The Record on Review

APA §706 requires reviewing courts to examine the "whole record." The record consists of the material the agency had before it when it made its decision—not support created after the agency made its decision. The reviewing court looks at the whole record, not just the evidence supporting the agency's decision. [52-53]

II. THE SUBSTANTIAL EVIDENCE TEST

The substantial evidence test, which governs review of formal agency adjudication and formal rulemaking, is the same standard that governs whether a judge should submit an issue to a jury rather than direct a verdict. That standard is whether such relevant evidence exists as a reasonable mind might accept as adequate to support a conclusion. The "whole record" requirement means that a decision might fail the substantial evidence test even though it is supported by some evidence, when that evidence is overwhelmed by evidence to the contrary. [53]

A. Witness Credibility

When an agency's decision is based, in whole or in part, on the credibility of the witnesses, the agency's decision is entitled to great deference because the reviewing court reviews only the paper record, without the opportunity to observe the demeanor of the witnesses. [53]

B. Agency Reversals of ALJ Decisions

When an agency reverses the decision of the trier of fact on appeal within the agency, the initial decision is part of the "whole record," and the reviewing court must take the reversal into account in deciding whether the agency's decision is supported by substantial evidence. [53-54]

III. DE NOVO REVIEW OF QUESTIONS OF FACT

Where agency adjudicatory factfinding procedures are inadequate or when new factual issues arise in an action to enforce nonadjudicatory agency action, the regulated party might be entitled to de novo review of the facts. De novo review means that the facts are retried in the court, and no deference is paid to agency factual conclusions. [54-55]

IV. REVIEW OF QUESTIONS OF LAW

There are competing traditions regarding judicial review of agency conclusions of law—one under which courts review questions of law de novo and another under which courts defer to agency interpretations of the statutes they administer. Courts have traditionally shown the greatest deference to agency decisions involving the applications of law to particular facts. Although the Court no longer distinguishes between issues of statutory authority to regulate and other statutory issues, traditionally courts have decided issues of agency statutory authority without deferring to the agency's interpretation of its enabling act. [55-56]

A. *Chevron*

In *Chevron, U.S.A., Inc. v. Natural Resources Defense Council, Inc.*, 467 U.S. 837 (1984), the Court stated that unless Congress has directly spoken to the precise issue in question, courts should defer to agencies on pure questions of statutory interpretation as long as the agency arrived at a reasonable or permissible construction of the statute. If Congress's intent is unclear or if Congress left a gap for the agency to fill, analysis moves to step two. [56-57]

B. Less Deferential *Chevron: Cardoza-Fonseca*

The Court sometimes states that under *Chevron*, the reviewing court should attempt to ascertain Congress's intent using "traditional tools of statutory construction." These include the language, structure, purpose, and legislative history of the statute being construed, and other interpretive devices such as the canons of statutory interpretation. *See INS v. Cardoza-Fonseca*, 480 U.S. 421, 447 (1987). [57]

C. *Chevron*: **Permissible Construction**

If a statute is ambiguous, or if Congress has left a gap for the agency to fill, an agency's interpretation is permissible under *Chevron* if it is "a sufficiently rational one to preclude a court from substituting its judgment for that of the [agency]." *Young v. Community Nutrition Institute*, 476 U.S. 974, 981 (1986). This is very deferential. [56-57]

D. **When *Chevron* applies**

Chevron applies to agency statutory interpretations rendered in relatively formal settings such as rulemaking and adjudication. Under *United States v. Mead Corp.*, 533 U.S. 218 (2001), it does not apply to agency statutory interpretations rendered less formally, such as in a ruling letter. In such cases, *Skidmore* deference may apply. Under *Skidmore*, courts defer to agency statutory interpretations on a sliding scale based on the formality of the process, the importance of agency expertise, and the degree to which the agency's reasoning is persuasive.

V. REVIEW OF QUESTIONS OF POLICY

1. **Informal rulemaking and informal agency action:** Courts review most agency policy decisions under the arbitrary and capricious test, which applies to informal rulemaking and informal agency action. The arbitrary and capricious test requires that agencies make decisions:

   1. "based on a consideration of the relevant factors," including alternatives to the agency's proposal;
   2. without "a clear error of judgment"; and
   3. under the correct legal standard. [58-59]
      The Court has also stated that:
   4. while the arbitrary and capricious inquiry is "searching and careful,"
   5. the standard of review is "a narrow one [and t]he court is not empowered to substitute its judgment for that of the agency."

   Citizens to Preserve Overton Park v. Volpe, 401 U.S. 402, 416-17 (1971). [59]

   As proof that they considered all relevant factors, courts require agencies to explain their decisions on major issues raised during the decisionmaking process. [60]

2. **The special case of the standard of review of deregulation:** Deregulation is normally reviewed under the same test that applies to the initial promulgation of the regulation being relaxed or rescinded. In most cases of informal rulemaking, this means the arbitrary and capricious test. The Court has rejected arguments that deregulation decisions should be reviewed under the same standard that governs a refusal to regulate in the first place. [61]

VI. REMEDIES ON JUDICIAL REVIEW

Reviewing courts have the power under APA §706 to "hold unlawful and set aside" agency action found not to meet the applicable standard of review. However, courts often remand matters to the agency for further consideration without ordering the agency to change its decision. This gives agencies the opportunity to cure any defects identified on judicial review. [61]

CHAPTER 5

AGENCY CHOICE OF POLICYMAKING MODE

I. CONSTITUTIONAL CONSTRAINTS ON CHOICE OF POLICYMAKING MODE

In most cases the choice between rulemaking and adjudication is left to Congress or to the agency under delegation from Congress. When an agency makes a decision applicable generally to an entire class of parties, a legislative procedure is sufficient to satisfy due process. *See Bi-Metallic Investment Co. v. State Board of Equalization*, 239 U.S. 441 (1915). However, under *Londoner v. Denver*, 210 U.S. 373 (1908), due process requires an adjudicatory hearing when the agency's decision is particularized to the situation of a regulated party. [67-68]

II. CHOICE OF POLICYMAKING PROCEDURE

The APA divides all agency action into two models—rulemaking and adjudication—but says very little about when each is required. Agencies must employ an adjudicatory process to issue orders against regulated parties. Agencies make rule-like determinations in both rulemaking and adjudication, and either is proper as long as the agency has the power to use the particular procedure and all procedural requirements are observed. [68-69]

A. Agency Discretion to Make Policy by Rule

Rulemaking is the preferred policymaking method for agencies because it allows agencies to make clear, comprehensive decisions in a legislative process in which the agency can benefit from extensive public input and thus make better policy decisions. Rulemaking is also fair because it establishes rules that govern all regulated parties at once rather than singling out parties at different times, which may occur when an agency brings an enforcement action against one regulated party at a time. [69]

B. Rulemaking and the Right to a Hearing

Agencies often use rulemaking to determine whether particular conduct violates a regulatory statute. Regulated parties have argued that when Congress establishes a hearing process to determine regulatory violations, the rulemaking violates their right to a hearing on all issues. This argument is usually rejected with a caveat that the agency must provide an opportunity for the party to argue that the rule should not apply in the particular case. [69-70]

C. Agency Power to Make Policy by Adjudication

Agencies often announce new rules of decision in an opinion arising from an adjudication. This practice has been challenged on the ground that the APA's definitions require rulemaking as the procedure for formulating general rules. The Supreme Court has rejected these challenges, although not definitively, stating that the choice between adjudication and rulemaking lies largely within the discretion of the agency. [71-72]

III. INFORMAL POLICYMAKING

A. Exemptions From §553

APA §553 exempts from all of its requirements rules that are in the areas of the military, foreign affairs, agency management, personnel, public property, loans, grants, benefits, and contracts. Section 553 also exempts, from its notice and comment requirements, nonlegislative rules such as interpretative rules, general statements of policy, and rules of agency organization or practice. Further, §553(b) allows agencies to dispense with notice and comment procedures when it finds that such procedures are "impracticable, unnecessary or contrary to the public interest." [72-73]

1. **Nonlegislative rule:** A nonlegislative rule is a rule that has no legal effect. Rather, it interprets existing legal obligations (interpretative rule) or states the agency's view on a matter of policy without creating legal rights or obligations (general statement of policy). Nonlegislative rules must be published in the Federal Register. Agencies may not give legal effect to nonlegislative rules. [73-75]

B. Policymaking by Manual or Other Internal Document

When an agency makes policy without going through either rulemaking or adjudication, the APA requires that any rule be published in the Federal Register or it may not be used against any party not having actual notice of it. APA §552(a)(1). *See Morton v. Ruiz*, 415 U.S. 199 (1974). [76-77]

C. Agencies' Obligation to Follow Their Own Procedural Rules

Agencies must.follow any procedural rules they have formally adopted through notice and comment procedures, but informally adopted rules may be ignored unless a party that the agency intended to benefit detrimentally relied upon the informally adopted procedural rule. *See American Farm Lines v. Black Ball Freight Service*, 397 U.S. 532 (1970); *Schweiker v. Hansen*, 450 U.S. 785 (1981). [77]

D. Informal Policymaking Generally: When May an Agency Act Without Adjudication or Rulemaking?

While agencies often decide policy matters and grant or deny applications or petitions informally (without using either an adjudicatory or rulemaking procedure), the statutory basis for this widespread practice is unclear. Because the APA appears to divide all agency actions between rulemaking and adjudication, this informal decisionmaking is often referred to as "informal adjudication." When an agency makes a decision informally, the only procedural requirements are notice of the decision and a brief statement of the reasons for the decision. *See* APA §555(e). [77-78]

CHAPTER 6

APA RULEMAKING PROCEDURES

I. APA §553 INFORMAL ("NOTICE AND COMMENT") RULEMAKING PROCEDURES

A. Basic Requirements of Informal Rulemaking

The basic requirements of informal rulemaking are: published notice of the proposed rulemaking, opportunity for public comment and, after consideration of the comments, publication of the final rule together with a concise general statement of the rule's basis and purpose. [82]

B. Notice

APA §553 requires notice of either the text of a proposed regulation or a description of the subjects or issues involved in the rulemaking. To prevent agencies from proposing one rule and then promulgating a completely different one, courts have required that the rules ultimately adopted be the logical outgrowth of the proposal, that they not substantially depart from the original proposal, or that the final rule may not materially alter the proposal. The cure for inadequate notice is a new notice and a new comment period. [82-84]

C. Meaningful Opportunity to Submit Comments

Some courts have interpreted APA §553(c)'s requirement that interested parties be allowed to submit comments on proposed rules to require a "meaningful" opportunity to participate. These courts have required agencies to provide notice of any data or studies upon which the agency relies. *See United States v. Nova Scotia Food Prods. Corp.*, 568 F.2d 240 (2d Cir. 1977); *National Black Media Coalition v. FCC*, 791 F.2d 1016 (2d Cir. 1986). Although nothing in the APA explicitly requires it, courts have held that for the opportunity to participate to be meaningful, interested persons must be allowed to respond to opposing comments. [84-85]

D. The Problem of Ex Parte Contacts in Rulemaking

Ex parte contacts consist of communications from interested parties to administrators outside the formalities of the comment process. While such contacts are barred in formal adjudication and formal rulemaking, the APA does not bar ex parte contacts in informal rulemaking. [85]

1. **Ban on ex parte contacts:** While some courts hold that ex parte contacts are generally not barred in informal rulemaking, some courts have ruled that ex parte contacts should not be allowed because they threaten the ability of other interested parties to participate meaningfully in the rulemaking process. Some courts suggest that agencies should consider only the comments presented through the notice and comment process because ex parte comments threaten the court's ability, on judicial review, to examine the true basis of agency decisions. Other courts have confined the ban on ex parte contacts to rulemakings that involve competing claims to a valuable privilege. [85-86]

2. **Remedy for ex parte contacts:** Even courts holding that ex parte contacts should not occur recognize that the realities of the political process mean that such contacts may occur. Thus, courts have held that if ex parte contacts do occur, any documents received and a summary of oral communications should be placed on the record. [86]

3. **Intragovernmental ex parte contacts:** The President, as chief executive, has a right to receive information from administrative officials regarding pending rulemakings, and a right to give input on the substance of rulemakings. It may also be appropriate for members of Congress to represent the interests of their constituents through ex parte contacts as long as they do not raise extraneous matters to pressure the agency in the rulemaking process. [87]

E. Prejudgment in Rulemaking

A decisionmaker in a rulemaking may be disqualified if it is shown by clear and convincing evidence that the decisionmaker has prejudged the issues to such a great extent that he or she has an unalterably closed mind, and thus will not consider the comments submitted in the rulemaking process. *See Association of National Advertisers, Inc. v. FTC*, 627 F.2d 1151 (D.C. Cir. 1979), *cert. denied*, 447 U.S. 921 (1980). [87-88]

F. The Concise General Statement

APA §553 requires agencies to explain their rules with a "concise general statement of their basis and purpose." The statement must respond to substantial issues raised by the comments and state the agency's views on major issues of law and policy. [88-89]

G. Publication of Final Rules

Agencies must publish final rules in the Federal Register. If a rule is not properly published, the rule is ineffective as to any party without actual notice of the rule. APA §552. [89]

H. Hybrid Rulemaking

Some enabling acts impose procedural requirements in addition to those included in §553. They usually consist of discovery, cross-examination of experts, and additional comment periods so that interested parties could comment on adverse comments submitted. Courts also imposed such requirements in complex rulemakings when they viewed §553 procedures as inadequate. In *Vermont Yankee Nuclear Power Corp. v. NRDC*, 435 U.S. 519 (1978), the Supreme Court ruled that courts may not require procedures in addition to those specified in either the APA or an enabling act because uncertainty over the correct level of procedure would lead agencies to overproceduralize, losing the benefits of the streamlined rulemaking process. This calls into question judicial imposition of the ban on ex parte communications in rulemakings as well as other judicially imposed procedural requirements. [89-90]

II. FORMAL RULEMAKING PROCEDURES: THE ADDITIONAL REQUIREMENTS OF APA §§556 AND 557

A. When is Formal Rulemaking Required?

Formal rulemaking, which is rulemaking conducted in a formal, adjudicatory procedure, is required when the agency's enabling act requires rules to be made "on the record after opportunity for an agency hearing." Because formal rulemaking is a cumbersome procedure, courts are loathe to find that it is required and agencies rarely use it. [91]

B. Formal Rulemaking Procedures

Formal rulemaking is conducted like a trial, with an administrative law judge or agency head presiding. Ex parte communications are prohibited. Parties are entitled to present their cases by oral or documentary evidence, and they are entitled to cross-examine opposing witnesses. The record produced at the hearing is the exclusive record for decision in formal rulemaking, and a detailed decision with findings of fact and conclusions of law is required. [91]

III. NEGOTIATED RULEMAKING

Under the Negotiated Rulemaking Act, agencies may formulate proposed rules through a process of formal negotiations among interested parties. If negotiations are successful, the agency normally proposes a rule in line with the negotiated consensus. Such rules are subject to normal notice and comment procedures, and the agency is free to change its mind and promulgate a final rule that differs from the rule agreed to in negotiations. [92]

IV. DIRECT FINAL RULEMAKING

If no adverse comments are expected, some agencies have employed a procedure called "direct final rulemaking" under which an agency publishes a final rule and specifies that it will go into effect unless the agency receives adverse comments. If the agency receives adverse comments, the direct final rulemaking is canceled, and the agency conducts a normal notice and comment process. While direct final rulemaking has not been tested in court, it will probably be upheld as a method for promulgating legislative rules as long as the receipt of adverse comments triggers notice and comment procedures. [92]

CHAPTER 7

AGENCY ADJUDICATION AND DUE PROCESS

I. ARTICLE III CONSTITUTIONAL LIMITS ON AGENCY ADJUDICATION

Agency adjudication appears to violate Article III's vesting of the judicial power of the United States in the federal courts. However, the federal courts have approved agency adjudication when it occurs under circumstances thought not to threaten the policies and values underlying Article III. [97]

Agency adjudication is most clearly permissible in public rights disputes, which are disputes between a private party and the government over such things as licenses or benefits. More recently, the Supreme Court has approved of agency adjudication of disputes between two private parties where the rights involved arise out of or are closely associated with a federal regulatory scheme and where the essential attributes of judicial power remain in the federal courts so that the role of the federal courts in the government is not threatened. The Court has found it important that agency orders must be enforced in court, and the parties have a choice between an Article III court and a non-Article III tribunal. The Court has rejected Justice Brennan's view that non-Article III adjudication is permissible only in the three narrow categories of territorial courts, military courts, and public rights disputes. *See Community Futures Trading Comm'n v. Schor*, 478 U.S. 833, 859 (1986) (Brennan, J. dissenting). [97-101]

II. DUE PROCESS AND THE ADJUDICATORY HEARING

A. **Property Interests** The first question in any due process dispute is whether the claim involves a protected interest, i.e., life, liberty, or property. While at one time interests such as government benefits were thought of as gratuities that could be withdrawn at any time, today such interests are considered property interests if claims to the benefit are evaluated under a definite set of criteria that create an entitlement to the benefit. In the absence of an explicit entitlement, less formal assurances or state practices may create an entitlement. [102-103]

B. **"Bitter With the Sweet"** In *Arnett v. Kennedy*, 416 U.S. 134 (1974), Justice Rehnquist, joined by two other members of the Court, argued that a civil service employee with a for-cause termination provision (the "sweet") should receive only the minimal process (the "bitter") specified in the statute granting the forcause entitlement. A majority of the Court rejected this argument, adhering to *Roth's* separation of procedure from substance. [103]

C A P S U L E   S U M M A R Y

C. Liberty   Some liberty interests are created, like property interests, by external law that creates an entitlement. For example, while prisoners have no constitutional right to parole, if state law creates an entitlement to parole, then a liberty interest is created and due process standards govern the procedures employed at parole hearings. Other liberty interests, such as the right to freedom of movement, are recognized as part of the constitutional definition of liberty and are thus created by the Due Process Clause itself. [104-105]

D. Determining What Process is Due   How much process is due is determined by applying the *Mathews v. Eldridge* balancing test and asking whether the procedures already provided are adequate. The *Mathews v. Eldridge* balancing test considers (1) the strength of the private interest affected by the government action; (2) the risk of an erroneous deprivation if additional procedure is not afforded; and (3) the government's interest in proceeding with no more process than already afforded. [105-106]

Sometimes, alternatives to a trial-like hearing in the agency in advance of the adverse action are held to satisfy due process. These alternatives include common law remedies, postdeprivation remedies more generally, and a consultative model of procedure. Agencies may not impose legally binding orders on regulated parties without following due process. [107-108]

E. The Right to a Neutral Decisionmaker [108]

1. **Bias:**   Due process is violated if a decisionmaker has a pecuniary interest in the outcome of the adjudication. Pecuniary interests can be direct, such as a decisionmaker who receives a portion of any fines levied in an adjudication, or indirect, such as a decisionmaker in competition with those subject to the agency enforcement. Bias may also exist if a decisionmaker feels pressure from agency superiors to decide in a particular way. [108]

2. **Prejudgment:**   Due process is violated if it appears that a decisionmaker in an adjudication has, in some measure, prejudged the facts or law of a particular case prior to hearing it. [109-110]

III. STATUTORY HEARING RIGHTS

Many statutes grant the right to a hearing to determine matters such as licenses and government benefits. [110]

A. The Statutorily Required Hearing Must be Genuine   When a statute grants an applicant a hearing on an application for a government benefit or license, the hearing must provide the applicant with a genuine opportunity to prevail. Under *Ashbacker*, the agency may not make it nearly impossible for the applicant to prevail before holding the hearing. *See Ashbacker Radio Corp. v. FCC*, 326 U.S. 327 (1945). [110]

B. Substantive Standards That Limit Hearings   Agencies with the power to engage in rulemaking may adopt substantive rules that limit the issues addressed at a statutorily prescribed hearing. The rules must be substantively valid. Because these rules are in tension with the party's statutory right to a hearing, courts have required that agencies provide an opportunity for parties to argue that a rule does not, or should not, apply to the particular case. [110-111]

C. Applications That Establish Ineligibility   In *United States v. Storer Broadcasting Co.*, 351 U.S. 192 (1956), the Court held that the Federal Communications Commission (FCC) is free to deny an application without a hearing when the application itself reveals that the license would be denied under a substantively valid statute or regulation. [111]

D. The Irrebuttable Presumption Doctrine The irrebuttable presumption doctrine held that when there was a liberty or property interest at stake, due process required a hearing on all issues, and a statute could not preclude a hearing on a central issue. This doctrine proved unworkable, and it was abandoned in *Weinberger v. Salfi*, 422 U.S. 749 (1975), when the Court upheld a provision of the Social Security Act that excluded widows who were married to a deceased worker for shorter than nine months from eligibility for survivors' benefits against a challenge that the statute created an irrebuttable presumption that a marriage shorter than nine months was a sham. [112-113]

CHAPTER **8**
SUBSTANTIVE POLICYMAKING IN AGENCIES

I. PERMISSIBLE CONSIDERATIONS IN AGENCY POLICYMAKING

Agencies are required to consider only the factors made relevant by their enabling acts and by other generally applicable statutes such as the National Environmental Policy Act (NEPA). Agencies should make policy by applying their expertise, in a reasoned fashion, to the factors made statutorily relevant. Agencies should not take factors into account that are not within the considerations made relevant by statute or valid regulation. [118]

II. COST-BENEFIT ANALYSIS

Cost-benefit analysis promotes reasoned decisionmaking by forcing agencies to quantify the effects of their actions in a more concrete fashion. While it has been argued that agencies should be required to conduct cost-benefit analysis regarding their major policy decisions and should not adopt a policy unless the benefits outweigh the costs, courts will not require cost-benefit analysis unless statutorily required. Courts have not read general standards such as "reasonably necessary or appropriate" as requiring cost-benefit analysis, perhaps in part because many costs and benefits are difficult to quantify and because Congress appears to prefer values other than efficiency in many regulatory programs. [119-120]

III. IMPACT STATEMENTS

Another method of forcing agencies to focus on the effects of their actions is to require the agency to prepare an impact statement, such as an environmental impact statement or a small business regulatory impact statement. Impact statements improve decisionmaking and provide an opportunity for opponents of the agency's plan to put pressure on the agency to change or abandon its plans due to undesirable effects. [120-121]

A. Environmental Impact Statements Under NEPA

NEPA requires federal agencies to prepare Environmental Impact Statements (EIS) regarding "major Federal actions significantly affecting the quality of the human environment." The EIS must detail the effects and include consideration of alternatives. [121]

B. Environmental Effects

In addition to traditional environmental effects, NEPA covers a broad range of effects on the human environment, such as displacement of social institutions and concentration of low-income residents in a neighborhood. For NEPA to apply, there must be a physical alteration of the environment and the matter must be within the agency's control. [121]

C. NEPA is Essentially Procedural

The EIS must be part of the record during agency consideration of its action, and courts have held that the agency must consider the environmental effects. Nothing in NEPA, however, requires that agency action be changed or abandoned due to environmental effects. [121-122]

IV. CONSISTENCY AND CLARITY REQUIREMENTS

Courts have, on judicial review, required agencies to operate under clearly stated substantive criteria and have required agencies to treat like cases alike.

A. Clarity

The clarity cases, which are in tension with decisions allowing agencies the discretion to decide issues on a case-by-case basis, hold that agency action may be taken only pursuant to clear criteria. Some courts have held that where property or liberty interests are at stake, clarity is required by due process. [122-123]

B. Agency Decisions Are Judged on the Reasons Stated by the Agency

Related to the clarity requirement is the well-established doctrine that agency decisions are evaluated, on judicial review, based on the reasons given by the agency at the time the decision was made, not on reasons first offered on judicial review. [123-124]

C. Consistency

Agencies are required to be consistent, i.e., to treat like cases alike, and must offer an explanation, when they treat like cases differently. [124]

D. Agencies Must Follow Their Own Rules

Agencies are required to follow their own rules, whether those rules have been adopted in a rulemaking proceeding or announced in the course of an agency adjudication, unless the agency has validly changed its rule. Agencies must apply their rules as written and may not change their rules by applying a rule in a manner inconsistent with the rule as written. *See Allentown Mack Sales and Service, Inc. v. NLRB*, 522 U.S. 359 (1998). However, courts often allow agencies to ignore rules that have not been formally adopted in a rulemaking or adjudication. [124-125]

E. Estoppel and Administrative Agencies

Except in extreme circumstances and where government funds are not involved, agencies are not estopped by the conduct or statements of agency officials. For example, if an agency official gives erroneous advice by misstating the eligibility requirements for a government program, the erroneous advice does not estop the agency from relying upon the program's actual requirements to deny claims. [125-126]

F. Nonacquiescence

Agencies sometimes refuse to acquiesce to legal rulings by lower federal courts. In such cases, the agency may follow the ruling in the circuit in which it was rendered but will adhere to its position in other courts with the possibility of prevailing with a favorable ruling in the Supreme Court. While intercircuit nonacquiescence seems appropriate in some circumstances, intracircuit nonacquiescence, in which an agency refuses to follow a decision of the court of appeals even within the circuit that rendered the decision, is difficult to defend. [126-127]

CHAPTER **9**

AGENCY ENFORCEMENT AND LICENSING

I. PROSECUTORIAL DISCRETION

A. Decisions Not to Prosecute or Regulate

Unless an enabling act contains standards under which an agency is required to prosecute a violator or regulate in an area, a decision not to prosecute or regulate is not reviewable. By and large, courts have concluded that the agency should be left to decide, in its expert judgment, which enforcement actions present the best use of agency resources. [132]

B. Potential Problems with Agency Prosecutorial Discretion

Unreviewable agency prosecutorial discretion presents the potential for subversion of congressional intent by applying different priorities than those that led Congress to pass the agency's enabling act. Agency prosecutorial discretion may allow an agency to play political favorites and may also lead the agency to select only easy targets for prosecution, leaving serious violations unaddressed. [132-133]

C. Discriminatory Enforcement

Subjects of agency enforcement sometimes claim that although they may have violated regulatory norms, the agency should not issue an enforcement order against them unless and until the agency issues enforcement orders against others (for example, competitors) engaged in the same practice. The standard for deciding whether a court should preclude an agency from enforcing an order until the agency orders others in the industry to halt the same practice is "patent abuse of discretion"—a very difficult standard to meet. As long as an agency can articulate a rational basis for its actions, the order will be enforced. [133-134]

D. Discriminatory Imposition of Sanctions

Courts have rejected claims that agencies have imposed overly harsh sanctions for violations, either when compared to sanctions imposed on others, or under agency policy regarding sanctions.

The Supreme Court has held that absent statutory restrictions, an agency is free to impose whatever sanctions are within its statutory power. [134]

E. Constitutionally Based Claims of Discriminatory Enforcement

An agency violates equal protection if it selects its enforcement targets based on a suspect classification. *See Yick Wo v. Hopkins*, 118 U.S. 356 (1886). When outspoken criticism of an agency or the program the agency administers triggers enforcement, regulated parties have unsuccessfully argued that the prosecution punishes or chills speech in violation of the First Amendment. [134-135]

II. LICENSING AND RATEMAKING

A. Occupational Licensing

Doctors, lawyers, optometrists, pharmacists, hair stylists, truck drivers, and many other professionals must obtain licenses from the state in order to practice their professions. [135]

1. **Licenses are property protected by due process:** Because discernible standards normally govern the grant, denial, renewal, and revocation of professional licenses, such licenses are protected by due process as property. [135]

2. **Bias due to self-interest: The problem of self-regulation:** Occupational licensing often presents the potential for bias due to self-interest because the licensing board may be dominated by one segment of a profession that seeks to avoid competition from another segment. If the members of the board have an interest in the outcome of a proceeding before it, due process may preclude them from hearing it. [136]

B. Broadcast Licensing Procedures

1. **"Public interest" standard for granting licenses:** The FCC decides whether to grant a broadcast license based on the very discretionary standard of public interest, convenience, and necessity. [136]

2. **Broadcast licensing hearing requirements:** The FCC is required to hold a full adjudicatory hearing before rejecting an application for a broadcast license. [136-137]

3. **Mutually exclusive applications: The *Ashbacker* rule:** When two applicants file competing applications, the FCC may not grant one of the applications without holding a hearing on the other. *See Ashbacker Radio Corp. v. FCC*, 326 U.S. 327 (1945). To meet this obligation, the FCC holds comparative hearings in which the relative merits of applicants are judged on a variety of factors such as diversification of ownership, involvement of ownership in the management of the station, the quality of proposed programming, and the character of the applicants. While comparative hearings were formerly held on renewal applications, recent legislation has created an entitlement to renewal absent inferior service or other violations by the incumbent licensee. [137-138]

4. **Restricting the scope of hearings by rule: *Storer*:** In *United States v. Storer Broadcasting Co.*, 351 U.S. 192 (1956), the Court held that the FCC may make the "public interest, convenience, and necessity" standard more specific with rules, such as multiple ownership rules

that restrict the number of stations owned by a licensee. The Court held that it did not violate the right to a full hearing to deny a license based on noncompliance with an FCC rule. [138-139]

C. Rate making Principles and Procedures Ratemaking is the procedure for setting rates in regulated industries such as electric power and telephone. Ratemaking has been conducted according to three different models: one in which rates set by the company are subject to challenge as "unreasonable," one in which rates are prescribed in a comprehensive formal ratemaking process, and one in which the company files tariffs that are barely examined by the agency unless someone challenges them. [142-144]

Chapter **10**

AGENCY INFORMATION GATHERING

I. INSPECTIONS

Many agencies monitor compliance with regulatory requirements by inspecting the subjects of regulation. To do so, the agency must have authority to inspect. Further, agencies are subject to constitutional constraints on information gathering. [149]

A. Administrative Authority to Inspect Regulated Businesses

The APA prohibits agencies from conducting inspections, or otherwise gathering information, without legal authority. APA §555(c). [149]

B. Constitutional Constraints on Agency Inspection

Agency inspections are subject to constitutional constraints, most notably those imposed by the Fourth Amendment. However, probable cause (in the criminal law sense) is not required for warrants to conduct inspections. In "pervasively regulated businesses," warrants may be unnecessary. [149]

1. **Normally, a warrant is required:** Under normal circumstances, a warrant is required before government agents may enter and inspect a business to monitor compliance with regulatory requirements. [149]

2. **Warrants for administrative inspections may issue without probable cause:** An agency may obtain a warrant merely by showing that normal legislative or administrative standards for conducting an inspection are met. The agency does not need probable cause. [149-150]

3. **Pervasively regulated businesses:** In cases where substantial regulatory interest would be threatened by imposing a warrant requirement, no warrant is required to inspect the premises of a business that is subject to pervasive regulation. [150]

C. Regulatory Inspections of Homes

Recipients of government benefits may be required to allow welfare caseworkers to inspect their homes as a condition of continued benefits. Also, warrants to inspect a home for compliance with a building code do not require probable cause in the criminal sense. Rather, warrants may issue if the agency establishes that the inspection is part of its normal regulatory scheme to monitor compliance with the relevant code. Finally, probation officers may, without a warrant or probable cause, search the homes of convicted criminals who have been placed on probation. [150-151]

D. Drug Testing

Drug testing programs are evaluated according to several factors, including the expectation of privacy of the individual tested, the degree to which the testing program invades that privacy, the importance of the governmental interest underlying the testing program, and the degree to which the testing program's standards ameliorate the potential for arbitrary selection of individuals to be tested. [151-152]

II. PRODUCTION OF INFORMATION AND DOCUMENTS

A. Agency Requests for Information or Documents

An agency may require regulated parties to provide information or documents as long as the demand is not too indefinite or burdensome, and the information sought is reasonably relevant to a matter of legitimate agency concern. Subjects of investigations normally cannot test the agency's jurisdiction in a proceeding to enforce a subpoena. [152]

B. Disclosure of Privileged Information or Trade Secrets

It is unclear whether agencies must respect recognized privileges such as the attorney-client privilege, the doctor-patient privilege, and the husband-wife privilege. Corporations, other entities (such as labor unions and partnerships), and the custodians of records for such entities, have no Fifth Amendment privilege against providing the government with information or documents. The government may be required, under the Takings Clause, to compensate a regulated party whose trade secret information is disclosed. [152-154]

III. THE PAPERWORK REDUCTION ACT

Before an agency may promulgate a new request for information, the agency must submit a proposal to Office of Information and Regulatory Affairs (OIRA) within the Office of Management and Budget (OMB). OIRA may reject the agency's proposal if it finds that the agency does not have a legitimate need for the information. The Paperwork Reduction Act (PRA) does not apply to requirements that one regulated party disclose information directly to another party. [154]

CHAPTER 11

PRIVATE ENFORCEMENT OF REGULATORY NORMS

I. THE CITIZENS' SUIT

A. Suits Against Violators

Citizens' suit provisions typically authorize "any citizen" or "any person" to seek damages, an injunction, or both against violations of the relevant statute by private parties and by government. This citizens' suit provision does not authorize a suit against the government for regulatory errors but only for conduct that violates the substance of a regulatory program, such as pollution by the government in violation of an environmental statute. [159]

B. Suits Against the Government as Regulator

Citizens' suit provisions typically provide for actions in the nature of mandamus against regulators when it is alleged that they have not fulfilled nondiscretionary regulatory duties. This provision is not a substitute for judicial review and may not be used to examine the substance of agency action. [159]

C. Standing Problems in Citizens' Suits

Plaintiffs in citizens' suits must meet all Article III standing requirements. Citizens' suit provisions may, however, overrule prudential limits on standing and place all "citizens" within the zone of interests of the relevant regulatory program. [160]

II. IMPLIED PRIVATE RIGHTS OF ACTION

If congressional intent to do so exists, a federal court may imply a right of action so that a private party can sue another private, party for violating a regulatory statute even if the regulatory statute itself provides only for enforcement by a federal agency. Contrary to older cases, the recent cases allow rights of action to be implied only if it appears that Congress intended courts to do so. The focus on congressional intent arises from arguments that those courts that implied rights of action without evidence of such intent were.usurping Congress's legislative function. [160-162],

III. ALTERNATIVE STATE REMEDIES AND REGULATORY PREEMPTION

A. Preemption of State Remedies

There is a presumption, rooted in federalism concerns, that state law is not preempted unless Congress's intent to do so is clear. Nonetheless, Congress may preempt state law explicitly, by providing in a statute that state law is preempted, or implicitly, by creating federal law that is so comprehensive it appears that Congress must have intended to displace state law that is within the "field" occupied by Congress. Further, state law in actual conflict with federal law, or which stands as an obstacle to the realization of federal policy, is preempted. [162-165]

B. The Primary Jurisdiction Doctrine

The primary jurisdiction doctrine requires that a claim within the substantive jurisdiction of an agency must be heard first by that agency even if the facts give rise to a claim otherwise cognizable in a court. A savings clause in a regulatory statute may prevent the primary jurisdiction doctrine from operating. [165-166]

CHAPTER 12

LIABILITY OF AGENCIES AND OFFICIALS

I. SOVEREIGN IMMUNITY AND SUITS AGAINST FEDERAL AGENTS AND AGENCIES

A. Common-law Sovereign Immunity

At common law, sovereign immunity barred damages actions against the government and government officials acting in their official capacities unless the government consented to the suit. [170]

B. The Federal Torts Claim Act

The Federal Tort Claims Act (FTCA) waived the sovereign immunity of the federal government for negligent or otherwise wrongful acts or omissions by the United States government or its employees. The FTCA creates federal government liability for "tort claims, . . . in the same manner and to the same extent as a private individual under like circumstances." 28 U.S.C. §2674. The FTCA is often used to pursue an action for damages when the conduct of administrators is allegedly tortious. [170-171]

C. Exceptions to FTCA Liability

The FTCA contains numerous exceptions and limitations, the most important of which is the discretionary-function exception. The Supreme Court has defined the discretionary-function exception as exempting actions from liability when the official has choice and when the action involves the "permissible exercise of policy judgment." In addition to law and policymaking functions, the courts have held that the discretionary-functions exception bars liability for errors in the planning stages of government operations. The Court has also been very skeptical of claims that the government should be held liable for negligence in performing inspections and similar regulatory functions. [171-173]

D. The *Feres* Doctrine

The Supreme Court has created a nonstatutory exception to the FTCA, called the "*Feres* Doctrine," for military activities. This doctrine basically bars all claims that are "incident to service" in the armed forces. [173-174]

II. LIABILITY OF INDIVIDUAL FEDERAL OFFICIALS

A. Common-law Immunities of Government Officials

In many situations, government officials are privileged to engage in conduct that, if performed by a private party, would be tortious. The courts have also recognized immunity from tort liability for federal government officials acting within the scope of their duties. Further, if a claim against a federal government official falls within the scope of the FTCA, the government is substituted as defendant, and the individual official is released from liability. [174-175]

B. Judicially Created Constitutional Tort Liability

The Supreme Court, in *Bivens v. Six Unknown Named Agents of Federal Bureau of Narcotics*, 403 U.S. 388 (1971), created a damages action against federal officials for constitutional torts. [175]

1. **Exceptions to *Bivens*:** The *Bivens* action is not available when there are "special factors counseling hesitation in the absence of affirmative action by Congress," or when Congress has provided an alternative remedy that it explicitly declared to be a *substitute* for the *Bivens* action. The existence of a comprehensive alternative remedial scheme has been considered a special factor counseling hesitation. [175-176]

2. **Immunities in *Bivens* actions:** Administrative officials performing judicial, legislative, and prosecutorial functions are absolutely immune from damages because at common law, judges, legislators, and prosecutors were absolutely immune from damages. Officials performing

functions not traditionally accorded an absolute immunity are protected by a qualified immunity. A plaintiff can overcome the qualified immunity by showing that the defendant violated a clearly established constitutional right of which a reasonable official should have known. [176-177]

III. LIABILITY OF STATE AND LOCAL GOVERNMENT OFFICIALS

State and local government officials can be sued in federal court under 42 U.S.C. §1983 for damages and injunctive relief for conduct violating the federal Constitution and laws. [178]

A. Eleventh Amendment

The Eleventh Amendment, as interpreted and applied by the Supreme Court, prohibits the federal courts from awarding damages against states and state government agencies. State officials can be enjoined from violating federal law and state officials can be held personally liable for damages, to be paid out of their own pockets. [178]

B. "And Laws" Actions

Section 1983 provides a cause of action against state officials who violate federal statutory law. However, when the federal statute contains a comprehensive remedial scheme that includes its own private right of action against violations, the Supreme Court has held that plaintiffs must use the particular statutory remedy and not the more general §1983 action. The Court has also held that the §1983 remedy for violating a federal statute is not available when the federal statute creates no enforceable rights. [178]

C. Immunities

Defendants in §1983 actions are protected by the same immunities that the courts have applied in *Bivens* actions., [178]

D. Municipal Liability

Municipalities are "persons" subject to suit under §1983, but they may be held liable only for municipal policy or custom and may not be held liable on a vicarious liability theory for the constitutional violations of their employees. [178-179]

CHAPTER **13**

FREEDOM OF INFORMATION AND OPEN MEETINGS

I. THE FREEDOM OF INFORMATION ACT (FOIA)

A. Public Right of Access to Agency Records

FOIA requires that agencies publish certain matters and allow public inspection, upon request, of all other "records" unless the records sought fall within one of FOIA's exceptions. [185]

1. **Agency records:** Agency records are those records that are created or obtained by the agency in the course of doing the agency's work and in the control of the agency at the time of the FOIA request. [185]

2. **Records "wrongfully withheld":** FOIA creates a legal claim when an agency "wrongfully withholds" agency records. [185]

3. **Special FOIA definition of "agency":** The FOIA definition of "agency" includes entities that may not be subject to other APA requirements, such as government corporations and executive branch entities that may collect information, but have no power to take actions having any legal effect. [186]

B. Exceptions to FOIA

FOIA contains nine categories of exceptions to the requirement that agencies disclose their records. *See* 5 U.S.C. §552(b)(1)-(9). The Supreme Court has stated repeatedly that FOIA exemptions should be narrowly construed. The exceptions include classified national defense and foreign policy records; records concerning agency personnel matters; privileged or confidential business or financial records; trade secrets; privileged or confidential commercial information; law enforcement records where disclosure would harm law enforcement efforts; internal agency memoranda; personnel, medical, or law enforcement records where disclosure would unduly invade privacy; and records protected against disclosure by any other statute. [186-188]

C. Disclosure of Exempt Records

Nothing in FOIA precludes an agency from voluntarily turning over records that FOIA exceptions would allow the agency to withhold. However, the Trade Secrets Act makes it a criminal offense for a government official to release information held to be within the FOIA trade-secrets exception. A person whose confidential information is threatened to be released by an agency has a "reverse-FOIA" cause of action under the APA's judicial review provisions (not the Trade Secrets Act itself) to prevent disclosure. [188]

D. The Privacy Act of 1974

The Privacy Act of 1974, 5 U.S.C. §552a, prohibits agencies from disclosing records "except pursuant to a written request by, or with the prior consent of, the individual to whom the record pertains." The Privacy Act also restricts the information agencies are allowed to collect on individuals. The Privacy Act's nondisclosure provisions do not apply to records required to be disclosed under FOIA. [189]

II. DISCOVERY FROM THE GOVERNMENT IN LITIGATION

The government has two special privileges that protect government records from discovery in litigation; evidentiary privilege and executive immunity (also known as executive privilege). [192]

A. Evidentiary Privileges

Evidentiary privileges protect records in sensitive categories like state secrets, military secrets, and sensitive foreign affairs matters. The court determines whether the material sought in discovery is protected by a privilege by balancing the litigant's need for the information against the government's interest in secrecy. [192]

B. Executive Immunity

When the executive branch claims immunity from the discovery process, the court balances the executive branch's need for confidentiality against the litigant's need for the material. When the

President invokes executive privilege, the burden is on the party seeking discovery to demonstrate that the material is essential to justice. [192]

IV. OPEN-MEETINGS REQUIREMENTS

A. The Sunshine Act

In the Sunshine Act, 5 U.S.C. §552b, the government requires all agencies (using FOIA's definition of "agency") that are headed by a "collegial body composed of two or more individual members," to announce their meetings at least one week in advance and to open those meetings to the public, unless a Sunshine Act exception applies. Agencies headed by a single individual are not subject to the Sunshine Act, even when the head of the agency meets with subordinates to discuss agency business. [192-193]

1. **"Meeting of an agency":** A gathering of agency members is a "meeting of an agency" with in the Sunshine Act if the members "jointly conduct or dispose of agency business." The Sunshine Act does not apply to meetings that are purely consultative in character when the agency does not purport to conduct business. [193]

2. **When may an agency meet in private?** The Sunshine Act contains ten categories of exceptions to its open-meetings requirement, most of which track the exceptions to FOIA's disclosure requirements. *See* 5 U.S.C. §552b(c)(l)-(8). A meeting may be closed pursuant to the Sunshine Act exceptions only by a public vote of a majority of the members of the agency. [193]

B. The Federal Advisory Committee Act (FACA)

FACA requires presidential advisory committees, which include private citizens as members, to comply with the Sunshine Act with regard to their meetings and with FOIA with regard to their records. Because it interferes with the President's ability to seek advice from private citizens, it has been argued that FACA violates the separation of powers. [193-194]

Chapter 1

INTRODUCTION TO STUDYING ADMINISTRATIVE LAW

ChapterScope —————————————————————————————

This chapter defines administrative law and introduces some key issues in administrative law, such as the sources of administrative law, methods for studying administrative law, the origins and roles of administrative agencies, and theories for understanding administrative law and agency behavior. The key points in this chapter are:

- **Defining administrative law:** Administrative law regulates the exercise of authority by executive officials, including officials of agencies that are formally independent of the executive branch.

- **Sources of administrative law:** Administrative law includes constitutional law, statutory law including the Administrative Procedure Act (APA), and common-law principles predating the APA.

- **Studying administrative law:** When studying administrative law, focus is usually on the sources of agency power, the constitutional limits on that power, the procedural requirements for exercise of agency power, and the availability and scope of judicial review of agency action.

- **Public interest versus public choice theories of regulation:** A fuller understanding of administrative law can be achieved by analyzing agency structure and agency action under the public interest and public choice theories of regulation.

    - **Public interest theory** analyzes administrative law with reference to the public policy goals of the government.

    - **Public choice theory** analyzes administrative law with reference to the political environment and realities of the administrative system.

I. WHAT IS ADMINISTRATIVE LAW?

Administrative law is the branch of law that regulates the exercise of authority by executive officials including officials of independent agencies. Administrative law originated in common-law actions directed at officials exercising government power, including mandamus, prohibition, and certiorari. Federal administrative law is largely a statutory and constitutional creation, although some pre-APA common-law elements survive. In this text the focus is on federal law, although most states have administrative law that resembles federal law.

A. The sources of administrative law

Administrative law derives mainly from four sources:

1. **The Constitution:** The Constitution of the United States limits the type of power that agencies may exercise and also places limits on the methods that agencies may employ to exercise that power.

2. **The Administrative Procedure Act:** The *Administrative Procedure Act (APA)* is a federal statute that prescribes the procedures agencies must follow and establishes the framework for judicial review of agency action.

3. **Particular agency enabling acts and other statutes:** The statute that establishes each agency and prescribes its mission (and other statutes directed at a particular agency) are important sources of law regarding a particular agency, and may even modify the APA with regard to that agency. Further, other statutes, such as the National Environmental Policy Act, may place obligations on agencies.

4. **Administrative common law:** Before the APA was enacted, common law regulating the exercise of government power had developed. Courts sometimes still refer to the common-law doctrines, often to explain the meaning or application of the APA.

B. **The study of administrative law**

In studying administrative law, it is helpful to focus on the following issues:

1. **The source of agency power:** You should identify the source of agency power (usually the agency's enabling act, which delegates power to the agency and describes the agency's jurisdiction) and understand the terms of the agency's power including any apparent or implicit limits on that power. Also, you need to be aware of the substantive terms of the agency's use of its delegated power—under what circumstances is the agency authorized or required to act?

2. **Constitutional limits on agency power:** You should be aware of potential constitutional limitations on agency power. The Constitution may limit the agency's power, either through specific provisions or through doctrines derived from the principle of separation of powers.

3. **The procedural requirements on the agency:** It is important to identify the procedural requirements placed on the agency. This is the heart of administrative law. Procedural requirements arise from the Constitution, the APA, administrative common law, the agency's particular statute, and other statutes that place obligations on administrative agencies.

4. **When is judicial review available?** The availability of *judicial review* is determined by application of the APA and the agency's particular statute, and it is important to be aware of when review is available and what actions are reviewable. Constitutional doctrines such as standing and ripeness, as well as administrative common law, can also influence the availability of judicial reveiw.

5. **What is the scope of judicial review?** The APA and the agency's particular statute determine the scope of judicial review—what standard the reviewing court applies. The scope of judicial review determines how deferential the reviewing court will be to the agency's decision.

6. **What enforcement mechanisms are available for the agency and for private parties?** Agency enforcement power may be limited by a particular statute, the APA, and the Constitution. Private parties may attempt to force agencies to bring enforcement actions or they may attempt to enforce regulatory norms themselves, without agency involvement.

II. THE ORIGINS AND ROLES OF ADMINISTRATIVE AGENCIES

A. The origins of the administrative state

The administrative state as we know it began in 1887 with the establishment of the first modern regulatory agency, the recently eliminated Interstate Commerce Commission. Antecedents to the administrative state have existed as long as the republic. For example, the first Congress authorized the President to appoint an official to estimate import duties. These were a very important source of income for the federal government and continue to be an important area of federal policy.

B. Agencies in the governmental structure

Most federal administrative agencies are within a department of the executive branch, in a chain of command with the President at the apex. Congress has designated some agencies, such as the Federal Communications Commission (FCC), as *independent agencies.* Independent agencies are not within any department of the federal government and are not under the supervision of the President or a cabinet officer.

C. The role of administrative agencies

Administrative agencies, as the name implies, administer government programs established by Congress.

D. Explanations for the growth of the administrative state

The administrative state has grown in response to the increased size and complexity of the economy and the increased demands from interest groups and voters for more regulation. As government programs have grown, so has the administrative state. New agencies have been established, and existing agencies have increased in size. Even with the wave of deregulatory thinking since the late 1970s, the overall size and scope of the federal government has not decreasd.

III. THE FUNCTIONS OF ADMINISTRATIVE AGENCIES

Administrative agencies perform a wide variety of functions in the United States at the local, state, and federal levels. As in most administrative law courses, this text concentrates on federal agencies.

A. Distribution of benefits

Administrative agencies distribute government benefits such as welfare, disability benefits, old-age benefits, medical care for poor people and seniors, and loan guarantees for home buyers and students. Agencies often adjudicate disputes that arise in these areas.

B. Granting of licenses and permits

Agencies rule on requests for licenses and permits in a wide variety of areas, including the construction and operation of nuclear power plants, logging on federally owned forest land, operation of stockyards, ownership and operation of television and radio stations, and the operation of commercial airlines.

C. Policymaking

Federal agencies make important policy decisions in a wide variety of areas. Congress often instructs an agency in very broad terms and leaves important matters to agency discretion, including whether to require automobiles to be equipped with seat belts, air bags, or both; how much of certain pollutants may be released into the air and water; the proper conditions for conducting elections to determine whether employees will be represented by a labor union; whether an interstate highway should be built through parkland; and the requirements for obtaining the various benefits, licenses, and permits administered or required by federal law in numerous areas.

D. Policymaking methods

Agencies make policy in a variety of ways, each of which is studied in depth elsewhere in this text. Policymaking methods include legislative *rulemaking, adjudication*, and informal procedures sometimes referred to as *informal adjudication*.

IV. PUBLIC INTEREST AND PUBLIC CHOICE EXPLANATIONS OF REGULATION AND THE STRUCTURE OF ADMINISTRATIVE AGENCIES

The *public interest* and *public choice* theories are the two major approaches to understanding and evaluating the work of agencies.

A. Public interest theory of regulation

Public interest theory explains administrative law based on traditional notions of the policy aims of regulation. Public interest theory holds that regulation is desirable in several, often related, situations.

1. **Externalities:** Regulation is desirable to prevent private parties from externalizing costs. For example, antipollution laws address the fact that polluters externalize the costs of their operations on people who live downwind or downstream of a pollution source.

2. **Creating and controlling monopolies:** Regulation is desirable to create monopolies when it is thought that competition would result in inadequate service to the public. Further regulation controls those monopolies so they provide adequate service and do not earn unreasonable profits. For example, in many areas government has granted a monopoly over the provision of electricity so that the electric company has an adequate incentive to wire all homes and businesses for electricity. The price and terms of the contract between the utility and its customers are then heavily regulated.

3. **Public goods:** Regulation is desirable when the producer of a valued good or service cannot force people to pay for the product. Payment for *public goods*, such as the national defense or scenic parkland, must be compelled through the tax system. Otherwise, no one would voluntarily pay, and the good would be underproduced.

4. **Information costs:** Inequalities of information in the marketplace might also justify government regulation in the form of mandatory disclosure. Consumers may value the information but be unable to bargain for it because of lack of market power or lack of sufficient information to even know what information to look for. This theory justifies, *inter alia*, food product labeling; efficiency ratings on products like automobiles, air conditioners, and refrigerators; and securities market disclosures.

B. Public interest theory of agency structure

Public interest theory evaluates the structure of agencies based on whether they are well suited to perform their functions. If the agency's function is to make policy in an area requiring scientific expertise, the structure should be designed to maximize the input of experts. If the agency's function is to award benefits or adjudicate disputes under a particular legal scheme, then the agency should be designed with process values in mind. In general, agencies should be structured to optimize the performance of those goals that are oriented to the public interest.

C. Public choice theory of regulation

Public choice theory explains regulation as a product of the political process in which parties with political power enlist government coercion to achieve goals that they could not achieve in a free market. One major reason for regulation, according to public choice theory, is the desire of government officials to increase their power and maximize their benefits from the regulatory scheme. Public choice observes that often the strongest impetus for regulation comes from government officials who see an opportunity to gain influence and make themselves more attractive in the future as highly paid employees in the industries they regulate.

Public choice rebuts each of the public interest explanations for regulation with an explanation based on political power.

1. **Externalities:** Public choice explains regulation of *externalities* as a victory of the more powerful party who could not prevent the other party's activity, either through the market or through traditional tort law such as nuisance. For example, there is no objective reason for preferring the interests of a quiet residential property owner over the interests of a noisy manufacturing business that residents dislike.

2. **Monopolies:** Public choice theorists are skeptical of claims that monopolies are necessary and view monopolies as governmentally enforced subsidization of politically powerful businesses. In the public choice view, utilities with monopoly rights tend to earn excessive profits, and the existence of the monopoly lowers the incentive to create more efficient and more desirable products and services. The ability of the public to politically resist monopoly creation is low because each consumer may suffer only a small negative effect from the monopoly.

3. **Public goods:** Public choice theorists see very few genuine public goods and view government compulsion in most public goods areas as tending toward overproduction of the good involved. For example, private schools and private parks exist, and they would be more efficiently provided if government did not use its power of taxation to create public competitors. Government intervention occurs because of the political power of the beneficiaries of the regulation.

4. **Information:** Public choice theorists suspect that forced disclosure of information results in overproduction of information—which means that consumers and producers are forced to pay for information they do not want. The market would determine how much information people want, and government intervention occurs because powerful consumer advocates lobby for tougher regulation (which in turn increases their support from consumers). Sometimes businesses lobby for more information disclosure. This occurs when producers of higher-quality products use government regulation to force competitors to disclose unfavorable facts.

D. Public choice and agency structure

Public choice theorists explain agency structure as created to maximize the influence of those parties, including members of Congress, most keenly interested in the output of the agency. When Congress wishes to maximize its own influence, it often creates an independent agency or otherwise structures the agency to insulate it from presidential control. Interest groups lobby for agency structure to increase their regulatory success. For example, labor unions lobbied to place authority over worker safety in the Department of Labor where they had the most influence, while business interests wanted authority placed in an independent agency to reduce the influence of organized labor.

E. Judicial power and administrative law

    1. Public interest: Public interest theories of administrative law see judicial review of agency action as providing a neutral forum for ensuring that agencies obey Congress's instructions, act rationally, and are not captured by powerful interests.

    2. Public choice: Public choice theories of administrative law see judicial review as a mechanism for enforcing the bargain arrived at in Congress or of satisfying constituencies that are concerned with unchecked agency power. For example, if powerful interests believe they will have greater success in an agency than in Congress, then public choice predicts that such interests will lobby for (and may get) weak judicial review, or no judicial review at all.

Quiz Yourself on ADMINISTRATIVE LAW FUNDAMENTALS

1. Is administrative law, especially administrative procedure, derived solely from the APA?

    _____

2. What functions do administrative agencies fulfill? _____

3. What are the differences between public interest and public choice theories of agency action?

    _____

Answers

1. No. While a great deal of administrative law grows out of the APA, administrative law also has sources in constitutional law (especially separation of powers norms) and in the common law of administrative review that governed before the passage of the APA. The particular statutes governing specific agencies are also important sources of administrative law. With regard to agency procedures, the APA, constitutional due process norms, and particular agency statutes all contribute to the procedural universe.

2. Administrative agencies distribute benefits, grant permits and licenses, and make and administer policy across a broad range of issues. As government regulation and government benefits distribution have increased, so have the number of agencies and the range of responsibilities of the agencies.

3. Public interest theories focus on the policy reasons for agency action, such as eliminating harmful pollution or redistributing wealth to poor people unable to acquire it in the market or through private charity. Public choice theories focus on the political activity that leads to agency action and are more likely to explain regulation and redistribution as the triumph of powerful interest groups who were able to use political clout to secure benefits for themselves from the legislature or agency. For example, while public interest theory would explain the regulation of rates in an industry as necessary to keep prices down while ensuring healthy businesses, public choice theory would explain rate regulation as government protecting businesses from competition that would tend to lower their prices.

Exam Tips on ADMINISTRATIVE LAW FUNDAMENTALS

Here are some important issues to keep in mind in connection with any administrative law exam:

☞ You should be clear on an exam about the *source of the law* that is relevant to the issues. Be explicit about when you are drawing on the *Constitution*, the *APA*, the *particular agency's statute*, some *other statute* or *traditional common-law* principles.

☞ Whenever an issue arises regarding agency power to act, look carefully at and draw upon the agency's *enabling act*.

☞ The political background often helps understand agency action.

   ☞ If, under public choice theory, it appears that an agency was *captured* by a powerful interest group, you might express skepticism about the agency's actions.

   ☞ On the other hand, if it appears agency experts are pursuing an important *public policy goal*, you might argue for deference to the agency.

CHAPTER 2

SEPARATION OF POWERS AND DISTRIBUTION OF ADMINISTRATIVE POWER

ChapterScope

This chapter analyzes the separation of powers problems raised by the administrative state and the distribution of power within the administrative state. The key points in this chapter are:

- **The nondelegation doctrine:** The Constitution vests the legislative power in Congress. The *non-delegation doctrine* prohibits Congress from delegating away its legislative power.

  - Congress often delegates discretionary power to administrative agencies, and the *nondelegation doctrine* regulates how much discretionary authority Congress may delegate to an agency.

  - The current understanding is that Congress must legislate an *"intelligible principle"* to guide the agency in its exercise of discretion.

- **The legislative veto is unconstitutional:** Congress attempts to control agencies through formal and informal means. One method of control that Congress employed is the *legislative veto*, under which a majority vote of some subset of Congress, usually one house, could veto an administrative action. The legislative veto was held unconstitutional as an attempt by Congress to legislate without meeting the constitutional requirements of bicameralism and presentment to the President.

- **Congress may not participate directly in the appointment or removal of executive officials:** The *Appointments Clause* provides for the appointment of officers of the United States by the President with Senate confirmation or, for inferior officers when specified by Congress, by the President alone, by a department head or by the courts.

  - Except for Senate confirmation and removal under the impeachment process, Congress may not participate directly in the appointment or removal of officers of the United States.

  - Congress may hire its own officials when their activities are in aid of legislation and not executive in nature.

- **Congress may legislatively restrict the President's ability to remove officials:** Congress may restrict (to a "for cause" or other similar standard) the President's ability to remove all but certain high-level executive officials. For very high-level officials, the President is entitled to unrestricted power to remove them.

- **Agencies may adjudicate public rights and some private disputes in closely regulated areas:** Congress may assign to administrative agencies the power to adjudicate *public rights* disputes (rights against the government). Congress also may grant agencies the power to adjudicate private disputes in closely regulated fields, so long as the *essential attributes of judicial power* remain in the courts.

I. THE NONDELEGATION DOCTRINE

The ***nondelegation doctrine*** prohibits excessive delegation of discretionary powers by the Congress to federal agencies. This doctrine stems from the concept of the ***separation of powers***. In its crudest form, separation of powers means that each branch of government is confined to exercising those powers within its particular sphere, and any attempt by one branch to exercise a power properly belonging to another branch violates the separation of powers. However, it is often difficult to identify which branch "owns" a particular function and which function a branch is exercising in any particular action. Thus, separation of powers analysis is often pragmatic rather than conceptual, asking whether the system is functioning properly rather than whether a power, by definition, belongs to a different branch.

A. The rule against the delegation of legislative power to the executive branch

1. **Historical origins:** Early cases stated that the Constitution absolutely prohibited the delegation of legislative authority from Congress to the executive branch. However, this did not mean that Congress could not assign discretionary authority to the executive branch, but only that any delegated authority had to be executive in nature and not legislative.

2. **Permissible delegations. "Filling up the details":** In several early cases, the Court upheld delegations on the ground that Congress had made the legislative decisions and the executive branch was merely filling in details or acting under Congress's instructions when certain facts were found to exist. Under this analysis, the discretion exercised by executive officials was not legislative but rather was discretion inherent in the execution of the laws.

   Examples: In *The Brig Aurora*, 11 U.S. (7 Cranch) 382 (1813), the Court upheld Congress's delegation to the President of the authority to lift an embargo of European trade when he found that the subjects of the embargo had. "ceased to violate the neutral commerce of the United States." In *Wayman v. Southard*, 23 U.S. (10 Wheat.) 1 (1825), the Court approved a delegation of power to the federal courts to make their own rules of procedure. In *Field v. Clark*, 143 U.S. 649 (1892), the Court upheld a delegation of power to the President to impose tariffs when the President found the need for the tariffs. Finally, in *United States v. Grimaud*, 220 U.S. 506 (1911), the Court rejected a rancher's challenge to a fine levied for violating a regulation restricting grazing that was promulgated by the Secretary of Agriculture under a broad delegated power to protect the national forests from "fire and depredations." In all these cases, the Court held that the delegation was permissible since only the power to "fill up the details" had been delegated.

B. The intelligible principle test

1. ***J. W. Hampton***: In *J. W. Hampton, Jr. & Co. v. United States*, 276 U.S. 394 (1928), the Court stated that a delegation is permissible when Congress "lay[s] down by legislative act an ***intelligible principle*** to which the person or body authorized to fix such rates is directed to conform." *Hampton*, 276 U.S. at 409. *Hampton* involved a challenge to Congress's delegation of authority to the President to alter tariffs when the President found that statutorily established tariffs did not equalize the costs of production between the United States and competing foreign countries. In the course of approving this delegation under familiar nondelegation doctrine concepts, the Court announced its new ***intelligible principle*** test.

2. **Loosening of nondelegation standards:** The intelligible principle standard appears to substantially loosen the constraints placed on agencies by the nondelegation doctrine. The Court's reliance on the existence of an "intelligible principle" to guide administrative action

acknowledges that agencies do not act mechanically when they "fill up the details" but actually exercise a great deal of discretion and judgment.

C. New deal strict application

The New Deal era witnessed an explosion in regulatory programs designed to achieve and maintain economic recovery. The Supreme Court greeted New Deal legislation with a great deal of skepticism, and in addition to many decisions invalidating state and federal legislation on other grounds, it struck down three federal statutory provisions on delegation grounds.

1. *Panama Refining and Schechter Poultry:* The National Industrial Recovery Act (NIRA) granted the President broad powers to regulate the economy during the Great Depression. One provision granted the President power to exclude petroleum products from interstate commerce if they were produced or marketed in violation of state restrictions. In *Panama Refining Co. v. Ryan*, 293 U.S. 388 (1935), this provision was declared unconstitutional on the ground that it contained no standards guiding the President's decision of whether to invoke his powers in a particular case. Another NIRA provision granted the President the power to approve and thus make legally binding codes of "fair competition" that would be drafted and submitted by private trade organizations. In *Schechter Poultry Corp. v. United States*, 295 U.S. 495 (1935), the Court invalidated this provision of the NIRA on essentially the same ground as it relied upon in *Panama Refining*, i.e., that it contained insufficient standards guiding the President's discretion over whether to approve a particular code of fair competition. The problem with both provisions, according to the Court, was that the President could legally decline to take action under any set of circumstances. (Schechter Poultry also relied on the fact that the codes were drafted by private groups.) A broadly stated set of statutory purposes was not sufficient to save the statute from invalidation under the nondelegation doctrine.

2. **Public process requirement:** The Court also faulted the NIRA for failing to require a public process for the formulation and approval of the codes of fair competition. The Court strongly criticized the grant to private organizations of the power to draft the codes and the lack of notice or public procedures for the carrying out of this legislative-type function. The Court noted that in other cases where broad delegations had been upheld (such as the delegation to the FCC of the power to act in the public convenience, interest, or necessity in regulating the broadcasting industry), the existence of statutorily mandated agency procedures was an important safeguard against the evils of delegation.

3. *Carter Coal:* In *Carter v. Carter Coal Co.*, 298 U.S. 238 (1936), the Court struck down a statute that authorized coal producers to elect local boards with power to set minimum prices for coal in their districts. The Court rejected this delegation out of hand, characterizing it as "legislative delegation in its most obnoxious form for it is not even delegation to an official or an official body . . . but to private persons whose interests may be and often are adverse to the interests of others in the same business." *Carter Coal*, 298 U.S. at 311.

D. The return to a lenient nondelegation doctrine

1. *Yakus* and "practical necessity": In the 1940s, the Court signaled a shift back to a more liberal attitude toward delegation. In *Yakus v. United States,* 321 U.S. 414 (1944), the Court upheld a delegation to an agency to fix "generally fair and equitable" rent and price ceilings. The Court stated that delegation of discretion to agencies was a practical necessity and that broad delegations of discretion were permissible so long as discernible boundaries of discretion

existed. In several cases following *Yakus*, the Court relied upon congressional purposes and effective legal and political controls to uphold statutes against delegation-based challenges.

2. **The dormant nondelegation doctrine:** The Court's recent hospitable attitude toward delegations, and the fact that no statutes have been struck down on delegation grounds since the 1930s, may mean that the delegation doctrine no longer poses a substantial bar to congressional delegation of discretion to agencies or to the President. Even though the Court continues to evaluate challenges to delegations on the "intelligible principle" standard, the Court always manages to find sufficient legislative guidance to withstand attack. Also, the presence of alternative legal and political safeguards against agency overreaching may; help validate an otherwise questionable delegation. *See Amalgamated Meat Cutters v. Connolly,* 337 F. Supp. 737 (D.D.C. 1971).

3. **The *Benzene* case: Nondelegation as statutory interpretation**

   a. ***Benzene's* holding:** In *Industrial Union Department, AFL-CIO v. American Petroleum Institute (The Benzene Cases),* 448 U.S. 607 (1980), the Court relied upon the nondelegation doctrine to narrowly construe the Occupational Safety and Health Administration's *(OSHA)* authority to prescribe occupational health and safety standards. The American Petroleum Institute, and others, challenged an OSHA regulation that severely reduced permissible occupational exposure to benzene, a carcinogen. The challengers argued that the rule was not adequately supported by evidence in the rulemaking record that the reduction was necessary to protect the health of exposed workers. The agency argued that it had a statutory duty to regulate carcinogens to, the lowest possible level of exposure that was technologically and economically feasible. The plurality rejected the agency's position and construed the statute, in part on nondelegation grounds, to require a threshold finding of a ***significant risk*** in the workplace before the agency was authorized to promulgate a workplace safety standard.

   b. ***Benzene* and the nondelegation doctrine:** The plurality stated that without the significant risk requirement, the statute might be unconstitutional under the nondelegation doctrine. The nondelegation violation here would apparently be the lack of guidance on when the agency was authorized or expected to pursue the goal of a virtually risk-free workplace. Unfortunately, from the plurality's opinion, it is actually difficult to see how the nondelegation doctrine is relevant to the case.

   c. **Justice Rehnquist's nondelegation concurrence:** Justice Rehnquist's *Benzene* concurrence argues that the statute violates the nondelegation doctrine because the agency's choice of when to pursue the goal of a virtually risk-free workplace is statutorily unconstrained. Justice Rehnquist's opinion extols the virtues of the nondelegation doctrine. He argues that the Court should reinvigorate the nondelegation doctrine because it (1) forces Congress, the representative branch of government, to make important policy choices; (2) increases the guidance under which agencies act; and (3) facilitates judicial review by requiring more definite statutory standards against which courts can measure administrative decisions. Justice Rehnquist's effort to revive the delegation doctrine failed, and he gained only the support of Chief Justice Burger in a later opinion attacking the same provision of the OSH Act.

4. **Post-*Benzene* nondelegation cases:** Since the *Benzene* case, the Court has rejected several delegation challenges.

   a. ***Touby v. United States:*** In *Touby v. United States,* 500 U.S. 160 (1991), the Court upheld a delegation of power to the Attorney General to place a drug on a list of controlled substances, thus creating criminal liability for the sale or manufacture of the drug. Touby argued that the intelligible principle test was too lenient in cases involving executive creation of criminal liability. The Court held that even if a more stringent test was required for delegations of the power to create crimes, the delegation in *Touby* satisfied it.

b. *Mistretta v. United States:* In *Mistretta v. United States,* 488 U.S. 361 (1989), the Court applied the intelligible principle test to uphold the Sentencing Reform Act, which delegated the authority to promulgate mandatory federal sentencing guidelines to the United States Sentencing Commission. The Court held that the act's declaration of purposes and goals, and its specification of the factors to be considered by the commission, provided a sufficient intelligible principle. The Court also rejected Justice Scalia's dissenting argument that the statute was unconstitutional because the Sentencing Commission was, in effect, a mini-legislature since it had no function other than promulgating the guidelines. For Justice Scalia, such a minilegislature was unconstitutional because its discretion was not incident to the performance of an executive function.

c. "Intelligible principle" as generalized instructions: It appears that under current law, relatively general statutory purposes or broadly stated instructions to agencies will supply an intelligible principle and thus meet the requirements of the nondelegation doctrine.

E. Attempted revival of the nondelegation doctrine: *Whitman v. American Trucking Associations, Inc.*

1. The D.C. Circuit directs EPA to create its own intelligible principle. In *American Trucking Associations, Inc. v. U.S. Environmental Protection Agency,* 175 F.3d 1027 (D.C. Cir. 1999), the D.C. Circuit attempted a revival of the nondelegation doctrine, but with a twist under which an agency could cure a violation of the nondelegation doctrine by adopting a construction of its statute limiting its own discretion.

a. The rules and statute at issue: The American Trucking Associations (ATA) challenged the EPA's promulgation of National Ambient Air Quality Standards (NAAQS) for ozone and particulate matter. The Clean Air Act (CAA) requires EPA to establish standards "requisite to protect the public health" with an "adequate margin of safety." ATA argued on judicial review of the NAAQS that the EPA's construction of the CAA violated the nondelegation doctrine.

b. The D.C. Circuit's holding: The D.C. Circuit found a violation of the nondelegation doctrine not so much because the statute lacked an intelligible principle but rather because EPA had not adopted an intelligible principle to confine its own discretion. The problem for the court was that there was no preexisting principle either in the statute or in any announced EPA rule that directed the choice among numerous possible levels for the various pollutants EPA regulates.

c. Remand to the agency: The court thus remanded the case to the EPA to allow that agency to construe the statute to avoid the constitutional violation. The court reasoned that under the Benzene case, a limiting construction might provide an intelligible principle for a statute that would otherwise be unconstitutional under the nondelegation doctrine, and that the agency ought to be given the first chance to adopt the limiting construction.

2. The Supreme Court reverses: The Supreme Court reversed the D.C. Circuit's decision and rejected its novel understanding of the nondelegation doctrine. *See Whitman v. American Trucking Associations, Inc.,* 531 U.S. 457 (2001).

a. **Reaffirmation of the intelligible principle test:** The Supreme Court reaffirmed the ***intelligible principle*** test for deciding whether a statute contains sufficient guidance to pass muster under the nondelegation doctrine and held that the CAA's language, requiring NAAQS that are "requisite to protect the public health" with an "adequate margin of safety," easily meets that test.

b. **Rejection of agency limiting construction as a cure for nondelegation violations:** To the Supreme Court, and to most observers of the decision, the D.C. Circuit's remand to the agency to create its own intelligible principle made no sense in light of nondelegation doctrine's primary purpose of ensuring that Congress makes the important legislative decisions. The Court stated that "[t]he idea that an agency can cure an unconstitutionally standardless delegation of power by declining to exercise some of that power seems to us internally contradictory. The very choice of what portion of the power to exercise ... would itself be an exercise of the forbidden legislative authority." Thus, the nondelegation doctrine remains, after *Whitman*, relatively toothless.

II. CONGRESSIONAL CONTROL OF ADMINISTRATIVE AGENCIES

A. **Informal congressional influence**

1 **Informal contacts with agency officials:** Members of Congress have numerous informal contacts with agency personnel to express their interests and the interests of their constituents in the outcome of agency action. Members of Congress also seek information from agency officials and summon them to committee hearings to explain their actions.

2. **Congressional influence on agency appointments:** Congress influences agency action by pressuring the President to appoint officials favored by members of Congress. These officials owe their agency positions to members of Congress who retain influence over their actions at the agency.

B. **Formal congressional influence** Congress can formally influence agency action through agency funding provisions in appropriations bills, by statutorily restricting agency action, and by overruling regulations under recent legislation that gives Congress sixty days to review major agency rules before they go into effect. Congress also attempts to increase its influence on agency action by creating independent agencies that are less subject to presidential control.

C. **The Legislative veto and review of regulations**

1. **The legislative veto defined:** Under the ***legislative veto***, Congress reserved the power to reject agency action (usually regulations) with a vote, depending on the particular provision, of both houses of Congress, by one house of Congress, or in some cases even by a single congressional committee. Legislative vetoes were not presented to the President for signature or veto. For several decades, Congress employed the legislative veto to control agency action.

2. **The *Chadha* decision:** In *Immigration and Naturalization Service v. Chadha*, 462 U.S. 919 (1983), the Supreme Court held a one-house legislative veto unconstitutional. In *Chadha*, the House of Representatives vetoed the decision of the Attorney General to suspend Chadha's deportation. (Suspension of deportation is a procedure under which an otherwise deportable

alien is allowed to remain in the United States due to extreme hardship to the alien or the alien's family.) The Court held that the one-house veto violated the ***bicameralism*** and ***presentment*** requirements of the Constitution. The Court held that bicameralism and presentment apply to all congressional actions that affect the legal rights and duties of persons outside the legislative branch. This was the case in *Chadha*, since the legislative veto required the Attorney General to deport Chadha when Chadha otherwise would have been allowed to remain in the United States.

3. **After *Chadha*, all legislative vetoes are unconstitutional**: The *Chadha* Court's reliance on bicameralism and presentment means that all legislative vetoes are unconstitutional. Thus, Congress's only method of nullifying agency action is through legislation that passes both houses of Congress and is presented to the President.

4. **Congressional review of regulations:** In a part of the Contract with America Advancement Act of 1996, Congress created a procedure in a new APA chapter (Chapter 8) under which agency rules can be rejected by a resolution that passes both houses of Congress and is presented to the President. The resolution must be introduced in Congress within sixty session days of Congress receiving notice of the rule, and major rules cannot become effective until after the sixty days have expired. This procedure meets the bicameralism and presentment requirements.

D. Congressional involvement in appointment and removal of executive officials

The Appointments Clause, Article II, Section 2, Clause 2 of the Constitution, provides:

> [The President] shall nominate, and by and with the Advice and Consent of the Senate, shall appoint . . . all other Officers of the United States, whose appointments are not herein otherwise provided for, and which shall be established by Law: but the Congress may by Law vest the Appointment of such Inferior Officers, as they think proper, in the President alone, in the Courts of Law, or in the Heads of Departments.

1. **Congress may not appoint administrative officials. *Buckley v. Valeo*:** In *Buckley v. Valeo*, 424 U.S. 1 (1976), the Court ruled that the Federal Election Commission (FEC) could not engage in ***executive functions*** such as ***rulemaking*** and ***enforcement*** because four of its six members were appointed by members of Congress (two by the president pro tempore of the Senate and two by the Speaker of the House). The Court held that only officers of the United States may exercise authority under the laws of the United States and that such officials must be appointed in accordance with the Appointments Clause of the Constitution. The Appointments Clause does not confer any appointment power on Congress or its members. The Court did allow the FEC to collect information and make reports to Congress. Those activities were held to be "merely in aid of legislation" and did not involve the exercise of authority pursuant to the laws of the United States in ways that would affect persons outside of Congress.

2. **Congressional influence over appointments:** Congress's powers, including power over the budget and other presidentially favored legislation, and the Senate's constitutional advice and consent power can effectively force the President to appoint persons as administrators who are favored by key members of Congress. Congress often formally influences appointments by requiring bipartisanship and by legislatively regulating the agency chairman's party.

3. **Congressional appointment of legislative officials:** The Court in *Buckley* did allow that Congress and its officials may participate in the appointment of officials who act merely in aid of legislation, such as officers who gather information or do research to help Congress decide whether and how to legislate. However, officials appointed by Congress may not exercise authority under the laws of the United States, such as prosecutorial or rulemaking

authority, because they have not been appointed in accordance with the Appointments Clause. Therefore, the FEC could not engage in rulemaking or enforcement activities but could receive information and make reports to Congress.

4. **Congress may not participate in the removal of administrative officials:** Other than removal via *impeachment* and conviction, the Constitution contains no provision regarding the removal of officials. The Court has held that officers of the United States may not be subject to removal by congressional action, except by impeachment by the House and conviction by the Senate.

   a. ***Bowsher v. Synar*:** In *Bowsher v. Synar*, 478 U.S. 714 (1986), the Court held that the *comptroller general*, an official subject to removal by joint resolution of Congress (with presentment to the President), could not exercise authority under the laws of the United States and thus could not establish potentially binding spending reductions under the Balanced Budget and Emergency Deficit Control Act of 1985. The Court held that this would violate the separation of powers because Congress would be interfering in the execution of the laws through the power to participate in the removal of an officer of the United States.

   b. **Congress may restrict removal of administrative officials to "good cause":** Congress may place statutory restrictions, such as "good cause," on the removal of administrative officials. Congress may also delegate the removal power to an official under presidential control. For example, in *Morrison v. Olson*, 487 U.S. 654 (1988), the Court upheld the Independent Counsel Act, under which a prosecutor appointed to investigate alleged wrongdoing by executive officials could be removed only by the Attorney General and only for cause.

5. **Members of Congress may not serve as administrative officials**

   a. **The Incompatibility Clause:** The Incompatibility Clause, Article I, Section 6, Clause 2 of the Constitution, forbids members of Congress from holding executive appointments during their terms in Congress.

   b. **Separation of powers:** In addition to violating the Incompatibility Clause, it would violate separation of powers for members of Congress to serve as administrators.

      Example: Congress designated certain members of Congress (formally in their private capacities as airport users) to serve on the Metropolitan Washington Airports Authority, a board that administers the airports in the Washington, D.C., area. The Supreme Court held that the arrangement violated the Constitution, either because the authority's work would amount to legislation by a subgroup of Congress without bicameralism and presentment or because it involved congressional participation in the execution of the law. *See Metropolitan Washington Airports Authority v. Citizens for Abatement of Aircraft Noise, Inc.*, 501 U.S. 252 (1991).

III. EXECUTIVE CONTROL OF ADMINISTRATIVE AGENCIES

Article II places the President at the apex of the executive branch and, therefore, the administrative hierarchy. Thus, the President should be able to exert a great deal of control over administrative officials and agencies. However, Congress attempts, in many different ways, to insulate administrative officials from presidential control.

A. Inherent executive power The Constitution vests all the executive power in the President of the United States. The power inherent in that grant, and in the office of the President, has historically not been very clear.

   1. The President's seizure of the steel mills: During the Korean War, after steel workers threatened to go on strike, President Truman issued an ***executive order*** directing the Secretary of Commerce to seize the nation's steel mills.

   2. The Court's invalidation of the seizure: The Supreme Court held that President Truman's order to seize the steel mills was invalid. The Court rejected the administration's arguments that the President's actions were within his power as commander-in-chief of the armed forces or within his power to enforce the laws. The Court noted that no statute authorized the seizure and that therefore the President was making, rather than simply enforcing, the law. *See Youngstown Sheet & Tube Co. v. Sawyer*, 343 U.S. 579 (1952).

   3. Justice Jackson's Steel Seizure concurrence: In his concurring opinion, Justice Jackson argued that the question of presidential power was more complicated and that the Court should have looked beyond the question of whether the President was acting pursuant to statutory authorization. Justice Jackson admitted that the President's power is at its greatest when acting pursuant to express or implied congressional authorization and at its weakest when acting contrary to Congress's will. Jackson argued that there is a category in the middle when the President acts with neither support nor disapproval from Congress. In such cases the President's power to act may be concurrent with Congress's, and the lack of congressional authorization does not necessarily mean that the President, when exercising power, is engaged in lawmaking.

   4. Legality of Executive Orders: More recent cases have made it clear that while the President has the inherent authority to manage the Executive Branch, the President does not have the authority to issue executive orders that are contrary to law. In *Chamber of Commerce v. Reich*, 74 F.3d 1322 (D.C. Cir. 1996), the Court of Appeals invalidated an order issued by President Clinton prohibiting federal agencies from contracting with companies that had hired permanent replacements for striking workers. The court found that Clinton's order was contrary to the National Labor Relations Act (NLRA), which allows employers to hire permanent replacements in some circumstances. However, in *Building & Construction Trades Dept., AFL-CIO v. Allbaugh*, 295 F.3d 28 (D.C. Cir. 2002), the Court of Appeals upheld an executive order issued by President George W. Bush prohibiting federal agencies from either requiring or forbidding their contractors to use a particular form of labor agreement known as a Project Labor Agreement. The court placed primary reliance on the President's inherent "supervisory authority over the Executive Branch." 295 F.3d at 33. The court also noted that Bush's order purported to apply only "to the extent permitted by law" thus avoiding conflict with the NLRA.

B. The unitary executive theory

The ***unitary executive theory*** holds that the Constitution vests all executive power in the President. Under this theory, any attempt by Congress to insulate officials and agencies from complete presidential control is suspect and probably unconstitutional. This theory (whose advocates include Justice Scalia) is attractive for its simplicity and apparent adherence to constitutional text but does not reflect governing law.

C. Presidential control of appointment of executive officials: The Appointments Clause

The President exerts a great deal of control over the executive branch through the power to appoint officers of the United States. The appointment of such officials must be made pursuant to the procedures specified in the ***Appointments Clause***. This clause provides that the President, with the advice and consent of the Senate, appoints officers of the United States, and Congress may specify that ***inferior officers*** are appointed by the President alone, by the heads of departments, or by the courts of law.

1. **Principal versus inferior officers:** The Appointments Clause distinguishes between officers of the United States who must be appointed by the President with the advice and consent of the Senate, and ***inferior officers*** who may be appointed pursuant to the alternative procedures specified in the clause. To distinguish them from inferior officers, those officers who must be appointed by the President are often referred to as ***principal or superior officers***. There is no clear substantive line between principal and inferior officers.

   a. **Principal officers:** Principal officers are high-level officials in the executive branch and heads of independent agencies. Cabinet members and commissioners of independent agencies are principal officers because there is no one in the government hierarchy between them and the President. There is not a great deal of caselaw about whether a particular government official is a principal, or inferior, officer.

   b. **Inferior officers:** Inferior officers are lower-level executive officials who are under the supervision of other executive officials beneath the President. In *Morrison v. Olson, supra*, the Court held that an independent counsel is an inferior officer. The independent counsel was appointed by a special panel of the United States court of appeals to investigate wrongdoing by executive branch officials and could be removed by the Attorney General for cause, but was not under the supervision of the Attorney General or any other executive branch official. The Court relied on the **limited scope and duration** of the independent prosecutor's appointment and the **Attorney General's removal power,** to hold that the independent prosecutor is not a principal officer. However, in *Edmond v. United States*, 520 U.S. 651 (1997), the Court held that judges on a Coast Guard Court of Criminal Appeals, whose appointments were not limited in scope or duration as was the appointment of the Independent Counsel, were nevertheless inferior officers, primarily because their work "is directed and supervised at some level by others who were appointed by Presidential nomination with the advice and consent of the Senate." 520 U.S. at 663. The Court emphasized that the factors relied upon in *Morrison* were not intended to be exclusive.

   c. **Appointment of Inferior Officers:** Unless Congress specifies otherwise, inferior officers are appointed via the same procedure as principal officers: by the President with the advice and consent of the Senate. However, the Appointments Clause allows Congress to specify, by legislation, that inferior officers may be appointed by the President alone, by the courts of law or the heads of departments, such as the Secretary of Transportation who appointed the judges in *Edmond*. In *Morrison v. Olson*, the Court held that because the Appointments Clause provides that courts of law may, pursuant to legislation by Congress, appoint inferior officers, a federal court may appoint an independent counsel. The courts of law may appoint inferior officials exercising executive authority.

   d. **Incongruous appointments:** The Court, in dicta in *Morrison v. Olson*, stated that there were constitutional limits to Congress's ability to assign the appointment of inferior officers under the Appointments Clause. The Court suggested that some appointments might be in congruous. For example, appointments made across departmental lines or by a court appointing an official to a position unrelated to law or legal processes (such as an undersecretary of a department) may be incongruous. Incongruous appointments may violate the separation of powers.

2. **Employees.** There are subordinate federal **employees** who are neither principal nor inferior officers and thus may be appointed pursuant to procedures other than those provided for in the Appointments Clause, such as a civil-service-type appointments process. "Employees" are low-level officials who are employed by the federal government but exercise no discretion or authority to administer federal law. Clerical workers and maintenance workers are paradigm examples of employees. Officials who exercise discretion and authority are **officers**, not employees. For example, in *Freytag v. Commissioner of Internal Revenue*, 501 U.S. 868 (1991), the Supreme Court held that "special trial judges" utilized by the United States Tax Court were "**officers of the United States**." Interestingly, the Supreme Court did not base its decision on the fact that the special trial judges could make final decisions in minor cases. Rather, the Court relied upon the discretion and authority involved in presiding over hearings even in cases in which the special trial judges could make only recommendations to tax court judges. Nevertheless, the D.C. Circuit, in *Landry v. FDIC*, 204 F.3d 1125 (D.C. Cir. 2000), held that administrative law judges who could only recommend agency action were **employees** and not **officers** simply because they could not make final decisions in any category of cases. The *Landry* court's distinction of *Freytag*, on the basis that *Freytag* was grounded upon the power of the special trial judges to make final decisions in some cases, does not appear to be faithful to the language of the opinion in *Freytag*.

D. Congressional involvement in appointment of officers of the United States

Because there is no provision in the Appointments Clause for congressional appointment power, Congress may not participate directly in the appointment of officers of the United States (principal or inferior) except through the Senate's advice and consent power.

E. Removal of executive officials

The Constitution does not mention the removal of officials except through impeachment, an extraordinary procedure under which the House charges and the Senate tries officials for "Treason, Bribery, or other high Crimes and misdemeanors:" Impeachment and conviction results in removal from office. Despite the absence of explicit constitutional authority, the Supreme Court has held that the President has the right to remove executive officials, subject to restrictions Congress may place on the President's removal power.

1. **Presidential power to remove executive officials:** In the absence of statutory restrictions, the President has the power to remove executive officials at will.

2. **Congressionally imposed restrictions on removal of officials:** Congress may, under certain circumstances, restrict the President's power to remove executive officials but Congress itself may not retain advice and consent power over removal of officials or participate in the removal of officials except through exercise of the impeachment power.

   a. *Myers v. United States*: In *Myers v. United States,* 272 U.S. 52 (1926), the Supreme Court ruled that Congress may not statutorily require the President to seek the Senate's permission before removing a local postmaster, an official considered to be performing purely executive functions. Although this case is often cited as establishing the President's unlimited constitutional power to remove purely executive officials, the holding is actually narrower, providing only that the Senate may not retain a role in the removal of such officials. In fact, the Court notes in dicta that Congress may restrict the removal of inferior officers.

b. ***Humphrey's Executor***: In *Humphrey's Executor v. United States*, 295 U.S. 602 (1935), the Court held that Congress may require a finding of cause before an official exercising ***quasi-legislative*** and ***quasi-judicial*** power may be removed. The Court distinguished *Myers* on the ground that Humphrey, as a federal trade commissioner, exercised legislative rulemaking and adjudicatory powers that were appropriately shielded from excessive presidential influence, while the postmaster in *Myers* exercised purely executive functions. In addition, Humphrey, as a commissioner of an independent agency, may not have been an inferior officer and thus, the *Myers* dicta allowing restrictions on removal of inferior officers might not have applied to him. Therefore, the quasi-judicial and quasi-legislative nature of the functions performed provided a constitutionally sufficient justification for restricting the President's removal of a principal officer.

c. ***Morrison v.* Olson and removal power:** *Morrison v. Olson*, 487 U.S. 654 (1988), holds that Congress may restrict the removal of an official exercising purely executive functions. In *Morrison*, the Court approved a provision of the Ethics in Government Act that confined the removal of an independent counsel to personal action by the Attorney General and only on a finding of "good cause." The Court rejected reading *Myers* as entitling the President to unlimited power to remove officials exercising executive functions. The Court also rejected reading *Humphrey's Executor* to confine Congress's power to restrict removal to officials exercising nonexecutive functions such as quasi-legislative and quasijudicial power. Thus, *Morrison* greatly increases Congress's power to restrict the President's ability to remove executive branch officials.

F. Separation of powers and the appointment and removal powers

Separation of powers mandates that one branch may not interfere with another branch's ability to carry out its constitutionally assigned functions.

1. ***Morrison v. Olson* and the appointment power:** In *Morrison v. Olson*, the Court decided that separation of powers was not violated by a federal court's appointment of an independent counsel to investigate the executive branch. The Court held that investigation and prosecution by an independent counsel appointed by a court of law would not threaten the President's ability to properly execute the laws.

2. ***Morrison v. Olson* and the removal power:** In *Morrison*, the Court stated that Congress may restrict the President's power to remove executive officials as long as the President's ability to carry out his constitutionally assigned functions is not compromised. The Court held that it is permissible to restrict the removal of an independent counsel to removal by the Attorney General for cause. The Court held that the "for cause" provision and the assignment of the removal power to the Attorney General did not violate the separation of powers standard.

3. Separation of powers and congressional involvement in appointment and removal: The Court has been very strict in its apparently absolute rejection of a formal role for Congress in the appointment and removal of officials outside of impeachment. Congress may not participate in the appointment and removal of officers of the United States; While. Congress may appoint officials who help Congress perform its legislative function, those officials may not engage in executive activity (which the Court defines as the exercise of authority under the laws of the United States).

G. Direct presidential supervision of administrative agencies

Presidents have long struggled to control and coordinate the activities of administrative agencies, while Congress has attempted to insulate agencies from presidential influence. There are several routes that presidents have taken to gain greater control of agencies.

1. **Executive orders requiring centralized control over agencies:** Every President since Jimmy Carter has, by executive order, required agencies to participate in a centralized review of regulatory proposals. President Reagan established centralized review by the Office of Management and Budget (OMB) in the White House; and that review has continued under subsequent administrations. As part of this regulatory review, agencies have been required to perform a *cost-benefit analysis* of their proposed regulations, and OMB has attempted to influence agencies to produce more cost-effective regulation.

2. **Budgetary control over agencies:** Agencies' budget requests are channeled through OMB, giving the President another method of controlling agencies. Congress, of course, is free to set an agency's budget at the level it prefers. In the case of at least one agency, the International Trade Commission (ITC), Congress has statutorily provided that the agency submit its budget directly to Congress without presidential review via OMB. This shields the ITC from presidential influence.

3. **The special case of the independent agencies:** Congress designates some agencies as "independent" in order to shield them from presidential influence and to maintain greater congressional influence over them. Congress states, in the enabling acts creating these agencies, that they are "independent" and not located in any department of the executive branch. These agencies are typically headed by commissioners appointed for a term of years by the President with the advice and consent of the Senate with removal by the President only for good cause. In recognition of the special position of the independent agencies, presidents have not attempted to control them nearly as much as the agencies within the executive branch. For example, President Clinton required independent agencies to participate in a centralized regulatory planning process, but he did not require them to submit their regulations to OMB for review.

4. **Patronage and civil service:** Through the *patronage* system, presidents historically maintained a great deal of control over the personnel within the executive branch.

   a. **Patronage defined:** In a patronage system, party loyalists (or persons recommended by party loyalists) are chosen to fill positions at all levels in a new administration.

   b. **Civil service system defined:** In the *civil service system* that exists today, all but the highest government positions are filled through a merit selection process. Further, civil service employees have statutory job security that protects them from replacement when a new administration takes over.

   c. **First Amendment limits on patronage:** The Supreme Court has held that the First Amendment limits the President's right to replace government officials for political reasons. Most government employees have the right to engage in political activity, such as party membership and voting, and they may not be fired for exercising that right. Therefore, the President may replace, for political reasons, only officers where the need for loyalty to the President outweighs the officials' interest in engaging in the political activity—such as officials in confidential positions and officials who engage in relatively high-level policymaking.

H. The line item veto: In an attempt to control spending, Congress passed the Line Item Veto Act, under which the President was granted the power to cancel certain items of spending and tax benefits contained in legislation. The President was first required to sign the bill in which the items were contained. Then, the President could cancel items by transmitting a message to that effect to Congress within five days of signing the bill. In a decision reminiscent of *Chadha*, the Supreme Court held this procedure unconstitutional since in effect it granted the President unilateral power to amend or repeal legislation. *See Clinton v. City of New York*, 524 U.S. 417 (1998). The problem with the Line Item Veto Act was that once the President signed the bill passed by Congress, the entire bill became law, and only further legislation by both Houses of Congress could amend or repeal it. The Court rejected the argument that the President was merely exercising delegated authority on the ground that when the President cancels an item so soon after signing the bill, the President is rejecting Congress's judgment, not furthering Congress's policy.

IV. ADJUDICATION WITHIN ADMINISTRATIVE AGENCIES

Agency adjudication raises a separation of powers problem. Because Article III vests the judicial power in the ***Article III courts***, it has been argued that administrative agencies usurp that power when they adjudicate cases. However, the Supreme Court has approved of a great deal of agency adjudication. While originally such approval was limited to three categories—public rights, territorial courts, and military courts—recent cases have approved much broader adjudication in non-Article III courts.

A. Public rights

The adjudication of ***public rights*** (claims against the government) may be assigned to administrative agencies. There are two related theories that justify using administrative power to adjudicate public rights disputes.

1. Adjudication not necessary: First, since historically public rights disputes could have been decided within the government without any adjudication, the government's choice of an adjudicatory procedure within an administrative agency has been held not to violate Article III. Even if due process property rights in government benefits now require adjudication, adjudication in an agency may satisfy due process.

2. Public rights did not exist at common law: Second, since claims against the government were barred at common law by ***sovereign immunity***, assigning their adjudication to administrative agencies does not deprive the Article III courts of any of their traditional jurisdiction.

B. Private rights

Adjudication of ***private rights*** disputes (legal disputes between private parties) in administrative agencies is suspect and may occur only under certain conditions.

1. *Crowell v. Benson*: *Crowell v. Benson*, 285 U.S. 22 (1932), was the first case in which the Supreme Court approved the adjudication of a private rights dispute by an administrative agency. *Crowell* involved workers' compensation-type claims by longshoremen against their employers. The *Crowell* Court relied heavily on the availability of judicial review to sustain the statute.

a. ***Crowell's* stringent requirements:** In *Crowell*, the Court imposed relatively stringent requirements, including *de novo review*, for questions of law and questions of jurisdictional fact (i.e., facts that determine whether the agency has jurisdiction over the dispute). It is now unclear whether the stringent requirements of *Crowell v. Benson* are, in light of more recent cases, still good law.

b. ***Crowell's* more lenient requirements:** The *Crowell* Court held that Article III allowed deferential judicial review of an agency's factual determinations concerning the details of employees' claims. First, the Court viewed the agency's function as similar to that of masters and juries who often aid Article III judges in their fact finding. Second, assigning the fact finding to an agency might actually preserve judicial power by not overwhelming the courts with numerous controversies, while maintaining judicial control through de novo review of questions of law and deferential review of the facts.

2. **Current law. A pragmatic test:** Today courts use a pragmatic test to determine whether the assignment of adjudicatory functions to an agency violates the separation of powers. Various factors determine whether the encroachment on the Article III courts' judicial power is so great as to threaten the separation of powers. There is no categorical bar to adjudication of private rights disputes in non-Article III tribunals.

3. ***Commodity Futures Trading Commission (CFTC) v. Schor:*** The most recent comprehensive application of the pragmatic test is *CFTC v. Schor*, 478 U.S. 833 (1986), which employed the following factors and approved agency adjudication of a private rights dispute:

   a. **Particularized area of law:** Agency adjudication is more likely to be constitutional if it involves a particularized area of law closely related to a federal regulatory scheme and does not cut across an entire class of traditionally judicially cognizable cases. Thus, in Schor, the Court approved agency adjudication of a small category of common-law claims that were closely related to the regulation of the business of marketing securities.

   b. **Court enforcement:** Any judgment in a private rights dispute should be enforceable only by the order of an Article III court.

   c. **Judicial review:** Judicial review of private rights disputes should be available in an Article III court under a standard of review that is stringent enough to ensure significant judicial involvement in resolution of the dispute. On questions of law, de novo review is preferable.

   d. **Other aspects of judicial power:** The administrative agency should have only those powers necessary to resolve the disputes within its jurisdiction and should not be empowered with attributes of pure judicial power—such as the power to issue writs of habeas corpus or the power to preside over jury trials.

   e. **Freedom to choose an Article III court:** Parties to a private rights dispute should retain the freedom to choose an Article III court, ensuring that they are voluntarily presenting their dispute to an administrative tribunal.

   Example: The Bankruptcy Code granted non—Article III bankruptcy courts jurisdiction of all common-law claims involving the bankrupt party. This was challenged as unconstitutional by a party to a contract in a dispute with a bankrupt entity. In *Northern Pipeline Construction Co. v. Marathon Pipeline Co.*, 458 U.S. 50 (1982), the Court held this jurisdictional grant to a non-Article III court unconstitutional because jurisdiction was over the whole range of commom-law actions and was not confined to a particular area of law.

Quiz Yourself on
SEPARATION OF POWERS AND DISTRIBUTION OF ADMINISTRATIVE POWER

4. Congress enacts a statute authorizing the President to grant favorable trade status to a foreign nation on a finding that the foreign nation "meets acceptable standards on human rights" or that favorable trade status is "in the best interests of the United States." Would this statute violate the nondelegation doctrine? _____

5. An amendment to the Internal Revenue Code provides that the Internal Revenue Service (IRS) must submit all proposed regulations to the House Ways and Means Committee. If the committee is silent, the regulations go into effect sixty days after submission. If the committee (by majority vote) disapproves of a regulation, then the effective date of the regulation is delayed a further 120 days to allow time to introduce (and possibly pass) a bill disapproving the regulation. Normal procedures regarding presentment to the President, veto, and override apply to this bill. If a disapproval bill does not become law within the 120 days, the regulation goes into effect. Is this a constitutional method of oversight? _____

6. Congress passes a statute stating that the President must have good cause before firing United States attorneys and that the Senate may, by a majority vote, reject presidential removal of United States attorneys. Are these restrictions constitutional? _____

7. Congress is upset about the way that the President is distributing highway funds, so in its new appropriations bill it provides that the comptroller general has the power to reject allocations of highway funds made by the Secretary of Transportation. Is this provision constitutional? _____

8. Congress is upset with the President's choices for United States attorneys, so it passes (over veto) a statute delegating the authority to appoint United States attorneys to the courts of appeals, each of which would appoint the United States attorneys for districts within their respective circuits. Is that constitutional? _____

9. The Federal Emergency Management Agency (FEMA) in the Department of Homeland Security (DHS) needs to hire more claims officers to process claims for disaster relief in the wake of disasters. Claims officers counsel disaster victims on which claims to file and how to file them. They also receive the claims and forward them, with a recommendation, to claims adjusters, who have authorty to grant or deny claims. Congress specifies by statute that the Director of FEMA, not the Secretary of DHS, "shall have the authority to hire claims officers." Is this a constitutional appointments process? _____

Answers

4. No. Under traditional nondelegation standards, the President's role can be seen largely as "filling up the details." Under the "intelligible principle" test, the requirement that the foreign nation "meets acceptable standards on human rights" is sufficient to pass muster under the nondelegation doctrine. The second half of the statute is a bit more problematic because the "best interests of the United States" standard is not very clear. In some contexts this might raise nondelegation concerns. However, a court might view the statute—invoking the universe of considerations that have long been relevant to presidents in trade matters—as supplying an adequate intelligible principle. Further, the President's traditional power in foreign relations makes the relative paucity of guidance more acceptable in this context than in other areas.

5. Probably not. The requirements that regulations be submitted to a House committee and that regulations do not go into effect until sixty days after submission are probably constitutional since they do not amount to much of an intrusion into the power of the executive branch and since they become law independent of the action of any unit of Congress. The bicameralism and presentment of the disapproval bill saves it from *Chadha* problems. The constitutionally suspect aspect of the statute is that the vote of the House Ways and Means Committee to disapprove the regulation further postpones the effectiveness of the regulation. Since this action has effects outside the legislative branch of government, it is probably legislative. Thus there would be a violation of *Chadha*'s requirement that any legislative action having legal effect must go through both houses and be presented 'to' the President. The argument in favor of the constitutionality of this scheme is that the action of the committee merely delays the effective date of the regulation. The regulation is not canceled without passage of a bill by both houses and presentment to the President; this meets *Chadha*'s concerns.

6. One may be, but not the other. The good-cause requirement is probably constitutional; the senatorial role in the removal process is not. Despite the predominant understanding of *Myers v. United States*, Congress has broad power to impose good-cause restrictions on the President's ability to fire executive officials. This is made clear from *Morrison v. Olson*, which allowed a good-cause restriction on the firing of an independent counsel. The argument against the good-cause restriction is that by restricting the President's ability to fire a member of the cabinet who reports directly to the President, it infringes on the President's ability to function as a separate, co-equal branch of government and thus violates the separation of powers. On the Senate's role, the cases are clear that Congress, or units of Congress, may not itself participate in the removal process. That provision is unconstitutional.

7. No. The comptroller general is removable by a joint resolution of both houses of Congress. Most of the functions of the comptroller general are in aid of the legislative process, and it is thus constitutional for that official to be removable by Congress. However, an official removable by Congress may not exercise authority under the laws of the United States, and this would include the power to disapprove of the Secretary of Transportation's allocation of highway funds.

8. Probably yes. The Appointments Clause allows Congress to grant the power to appoint "inferior officers" to the President alone, to the department heads, and to the courts of law. After *Morrison v. Olson* and *Edmond v. United States*, a United States attorney would probably by considered an inferior officer since the United States attorney is subject to the control of the Attorney General and must follow Justice Department policies. As an inferior officer, the United States attorney is subject to appointment by the courts of law. The two arguments against this statute are: a United States attorney is a principal officer and must be appointed by the President with the advice and consent of the President, and the presidential appointment of United States attorneys is necessary to preserve the

President's power under a separation of powers analysis. Note that Congress may not grant appointment power for inferior officers to officials not listed in the Appointments Clause and may not itself participate in the appointment of officers of the United States except through Senate confirmation of presidential appointments.

9. Probably yes. Because they lack significant discretion and authority to administer the law, the claims officers would probably be considered "employees" not officers of the United States covered by the Appointments Clause. The contrary argument, based on the Supreme Court's decision in *Freytag*, would be that processing claims and making recommendations means that they are officers covered by the Appointments Clause and thus must be appointed either by the President with the advice and consent of the Senate, or by the Secretary of DHS if Congress so specifies. The D.C. Circuit's *Landry* decision supports the argument that they are employees.

Exam Tips *on*
SEPARATION OF POWERS AND DISTRIBUTION OF ADMINISTRATIVE POWER

☞ In nondelegation doctrine issues, it often is useful to address the history of the doctrine and explain how it has evolved from a strict, categorical approach to the current intelligible principle standard.

    ☞ Point out that the nondelegation doctrine is a very lenient standard and that no statute has failed the intelligible principle test in recent years. Mention the *Whitman* case as the most recent example.

    ☞ If a question calls for an extended discussion of the nondelegation doctrine, it is helpful to ground that discussion in Justice Rehnquist's analysis in his *Benzene* concurrence of the normative bases for the doctrine, most importantly that Congress makes the basic policy choices.

    ☞ It also may be useful to discuss the nondelegation doctrine in light of larger separation of powers concerns such as those raised in Justice Scalia's *Mistretta* dissent.

☞ In all separation of powers questions, start the discussion by identifying and applying any relevant constitutional provisions, such as the bicameralism and presentment clauses with regard to the legislative veto or the Appointments Clause in appointment and removal cases. Then go on to discuss more general separation of powers concerns that arise in cases involving issues such as the legislative veto, appointment and removal powers, presidential control and the like.

☞ In many appointment and removal cases, it is important to understand the remedy—the Court usually prohibits an official from exercising a power instead of holding that the method of appointment or removal was unconstitutional.

    ☞ For example, point out that any official appointed by or removable by Congress cannot exercise powers reserved to "officers of the United States" since "officers of the United States" only may be appointed in accordance with the Appointments Clause and may not be removed by Congress.

☞ If relevant, mention that Congress may appoint and remove its own officials.

☛ In cases involving Congress's power to restrict the President's power to remove executive officials, be sure to analyze the issue in light of Congress's broad power to restrict removal that the Court recognized in *Morrisson v. Olson*. While a discussion of the "quasi-legislative" and "quasijudicial" language of *Humphrey's Executor* might be appropriate, *Morrisson* better represents current law.

☛ When discussing the constitutionality of locating adjudication within administrative agencies, be sure to explore the different treatment accorded public rights and private rights and be sure to analyze the issue in light of the factors stated in *CFTC v. Schor*, including that the agency adjudication occurs in a particularized area of law related to a regulatory scheme, that orders are enforceable only in court, that effective judicial review is available, and that the essence of the judicial power is not delegated to the agency.

CHAPTER 3

THE AVAILABILITY OF JUDICIAL REVIEW OF ADMINISTRATIVE DECISIONS

ChapterScope

This chapter explores the availability of judicial review of administrative decisions mainly under the Administrative Procedure Act, but also with reference to review of constitutional challenges to administrative action. The key points in this chapter are:

- **Jurisdiction:** A petition for review must be brought in a court with jurisdiction over the action. Jurisdiction involves which court can hear the petition for review and not whether the particular agency action is reviewable. Jurisdiction is thus distinct from reviewability.

- **APA grant of judicial review:** Chapter VII of the APA, §§ 701-706, grants a right to obtain judicial review of "agency action made reviewable by statute and *final agency action* for which there is no adequate remedy in a court" to persons "*suffering legal wrong* because of agency action, or *adversely affected or aggrieved* by agency action within the meaning of a relevant statute."

- **Presumption of reviewability** with exceptions. There is a strong legal presumption in favor of judicial review of agency action meeting the above-stated criteria, but that presumption may be rebutted in two ways:

  - **Statutes precluding judicial review:** Judicial review is not available if a statute explicitly precludes judicial review. APA §701(a)(1).

  - **Agency action is "committed to agency discretion by law":** Judicial review is not available if agency action is committed to agency discretion by law. APA §701(a)(2).

    - This exception is satisfied in three categories of cases: (a) where the governing statute *supplies no law or clear standards* for a court to apply to judge the correctness of agency action; (b) where the governing statute appears to *vest unreviewable discretion* in the agency; and (c) where the agency action falls into a category of agency action that has *traditionally been unreviewable*.

- **Standing to seek judicial review:** Parties seeking judicial review must satisfy APA and constitutional tests for standing.

  - The basic constitutional test for standing is that the party seeking judicial review must have suffered an "*injury in fact*" that was "*fairly traceable*" to the challenged conduct such that the injury is *remediable* by judicial action.

  - For standing under the APA, the party also must be within the *zone of interests* addressed by the regulatory statute.

- Only *final agency action* is reviewable. Further, the case must be *ripe* and not *moot*, and administrative remedies must be *exhausted*.

- The requirement of "final agency action" means that judicial review may not be sought before agency action is final.

- Even final agency action may not be ripe for review if it is not *fit* for review and if the petitioner would not suffer **hardship** by waiting for the action to become ripe.

- A petition for judicial review may not be brought until administrative remedies have been exhausted, although this is a somewhat flexible doctrine.

- Finally, if a petition for review is brought after the challenged agency action has ceased to have any adverse effects on the petitioner, the action may be moot.

I. JURISDICTION

The petition for judicial review must be brought in a court that has *jurisdiction* over the claim.

A. Federal court jurisdiction over petitions for judicial review

The federal courts generally have jurisdiction over petitions for review of federal agency action under two statutory sources.

1. **Specific review statutes:** Agency enabling acts often grant a right of judicial review and explicitly create federal court jurisdiction over petitions for review. Most such statutes grant jurisdiction over petitions for review to the courts of appeals. *See, e.g.*, The Federal Trade Commission Act of 1914, 15 U.S.C. §41(c). A few grant jurisdiction to the district court. *See, e.g.*, 42 U.S.C. §405(g), granting jurisdiction over review of social security determinations to the district courts.

2. **Federal question jurisdiction, 28 U.S.C. §1331:** If Congress has not provided for judicial review in an agency's enabling act, a party who meets APA and constitutional standing requirements can bring an action for judicial review in the district court under the Judicial Code's grant of district court jurisdiction over civil actions arising under federal law, 28 U.S.C. §1331. Claims for review of agency action arise under federal law, easily meeting the test for jurisdiction under § 1331. In the past, there was an amount in controversy requirement for cases brought under federal question jurisdiction but that requirement has been repealed. Thus any petition for judicial review that meets other jurisdictional requirements may be brought to a federal court regardless of how little is at stake in monetary value.

B. The distinction between jurisdiction and reviewability

It is important to understand that *jurisdiction* and *reviewability* are separate issues, and the existence of one does not necessarily imply the existence of the other.

1. **Jurisdiction:** Jurisdiction involves whether a particular court has the authority to hear a class of disputes. The fact that federal courts have jurisdiction over federal questions does not mean that all challenges to agency action based on federal law are reviewable.

2. **Reviewability:** Reviewability is the equivalent of the existence of a cause of action, and involves whether a claim exists that may be brought in a court with jurisdiction. An action is reviewable only if, as elaborated below, a particular statute makes the agency action

reviewable or if the action meets the requirements of APA §704. The fact that an agency action is reviewable does not answer the question of which federal court, if any, has jurisdiction over the claim.

C. Deciding which court is the proper forum for judicial review

1. **Rule of thumb:** It has long been said that there is a rule of thumb that the court of appeals has jurisdiction when an administrative record exists, and the district court has jurisdiction when a record does not exist. As agency procedures become more formal, an adequate administrative record is more likely to exist, and it becomes more likely, that the court of appeals will be the proper forum for judicial review. When no adequate record exists, the district court's trial procedures are thought necessary to create one. This rule of thumb has been undermined by recent developments discussed below.

2. **Specific statutes:** In most cases the choice between the court of appeals and the district court is simple because the agency's governing statute identifies the proper forum for judicial review. Most statutes provide for review of administrative action in the court of appeals. The most notable exception is the Social Security Act, 42 U.S.C. §405(g), which provides for district court review of orders denying or terminating benefits even though the agency has conducted a formal adjudication. In the absence of statutory authority for choosing the court of appeals, the federal question jurisdiction provision of 28 U.S.C. § 1331 directs review to the district court.

3. **Presumption in favor of review in the court of appeals:** Courts interpret specific statutes, whenever possible, to direct review to the court of appeals even in cases of informal agency action where there is no formal agency record. There are two reasons for this preference.

   a. **Judicial economy favors appellate review:** Judicial economy favors review in the court of appeals. If review is available in the district court, the losing party can appeal the district court's decision to the court of appeals. Two levels of judicial review signify greater delay and more resources devoted to review. *See Florida Power and Light, Co., v. Lorion*, 470 U.S. 729 (1985).

   b. **The court reviews the agency's record:** The Supreme Court has stated, as a fundamental principle of administrative law, that a reviewing court should judge the agency's action on the record that was before the agency and not based on one created during litigation. *Camp v. Pitts*, 411 U. S. 138 (1973); *Florida Power and Light Co., v. Lorion*, 470 U. S. 729 (1985). Thus, the Court has rejected the argument that a district court's trial procedures are necessary to assemble a record adequate for review because it conflicts with this fundamental principle.

   c. **Limits to the presumption:** The presumption favoring court of appeals review of agency action is limited to when a statute exists that can be construed to grant jurisdiction over the cases to the court of appeals. *See, e.g., Harrison v. PPG Industries, Inc.*, 446 U.S. 578 (1980) (construing the Clean Air Act's grant of court of appeals jurisdiction over "final agency action" to include *informal agency action*). Absent such a statute, the only source of federal jurisdiction would be the general federal question statute, which provides for district court review.

II. REVIEWABILITY

A. Presumption in favor of judicial review

There is a longstanding presumption that judicial review of agency action is available. This presumption may be rebutted in a variety of ways as discussed below.

1. **Why the presumption exists:** The APA's judicial review provisions create a presumption in favor of judicial review of agency action. This presumption is consistent with the judiciary's role in protecting individuals from arbitrary exercises of government power. Judicial review is thought to be necessary to keep agencies within the bounds established by Congress.

2. **Pre-APA law on reviewability:** The presumption in favor of judicial review of agency action did not exist before the APA was enacted, and many agency decisions were not subject to judicial review. Common-law writs, such as mandamus, were available to challenge only nondiscretionary (or ministerial) agency action. Any hint of executive discretion would lead federal courts to deny reviewability. *See Decatur v. Paulding*, 39 U.S. (14 Pet.) 497 (1840). Although some pre-APA courts favored judicial review of any allegation of official illegality, *see American School of Magnetic Healing v. McAnnulty*, 187 U.S. 94 (1902), the dominant pre-APA view held that review was available only when Congress explicitly provided for review. *See, e.g., Switchmen's Union v. National Mediation Board*, 320 U.S. 297 (1943).

B. APA §704's grant of judicial review

APA §704 provides for judicial review of "[a]gency action made reviewable by statute and final agency action for which there is no other adequate remedy in a court." This statute creates a strong presumption of reviewability of **final agency action**. In essence it provides a cause of action for judicial review of final agency action when no other statute provides for review. The key provisions of §704 may be understood as follows:

1. **Agency action made reviewable by statute:** This somewhat redundant provision merely states that if a statute other than the APA, such as an agency enabling act, provides for judicial review of a particular agency action, the action is reviewable. It also suggests that, absent contrary statutory provisions, the requirements of Chapter VII of the APA, including the standards of judicial review, govern the remaining issues in judicial review. APA standards of review are discussed in Chapter 4.

2. **Final agency action for which there is no other adequate remedy in a court:** This provision creates a general entitlement to judicial review of final agency action. The standards for determining when an agency action is final are discussed below in the ripeness section. The requirement that there be "no other adequate remedy in a court" means that if Congress has provided a remedy other than APA judicial review for a particular agency action, APA review is not available unless the alternative remedy is not adequate. If a court finds the other remedy inadequate, then review is presumptively available under APA standards of review.

3. **Agency action:** Review under the APA is available only for "agency action." "'[A]gency' means each authority of the United States" except, inter alia, Congress, civil and military courts, and the governments of territories and possessions of the United States. APA §551(1). Despite the absence of an explicit exemption, the Supreme Court has decided that the President is not an agency within the meaning of the APA. *Franklin v. Massachusetts*, 505 U.S. 788 (1992). Further, the Supreme Court has required that the petitioner identify a particular agency action that is

being challenged, holding that APA review is not available to challenge the general manner in which an agency regulates. *See Norton v. Southern Utah Wilderness Alliance*, 542 U.S. 55 (2004).

C. Statutory preclusion of review: APA §701(a)(1)

APA §701 specifies two situations in which APA judicial review is not available: when "*statutes preclude judicial review*" and when "*agency action is committed to agency discretion by law.*"

1. **Explicit preclusion of review:** APA §701(a)(1) provides that judicial review is not available when "statutes preclude judicial review." Normally, for a statute to preclude judicial review, it should explicitly mention judicial review. The best example of such a statute was old §211(a) of the Veterans' Administration Act, which provided that the "decisions of the [Veterans' Administration] on any question of law or fact under any law administered by the Veterans' Administration . . . shall be final and conclusive and no other official or any court of the United States shall have power or jurisdiction to review any such decision[.]" A statute like this precludes review of administrative action. However, a statute that precludes review of agency action does not preclude a constitutional challenge to the statute itself, since in such a case the Court reviews a decision by Congress, not the agency. *See Johnson v. Robison*, 415 U.S. 361 (1974).

2. **Implicit preclusion of review:** Courts have found that statutes implicitly preclude review when the statutes channel review in particular ways or on behalf of particular parties.

   a. **Implicit preclusion by confining review to particular agency action:** When Congress explicitly grants review of a particular set of agency actions, this may implicitly mean that Congress has precluded review of other, related, agency actions.

      Example: An agency has the power to suspend and revoke licenses to sell a product. If a license is suspended, the process continues and culminates either in revocation or a decision against revocation, at which time the suspension ends. If the agency's enabling act explicitly provides for review of decisions regarding revocation, there is an argument that Congress has implicitly precluded review of suspension orders.

   b. **Implicit preclusion by channeling review to specific avenues of review:** When Congress specifies a particular avenue of review it may implicitly mean that Congress meant to preclude other avenues of review.

      Example: Certain undocumented immigrant workers were given the right to apply for a work permit under a special program. The statute creating the special program stated that a denial of a permit under the program could be judicially reviewed as a defense in an action to deport the immigrant. This provision gives rise to an argument that immediate judicial review of the denial of the work permit was implicitly precluded by the grant of judicial review in the context of a deportation proceeding.

   c. **Implicit preclusion by granting of standing to seek review to a particular class of parties:** When Congress grants **standing** to seek review to a particular class of parties, this may implicitly mean that Congress meant to preclude other parties from seeking review.

   d. **Implicit channeling preclusion exists only when Congress is very explicit concerning review:** Implicit preclusion due to channeling of review occurs only when an agency's enabling act is very explicit about who can obtain review, is very explicit about how review should be sought, or both.

Example: *Block v. Community Nutrition Institute*, 467 U.S. 340 (1984). In *Block*, consumers and a nonprofit nutrition advocacy group sought review of a decision by the Secretary of Agriculture that increased the price of certain milk products. A milk handler also sued. The statute specified that milk handlers could obtain judicial review but only after they exhausted remedies provided by the Secretary. The Court held that under these circumstances, review on behalf of parties other than milk handlers was implicitly precluded by the statute that granted review only to milk handlers and channeled that review through the administrative process.

e. *Bowen v. Michigan Academy of Family Physicians.* **Channeling may not prevent challenges to the administration of a program as a whole or to other parts of a program:** A statute that channels review of individual determinations under a program might not bar review directed at the administration of the program as a whole. Channeling review of determinations under one portion of a statute does not necessarily preclude review of determinations under another portion of the program. In *Bowen v. Michigan Academy of Family Physicians*, 476 U.S. 667 (1986), the Court stated as a principle of administrative law that the fact that some administrative actions are made reviewable by statute does not, by itself, support an inference that other actions under the same program are not reviewable.

f. **An explicit channeling provision may not bar general attacks on the administration of a program:** Even an explicit statutory bar of judicial review of determinations on the merits of individual cases may not bar review of general challenges to the administration of the program.

Example: *McNary v. Haitian Refugee Center, Inc.*, 498 U.S. 479 (1991). In *McNary*, a statute creating a new category of legal immigrant workers provided that "There shall be no . . . judicial review of a determination respecting an application for adjustment of status under this section except in accordance with this subsection" and that "there shall be judicial review of . . . a denial [of the new status] only in the judicial review of an order of exclusion or deportation[.]" Despite the explicit language of the statute, the Court held that as long as no individual status determination was challenged, the statute did not bar disappointed applicants and their advocates from pursuing, in a class action, constitutional and statutory challenges to the procedures used in the program as a whole.

D. **Committed to agency discretion by law: APA §701(a)(2)**   APA §701(a)(2) bars judicial review of agency action "committed to agency discretion by law." That provision, a descendant of the now-abandoned notion that discretionary administrative action was never reviewable, can be understood in three different ways — all of which reinforce the idea that certain decisions have been left to agency discretion and are free from judicial review.

1. **The three ways of understanding "committed to agency discretion":** There are three ways of understanding unreviewability based upon the conclusion that "agency action is committed to agency discretion by law." These are the "no law to apply" approach, the "deeming clause" approach, and the "traditionally unreviewable" approach.

a. **"No law to apply":** The original understanding of "committed to agency discretion by law" is that judicial review is not available when the governing "statutes are drawn in such broad terms that in a given case there is no law to apply." Judicial review is not possible in such cases because there is no discernible statutory standard against which to judge the legality of agency action. Because Congress normally attempts to give agencies statutory guidance, this exception to reviewability of final agency action is rarely met.

Example: *Webster v. Doe.* In *Webster v. Doe*, 486 U.S. 592 (1988), the Supreme Court held that the decision to fire an employee of the Central Intelligence Agency (CIA) was committed to the discretion of the director of the CIA because the governing statute, which provided that the director had the power to terminate the employment of CIA employees "whenever he shall deem such termination necessary or advisable in the interests of the United States," was so vague that it did not supply courts with law to apply in order to determine whether the director's decision was within statutory bounds.

b. **"Deeming clauses." The vesting of unreviewable authority in an agency official:** Review is also "committed to agency discretion by law" when the statute suggests that Congress intended for the agency to have final authority over adecision. Such statutory provisions may be referred to as "deeming clauses."

Example: In *Webster v. Doe*, the statutory language, by stating that the director may terminate employees when he "***deem[s]***" it in the interest of the United States, assigned final authority to dismiss CIA employees to the director. The statute does not state that it must actually be in the national interest to terminate the employee — only that the director must ***deem*** it to be so. The Court observed that "[t]his standard fairly exudes deference to the Director." *Webster v. Doe*, 486 U.S. at 600.

Example: In *Lincoln v. Vigil*, 508 U.S. 182 (1993), an agency's allocation of funds from a lump-sum appropriation was held committed to agency discretion by law partly on the "deeming clause" theory but without an explicit deeming clause. The Court found that a lump-sum appropriation was a congressional determination that the agency, within broad parameters, should determine how to spend the money. In essence, the Court held that the lump sum appropriation was an implicit "deeming clause" under which Congress grants unreviewable discretion to the agency to decide how to apportion the lump sum.

c. **Decisions traditionally not reviewable. Justice Scalia's *Webster* dissent:** The Court has also held that there are categories of administrative decisions that are unreviewable under the "committed to agency discretion by law" provision because these categories have traditionally been held to be committed to agency discretion. This categorical approach originated in Justice Scalia's attempt, in his *Webster v. Doe* dissent, to explain the meaning of the words "by law" in the phrase "committed to agency discretion by law." Justice Scalia stated that "by law" refers to a body of common law of reviewability under which certain subject matter categories of agency action were traditionally unreviewable.

Example: In *Lincoln v. Vigil*, the Court held that allocation of funds from a lump-sum appropriation is not reviewable, in part, because it is "another administrative decision traditionally regarded as committed to agency discretion." *Lincoln v. Vigil*, 508 U.S. at 191. The Court had meager evidence for the tradition (it cited only a 1975 opinion of the comptroller general), but it nonetheless held that agency decisions allocating funds from lump-sum appropriations were unreviewable.

d. **The "deeming clause" and "traditionally unreviewable" approaches are creations of the Supreme Court not provided for in the APA:** Neither the text nor the legislative history of APA §701(a)(2) bear the meaning ascribed to it under the "deeming" and "traditionally unreviewable" approaches. The legislative history, and the caselaw until *Webster v. Doe*, support only the original "no law to apply" interpretation.

2. **Relationship between "committed to agency discretion by law" and the nondelegation doctrine:** It may appear that the "no law to apply" branch of unreviewability entails an automatic violation of the nondelegation doctrine. However, there are two reasons why the lack of law to apply does not automatically violate the nondelegation doctrine's insistence that Congress supply an intelligible principle when delegating legislative power to administrative agencies. First, not all agency action involves delegated legislative power.

    Example: *Webster v. Doe* involved the power to terminate executive employees. The power to terminate an executive employee is an executive function. Thus, the discretion granted in that case did not violate the nondelegation doctrine. Second, although there may be "no law to apply" for reviewability purposes, this does not necessarily mean that a statute does not contain an intelligible principle. Congress's general purpose may supply enough guidance to satisfy the intelligible principle standard without providing sufficient guidance to allow meaningful judicial review.

E. **The special case of the unreviewability of the exercise of prosecutorial discretion** The Supreme Court has been especially reluctant to allow judicial review of agency decisions involving when to regulate or whom to prosecute for violations within the agency's jurisdiction. The Court has analyzed these issues under the heading of ***prosecutorial discretion***.

1. **The presumption against review of exercises of agency prosecutorial discretion:** The Supreme Court has created, under APA §701(a)(2), a strong presumption that prosecutorial discretion decisions are unreviewable as "committed to agency discretion by law."

    a. ***Heckler v. Chaney:*** In *Heckler v. Chaney*, 470 U.S. 821 (1985), the Court held that §701 (a)(2) barred review of the Food and Drug Administration's (FDA) decision not to take enforcement action against states that administered capital punishment by the lethal injection of drugs that were not approved for that particular use. The Court held that it was up to the agency to balance the various factors that are relevant to the agency's decision whether to take action against a particular violation of law administered by the agency and that ordinarily no judicial review is available of the decision not to take enforcement action.

    b. **Prosecutorial discretion in labor law:** In order for a charge of an unfair labor practice to go forward, the general counsel of the National Labor Relations Board (NLRB) must file a complaint with the NLRB.

        i. **Unreviewability of decisions not to file:** A decision by the general counsel not to file an unfair labor practice complaint with the NLRB is "final" under the statute creating the NLRB. The Court has held that the decision not to file an unfair labor practice charge is an unreviewable exercise of agency prosecutorial discretion. *See NLRB v. Sears, Roebuck & Co.*, 421 U.S. 132, 136-38 (1975).

        ii. **Unreviewability of settlements before hearing:** The general counsel's unreviewable discretion to decide whether to file a complaint extends to a decision to withdraw a complaint before a hearing. Therefore, if the general counsel reaches a settlement with the employer before a hearing is held, the terms of the settlement are not subject to judicial review. *See NLRB v. United Food and Commercial Workers*, 484 U.S. 112

(1987). The Court reinforced its decision in *Food and Commercial Workers* with the channeling argument that review of settlements was unavailable because the labor laws grant review of some decisions but not the decision to withdraw a complaint before the hearing.

  iii. Reviewability of dismissal pursuant to a settlement: If a settlement has been reached after a hearing or some other proceeding before the agency has been held, then the decision to settle might be reviewable. This is because to settle the case once proceedings before an agency have begun, the agency must issue an order dismissing the case pursuant to the settlement. Such an order would be final agency action subject to judicial review. However, courts are likely to be very deferential in reviewing orders dismissing enforcement actions as part of settlement agreements.

2. **How to rebut the presumption against review of agency exercises of prosecutorial discretion:** The presumption against review of prosecutorial discretion may be rebutted if the agency's enabling act requires the agency to bring enforcement action under certain specified circumstances or within a certain time period. Prosecutorial decisions are reviewable when "the substantive statute has provided guidelines for the agency to follow in exercising its enforcement powers." *See Heckler v. Chaney*, 470 U.S. at 832.

  a. ***Dunlop v. Bachowsk.* Review of prosecutorial decisions:** In *Dunlop v. Bachowski*, 421 U.S. 560 (1975), the Court held that the Secretary of Labor's refusal to bring a lawsuit challenging the results of a union election was reviewable because, under specified circumstances, the relevant statute required the Secretary to sue. The statute provided that if the Secretary finds probable cause to believe that the law governing union elections was violated, the Secretary "*shall*, within sixty days, after the tiling of such complaint, bring a civil action against the labor organization as an entity in the District Court of the United States." *Dunlop*, 421 U.S. at 563. While the *Heckler* Court stated that in *Dunlop* "the statutory language supplied sufficient standards to rebut the presumption of unreviewability," it is difficult to locate such a finding in the actual *Dunlop* opinion. *See Heckler*, 470 U.S. at 833.

  b. ***Dunlop v. Bachowski.* Review is very narrow:** When reviewable, prosecutorial decisions are likely to be reviewed very deferentially. The agency's decision is upheld unless the administrator fails to provide plausible or rational reasons for the failure to prosecute. In *Dunlop*, for example, the Court may have felt compelled by the statute's mandatory language ("shall . . . bring a civil action") to review the decision not to sue, but the Court clearly stated that the review is to be very deferential, insisting only that the Secretary articulate rational reasons for failing to bring the required civil action.

F. **The distinction between APA §701(a)(1) and §701(a)(2)** Because all three of the variations on the meaning of "committed to agency discretion by law" in §701(a)(2) arguably involve some measure of congressional intent to preclude judicial review, it may be difficult to distinguish §701(a)(2) from situations in which "statutes preclude judicial review" under §701(a)(1). The only clear distinction is that §701(a)(1) statutory preclusion exists only when the statute mentions judicial review. Typically, statutes relied upon to establish that a matter is committed to agency discretion by law do not mention judicial review at all.

G. Preclusion of review of constitutional questions

The Court has not decided whether Congress may preclude judicial review of constitutional challenges to agency action. Because precluding judicial review of constitutional challenges itself raises a serious constitutional question, courts have interpreted statutes precluding judicial review to preclude review only of nonconstitutional questions, while preserving review of constitutional issues. For example, in *Johnson v. Robison*, 415 U.S. 361 (1974), the Court held that a statute barring review of decisions of the Veterans' Administration did not bar a constitutional challenge to the statute the VA was charged with administering. *See also Webster v. Doe*. Justice Scalia, in his dissent in *Webster*, argued that Congress has the power to preclude review of constitutional issues. The issue will only be resolved authoritatively if Congress unmistakably bars the review of constitutional challenges.

III. STANDING TO SECURE JUDICIAL REVIEW

A party seeking judicial review must have standing to sue. In order to have standing the plaintiff must be injured by the challenged conduct and must stand to gain from a favorable ruling. Standing problems arise most often in actions seeking injunctive (or similar) relief regarding an agency's treatment of a party other than the one seeking review. It may be unclear whether the agency's action has injured the party seeking judicial review and whether holding the agency action unlawful (and setting it aside) will alter the plaintiff's situation. Standing is rarely if ever a problem when the regulated party seeks judicial review.

A. The constitutional underpinnings of the standing doctrine

Core standing requirements derive from constitutional limits on the powers of the federal courts. There are also judicially created standing doctrines referred to as ***prudential limitations on standing***.

1. **Cases and controversies:** Article III of the Constitution limits federal court jurisdiction to "cases" and "controversies." In order to meet Article III's case or controversy requirement, the plaintiff must be seeking to redress an ***injury*** that is sufficient to bring a claim before a court. The injury must have been ***caused*** by the challenged government conduct. The injury must be such that it will be ***remedied*** by a favorable judgment.

2. **Prudential limitations on standing:** The federal courts have imposed additional standing requirements beyond the constitutional minimum. These requirements (called "prudential" limitations) are, according to the Supreme Court, necessary to confine the courts to their proper role in government. Prudential limitations prevent courts from deciding "abstract questions of wide public significance," especially when "judicial intervention may be unnecessary to protect individual rights." *Warth v. Seldin*, 422 U.S. 490, 499-500 (1975).

B. Constitutional standing: the "injury-in-fact fairly traceable" test

The basic constitutional requirement for standing is that the plaintiff has suffered an ***injury-in-fact that is fairly traceable to the challenged conduct and redressable by a favorable judgment***. While these requirements appear relatively simple and straightforward, they have been applied so inconsistently over the years that it is very difficult to generalize from the decisions. The most one can hope for is to understand the arguments in the cases and try to make sense of their reasoning.

1. **Injury-in-fact:** The most basic requirement for standing is that the plaintiff must have suffered an injury. To satisfy this requirement, the plaintiff must be "significantly affected" by the challenged conduct.

   a. **An abstract interest is not sufficient for standing:** Persons or groups with an abstract interest in a regulatory scheme do not have standing without an actual injury. In *Sierra Club v. Morton*, 405 U.S. 727 (1972), the Court held that an abstract interest in environmental protection, which led to opposition to a development plan for parkland, was not a sufficient injury for standing purposes. The Court stated that, for standing purposes, only a person who had used and planned to continue using the parkland in its undeveloped state would have a sufficient injury to bring suit to prevent the development.

   b. **Common-law injuries, aesthetic injuries, economic injuries, and deprivations of rights are sufficient for standing:** The easiest case for the existence of standing is an injury to an interest that is protected under the common law. Injuries to aesthetic and economic interests are enough for standing. Deprivation of rights, such as the right to speak, can also suffice for standing. The Court has also held that government refusal to provide information is sufficient injury for standing, at least where the information might be useful, for instance in deciding how to vote in an upcoming election. In all cases it is vital for standing that the plaintiff actually be affected by the allegedly illegal conduct.

   c. **Deprivation of statutorily created rights can also confer standing:** Congress can create rights, the deprivation of which may be sufficient for standing. For example, in *Havens Realty Corp. v. Coleman*, 455 U.S. 363 (1982), the Court held that an African American "tester," who did not intend to rent an apartment, was injured when the landlord lied and said that no apartment was available, because Congress has given all persons the right to receive truthful information about apartment availability, without regard to race.

   d. **Members of Congress may have standing to sue over interference with their powers:** Members of Congress are injured when their lawmaking powers are interfered with, and such injury may be sufficient for standing. Members of Congress have sued over the legality of the pocket veto and over alleged violations of the Origination Clause, under which revenue-raising bills must originate in the House of Representatives. The D.C. Circuit has held that injury sufficient for standing exists in such cases. *See generally Moore v. United States House of Representatives*, 733 F.2d 946 (D.C. Cir. 1984). The Supreme Court has not decided on congressional standing in the abstract, although it did rule against congressional standing to challenge the **Line Item Veto** Act before the President had exercised the veto power granted in the Act. *See Raines v. Byrd*, 521 U.S. 811 (1997). Cf. *Walker v. Cheney*, 230 F. Supp. 2d 51 (D.D.C. 2002) (Comptroller General lacks standing to sue to compel Vice President to turn over documents to members of Congress).

2. **The injury must be "fairly traceable" to the challenged conduct:** The injury must be "fairly traceable" to the challenged conduct, or in other words, the conduct challenged must have actually caused the injury. While the concept of causation is not a difficult one to grasp, the cases do not analyze causation in a consistent fashion.

   a. ***SCRAP* and *EKWRO*:** *United States v. Students Challenging Regulatory Agency Procedures (SCRAP)*, 412 U.S. 669 (1973) and *Simon v. Eastern Kentucky Welfare Rights Organization, Inc. (EKWRO)*, 426 U.S. 26 (1976), appear to apply different standards with regard to traceability. In *SCRAP*, the Court held that increased litter in parks was traceable to a generally applicable rail freight rate hike approved by the Interstate Commerce Commission that made shipping trash for recycling more expensive. In *EKWRO*, the Court held that the lack of availability of free medical care was not traceable to the Internal Revenue Service's (IRS's) lax enforcement of requirements for charitable status under which hospitals are required to provide free medical care to indigents. It is difficult to see how the causation in *SCRAP* is any stronger than in *EKWRO*.

b. ***Warth* and *General Contractors*:** Another pair of cases further illustrates the inconsistencies in Supreme Court standing doctrine: *Warth v. Seldin*, 422 U.S. 490 (1975) and *Northeastern Florida Chapter of Association of General Contractors v. Jacksonville*, 508 U.S. 656 (1993). In *Warth*, the Court rejected builders' and potential residents' claims that zoning laws prevented low-income housing from being built in a town. The builders could not identify a project that had been turned down, and thus potential residents could not establish that they were injured by the zoning laws. In *General Contractors*, the Court allowed white contractors, who had never been turned down for a contract, to challenge a minority set-aside program. The Court reconceptualized the interests affected and ruled that the contractors had standing since they were injured in their ability to compete on an equal footing with minorities entitled to the preference. Not only is the standard for causation loose in *General Contractors*, it is difficult to see how the contractors met the basic requirement of injury as applied in *Warth* since they could not identify contracts that they lost (but might have won) because of the set-aside program.

c. **Causation, redressability, and the treatment of third parties:** As the Court has stated explicitly, it is more difficult to establish standing when the party seeking review challenges an agency's treatment of a third party. *See Lujan v. Defenders of Wildlife*, 504 U.S. 555 (1992). There are problems of causation and redressability. The action of a third party (and not the government's actions) may independently cause the plaintiff's injuries and ordering the government to act differently may not change the third party's conduct in a way that is beneficial to the plaintiff.

3. **Redressability:** To have standing the plaintiff must show that the remedy sought will redress the injury. The issue of redressability looks at whether the plaintiff has a personal stake in the outcome of the litigation such that the plaintiff will benefit if the court grants relief. Redressability is thus the flip side of causation: if ending the challenged conduct would cure the injury then, obviously, the challenged conduct caused the injury.

a. **Redressability in *SCRAP* and *EKWRO*:** In *SCRAP*, the redressability question was whether reducing freight rates would lead to more recycling, and thus less litter, in the parks. The Court ruled in favor of redressability. In *EKWRO* the redressability question was whether better IRS enforcement of the requirement that charitable hospitals treat indigents would actually lead to the hospitals treating more indigents. Here the Court ruled against redressability, holding that it was not clear that the hospitals would treat more indigents. Rather, they might simply forego tax-exempt status.

b. **Redressability and the inability of a court to order effective relief:** An injury is not redressable when a court is without power to craft an enforceable order against the official engaged in the illegal conduct. In *Lujan v. Defenders of Wildlife*, 504 U.S. 555 (1992), a plurality held that since a remedy would require the cooperation of federal agencies who were not parties to the case, the injury was not redressable because a court cannot issue a judgment against a nonparty. However, in *Franklin v. Massachusetts*, 505 U.S. 788 (1992), a majority of the Court found redressability even though the President, who was not a party to the case, was the official responsible for the conduct that was complained of. The Court stated that it expected that the President would act in accordance with the Court's decision on the merits even though it doubted that a court could issue a binding order against the President.

c. Redressability: past and present harm: A plaintiff seeking relief against past harm may lack standing on **redressability** grounds if the harm is not continuing and the plaintiff is not entitled to damages or any other form of compensation for the past harm. For example, in *Steel Company v. Citizens for a Better Environment*, 523 U.S. 83 (1998), the Court rejected standing for an environmental group that challenged the Steel Company's failure, in the past, to provide required information to the EPA concerning the presence of hazardous waste. The Court ruled that remedies such as a declaration that the company had violated the law in the past and even the imposition of civil fines (which would go to the government, not the plaintiff) based on past violations were insufficient for standing because they did not **redress** any present harm suffered by the plaintiff. However, the deterrent effect of a civil penalty toward future violations has been held sufficient to satisfy the redressability requirement. *See Friends of the Earth, Inc. v. Laidlaw Environmental Services, Inc.*, 528 U.S. 167 (2000). This conclusion seems to be in tension with the apparently contrary view of the Court in *Steel Company*.

C. Administrative law standing: The old "legal right" test

Early administrative law standing cases allowed review only on behalf of parties whose own legal rights had been allegedly violated by agency action. Parties injured by agency treatment of others lacked standing to seek judicial review. Cases involving regulation of competitors best illustrate the limits on standing implicit in the legal right test: a business entity's claim would be rejected when the regulation of a competitor (or lack of a legally required regulation) gives the competitor an unfair advantage in competition on the ground that the plaintiff did not have a legal right to protection from the competition.

1. *Alexander Sprunt & Son, Inc. v. United States:* In *Alexander Sprunt & Son, Inc. v. United States*, 281 U.S. 249 (1930), the Court rejected a claim that the Interstate Commerce Commission (ICC) had set railroad shipping rates for Sprunt's competitors too low, thereby injuring Sprunt's business. The Court stated that even though Sprunt was injured, Sprunt did not have standing because Sprunt's only legal right was to be charged reasonable rates itself. That legal right was not implicated when the ICC lowered the rates charged to Sprunt's competitors.

2. The legal right test was not constitutionally required. *FCC v. Sanders Bros. Radio Station***:** In 1940 the Court ruled that Congress had the power to override the legal right test and appoint competitors as *private attorneys general* to vindicate the public interest by keeping agencies within legal bounds. This means that the legal right test was not of constitutional pedigree. If it was, Congress could not override it. In *FCC v. Sanders Bros. Radio Station*, 309 U.S. 470 (1940), the Court held that Sanders Bros, had standing to challenge the award of a radio station license to a competitor because Congress had statutorily granted a right to judicial review of FCC orders to any person whose "interests are adversely affected" by an order of the FCC.

3. **Criticisms of the legal right test:** The legal right test for standing was criticized because it required the plaintiff to establish a key element of the claim on the merits (whether his or her legal rights were implicated) at an early stage of the litigation, just to establish standing. This criticism led to the abandonment of the legal right test in favor of the *zone of interests* test as discussed below.

D. **Standing in administrative law under the APA: APA §702 and the zone of interests test**

   1. **It is unclear how much the APA expands upon the legal right test:** APA §702 states, in part, that "[a] person suffering legal wrong because of agency action, *or adversely affected or aggrieved by agency action within the meaning of a relevant statute*, is entitled to judicial review thereof."

      a. **The violation of a legal right satisfies the first clause of APA §702:** The first clause of APA §702 is the legal right test. Thus, the APA grants standing to anyone whose legal rights are violated by agency action.

      b. **When is a party adversely affected or aggrieved within the meaning of a relevant statute?** The second clause of §702, italicized above, appears to liberalize standing beyond the legal right test to all those injured by the agency action, but is limited by the phrase "within the meaning of a relevant statute." While courts have not looked to statutes to determine who is an "adversely affected or aggrieved" party under the APA, the zone of interests test (discussed below) limits APA standing to those parties whose interests were important to Congress in formulating the regulatory scheme.

   2. ***Data Processing* and the zone of interests test:** In *Association of Data Processing Service Organizations, Inc. v. Camp*, 397 U.S. 150 (1970), the Court held that to have standing the plaintiff must show two things: a constitutionally sufficient injury and that "the interest sought to be protected by the complainant is arguably within the zone of interests to be protected or regulated by the statute or constitutional guarantee in question." *Data Processing*, 397 U.S. at 153.

      a. **Rejection of the legal right test:** The *Data Processing* Court discarded the legal right test on the ground that it went to the merits and should not be relevant for purposes of standing.

      b. **Application of the zone of interests test in *Data Processing*:** The zone of interests test limits standing to a subset of those injured by the challenged action but is broader than the legal right test. *Data Processing* presented the classic competitor's challenge to administrative action. The comptroller of the currency allowed national banks to sell certain data-processing services to their customers and to other banks. The data processors, competitors of the national banks in the data processing field, challenged the comptroller's ruling as violating statutory restrictions on the activities of national banks. The Court held that because the statute regulating banks was concerned not only with the financial health of the banks themselves but also with the interests of parties in competition with banks, the data processors were within the zone of interests of the statutory scheme and thus had standing to seek judicial review.

      c. **The zone of interests test takes a political view of standing:** The zone of interests test takes a political, rather than legal, view of standing because it asks not whether the plaintiff has a legal right at stake but rather whether the plaintiffs interests were considered by Congress or the regulatory body.

3. **The zone of interests test is alive:** Although the zone of interests test appeared to fall into disuse after *Data Processing*, it has enjoyed something of a revival in recent years. In *Air Courier Conference of America v. American Postal Workers Union*, 498 U.S 517 (1991), the Court denied standing to postal workers who challenged the Postal Service's decision to give up its monopoly over international remailing services—a method for saving money over airmail rates when sending a large volume of mail overseas. The Court held that postal workers were not within the zone of interests of the statute that created and regulated the United States Postal Service's monopoly over the mail. The only issue considered by Congress, according to the Court, was the public interest in an efficient mail service. However, in most cases in which it has come up, the Court has found that the party challenging agency action is within the zone of interests. *See, e.g., Federal Election Comm'n v. Akins*, 524 U.S. 11 (1998) (voters are in the zone of interests of election laws requiring political committees to disclose information); *National Credit Union Admin. v. First Natl. Bank & Trust Co.*, 522 U.S. 479 (1998) (competing banks are within the zone of interests of statute regulating the scope of credit unions' business); *Bennett v. Spear*, 520 U.S. 154 (1997) (ranchers and others seeking to limit reach of the Endangered Species Act are within the zone of interests addressed by the Act because the Act's citizen suit provision allows suits by "any person").

E. Prudential limits on standing

The prudential limits on standing are judge-made doctrines that limit access to the federal courts beyond the basic constitutional standing requirements.

1. **The plaintiff may not raise a generalized grievance:** The federal courts should not hear a case involving a *generalized grievance*, challenging government action that affects many people to a small degree. The generalized grievance rule is applied most strongly in challenges to government action brought by people in their capacity as taxpayers. A generalized grievance is one that should be resolved by the political branches, not by the courts.

   a. **Generalized grievance in *SCRAP*:** In *SCRAP*, the Court stated that the fact that many people are injured by government action should not prevent standing, lest the most widespread and injurious government illegalities become beyond judicial reach.

   b. **Generalized grievance in taxpayer cases:** The generalized grievance doctrine bars suits by taxpayers challenging how government spends its revenues. Since the plaintiffs only injury in these cases is an injury suffered by all citizens or taxpayers, the Court has held that the issue should be resolved in a political, rather than legal, forum.

   c. **The generalized grievance doctrine has not barred Establishment Clause challenges:** - Despite the generalized grievance doctrine, taxpayers have been allowed to challenge government spending as violating the First Amendment's ban on establishment of religion. *Flast v. Cohen*, 392 U.S. 83 (1968). This is because the Establishment Clause is a constitutional restriction on the taxing and spending power. There is a sufficient nexus between the taxpayer status and the claim so that the generalized grievance bar should not apply.

   d. **Later cases apply the generalized grievance doctrine to Establishment Clause challenges:** In *Valley Forge Christian College v. Americans United for Separation of Church and State*, 454 U.S. 464 (1982), the Court held that taxpayers could not, due to the generalized grievance doctrine, challenge a government department's decision to transfer surplus property to a religious school. This and other cases make it unclear whether the Establishment Clause exception to the generalized grievance doctrine survives.

2. A plaintiff may not assert the rights of a third party: A party must assert his or her own rights and may not litigate the rights of a third party even if the plaintiff is injured by the violation of the third-party's rights.

Examples: A shopkeeper has many customers who use food stamps, and her sales decrease significantly after the government allegedly illegally cuts off the food stamps of many of the customers. The drop in sales indicates that she is injured by the cutoff of food stamps to her customers. However, she may not have standing to challenge the food stamp cutoff because she would be asserting the rights of third parties—the food stamp recipients. She may also have a zone of interests problem since it is uncertain whether the food stamp program is concerned with the well-being of those who sell food to food stamp recipients. (She would have standing to challenge a government decision that she could no longer accept food stamps since that affects her own legal rights.) To overcome the prudential problems, she would have to establish an exception to the bar against third-party standing, and she would have to show (through the statute or legislative history) that shopkeepers' interests were within the zone of interests of the food stamp program.

a. The reasons for the ban on asserting the rights of third parties: The ban on asserting third-party rights keeps the courts out of disputes in which the persons primarily affected—those whose rights are actually at stake—have decided not to assert their rights. Further, the actual rightholder may have a greater incentive and greater ability to assert the rights than another party, who although injured, may not be as seriously affected and may not have complete information. Finally, third-party litigation may duplicate litigation between the government and the rightholder, and the rightholders should have the primary opportunity to assert their own rights.

b. Exceptions to the ban on asserting third-party rights

i. Close relationships: Plaintiffs may assert the rights of a third party when the plaintiff has a close relationship with the third party whose rights are at stake and a strong incentive to litigate to protect those rights.

Examples: Health care providers have been allowed to litigate the right of their patients to receive contraceptives or abortions because they are in a confidential relationship with their patients and the providers' own professional success depends upon their ability to provide the products or services.

ii. Impediment to asserting the rights: Third-party standing has also been allowed when the rightholders suffer from an impediment preventing or discouraging them from asserting their first-party rights.

Examples: Persons seeking abortions and contraceptive products and services might have privacy interests that prevent or discourage them from litigating their rights. Similarly, during the civil rights movement (and perhaps even today) African Americans seeking to vindicate their right to live in a previously segregated community might have feared reprisals from whites seeking to maintain segregation. Under such circumstances, courts have allowed third parties with close relationships to the rightholders to litigate the claims.

iii. First Amendment overbreadth claims: In the First Amendment context, the Court has allowed parties to argue that a statute that might constitutionally be applied to them is unconstitutional as applied to others; thus it should be struck down as overbroad on the theory that the existence of the overbroad statute chills the exercise of important First Amendment rights.

c. Tension between ban on asserting third-party rights and the demise of the legal right doctrine in standing: The ban on asserting a third-party's rights is in tension with the elimination of the legal right test for injury and the substitution of the zone of interests test. Under the zone of interests test, parties are allowed to challenge agency action without alleging that their own legal rights are at stake. The only legal rights at stake may be the rights of a third party whose treatment by the government caused the injury to the plaintiff.

3. Congress may overrule the prudential limitations: Since prudential limitations on standing are judge made and not constitutionally compelled, Congress has the power to overrule them. However, Congress may not expand standing beyond constitutional limits. Enactments regarding standing must be examined for constitutionality, as discussed below.

a. Overruling prudential limitations: As long as constitutional injury, causation, and redressability requirements are met, Congress may constitutionally grant standing for parties to litigate third-party rights and for citizens to litigate generalized grievances. Congress can easily bring a party within the zone of interests of a statute by mentioning that party's interests either in the statute or in the legislative history. Thus, it appears that Congress has broad power to expand standing.

b. The prudential limitations sometimes mask constitutional limitations on standing: The prudential limitations, especially the bar on asserting generalized grievances, might mask constitutional standing problems. In such cases, Congress may not overrule the limitations. For example, even if Congress overrules the generalized grievance doctrine by giving all citizens the right to challenge an agency's actions, those citizens still must meet the constitutional injury, traceability, and remediable standing requirements. Further, the Court (in an opinion by Justice Scalia) has characterized the bar against asserting generalized grievances as deriving from constitutional standing limitations. It is unclear if the Court agrees with Justice Scalia's characterization. *See Lujan v. Defenders of Wildlife,* 504 U.S. 555 (1992).

Examples: In many recent environmental statutes, Congress has granted a right to sue over violations to "any citizen." These are called ***citizens' suit*** provisions. In *Lujan,* the Court made it clear that the normal injury and redressability requirements apply to citizens' suits. Congress cannot overrule constitutional standing requirements.

4. Associational standing: Associations, such as interest groups and trade associations, have standing to litigate their own claims and also the claims of their members. When an association sues on its own behalf, it must meet normal standing requirements, i.e., it must have an injury that is traceable to the challenged conduct such that a remedy will cure the injury. For an association to sue on behalf of its members, it must establish (1) that the members themselves would have standing to sue; (2) that the interests the association is suing over are within the association's purpose; and (3) that the litigation will not be adversely affected by the absence of individual plaintiffs. *Hunt v. Washington State Apple Advertising Comm'n,* 432 U.S. 333 (1977).

IV. THE TIMING OF JUDICIAL REVIEW: RIPENESS, EXHAUSTION, AND MOOTNESS

Judicial review may be sought only when the claim is ripe, when administrative remedies have been exhausted, and before the claim becomes moot. Claims may not be brought too early (ripeness), too late (mootness), and (in some cases) without first exhausting administrative remedies.

A. The constitutional underpinnings of ripeness and mootness

The ripeness and mootness doctrines derive from the constitutional requirement of a "case or controversy." When a case is brought too early or too late, either there is not yet an injury sufficient for standing or the injury has ended, and a favorable judgment will not remedy it.

Examples: If a person brings a petition for judicial review of a regulation before the agency has attempted to enforce the regulation against the petitioner, the action may not be ripe because the petitioner has not yet been injured by the regulation. If the agency repeals the challenged regulation, the case is moot because the petitioner is no longer injured.

B. Ripeness in administrative law: The APA's grant of review of "final agency action"

APA §704 grants a right to judicial review of *"final agency action"* for which there is no other adequate remedy in a court. The "final agency action" provision is essentially a ripeness requirement, which excludes from review any agency action that is not yet complete. There are also ripeness requirements in addition to the APA's finality requirement.

1. **Finality, ripeness, and judicial review of agency adjudications:** Agency adjudications are final when the adjudicatory process in the agency has completely ended (including whatever appellate review is legally required within the agency), and the agency has issued its order.

2. **Finality, ripeness, and judicial review of agency rules:** A rule may be ripe for judicial review upon promulgation (before enforcement) if the issues are *fit* for judicial review and the party seeking review would suffer substantial *hardship* if review was delayed until after enforcement. *Abbott Laboratories v. Gardner*, 387 U.S. 136 (1967). If the fitness and hardship tests are not met, a party subject to a rule must wait to challenge the rule as a defense in an agency-initiated enforcement proceeding.

    a. **Is the promulgation of a rule final agency action under APA §704?** The promulgation of a rule pursuant to §553's notice and comment rulemaking provision is final under APA §704 in the sense that it is the end of the process of formulating the rule. There are no further administrative steps needed to give the rule the force of law. Further, requiring an enforcement order before judicial review may be sought would restrict judicial review to orders, and the APA does not confine the availability of judicial review to review of "orders." However, because of the independent problem of ripeness, the Supreme Court allows pre-enforcement review of regulations only when the fitness and hardship tests are met.

    b. **Fitness:** An issue is fit for pre-enforcement judicial review if no further factual development is necessary for the issue to be resolved. *Purely legal issues* are fit for judicial review pre-enforcement.

    c. **Hardship:** There is sufficient hardship to warrant pre-enforcement judicial review if it would be very expensive to comply with the regulation immediately (which might ultimately be overturned) and if special problems would arise for a party who violated the regulation to provoke an enforcement action (in order to get judicial review of the rule).

Examples: In *Abbott Labs*, a regulation was promulgated requiring drug manufacturers to use the generic name, along with the trade name, of medication *every time* the trade name appeared on the drug's packaging. The drug manufacturers immediately challenged the "every time" requirement, and the only issue in the case was whether the Food and Drug Administration (FDA) had statutory authority for the "every time" requirement. The Court held that this legal issue was *fit* for pre-enforcement review because it was the *purely legal issue* of whether the statute allowed for the "every time" requirement.

Hardship: The second issue in *Abbott Labs* was whether there was sufficient **hardship** to justify immediate judicial review. The Court held that the hardship was sufficient because it would be very costly for the drug manufacturers to print new labels and destroy those already in stock; violation of the regulation carried with it the risk of criminal penalties and seizures of improperly labeled medication. It would damage the drug manufacturers' reputations to willfully violate an agency regulation if they ultimately lost on judicial review.

    d. Absence of fitness: An issue is not fit for immediate judicial review when it is unclear what the regulation means or when it is likely to be applied.

    Examples: In a companion case to *Abbot Labs*, *Gardner v. Toilet Goods Association, Inc.*, 387 U.S. 158 (1967), a cosmetics manufacturer sought immediate review of a regulation requiring cosmetics manufacturers to permit FDA inspectors to have "free access" to certain manufacturing facilities. The Court held that the issue was not fit for review because it was unclear when the FDA would actually order inspections.

    e. Absence of hardship: There is not sufficient hardship for immediate judicial review if the regulation promulgated would not be expensive to comply with and if there are no substantial impediments to challenging the legality of the regulation on judicial review of an enforcement action.

    Examples: In *Toilet Goods*, the regulation provided that the cosmetics manufacturers must allow inspections or lose the certifications that allowed them to market their cosmetics. The Court held that there was not sufficient hardship for immediate judicial review because the regulation did not actually require the manufacturers to change their behavior, and they could promptly challenge any suspension of certification services on judicial review.

3. When are informal agency actions final? When an informal agency action has the effect of granting or denying permission to take a requested course of action, a court might consider it final agency action even though the decision was made without any formal procedures.

    a. *Overton Park* was final agency action: The Secretary of Transportation's approval of the route and design of the interstate highway involved in the *Overton Park* case was final agency action, despite the fact that it was made without a rulemaking or adjudicatory procedure.

    b. Informal responses to inquiries may also be final agency action: If an agency responds informally to an inquiry from a regulated party that a certain course of conduct would violate the law or is subject to a specified regulatory burden, the agency's response may be final and subject to immediate judicial review. *See National Automatic Laundry and*

Cleaning Council v. Shultz, 443 F.2d 689 (D.C. Cir. 1971). The determination of whether such agency action is final is similar to the "fitness and hardship" tests that govern whether review of a regulation may be sought immediately upon promulgation, without waiting for an enforcement action.

Examples: A national bank asks the comptroller of the currency whether it may offer a new banking product without violating the restrictions imposed on the activities of such banks by federal statutes and regulations. The comptroller of the currency, who is in charge of enforcing the restrictions on national banks, answers by letter that the bank would be violating the law if it offered the product. Because the informal ruling has the effect of denying the bank permission to offer the product, immediate judicial review may be available. *See First National Bank of Chicago v. Comptroller of the Currency*, 956 F.2d 1360 (7th Cir. 1992). *See also Air Brake Systems, Inc. v. Mineta*, 357 F.3d 632 (6th Cir. 2004) (review of agency web site posting stating that plaintiff's antilock braking system for trucks did not meet NHTSA's safety standards was not reviewable because it was tentative and based on incomplete information and because it had no legal consequences).

4. **When can agency inaction or refusal to act be ripe for review?** If the agency answers a request for action with a firm statement that it has decided not to act, that decision can be a "final agency action" subject to judicial review. However, if an agency has not answered a request for action or has explained its inaction as necessary to further study whether action is appropriate, inaction may not be final agency action subject to judicial review.

   a. **Whether inaction is final agency action is a factual inquiry:** Generally, whether agency inaction has ripened into a refusal to act is a factual question concerning the significance of inaction in the particular context. *See Oil, Chemical & Atomic Workers Union v. OSHA*, 145 F.3d 120 (3d Cir. 1998). Courts are reluctant to review agency action for excessive delay because such review infringes on the agency's prosecutorial discretion. Nonetheless, in extreme cases in which an agency has delayed excessively when it is statutorily required to act, a court may find the delay reviewable and order the agency to act. *See Public Citizen Health Research Group v. Chao*, 314 F.3d 143 (3d Cir. 2002). It is unclear, however, whether, in some contexts, review of agency inaction for excessive delay is consistent with ripeness concerns and with the general unreviewability of prosecutorial discretion.

   b. **If the agency is required to act in an emergency, inaction might be final:** If an agency is required to act in an emergency (and a member of the public petitions for agency action claiming that there is an emergency), agency inaction may amount to a final rejection of the claim of an emergency and thus might be ripe for judicial review. *See Environmental Defense Fund v. Hardin*, 428 F.2d 1093 (D.C. Cir. 1970); *Environmental Defense Fund v. Ruckelshaus*, 439 F.2d 584 (D.C. Cir. 1971).

Examples: The Secretary of Agriculture has the power, on a finding of an imminent hazard to the public, to order an immediate suspension of the registration of a pesticide and to continue the suspension during the cancellation process. The environmental groups in the EDF cases also petitioned for immediate suspension of the registration of the pesticide. More than a year after the petition for suspension was filed, the Secretary had not acted on it. The court of appeals held that delay in granting a suspension is reviewable since the delay is tantamount to a denial of suspension because the delay indicates that the Secretary does not agree with the petitioner that there is an imminent hazard to the public. However, the court found it necessary on two occasions to remand the suspension issue to the Secretary for findings so that it could effectively review the Secretary's decision.

  c. **Inaction, even if ripe, may not be reviewable:** If agency inaction occurs in the context of an exercise of an agency's prosecutorial discretion, then even if the agency inaction amounts to a final decision not to act, the agency's inaction will not be reviewable unless the agency's statute meets the requirements for review of prosecutorial discretion, i.e., it must contain criteria under which the agency is required to act.

C. Exhaustion of administrative remedies prior to seeking judicial review

One of the oldest, most established doctrines in administrative law is that challengers must exhaust remedies within the agency before seeking judicial review. Courts have applied this doctrine most strongly in cases of agency adjudication where there are normally one or two appeals available within the agency. However, in APA cases, there is no general *exhaustion* requirement beyond the APA §704's finality requirement; if an agency action is final within that section, judicial review under the APA is timely. *Darby v. Cisneros*, 509 U.S. 137 (1993).

  1. **Lack of agency jurisdiction can be raised only on review of the final agency order:** A party who claims that an agency lacks jurisdiction to subject the party to an enforcement hearing must await a final agency order and challenge the agency's jurisdiction on judicial review. The regulated party may not seek an injunction against the hearing. *Myers v. Bethlehem Shipbuilding Corp.*, 303 U.S. 41 (1938).

  2. **Exhaustion is required except in three narrow circumstances:** In non-APA cases, exhaustion of available administrative remedies is required unless (1) exhaustion would cause undue prejudice to the protection of the rights at issue; (2) the administrative agency lacks power to grant effective relief; or (3) the exhaustion would be futile because the administrative body is biased. *See McCarthy v. Madigan*, 503 U.S. 140 (1992).

  Examples: A prisoner sues prison officials for damages because of alleged unconstitutional conditions in the prison. There is an administrative process within the prison under which an order to improve the conditions can be issued, but no damages can be awarded. The prisoner is not required to exhaust administrative remedies because the remedy sought in the lawsuit — damages — is not available in the administrative proceeding. *McCarthy v. Madigan*, 503 U.S. 140 (1992).

  3. **The exhaustion doctrine serves several important policies:** The policies behind the exhaustion requirement include avoiding needless judicial intervention into administrative affairs, allowing an agency to correct its own errors, and sharpening the issues and the record for judicial review. *See McCarthy v. Madigan.*

  4. **In APA cases, there is no exhaustion requirement in addition to the criteria under APA §704:** APA §704 states that an agency action is final even if further appeal within the agency is available "unless the agency otherwise requires by rule and provides that the action meanwhile is inoperative, for an appeal to superior agency authority." In APA cases, exhaustion is required only of those remedies expressly required to be exhausted by. statute, or when an agency rule requires appeal before review and when the administrative action is made inoperativepending that review. *Darby v. Cisneros*, 509 U.S. 137 (1993). If APA §704 is met, no further exhaustion is required.

D. Mootness: When is it too late to seek review?

    1. A case is moot if there is no longer a live controversy between the parties: If a party is no longer subject to an agency rule, or if the agency repeals the rule, a claim for judicial review of the rule may be moot.

    Examples: A prisoner seeks injunctive relief to improve prison conditions. While the suit is pending, the prisoner's sentence ends, and he is released. The prisoner's injunctive claim is moot.

    2. Exceptions to the mootness doctrine: Mootness is a flexible doctrine, and moot cases are allowed to continue under certain circumstances.

        a. "Capable of repetition yet evading review": The most prominent exception to the mootness doctrine is when the claim is "capable of repetition yet evading review." These cases often involve inevitable mootness when the time necessary for litigating the claim is longer than the time the plaintiff will have an actual controversy.

        Examples: A pregnant woman seeks an injunction against a law that restricts abortion. While the case is still pending, she either gives birth or has an abortion. The case is not moot because all such claims will be moot by the time they are resolved.

        b. The defendant voluntarily ceases the challenged conduct: A moot case may be allowed to proceed where the mootness is caused because the defendant voluntarily ceases the challenged conduct. The courts have reasoned that as long as the defendant could resume the challenged conduct, the case should be allowed to go forward, lest all efforts at resolution are frustrated by voluntary cessation until after the case is dismissed for mootness. This exception is not satisfied if an agency is forced to change its rules — for example by a statutory amendment by Congress — because then the agency is not free to resume the challenged conduct.

Quiz Yourself on
THE AVAILABILITY OF JUDICIAL REVIEW
OF ADMINISTRATIVE DECISIONS

10. Does the existence of federal question jurisdiction, without an amount in controversy requirement, mean that judicial review is available for all agency action? _____

11. Assume Congress enacts a food stamp program that provides for three categories of food stamp assistance: emergency assistance, interim assistance, and regular assistance. Emergency assistance is provided on the day of an application when the applicant establishes, to the satisfaction of a caseworker, that the applicant is in dire need of assistance. Interim assistance is provided within ten days of an application for regular assistance when a caseworker concludes that it is likely that the agency will grant the application for regular assistance. Regular assistance is granted when, after full review, eligibility is established under program guidelines. The statue grants judicial review of denials of interim and regular assistance. The statute does not mention review of denials of emergency assistance. Are denials of emergency assistance reviewable? _____

12. Assume the same situation as above except that Congress has provided for review of denials of emergency and regular benefits but not interim benefits. How would the arguments against reviewability differ? _____

13. Regarding the same food stamp program, suppose a person files for emergency assistance and then after a week has still not received an answer. Can the applicant obtain judicial review of the failure to answer? _____

14. A statute provides that "the Administrator of the Environmental Protection Agency shall, in his discretion, designate those toxic waste sites that shall be given priority treatment" under the laws regulating the cleanup of toxic wastes. Priority treatment means that the site is cleaned up immediately, while normally the EPA delays cleanup while it tries to assign responsibility and recover cleanup costs in advance. A group of neighbors (near a particularly bad toxic waste site) sue the administrator when the administrator decides not to designate the site for priority treatment. Is the administrator's action subject to judicial review? _____

15. What would be the proper response to a petition for review filed against the Administrator of OSHA alleging that "the Administrator has failed to take adequate steps to ensure that all Americans work in a safe and healthful environment as required by statute"? _____

16. AT&T is upset that the FCC is giving favorable treatment to MCI and Sprint regarding rate regulation and the tariff-filing requirement. AT&T wants to sue the FCC. Would AT&T have standing to sue? _____

17. In order to receive federal funds under the Aid to Families with Dependent Children program (AFDC), states are required to take action to establish paternity and to secure child support orders from non-custodial parents (usually fathers) of children receiving AFDC benefits. Child support orders usually exceed the amount of AFDC benefits that are provided in the absence of a child support order. Further, without a paternity determination, a child cannot inherit from the estate of a noncustodial father. Does a child have standing to sue the state over the state's failure to attempt to establish paternity and the state's failure to seek a child support order against the child's noncustodial father? _____

18. A new regulation requires cigarette makers to disclose the ingredients of cigarettes on the package. The penalty for noncompliance is a substantial fine and seizure of all cigarettes in commerce not containing the proper labeling. Can the cigarette makers get immediate judicial review of this regulation upon its promulgation? _____

Answers

10. No. It is important to maintain the distinction between jurisdiction and reviewability. Jurisdiction means that a court may hear a claim, assuming a claim is available. Reviewability is concerned with whether, assuming jurisdiction, a particular agency action can be reviewed. While any claim alleging that an administrator has failed to obey the statute governing her agency may arise under federal law for the purposes of federal question jurisdiction, there are many claims that ultimately cannot be brought because the challenged agency action is unreviewable.

11. Maybe not. There are two sets of arguments against review. First, it can be argued that the denial of emergency assistance is not final since the agency will ultimately decide whether the person is entitled to regular or interim benefits. Against this, it can be argued that the denial of emergency benefits amounts to a final determination that the applicant does not meet the criteria for emergency benefits. The second argument is that by providing for judicial review of denials of interim benefits and regular benefits, Congress has implicitly precluded review of denials of emergency benefits. This argument could be strengthened or weakened with evidence from the legislative history and practice regarding other, similar, programs.

12. Now the arguments against reviewability are much stronger. First, interim benefits determinations look even more like tentative decisions regarding the application than do emergency benefits determinations. Because interim-benefits determinations are completely tied to the likelihood that regular benefits will be granted, the decision to deny interim benefits does not seem final. Second, the fact that Congress granted reviewability over one form of temporary relief (emergency) but not another (interim) is strong evidence that Congress did not intend for there to be review of interim determinations. There would be a strong argument that Congress precluded review of interim benefits determinations.

13. Maybe. It can be argued that the failure to answer a petition for immediate, emergency action is ripe for review as a refusal after a resonable time has expired, and that a week is too long for a response to a petition for emergency food aid.

14. Probably not, on the grounds that the agency action is committed to agency discretion by law. First, the statute does not contain a standard under which the administrator is supposed to decide which sites are given priority treatment. Thus, there may be "no law to apply." Law to apply may, however, be found in the goals of the cleanup program as a whole. Second, the statute explicitly places the priority status determination in the "discretion of the Administrator." This provision may be a "deeming" clause under which judicial review is precluded. Third, it can be argued that this is a decision like prosecutorial discretion because it involves a delicate and expertise-laden balancing of the priorities of the agency. Thus, it is in a category of determinations that are traditionally unreviewable.

15. The court may, under *Norton v. Southern Utah Wilderness Alliance*, dismiss the claim because the claim does not identify "agency action" with sufficient particularity to merit judicial review.

16. Probably yes. Under the legal right test, AT&T would not have had standing because AT&T has no legal right to have its competitors regulated properly. However, under *Data Processors*, AT&T could have standing if it could show that it is injured by the agency action and that it is within the zone of interests in the sense that competitors' interests are relevant to the regulatory scheme governing long distance telephone service. Since AT&T is in direct competition with MCI and Sprint in the long-distance market, AT&T is probably injured by a loosening of regulatory requirements on its competitors. The more tricky question is whether competitors' interests were relevant when the system of long-distance rate regulation was established. It is likely that such interests were relevant so that AT&T would meet the zone of interests test and have standing to challenge the FCC's treatment of its competitors.

17. Possibly. There are several ways to look at this question. Answering it is difficult because of the lack of consistency in the Supreme Court's standing cases. On the one hand, there are cases that support the argument that standing is lacking because the child's economic difficulties are caused by the non-custodial parent and not by the state. Redressability is also a problem because even if the state tried, it might not be able to establish paternity or procure an enforceable child support order. On the other hand, if you view the child as having a right arising from the state's attempt to establish paternity and to procure the support order, if the state fails to try, you can argue that the injury arises from the state's

failure to act. That injury is then sufficient to confer standing in a suit to force the state to try. In general, the Supreme Court has been skeptical of injury in cases like this. Because the purpose of the statute is to force states to try to procure paternity judgments and support orders for persons who are eligible for AFDC benefits, the plaintiff is in a class of the intended beneficiaries of the statute and might have an injury—even if he or she cannot establish that the state would have been successful in the particular case.

18. Maybe. The question is whether the case is ripe for review. Review should normally await an enforcement action, when the illegality of the regulation could be raised as a defense. In *Abbott Labs*, the Supreme Court decided that a regulation can be reviewed pre-enforcement if the issue is "fit" for review, and the regulated party would suffer substantial "hardship" if review was postponed. Here, the issue is probably fit since the only issue is likely to be whether the agency has the legal authority to impose the rule. There is also probably sufficient hardship since printing the labels would be expensive and reveal information that the company would prefer to keep secret. Further, a substantial fine and destruction of stock without proper labels would also be sufficient hardship.

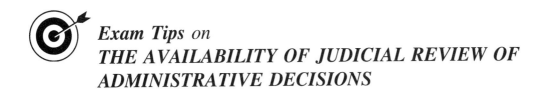

Exam Tips on THE AVAILABILITY OF JUDICIAL REVIEW OF ADMINISTRATIVE DECISIONS

☛ Be sure to keep the issues of jurisdiction and reviewability separate. You are more likely to be asked about reviewability than about jurisdiction.

   ☞ If jurisdiction is an issue, mention the old "rule of thumb" and then explain that jurisdiction depends mainly on what court has jurisdiction by statute.

   ☞ Point out that the Supreme Court favors jurisdiction in the court of appeals for reasons of judicial economy and thus if there is a statute that can be construed to give jurisdiction to that court, the Supreme Court will probably read it to do so.

☛ When discussing whether an agency action is reviewable, be sure to discuss whether the action is final, whether there are any ripeness problems, and whether either of the sections of APA §701 (a) affect reviewability.

   ☞ However, if the action is obviously reviewable, don't waste time discussing reviewability in depth—it is probably not being asked about.

☛ For statutory preclusion of review, be sure to look for both explicit and implicit preclusion.

☛ If there is statutory preclusion, be sure to evaluate whether the particular action over which review is sought is within the scope of the precluding statute.

   ☞ If the statute precludes review of particular decisions such as a denial of government benefits, analyze whether the party seeking judicial review is challenging the type of decision specified in the statute or whether the party seeking judicial review is challenging something else, such as the way the entire program is being administered.

☞ In cases involving global challenges to the way an entire program is being administered, point out that the Court, in the *McNary* decision seems open to arguments that global challenges are not precluded by statutes disallowing review of individual denials of benefits.

☞ In evaluating whether an action is committed to agency discretion by law, be sure to look for all three ways in which that can happen; no law to apply, a deeming clause, and a category traditionally not subject to judicial review.

☞ Make clear that these three understandings are related, that each tend to support the other, and that all involve evidence that Congress did not intend to subject the agency action to review.

☞ Look for arguments that the challenged agency action is akin to prosecutorial discretion. If it is, analyze reviewability under that line of cases.

☞ Remember that there is serious doubt about whether review of constitutional issues may be barred.

☞ Be sure the party seeking to challenge agency action has standing. Look for injury, causation, redressability, zone of interests, and the prudential limitations. Since the precedent in this area appears inconsistent, marshal arguments from both sides to show that you understand the issues even if the conclusion is not obvious.

☞ When the party seeking to challenge agency action is not the regulated party, be sure to discuss the zone of interests test and how it differs from the legal rights test.

☞ If there is a citizen suit provision, point out that everyone given permission to sue under that provision is probably within the zone of interests.

☞ In cases arising under statutes other than the APA, point out that the zone of interests test might not apply, since the zone of interests test may be based on the language of APA §702.

☞ Also, look for redressability problems—will the court be able to provide an effective remedy?

☞ The prudential limitations, including the ban on asserting the rights of third parties and the ban on litigating a generalized grievance, are subject to repeal by Congress.

☞ Look for repeal, such as by a citizen suit provision.

☞ Remember, however, that Congress may not override constitutional standing doctrines.

☞ Ripeness questions often arise when it appears that the agency's consideration is not complete. A common ripeness issue is whether a court should review a regulation before the agency has tried to enforce it. Use the *Abbott Labs* **fitness** and **hardship** tests. The differences between *Abbott Labs* and the *Toilet Goods* case are useful in applying the fitness and hardship test.

☞ An attempt to force an agency to act may raise ripeness questions. If you are asked whether an agency can be compelled to act, be sure to address whether the agency's failure to act is ripe.

☞ Agency inaction, as in a refusal to act, may not be ripe for review if the agency is still deciding whether to act although there may be a factual argument that the agency has delayed so long that its delay amounts to a decision not to act.

☞ If exhaustion of administrative remedies is an issue, apply the factors from the *McCarthy* opinion. However if agency action is final under the APA, those factors may not apply and the only issue may be whether a statute or regulation requires that certain remedies be exhausted.

CHAPTER 4

JUDICIAL REVIEW OF ADMINISTRATIVE DECISIONS

ChapterScope

This chapter examines the substance of judicial review of agency action including how to decide which APA standard of review applies, and what each standard means when applied to various types of agency action. The key points in this chapter are:

- **Standards of judicial review are prescribed by APA §706:** Unless the agency's particular statute states otherwise, the standard of review of agency action is determined by applying APA §706.

  - The *substantial evidence test* applies to *formal* adjudication and formal rulemaking.

  - **Arbitrary and capricious review** is available in most other circumstances.

  - **De novo** review applies rarely, when new factual issues properly arise for the first time on judicial review or when agency adjudicatory procedures are inadequate.

- **The reviewing court looks at the whole record:** APA §706 directs reviewing courts to examine the whole record when conducting judicial review, not merely those parts of the record that support the agency's action.

  - The record consists of the information the agency had before it at the time it made its decision.

  - Post hoc rationalizations for agency action are disfavored because the agency's action is judged on the record available at the time the decision was made.

- **Substantial evidence means such relevant evidence as a reasonable mind might accept as adequate to support a conclusion.**

  - The substantial evidence test, under which agency factual determinations in adjudicatory hearings are reviewed, requires that agency decisions be supported, on the record as a whole, by enough relevant evidence as a reasonable mind might accept as adequate to support the agency's conclusion.

  - The substantial evidence test is the same standard under which courts review jury verdicts.

- **Questions of law were traditionally for courts to decide.** Traditionally, courts deferred to agency factual conclusions and agency policy decisions, but held that issues of law were for the courts to resolve with some, but not much, deference to agency views.

- **The *Chevron* doctrine instructs courts to defer to agency decisions of statutory interpretation.** Contrary to the traditional view, the Supreme Court's *Chevron* decision appears to instruct courts to defer to any plausible agency statutory interpretation unless Congress's intent on the matter is unmistakably clear.

- Application of the *Chevron* standard has been inconsistent. Later cases are in conflict over whether courts should look beyond Congress's clearly expressed intent and attempt to ascertain Congress's intent using **traditional tools of statutory interpretation**.

- When decisions of law are made informally, a lower level of deference, known as *Skidmore* deference may apply.

- **Policy decisions and informal rulemakings are reviewed under the arbitrary and capricious test.**

  - For agency action to survive review under the arbitrary and capricious test, the agency must apply the correct legal standard, consider all relevant factors, evaluate alternatives, and explain their conclusions on issues raised in the decisionmaking process. In addition, the decision reached must not be so irrational that the court cannot help but conclude that the decision was not the product of the application of agency expertise to the problem.

I. STANDARDS OF JUDICIAL REVIEW UNDER THE APA

The APA, which governs judicial review of agency action, establishes the standards under which courts evaluate agency action. However, in many cases the agency's enabling act contains a provision establishing a standard of review that differs from the applicable APA standard. The enabling act provision takes precedence over the APA standard.

A. APA §706 and standards of review

APA §706 directs courts to "hold unlawful and set aside" agency action contrary to the Constitution, in excess of statutory authority, and taken without observance of procedural requirements. It also authorizes courts to review the legality of agency action under three standards:

arbitrary, capricious, an abuse of discretion or otherwise not in accordance with law; (§706(2)(A))

unsupported by substantial evidence in a case subject to sections 556 and 557 of this title or otherwise reviewed on the record of an agency hearing provided by statute; (§706(2)(D)) and

unwarranted by the facts to the extent that the facts are subject to trial de novo by the reviewing court (§706(2)(E)).

B. How to decide which provision of §706 applies

Those provisions of §706(2) with no textual guidance on when they apply are applicable to all reviewable administrative action. Others apply only to those administrative actions specified in the provision. The three most important substantive review provisions of §706 apply as follows:

1. The substantial evidence test applies only to formal adjudication and formal rulemaking: Section 706(2)(D) states that the **substantial evidence test** applies only to cases "subject to sections 556 and 557 of this title or otherwise reviewed on the record of an agency hearing provided by statute." Sections 556 and 557 are the *formal adjudication and formal rulemaking* provisions of the APA, and thus the substantial evidence test applies only to formal adjudication and formal rulemaking.

Example: A statute states that the Department of Agriculture shall conduct "public hearings" before issuing regulations governing the price of milk. Even though the statute requires hearings, the substantial evidence test does not apply because the statute does not require formal procedures under §§556 and 557, and because the statute does not explicitly require rulemaking "on the record after hearing."

2. **De novo review is available only when, under traditional administrative law principles, a party is entitled to trial de novo in the reviewing court:** Section 706(2)(E) provides that agency determination of facts should be overturned if "unwarranted by the facts to the extent that the facts are subject to trial de novo by the reviewing court." Section 706 does not tell us when "the facts are subject to trial de novo by the reviewing court." The Supreme Court has specified that de novo review is available only when:

   (1) the [agency] action is adjudicatory in nature and the agency factfinding procedures are inadequate or
   (2) issues that were not before the agency are raised in a proceeding to enforce nonadjudicatory agency action. *Citizens to Preserve Overton Park, Inc. v. Volpe*, 401 U.S. 402 (1971).

3. **The arbitrary and capricious test applies to all agency action:** Section 706(2)(A), which provides that agency action should be set aside if it is "arbitrary, capricious, an abuse of discretion, or otherwise not in accordance with law," contains no limitation on its applicability. Therefore, it applies to all reviewable administrative action.

   Example: The Bureau of Land Management approves a plan to harvest timber on 10,000 acres of federal land. The Bureau made this decision informally, i.e., there was no rulemaking or adjudication. The decision is subject to review under the ***arbitrary and capricious test***.

4. **If substantial evidence or de novo review is available, it governs:** Because the substantial evidence and de novo standards are considered more demanding on the agency than the arbitrary and capricious test, the arbitrary and capricious test is a fall-back position for those seeking judicial review of agency action. Parties seeking judicial review will always prefer the least deferential standard available.

C. **The record on review: what it consists of and what the court examines**

APA §706 requires reviewing courts to examine the whole record.

1. **The record on review consists of the material the agency had before it when it made its decision:** Reviewing courts should not look beyond the ***record*** that was before the agency at the time the agency made its decision. The agency may not support its decision with information that it did not have at the time it made its decision or with post hoc rationalizations that were not offered at the time the decision was made. Further, courts prefer to look at the actual documents and other materials the agency had before it. Affidavits (or other evidence of the basis of the agency's decision created for the judicial review litigation) are disfavoured and should only be used when it is not possible to create an adequate record out of the material that the agency had before it at the time it made its decision.

   Example: In *Overton Park*, the Secretary of Transportation approved the design of the disputed highway without any set procedures and announced the decision in a press release. The challengers sued the Secretary in the district court. The court based its review largely on testimony and affidavits of the officials involved in making the decision. The Supreme Court remanded the case to the district court with instructions that the district court examine the documents and other materials that were before the agency when it made its decision, rather than the affidavits that had been prepared for the litigation. The Court stated that lower courts should start with the materials that were before the agency and should require litigation affidavits and other post hoc materials only when necessary to supplement the record.

2. **The reviewing court looks at the whole record, not just the evidence supporting the agency's decision:** APA §706 overrules pre-APA practice and requires that a court conducting judicial review "shall review the whole record or those parts of it cited by a party" and not only the evidence supporting the agency's action. Thus, agency action supported by some evidence might be overturned on review if there is overwhelming evidence in the record opposing the agency's action.

II. REVIEW OF QUESTIONS OF FACT AFTER AGENCY ADJUDICATION: THE SUBSTANTIAL EVIDENCE TEST

The substantial evidence test is the standard of review for formal agency adjudication and formal rulemaking conducted under APA §§556 and 557 (or conducted on the record after a hearing pursuant to the agency's enabling act). In addition, some enabling acts specify that the substantial evidence test applies to that particular agency's informal rulemaking.

A. The substantial evidence test

1. **Substantial evidence defined:** Substantial evidence means "such relevant evidence as a reasonable mind might accept as adequate to support a conclusion." *Consolidated Edison Co. v. NLRB*, 305 U.S. 197, 229 (1938). This standard is the same standard that is employed to determine whether there is sufficient evidence to submit an issue to a jury; substantial evidence is lacking when a judge would direct a verdict on the ground that a reasonable jury could only have one view of the facts. *NLRB v. Columbian Enameling and Stamping Co.*, 306 U.S. 292 (1939).

2. **Substantial evidence review of the "whole record":** A court performing a substantial evidence review must look at the whole record, not only the evidence supporting the agency's decision, which was the pre-APA practice. A decision might fail the substantial evidence test, even thought it is supported by some evidence, when that evidence is overwhelmed by other evidence to the contrary.

B. The substantial evidence test applied

A court performing substantial evidence review examines the evidence that was before the agency and determines, in a rather uncomplicated way, whether the agency's decision was reasonable in light of the evidence on the record. Two situations merit special attention.

1. **Agency witness credibility determinations:** When an agency's decision is based (in whole or in part) on the credibility of witnesses, the agency's decision is entitled to great deference because the reviewing court reviews only the paper record without the opportunity to observe the demeanor of the witnesses. If the agency's decision relies on witness credibility, it takes a great deal of contrary evidence to convince a court that the agency's decision lacks substantial evidence.

2. **Agency reversals of ALJ decisions:** In most agencies, initial adjudicatory decisions are made by an Administrative Law Judge (ALJ) and must be appealed to a higher level within the

agency (often to the heads of the agency) before judicial review may be sought. The initial decision of the ALJ is part of the record of agency proceedings that are reviewed in court. Therefore, when an agency reverses the decision of the trier of fact on appeal within the agency, the reviewing court must take the reversal into account in deciding whether the agency's decision is supported by substantial evidence. The ALJ's decision weighs against the agency's decision.

a. *Universal Camera*. **Agency reversal of ALJ credibility findings:** Because witnesses appear only before the ALJ, a special problem arises when an agency reverses an ALJ's decision that is based, in whole or in part, on witness credibility. In *NLRB v. Universal Camera Corp.*, 179 F.2d 749 (2d Cir. 1950), the court of appeals held that it could not take into account the fact that the agency had reversed the ALJ, even when the reversal was based on a credibility determination. The court found itself unable to formulate an appropriate standard of review that would take the ALJ's decision into account and remain consistent with the requirements of the substantial evidence test.

b. *Universal Camera* **in the Supreme Court:** The Supreme Court disagreed with the court of appeals and held that because the initial decision is part of the record under the APA, the reviewing court must take the initial decisionmaker's opinion into account when deciding whether the agency's conclusions are supported by substantial evidence. *See Universal Camera Corp. v. NLRB*, 340 U.S. 474 (1951). The Court noted that Congress, in passing the APA's "substantial evidence on the record as a whole" provision, intended to make judicial review somewhat less deferential.

c. **The importance of credibility determinations in** *Universal Camera*: The Supreme Court, in remanding the case to the court of appeals, observed that "evidence supporting a conclusion may be less substantial when an impartial, experienced examiner who had observed the witnesses and lived with the case has drawn conclusions different from the Board's than when he has reached the same conclusion." *Universal Camera*, 340 U.S. at 496.

d. *Universal Camera* **on remand:** On remand, the court of appeals held that since the initial decision was based in part on a credibility determination, the agency's reversal of that decision was not proper because the ***evidence supporting the agency's decision was not enough to overwhelm the credibility findings of the ALJ***. *See NLRB v. Universal Camera Corp.*, 190 F.2d 429 (2d Cir. 1951). The concurring opinion on remand argued that the court's decision went too far in protecting ALJ credibility decisions from reversal by agencies. The strongest argument against the majority on remand is that APA §557(b) states that "[o]n appeal from or review of the initial decision, the agency has all the powers which it would have in making the initial decision except as it may limit the issues on notice or by rule."

III. DE NOVO REVIEW OF QUESTIONS OF FACT

A. De novo review applies only in rare circumstances

De novo review applies only in two rare circumstances: (1) where agency adjudicatory factfinding procedures are inadequate and (2) where new factual issues arise in an action to enforce non-adjudicatory agency action.

B. De novo review defined

De novo review means that the reviewing court considers the facts and reaches its own decision without deferring to the conclusions of the agency. Usually, in de novo review of facts, the facts are retried in the district court.

IV. REVIEW OF QUESTIONS OF LAW

A. Competing traditional standards of review of agency conclusions of law

There are competing traditions regarding judicial review of agency conclusions of law.

1. **De novo review of law:** Questions of law were traditionally reviewed de novo by courts on the theory that it is the judicial role to declare the law.

2. **Deferential review of law:** There is also a competing tradition that courts defer to reasonable agency interpretations of law because agency expertise assists in understanding Congress's statutory commands and other legal issues within the agency's jurisdiction.

B. Application of law to particular facts

Courts have traditionally shown the greatest deference to agency decisions involving the applications of law to particular facts. Such decisions are affirmed if they enjoy "warrant in the record" and a "reasonable basis in law." *NLRB v. Hearst Publications, Inc.*, 322 U.S. 111 (1944).

1. **Competing traditions in the *Hearst* case:** In *Hearst*, the Court reviewed the NLRB's determination that people selling newspapers on the street were employees of the newspaper company entitled to the protections of federal labor laws.

   a. **Definition of "employee" is for the courts:** In the first part of its *Hearst* opinion, applying traditional methods of statutory interpretation, the Court upheld the Board's decision not to apply the tort law definition of "employee" in determinations of employee status under the labor laws. The Court did not appear to defer to the Board at all. Rather it decided **de novo** that Congress did not intend for the tort law definition to apply.

   b. **Application of the definition is for the agency:** In the second part of its *Hearst* opinion, the Court reviewed the Board's decision that the particular newspaper vendors were employees. In that part of the opinion, the Court was highly deferential to the Board's decision and stated that "where the question is one of specific application of a broad statutory term . . . the reviewing court's function is limited." *Hearst*, 322 U.S. at 131.

C. Issues of statutory authority

1. **Tradition of nondeference:** Traditionally, courts have decided issues of statutory authority without deferring to an agency's interpretation of its enabling act. *Addison v. Holly Hill Fruit Products, Inc.*, 322 U.S. 607 (1944), illustrates this doctrine.

   a. **The *Holly Hill* issue:** In *Holly Hill*, agricultural workers and employees engaged in canning agricultural products "within the area" of agricultural production were exempted by Congress from the requirements of the Fair Labor Standards Act. The Act left it to the Administrator to determine the size of the area of agricultural production.

b. **The Administrator's ruling in *Holly Hill*:** The Administrator ruled that canning operations with more than seven employees would not be exempt even if they were in the "area" of agricultural production as previously defined by the Administrator.

c. **The Court's *Holly Hill* decision:** The Supreme Court, using traditional statutory interpretation methods, held that once the Administrator determined the "area" of agricultural production, there was no statutory authority to exclude canning operations from the exemption based on the size of the operation. The Court held that there was no occasion for deference to the agency since this was an issue of statutory authority.

2. **Current law on statutory authority:** The Court no longer distinguishes between issues of statutory authority and other statutory issues. Issues of statutory authority are analyzed, like other issues of statutory interpretation, under the ***Chevron doctrine*** outlined below.

D. **Pure questions of statutory interpretation: the *Chevron* test**

1. ***Chevron*:** In *Chevron, U.S.A., Inc. v. Natural Resources Defense Council, Inc.*, 467 U.S. 837 (1984), the Court stated that unless Congress has ***directly spoken to the precise issue in question***, courts should defer to agencies on pure questions of statutory interpretation as long as the agency arrived at a reasonable or permissible construction of the statute.

   a. **Identifying a pure question of statutory interpretation:** Pure questions of statutory interpretation are those issues that involve only the meaning of the words of the statute. They do not involve applying those words to a particular situation.

   Example: The clean air statute involved in *Chevron* regulated permits for the discharge of pollution from a "stationary source." In *Chevron*, the Court reviewed the Environmental Protection Agency's (EPA) definition, contained in a regulation, of the statutory term "stationary source" (under which an entire factory complex, which might contain several buildings and numerous smokestacks, cold be a single stationary source). The challengers argued that each smokestack must be regulated as a separate stationary source. Whether the statutory term—"stationary source"—could bear the meaning ascribed to it by the EPA was deemed, by the Court, a "pure question of statutory interpretation."

   b. **The test applied in *Chevron*:** The Court held that Congress had not directly spoken to the precise issue of whether each smokestack must be regulated as a stationary source, that the term "stationary source" was ambiguous, and that the agency's definition was permissible because it fell within the range of meanings that "stationary source" could bear.

2. **The *Chevron* two-step analysis:** Under *Chevron*, judicial review of agency interpretations of statutes proceeds in two steps.

   a. ***Chevron* step one:** Step one of *Chevron* asks whether Congress has directly spoken to the precise question at issue. If so, Congress's intent prevails. If the agency's interpretation conflicts with Congress's intent, the court should overrule the agency and replace the agency's interpretation with Congress's intent. If Congress's intent is unclear, or if Congress explicitly left a gap for the agency to fill, then the analysis moves to step two.

   b. ***Chevron* step two:** If the reviewing court concludes, in step one, that the statute is ambiguous because Congress has not directly spoken to the precise issue in question, then in a case involving implicit delegation of interpretive authority due to inadvertent ambiguity the reviewing court asks whether the agency's interpretation is "permissible." An interpretation is permissible if it is "a sufficiently rational one to preclude a court from substituting its judgment for that of the [agency]." *See Chemical Manufacturers Association v. NRDC*, 470 U.S. 116 (1985); *Young v. Community Nutrition Institute*, 476 U.S. 974 (1986). This is very deferential. Justice Stevens, the author of *Chevron*, sharply attacked this approach (in his dissent in *Young*) as inconsistent with the judicial role in statutory interpretation. In the case of explicit delegations, *Chevron* stated that the step two standard is that the agency interpretation may not be "arbitrary, capricious, or manifestly contrary to the statute." In *Household Credit Services, Inc. v. Pfennig*, 541 U.S. 232 (2004), the Court explained that under this standard, agency interpretations should be upheld if they are "rational" and "reasonable." It is unclear whether the distinction between explicit and implicit delegations of interpretative authority will ever make a difference to the outcome of a case.

c. **Less deferential formulations of *Chevron* step one:** In subsequent cases, the Court sometimes applies a less-deferential version of step one under which the reviewing court should attempt to ascertain Congress's intent using ***traditional tools of statutory construction*** including the language, structure, purpose, and legislative history of the statute being construed and other interpretive devices such as the canons of statutory interpretation. *See INS v. Cardoza-Fonseca*, 480 U.S. 421 (1987); *Dole v. United Steelworkers of America*, 494 U.S. 26 (1990). Under the less-deferential version of step one, courts are more likely to find congressional intent on a matter and thus are more likely to reverse the agency.

d. **The current view of *Chevron* step one:** It is difficult to arrive at a uniform view of how the Supreme Court applies *Chevron* step one at present. In some cases, the Court looks for the "plain meaning" of the statute under review, and appears less concerned with whether the statutory meaning would be different if traditional tools of statutory interpretation were applied. *See MCI Telecommunications Corp. v. A.T.&T.*, 512 U. S. 218 (1994). In other cases, the Court uses traditional tools of interpretation, and it is difficult to distinguish between pre- and post-*Chevron* practice. For example, in 2000, the Court based its holding that the FDA lacked jurisdiction to regulate tobacco on the structure of the statute and overall purpose of Congress, without regard to the statutory language. *See FDA v. Brown & Williamson Tobacco Corp.*, 529 U.S. 120 (2000). And in some cases, the Court has relied on canons or rules of statutory interpretation. *See Dole v. United Steelworkers*, 494 U.S. 26, 36 (1990) (applying "[t]he traditional canon of construction, noscitur a sociis" to determine unambiguous meaning of Paperwork Reduction Act); *Barnhart v. Thomas*, 540 U.S. 20, 26 (2003) (applying "rule of the last antecedent" to determine meaning of Social Security Act).

3. **When does *Chevron* apply?** *Chevron* applies to many, but not all agency decisions involving statutory interpretation.

a. **Less formal agency interpretive procedures:** *Chevron* applies to agency decisions on statutory construction arrived at in the course of rulemaking and adjudication. *Chevron* deference does not apply to agency statutory interpretations rendered less formally. For example, in *Christensen v. Harris County*, 529 U.S. 576 (2000), the Court held that *Chevron* deference did not apply to an interpretation contained in an "Opinion Letter" that an agency wrote in response to a letter from a regulated party asking whether the statute administered by the agency permitted a particular course of conduct. Similarly, in *United States v. Mead Corp.*, 533 U.S. 218 (2001), the Court refused to accord *Chevron* deference to a statutory interpretation contained in a Customs Service "ruling letter" which, although it represented the agency's official position, was not based on "a process of rulemaking or adjudication."

In both cases, the Court held that a lesser form of deference, known as *Skidmore* deference, applied, under which agency interpretations are "entitled to respect . . . but only to the extent that those interpretations have the 'power to persuade." *See Christensen*, 529 U.S. at 588 (quoting *Skidmore v. Swift & Co.*, 323 U.S. 134, 140 (1944)). Under *Skidmore*, courts decide how much to defer to agency interpretative decisions based on "the thoroughness evident in its consideration, the validity of its reasoning, its consistency with earlier and later pronouncements, and all those factors which give it power to persuade, if lacking power to control."

b. **Agency authority to "administer" the statute being interpreted:** *Chevron* applies only to statutes administered by the agency whose interpretation is at issue. Agency interpretations of the APA, for example, should not receive *Chevron* deference because no agency is charged with administering the APA. Likewise, if a statute's primary method of enforcement is through civil actions brought in court, agency views on the meaning of the statute will not receive *Chevron* deference. *See Adams Fruit Co. v. Barrett*, 494 U.S. 638 (1990). In such cases, the statute is "administered" by the courts, not the agency.

c. **Consistency and contemporaneity of interpretation:** The applicability of *Chevron* deference may be affected by the lack of consistency of the agency's current interpretation with prior agency interpretations. Although the Court has stated that agency interpretations are not "carved in stone" and thus may be changed when appropriate, the existence of a longstanding contrary interpretation may lead courts to question the validity of any reinterpretation, especially if the prior interpretation received prior court approval, *see Maislin Industries, U.S. Inc. v. Primary Steel, Inc.*, 497 U.S. 116 (1990), or appears to be more consistent with other action taken by Congress and the agency. *See FDA v. Brown & Williamson Tobacco Corp.*, 529 U.S. 120 (2000) (characterizing longstanding interpretation of food and drug laws as not giving the FDA authority to regulate tobacco as evidence that Congress did not intend to grant the FDA general regulatory power over tobacco). *See also Barnhart v. Thomas*, 540 U.S. 20 (2003) (longstanding agency interpretation entitled to greater deference). On the other hand, the Court has applied full *Chevron* deference to an interpretation of a statute that was rendered 130 years after the statute being interpreted was enacted. The Court stated that the delay was not relevant as long as ambiguity in the statute left a gap for the agency to fill. *See Smiley v. Citibank*, 517 U.S. 735 (1996).

d. **Interpretations of agency regulations:** Courts defer to agency interpretations of their own regulations, but not under *Chevron*. Rather, such deference has been based on the Court's decision in *Bowles v. Seminole Rock & Sand Co.*, 325 U.S. 410 (1945). *See Martin v. Occupational Safety and Health Review Commission*, 499 U.S. 144 (1991). Under *Seminole Rock*, a court defers to an agency's interpretation of its own regulations "unless it is plainly erroneous or inconsistent with the regulation." 325 U.S. at 414.

V. REVIEW OF QUESTIONS OF POLICY

Courts most often review agency policy decisions under the arbitrary and capricious test, which applies to informal rulemaking and informal agency action. Policy decisions made in formal rulemaking and adjudication are statutorily subject to substantial evidence review; they are reviewed under the substantial evidence test. It is unclear whether, with regard to policy questions, there is any practical difference between substantial evidence review and arbitrary and capricious review.

A. Defining a "policy decision"

A policy decision is a decision by an agency that determines whether regulation is necessary or desirable and what level or form of regulation is appropriate.

Example: When the EPA decides what level of a pollutant should be allowed into the atmosphere, it is making a policy decision. By contrast, when the EPA decides whether it has statutory authority to address an issue (for example, indoor air pollution due to secondhand tobacco smoke), it is making a decision of statutory interpretation. When it decides which indoor premises should be regulated or what level of ventilation should be required in an area where smoking is allowed, it is back to making a policy decision.

B. The arbitrary and capricious test

1. **Arbitrary and capricious defined:** The arbitrary and capricious test requires that agencies make decisions:

    1. "based on a consideration of the relevant factors," including alternatives to the agency's proposal suggested by the record;
    2. without "a clear error of judgment"; and
    3. under the correct legal standard.

    Overton Park, 401 U.S. at 415-16.

2. **Conducting an arbitrary and capricious review:** When conducting an arbitrary and capricious review, courts must keep in mind that:

    1. while the inquiry is "searching and careful"
    2. the standard of review is "a narrow one [and t]he court is not empowered to substitute its judgment for that of the agency."

    Overton Park, 401 U.S. at 416.

3. **Arbitrary and capricious standard applied. Hard look review:** The arbitrary and capricious standard is sometimes referred to as a "hard look review" because the court takes a hard look at the agency's policy decision and because the agency is required to take a hard look at viable alternatives to its chosen course, based on the record.

    a. **Agencies must apply the correct legal standard:** On judicial review, courts require agencies to apply the correct legal standard to the policy questions decided. For example, in *Overton Park*, the Supreme Court held that the district court, on remand, must "consider whether the Secretary properly construed his authority to approve the use of park land as limited to situations where there are no feasible [or prudent] alternative routes." *Overton Park*, 401 U.S. at 416.

    b. **Agencies must consider the relevant factors:** Agencies must consider the relevant factors, i.e., those factors made relevant under the correct legal standard. In *Overton Park*, this meant that the agency was required to consider the amount of disruption the highway would cause to the park and whether other proposals would cause the same problems.

    c. **Agencies must consider alternatives to their proposals:** An element of reasoned decisionmaking is the requirement that agencies consider those alternatives to their proposals that the record suggests. In the *Airbags Case*, for example, the agency erred by not considering mandatory airbags or mandatory nondetachable seatbelts as alternatives to the detachable belts that the agency thought would not increase automobile safety. *See*

Motor Vehicle Manufacturers Association v. State Farm Mutual Automobile Insurance Co. (The Airbags Case), 463 U.S. 29 (1983). In *Scenic Hudson*, the Second Circuit faulted the Federal Power Commission (FPC) for not adequately considering a gas turbine power plant as an alternative to a hydroelectric plant planned for the Hudson River. *Scenic Hudson Preservation Conf. v. FPC (I & II)*, 354 F.2d 608 (2d Cir. 1968) and 453 F.2d 463 (2d Cir. 1971), *cert. denied*, 407 U.S. 926 (1972).

   d. Agencies must explain their conclusions on issues raised in the decisionmaking process: As proof that they considered all relevant factors, courts require agencies to explain their decisions on major issues that are raised during the decisionmaking process. This includes an explanation adequate to establish that the agency considered relevant factors, that it considered alternatives, and that it considered the comments made during the rulemaking process.

   Example: The FDA established standards for the preparation of smoked fish because of reports of illnesses caused by the failure of the smoking process to eliminate bacteria. The producers of a particular species of fish submitted scientific data indicating that their particular fish is safe without the FDA's preferred process and that the economic viability of their product would be destroyed if they were required to use the preferred process for their fish. The FDA promulgated a uniform rule applicable to all species of fish without explaining why it rejected the data offered by the producers of that particular kind of fish. This, according to the court of appeals, made the rule invalid. *See United States v. Nova Scotia Food Prods. Corp.*, 568 F.2d 240 (2d Cir. 1977).

C. Standard of review of informal rulemaking

   1. The usual case. Arbitrary and capricious: The standard of review for informal rulemaking conducted under APA §553 is the arbitrary and capricious test. APA §706(2)(A). Dicta to the contrary in *Overton Park and Lincoln v. Vigil*, 508 U.S. 182 (1993), are incorrect.

   2. Substantial evidence review of informal rulemaking

   a. When substantial evidence review applies to informal rulemaking: Substantial evidence review applies to informal rulemaking only when specified by a particular regulatory statute.

   b. Does substantial evidence review make a difference? A great deal of doubt has been expressed over whether there is any detectable difference between substantial evidence review and arbitrary and capricious review of informal rulemaking. Substantial evidence review may allow for greater judicial scrutiny of the scientific or factual bases of agency rulemaking. This might help explain the result in the *Benzene* case where the Court closely scrutinized the scientific basis for the OSHA rule under review.

D. Standard of review of informal agency action

Courts review informal agency action (action for which there is no procedure specified) under the arbitrary and capricious test. Informal agency action is sometimes referred to as informal adjudication.

Example: The Secretary of Transportation's approval of the highway route in *Overton Park* was made without a rulemaking or adjudicatory procedure, and the Court held that it was subject to review under the arbitrary and capricious test.

E. The special case of deregulation: standard of review

Deregulation—the revocation or rescission of a regulation—is normally reviewed under the same test that applies to the initial promulgation of the regulation. In most cases of informal rulemaking, this means the arbitrary and capricious test.

1. **The argument for a more lenient standard of review of deregulation in the *Airbags Case:*** In the *Airbags Case*, it was argued that deregulation was analogous to a decision not to regulate and therefore should be unreviewable or reviewed on a very deferential standard.

2. **The Court's rejection of a more lenient standard of review of deregulation:** The Court rejected the argument for a more lenient standard of review of deregulation and held that the rescission of a rule is subject to the same standard of review as the promulgation of a rule.

    a. **The Motor Vehicle Safety Act:** The Motor Vehicle Safety Act subjects orders "establishing, amending, or revoking" an automobile safety standard to judicial review under APA §706. Because the Act equates orders revoking regulations with orders establishing regulations, the Court found that it should treat deregulation the same as regulation for purposes of judicial review.

    b. **The APA:** The APA itself (§551(5)) provides that revocation of a rule is done through rulemaking. Since the APA subjects all rulemaking to judicial review under §706, the structure of the APA also suggests that the revocation of a rule should be subject to the same standard of judicial review as the initial promulgation of a rule.

VI. REMEDIES ON JUDICIAL REVIEW

A. Courts may hold agency action substantively void

Reviewing courts have the power under APA §706 to "hold unlawful and set aside" agency action found not to meet the applicable standard of review. In many situations, courts do just that: they hold regulations null and void or order agencies to pay benefits or award permits unlawfully withheld. However, especially in rulemaking that involves policy questions, courts often choose to remand matters to the agency for further consideration without ordering the agency to change its decision.

B. Courts prefer procedural grounds

Courts prefer to rest the rejection of agency policy decisions on procedural grounds such as inadequate notice or inadequate opportunity to comment. Even when the problem is the lack of support in the record for the agency's action (which means that on the record before the agency the decision was arbitrary or capricious), courts often characterize this substantive failing as the procedural sounding problem of an inadequate record.

C. Remand to the agency is often the chosen remedy

Courts often remand matters to agencies for further consideration.

1. **Reasons for remanding:** Courts remand matters to agencies in order to give agencies the opportunity to cure the defects identified on judicial review. This includes the sufficiency of the record, and courts often give agencies another.opportunity to assemble a record adequate to support the chosen regulatory action.

2. **Reluctance to substantively reject agency decisions:** Courts shy away from direct substantive rejection of an agency's policy decision because agency decisions on matters of policy implicate agency expertise. Courts do not wish to appear to be substituting their judgment for that of the experts.

D. Remand may, in practice, amount to rejection

Remand of a matter to an agency may effectively amount to rejection because the agency may not actually reconsider the matter. Remand entails delay. Over time, agency enthusiasm for the initial decision may have faded with the emergence of new problems and new priorities—especially if a new administration has taken office.

E. After remand or rejection, the agency may start again

Even after a court rejects an agency policy decision as arbitrary or capricious (unless the court bases the rejection on a lack of agency power to act in the area or a statutory bar to the agency's policy choice), the agency may have the power to issue a new notice of proposed rulemaking and promulgate the same or a similar rule based on a new record.

1. **If remand was due to an inadequate record, the agency may assemble a better record:** If the reviewing court's rejection of a rule was for legal reasons unrelated to the record (such as lack of legal authority or improper statutory interpretation), action by Congress may be necessary before the agency can promulgate a new rule to achieve the same policy result.

Quiz Yourself on *JUDICIAL REVIEW OF ADMINISTRATIVE DECISIONS*

19. The Department of Agriculture decided to create a new method of regulating milk prices. Wanting the widest possible input, it decided to hold public hearings in eight locations around the country. The Secretary of Agriculture and other department officials were present at all eight hearings. The hearings were open to the public, and all attendees were allowed to address comments to and ask questions of the Secretary and the other officials present. After the rule was promulgated under APA §553, a milk producer from Wisconsin challenged the rule as not supported by substantial evidence. Is substantial evidence the proper standard for judicial review? _____

20. Does the arbitrary or capricious standard always apply? _____

21. The Bureau of Land Management approves a plan to harvest timber on ten thousand acres of federal land. This decision was made informally (there was no rulemaking or adjudication), and the decision was explained in a press release issued by the director of the Bureau. The decision is challenged on judicial review under the arbitrary and capricious test, and the Bureau asks the court to affirm its decision based exclusively upon affidavits from the Director and her assistants regarding the basis of the decision. Is this the proper procedure? _____

22. On review of the denial of a social security disability benefits claim, the agency argues that its doctor's testimony that the claimant was not disabled provides (on its own) substantial evidence to support the

claim, and therefore the court need look no further into the record. Is this a good argument? _____

23. In determining the amount of food stamps to which a claimant is entitled, the statute requires the Department of Agriculture to consider "the resources available to the family unit." The department has recently decided, in a §553 rulemaking, to change its definition of "family unit" and place children who are unrelated (e.g. stepchildren) in the same "family unit," thus reducing benefits to the stepsiblings of children who are receiving child support payments. A claimant, whose claim was denied based on child support payments to a stepsibling, sues claiming that the statute does not allow stepsiblings to be included in the same "family unit." What is the standard of review for the definition of "family unit?" _____

24. In response to revelations that airbags have killed and injured children and smaller adults, the National Highway Transportation and Safety Administration (NHTSA) decided, in a §553 rulemaking, to rescind the regulation requiring dual airbags in all cars. It also allowed those cars already manufactured with dual airbags to be equipped with on/off switches. The automobile insurers submitted comments, supported by scientific research, urging the retention of the airbag rule. They argued that redesigned airbags that did not deploy with so much force, combined with adjustments to the design of automobile dashboards, would resolve the problem. In its concise general statement, the agency did not mention the comments submitted by the insurers. Are the rescission of the airbags rule and the adoption of the switch requirement, arbitrary and capricious? _____

Answers

19. No. Despite Supreme Court dicta to the contrary, the proper standard of review of rules promulgated pursuant to APA §553 is the arbitrary or capricious standard of APA §706(2). The fact that the department held public hearings does not change this because the substantial evidence test applies only to rules made pursuant to APA §§556-557 and rules made "on the record after hearing" (not to rules made pursuant to §553 even if the agency elects to hold informal public hearings of the sort held in this case). "On the record after hearing" means rules made pursuant to a trial-type procedure, not §553 procedures augmented with public hearings.

20. Yes. Some of the standards or review enumerated in APA §706 contain explicit textual limitation on when they apply while others do not. The arbitrary and capricious test contains no such limitation, which means that it applies to all reviewable agency action. However, because the arbitrary and capricious test is the most deferential APA standard of review, the person seeking judicial review will always prefer to have another, less deferential, standard apply—such as the substantial evidence test or de novo review.

21. No. The court should review the record that was before the agency at the time the decision was made. APA §706 instructs reviewing courts to look at the "whole record" that was before the agency. It is a principle of administrative law that agency action must stand or fall based on the record that the agency considered when it made its decision. Even when the decision is made informally, courts should first look at the actual material the agency considered when it made its decision and should receive affidavits regarding the decisionmaking process only when the administrative record does not adequately reveal the basis for the agency's decision.

22. No. Under APA §706, the reviewing court is instructed to review the whole record, not merely those parts of it that support the agency. If there was enough evidence (especially documentary evidence), contrary to the agency's doctor's testimony such that a reasonable person would not accept the agency's conclusion, then the agency's decision would not be supported by substantial evidence. This reverses the pre-APA practice under which some courts looked only at the evidence supporting the agency to determine whether the agency's decision was supported by substantial evidence.

23. There are two competing traditions. On one view, the definition of "family unit" is an issue of law for courts to resolve—with some moderate deference to the agency's view. The other tradition is for a highly deferential review, especially if the case involves applying the definition to the particular household. Under *Chevron*, the court would ask whether Congress has directly spoken to the issue. Some members of the Supreme Court would insist that only the plain meaning of the statute should be consulted on this question; others would look more broadly into traditional tools of statutory interpretation such as statutory structure and legislative history. Since there is no definition of "family unit" in the statute, the Court would likely hold that Congress has not directly spoken to the issue, and the inquiry would shift to *Chevron* step two under which the Court would ask whether the agency's definition is a permissible construction of the statute. This is a very deferential standard, and the agency's construction is permissible unless it is substantially irrational.

24. Possibly. To argue that they were arbitrary and capricious, the challengers should urge the court to carefully review the record before the agency. It appears that the agency's decision is arbitrary and capricious because the agency did not consider alternatives to complete rescission, and it did not adequately explain its decision. The agency unecessarily gave up the lifesaving benefits of airbags that supported its initial requirement without considering a less-drastic alternative and without explaining why it concluded that the lower-force airbags were not sufficient to solve the problems and preserve safety. Further, the agency did not explain why both rescission of the dual airbags requirement and the on/off switch were necessary and may not have considered the alternative of the on/off switch only.

Exam Tips *on*
JUDICIAL REVIEW OF ADMINISTRATIVE DECISIONS

☛ Always look carefully at APA §706 to determine which standard of review applies to the particular agency action challenged.

   ☞ If the predicates for substantial evidence review (agency decision under formal procedures or "on the record after hearing") are present, substantial evidence review applies. In a close case, it might be useful to spend time analyzing whether substantial evidence review applies.

   ☞ De novo review is rarely available and not likely to be tested on. However, if it appears that a predicate for de novo review is present, be sure to state the grounds—where agency adjudicatory factfinding procedures are inadequate and where new factual issues arise in an action to enforce non-adjudicatory agency action—and be sure to explain that under de novo review, the reviewing court makes a fresh determination of the facts subject to de novo review.

☞ If no predicate for either substantial evidence review or de novo review is present, use the arbitrary and capricious test, and explain that this test always applies since it has no predicate.

☛ When applying any standard of review, remember that under-APA §706, the court looks at the ***whole record***, not just those parts of the record that support the agency. Thus, if an exam calls for review of a particular agency action, be sure to address the complete record.

☛ The substantial evidence test applies to formal adjudication and formal rulemaking done under §§556 and 557 or otherwise "on the record after hearing."

☞ Point out that except where §§556 and 557 are specified, courts rarely find that substantial evidence review applies—the hearing must truly be "on the record" in the sense of a formal adjudicatory-type hearing.

☞ If the substantial evidence test applies, state the definition of the test ("such relevant evidence as a reasonable mind might accept as adequate to support a conclusion") and be sure to look at the whole record and discuss whether the evidence against the agency's decision substantially outweighs the evidence on the other side.

☛ On issues of law, remember that there are competing traditions.

☞ If the issue is one of pure statutory interpretation, apply the two-step *Chevron* standard and be sure to describe the more and less deferential versions of step one.

☞ Unless the question really calls for it, don't spend too much time on step two.

☞ If the issue is not a pure question of statutory interpretation, it may be an application of law to a particular situation, which gets deferential, "reasonable basis and warrant in the record," review.

☛ Watch for situations in which *Chevron* does not apply because of the informality of the agency process leading to the interpretation. With informal interpretations, apply *Skidmore* deference.

☛ On issues subject to arbitrary and capricious review, be sure to state the standard as laid down in *Overton Park* and then apply the test to the issues at hand.

☞ Be sure that the agency applied the correct legal standard, considered all relevant factors, considered alternatives, and explained its decision adequately, which includes stating conclusions on the major issues raised.

☛ When grounds for setting aside agency action exist, discuss the appropriate remedy—should the court remand the issue to the agency for further consideration, should the court allow the agency to supplement the record, or should the court simply rule that the agency may not do what it proposes?

Chapter 5

AGENCY CHOICE OF POLICYMAKING MODE

ChapterScope

This chapter examines the rules and doctrines that govern an agency's choice of policymaking mode. The major policymaking procedural models are rulemaking and adjudication, but agencies also make policy informally, i.e., without going through either an adjudicatory or legislative process. The main points in this chapter are:

- Due process requires notice and an adjudicatory hearing when agency action affects a particular party and is based on facts specific to the situation of that party. These facts are referred to as "adjudicative facts."

- Where agency action is based on conditions common to many parties in an area, such as the value of all property in a city, such general facts are referred to as "legislative facts" and a legislative process is constitutionally sufficient.

- The main APA policymaking tools are rulemaking and adjudication.

  - Agencies have a great deal of discretion over which mode to use, although adjudication may be required before an agency may issue an order directed at a particular party.

  - Where no particular procedural model is statutorily or constitutionally required, agencies may make policy informally, i.e., without using either an adjudicatory or rulemaking process.

    - In such cases, the agency must give notice of its decision and provide a brief explanation.

    - An agency may not rely on an unpublished rule against any member of the public who lacks actual notice of the rule.

- Agencies, like common-law courts, often announce new rules in the course of deciding matters in adjudication.

  - The Supreme Court has allowed agencies to make rule-like decisions in the course of adjudication on two theories, first that the practice is within the traditional adjudicatory process and second that subsequent parties are ordered to follow the rule in a proper adjudication.

- There are policy reasons, including fairness to all regulated parties and superior fact-finding devices, favoring rulemaking as the procedure for formulating general policy-oriented rules.

- The APA exempts several types of rules, such as policy statements and interpretative rules, from notice and comment procedures.

  - For a rule to fall within an exemption, it must not be legislative, i.e., it must not add to or change existing legal obligations.

- If an agency is required to make rules "on the record after opportunity for an agency hearing" the agency must employ ***formal rulemaking*** procedures under which rulemaking is conducted in an "on the record" adjudicatory proceeding. This procedure is disfavored, and courts construe statutes, whenever possible, not to require it.

■ Agencies must follow their own formally promulgated procedural rules; and they also must follow informally promulgated procedural rules when a member of the public has relied on the rule and has been prejudiced by the agency's failure to follow it.

I. CONSTITUTIONAL CONSTRAINTS ON CHOICE OF POLICYMAKING MODE

The choice between rulemaking and adjudication is influenced heavily by constitutional due process concerns. Under certain narrow circumstances, *due process* requires adjudication. In most cases, however, the choice between rulemaking and adjudication is left to Congress or to the agency under delegation from Congress.

A. *Londoner v. Denver*

In *Londoner v. Denver*, 210 U.S. 373 (1908), the Court held that an agency, with delegated authority to tax property owners for street paving, was constitutionally required to hold individual hearings. The agency taxed the property owners based on the benefit conferred on the particular piece of property. Because the agency's decision was particularized to the situation of each property owner, the Court held that due process requires a hearing with the right to present arguments and evidence.

B. Due process and adjudicative facts

When an agency regulates a party based on the particular situation of that party, due process requires that the party be given an adjudicatory hearing to present its version of the facts. The particularized facts are referred to as **adjudicative facts** because they are the type of facts that are found through an adjudicatory process that focuses on the particular situation of a single or small number of parties.

C. *Bi-Metallic Investment Co. v. State Board of Equalization*

In *Bi-Metallic Investment Co. v. State Board of Equalization*, 239 U.S. 441. (1915), the Court held that when an agency imposes a tax on an across-the-board basis, without attention to the particulars of any taxpayer, due process does not require individualized hearings. In *Bi-Metallic*, an agency increased the value of all taxable property in the city of Denver by 40 percent. The Court rejected a due process challenge to the lack of hearings stating that when "more than a few people" are affected, legislative procedures are sufficient and the normal channels of government account-ability provide the only practical safeguard.

D. Legislative facts and due process

Due process does not require hearings when agencies make across-the-board decisions based on general factual conditions and not the particular situation of any particular regulated party. This type of fact is referred to as a *legislative fact* because it is the kind of fact normally found legislatively.

Example: A Virginia statute gave the Highway Commission the power to determine when public safety required railroads to remove a grade crossing and build a railroad bridge over a highway. This determination was made without notice or a hearing. The statute did not provide for judicial review, although the Virginia Supreme Court had stated that equity review for "arbitrary" action was available. In *Southern Railway v. Virginia*, 290 U.S. 190 (1933), the railway company challenged this statute as violating due process by not providing for a hearing on the safety of the crossing in advance of the order that the railroad remove the crossing and construct a bridge. The Court held that this procedure violated due process by not allowing a hearing and judicial review. The Court rejected the argument that administrative action without a hearing was constitutional because the Virginia legislature might have taken the same action without a hearing. The Court stated that even if that were true, it does not follow that an administrative officer (without the fact-finding and deliberative procedures of a legislature) was free to make such a determination without a hearing. The Court also held that the power of a court of equity to overturn the decision as "arbitrary" was too uncertain to provide due process.

Southern Railway moves beyond *Londoner* in one respect: it supports a claim that the argument for a hearing is strengthened by the fact that an administrator, as opposed to the state legislature itself, is making the decision. Thus, even if the removal of a particular grade crossing was a proper subject for the Virginia legislature employing a legislative process, an administrator making the same decision is required by due process to employ an adjudicative process.

II. CHOICE OF POLICYMAKING PROCEDURE

Agencies make policy in both rulemaking and adjudication. When agencies make policy through a legislative rule, then the only issue in a subsequent enforcement action is whether the regulated party violated the rule. When agencies make policy in adjudication, they act much like common law courts—announcing new "rules" in the course of deciding the particular case before the agency.

A. The APA and the choice of policymaking mode

The APA does not explicitly regulate the choice of policymaking mode, but its definitions of "adjudication" and "rulemaking" provide some guidance on the choice of policymaking mode. In addition to the APA and the Constitution, an agency's enabling act may prescribe a particular policy-making mode.

1. **APA policymaking tools:** The APA explicitly provides for two policymaking models: rulemaking and adjudication.

   a. **APA definition of rulemaking:** *"Rulemaking"* is defined as the "agency process for making, amending or repealing a rule." APA §551(5). *"Rule"* is defined as "the whole or a part of an agency statement of general or particular applicability and future effect designed to implement, interpret, or prescribe law or policy . . . ." APA §551(4).

   b. **APA definition of adjudication:** *"Adjudication"* is defined as the "agency process for the formulation of an order." APA §551(7). *"Order"* is defined as "the whole or a part of a final disposition, whether affirmative, negative, injunctive, or declaratory in form, of an agency in a matter other than rulemaking but including licensing." APA §551(6). In short, the APA provides that everything that is not a rule is an order, and the process for formulating an order is adjudication.

2. **The APA and agency choice of policymaking model:** The APA itself does not explicitly state when agencies must engage in rulemaking or adjudication to make policies. However, agencies must employ an adjudicatory process to issue orders against regulated parties.

a. **Rulemaking or adjudication.** Agencies make rule-like determinations in both rulemaking and adjudication, and either is proper as long as the agency has the power to use the particular procedure and all the procedural requirements are observed.

b. **Agencies must employ a valid procedure:** If an agency makes a rule, it must employ *some* valid procedure, normally rulemaking or adjudication, for any significant policy decision. For example, in *Sugar Cane Growers Cooperative of Florida v. Veneman*, 289 F.3d 89 (D.C. Cir. 2002), the court held that the promulgation of a plan, after informal consultation with some affected parties, for submitting and accepting bids for a program involving subsidies for plowing under surplus crops, which included the "procedures all applicants must follow, the payment limitations of the program, and the sanctions that will be imposed on participants if they plant more in future years" was a rule that should have been promulgated pursuant to §553. The court rejected the agency's harmless error argument—that the agency would have arrived at the same result had it engaged in notice and comment rulemaking. That argument, concluded the court, would amount to a virtual repeal of §553 because it would be extremely difficult to prove that the agency would have made a different decision had it followed the APA. *See also Utility Solid Waste Activities Group v. EPA*, 236 F.3d 749 (D.C. Cir. 2000) (correction of "technical errors" in rule without notice and comment cannot be excused as harmless error).

B. Agency discretion to make policy by rule

If an agency has statutory authority to make rules, then rulemaking is obviously an appropriate procedure for making policy. Because rulemaking has several legal and policy advantages over adjudication and informal policymaking, courts prefer policymaking by rule. In doubtful cases, courts are likely to rule in favor of agency authority to make rules.

1. **Advantages to making policy by rule:** There are several recognized advantages to making policy by rule.

   a. **Clarity:** Policy decisions promulgated in a rule are likely to be clearer and more definite than informal policy or policy made through adjudication. Increased clarity, in turn, better informs regulated parties of their legal duties and provides administrative law judges and courts with more guidance in enforcement actions and on judicial review.

   b. **Better decisions:** Policy decisions promulgated through rulemaking may be better than other decisions for two reasons. First, the legislative notice and comment process allows for greater public input into the decision and thus the agency may be better informed. Second, the legislative form of the rules may allow for a better-crafted decision, with exceptions when appropriate.

   c. **Comprehensive decisionmaking:** Rules allow agencies to impose comprehensive decisions at once on all similarly situated regulated parties. Comprehensive decisionmaking can save agency resources because the agency does not have to repeatedly establish the same point in numerous adjudications.

   d. **Fairness:** Policymaking by rule is fairer to regulated parties because it gives them better advance knowledge of their legal duties and avoids the singling out that occurs when an agency announces a new policy in an enforcement proceeding against one party who may be the only party subject to the new policy until further enforcement proceedings are brought.

e. Expedited hearings: Policymaking by rule allows an agency to establish its regulatory regime in a single rulemaking proceeding and then apply it to regulated parties in adjudications where the only issue will be whether the regulated party violated the rule. This is more efficient than forcing the agency to relitigate its policy in each adjudication.

2. **Arguments against agency power to make policy by rule:** In those cases in which agency statutory rulemaking power is in doubt, regulated parties make several arguments against agency authority to make policy by rules.

    a. Congressional intent: If the agency's organic statute appears to contemplate an adjudicatory process, regulated parties argue that Congress did not intend for the agency to have rule-making power. The argument is that Congress intended that the agency hold a hearing on all issues, including whether the party's conduct violated the statute.

    b. "Right to a hearing" on all issues: Related to congressional intent, regulated parties have argued that when Congress establishes a hearing process to determine regulatory violations, Congress grants regulated parties a right to a hearing on all issues—including whether the alleged conduct violated the statute. By making a binding rule that defines certain conduct as a violation, the agency is depriving the regulated party of the hearing granted by Congress on that issue.

    c. Longstanding agency practice: In certain cases, most notably regarding the Federal Trade Commission (FTC), some agencies long believed that they lacked power to make binding rules and instead were required to use an adjudicatory process to make binding policy. When an agency changes its mind, the regulated parties argue that the longstanding agency belief against rule making authority is evidence against agency power to make rules.

    d. When in doubt, rule against agency power: It has also been argued that because agencies have only those powers granted to them by Congress, courts should (when in doubt) rule against agency power to prevent the executive branch from seizing power not delegated to it.

3. **Courts favor agency rulemaking power:** In general, courts have resolved doubts in favor of agency rulemaking power. Thus, so long as some statutory provision can be interpreted to grant rulemaking power and there is no compelling evidence to the contrary, courts are likely to recognize agency power to make policy through the issuance of binding rules. Note, however, that when an agency rule decides an issue that would otherwise be addressed at a hearing, courts usually require the agency to allow regulated parties to argue that special circumstances mean the rule should not apply to the particular case.

Examples: The FTC has broad jurisdiction to order businesses to "cease and desist" from engaging in "unfair or deceptive acts or practices" in interstate commerce. For the first fifty years or so of its existence, the FTC formulated "cease and desist" orders through an adjudicatory process during which the FTC established both that the challenged practice violated the act and that the defendant had engaged in the unfair or deceptive practice. In the 1960s, the FTC decided to promulgate trade regulation rules that would establish that a particular practice was "unfair or deceptive," thus leaving for the hearing only the issue of whether the defendant had engaged in the practice. In 1971, the FTC adopted its first trade regulation rule, the so-called Octane Posting Rule, which specified that it was unfair and deceptive for sellers of gasoline to fail to post the octane rating of their products. In *National Petroleum Refiners Association v. FTC*, 482 F.2d 672 (D.C. Cir. 1973), *cert. denied*, 415 U.S. 951 (1974), the court of appeals held that the FTC had the power to make binding trade regulation rules. The court focused primarily on a provision of the FTC Act that gave the FTC the power to make rules and regulations, although the petroleum refiners argued that Congress intended only to give the agency the power to make procedural rules and not substantive ones.

The *National Petroleum* court found it persuasive that the FTC hearing process would be simplified, that regulated parties would have more certain knowledge of regulatory requirements, and that all members of an industry would be regulated at once if the FTC could make substantive rules—leaving for the hearing only the issue of whether the rules were violated. These advantages appeared so significant to the court that it resolved its doubts concerning the agency's rulemaking power in the agency's favor. In response to the argument that this procedure deprived the regulated parties of their right to a hearing to contest the issue of whether a particular practice is unfair or deceptive, the court stated that the party must be allowed an opportunity to argue that, due to special circumstances, the trade regulation rule should not be applied. Note also that because the FTC's jurisdiction is so broad, members of Congress became concerned, and Congress has legislated limits to the FTC's rulemaking power several times since the FTC began promulgating trade regulation rules.

C. Agency power to make policy by adjudication

Some agencies, most notably the NLRB, make policy primarily through an adjudicatory process in which new rules of decision are announced in the course of deciding particular adjudicatory matters. Because the APA's definitions appear to contemplate rulemaking as the procedure for formulating general rules, general rules stated as part of a decision in an adjudication have been attacked as having been promulgated without a proper rulemaking procedure. The Supreme Court has rejected these challenges, although not definitively, stating that the choice between adjudication and rulemaking lies largely within the discretion of the agency.

1. **Rulemaking in adjudication.** *Excelsior Underwear, Inc.:* In *Excelsior Underwear, Inc.*, 156 N.L.R.B. 1236 (1966), the NLRB held an adjudicatory hearing on a union's challenge to the fairness of a union representation election. The union challenged the election as unfair because the union had not been provided with a list of the names and addresses of the employees eligible to vote in the election. The NLRB approved the election but stated in its opinion that in all such elections beginning thirty days after the issuance of the opinion, employers must provide the list to the union. This reversed a prior NLRB ruling that held that providing the list was not necessary to ensure a fair election.

    a. *Excelsior* **looks like a rule. Generality:** The requirement that employers provide unions with a list of employees in *Excelsior* looks like a rule because it was stated as a general requirement applicable to all union representation elections.

    b. *Excelsior* **looks like a rule. Prospectivity:** The decision in *Excelsior* also looks like a rule because it was made prospectively and was not even applied to the election challenged in *Excelsior* itself.

    c. *Excelsior* **does not look like an order:** Because the rule in *Excelsior* was not applied to the election challenged in the case, *Excelsior* has been attacked as improper because no "order" was issued requiring the employer in that case to provide the list. Therefore, since *Excelsior* does not appear to be an order, it is argued that it must be a rule, and thus the procedure was improprer.

2. ***Excelsior* in the Supreme Court. *Wyman-Gordon*:** In *NLRB v. Wyman-Gordon Co.*, 394 U.S. 759 (1969), the NLRB ordered the employer to provide the union with a list of employees' names and addresses. The reasoning in the order consisted mainly of a citation to *Excelsior*. The employer challenged the order in court, arguing that the *Excelsior* rule was invalid because it was a rule and had not been promulgated in a rulemaking proceeding. A divided Supreme Court upheld the order in *Wyman-Gordon*, but a majority did not agree on the grounds.

   a. **Justice Fortas: *Wyman-Gordon* was a valid order and *Excelsior* is irrelevant:** Justice Fortas, joined by three other Justices, stated that the NLRB's order that Wyman-Gordon turn over the list in its election was a valid order and that the NLRB's reliance on *Excelsior* was irrelevant. Justice Fortas opined that agencies may, in the course of deciding cases, announce general rules and rely upon them as stare decisis. In his view this was not important in order to determine whether the order that Wyman-Gordon turn over the list was valid. The only vital factor to Justice Fortas was that "the Board in an adjudicatory proceeding directed [Wyman-Gordon] itself to furnish the list." *Wyman-Gordon*, 394 U.S. at 766. Justice Fortas also stated that the procedure in *Excelsior* itself was invalid. Because the NLRB did not apply the new requirement to the parties in *Excelsior* itself, the NLRB was legislating and should have used a rulemaking procedure.

   b. **Justice Black. *Excelsior* was a valid adjudication:** Justice Black's opinion, joined by two others, disagreed with Justice Fortas and held that it was proper for the NLRB to rely on *Excelsior*'s rule that employers furnish the list of employees because courts often announce new rules and make them prospective out of concerns for fairness or orderly administration. To Justice Black, the NLRB's decision was within the traditional bounds of the adjudicatory process. Because the NLRB followed proper adjudicatory procedures, the NLRB did not violate the APA by announcing the new "rule" in the course of adjudication. Justice Black also disagreed with Justice Fortas's argument that the order in *Wyman-Gordon* was proper regardless of the legality of the *Excelsior* decision. To Justice Black, this reasoning would free the NLRB from all procedural constraints in formulating policy.

   c. **Justices Douglas and Harlan. The NLRB should have used rulemaking:** Justices Douglas and Harlan both argued, in dissent, that the NLRB should have used a rulemaking procedure. Both argued that the NLRB's prospective rule in *Excelsior* was improper because prospective rulemaking is not within the APA's definition of adjudication. Rather, the only APA process for making prospective rules is rulemaking, and since the NLRB in *Wyman-Gordon* relied on the rule announced in *Excelsior*, the order in *Wyman-Gordon* was also invalid.

3. ***Bell-Aerospace* and discretion to make policy by adjudication:** In *NLRB v. Bell Aerospace Co.*, 416 U.S. 267 (1974), the Supreme Court unanimously upheld the NLRB's power in an adjudication to change its standard for determining whether certain employees (buyers) were managers. The Court stated that the choice between rulemaking and adjudication is a matter of agency discretion. The Court rejected the argument that because the new standard would be different from its prior rulings and because the new standard would be in the nature of a general rule, the NLRB was required to use rulemaking. However, the Court also noted that the question in *Bell Aerospace* was particularly suited to case-by-case adjudication. Thus, the Court did not adopt, as a general matter, Justice Black's reasoning in *Wyman-Gordon*.

4. Summary. Adjudication and general rules: The decision whether to use rulemaking or adjudication lies largely within the discretion of the agency. However, the Supreme Court has never definitively approved the making of prospective general rules in an adjudicatory process. Because the opinion in *Bell Aerospace* stresses the fact-specific nature of the inquiry into whether the employees are managers, it is dangerous to generalize from the holding in *Bell Aerospace* to a principle that agencies are free to make general rules in adjudication. In fact, the Court specifically disavowed deciding that issue.

III. INFORMAL POLICYMAKING

There are many situations in which agencies make policy without using either rulemaking or adjudication. Under some circumstances, agency action in the nature of rulemaking falls within an exception to APA §553's notice and comment requirements. In other cases, by statute or traditional practice, agencies act informally—making decisions without any formalized procedure. Under some circumstances, however, informal policymaking may violate the APA. In such cases, agencies must engage in a more formal policymaking process before their rules can be given legal effect.

A. Exemptions from §553

APA §553 contains several exemptions from its ***notice and comment*** procedures. This means that there are types of rules that agencies may make without going through notice and comment procedures.

1. Exemptions from all of §553: Section 553(a) states that §553 does not apply to military or foreign affairs functions; to matters relating to agency management or personnel; or to public property, loans, grants, benefits, or contracts. Thus, in these areas, agencies are free to make rules without regard to any of §553's requirements.

2. Section 553 exemptions for "nonlegislative" rules: APA §553(b) exempts ***interpretative rules, general statements of policy***, and rules of agency organization or practice from notice and comment requirements. These exempt rules are often referred to collectively as "nonlegislative rules." Further, §553(b) allows agencies to dispense with notice and comment procedures when it finds that such procedures are "impracticable, unnecessary or contrary to the public interest."

   a. Definition of "legislative rule": A *legislative rule* is a rule that adds to or changes legal requirements. A legislative rule effects an actual change in existing law or policy, and it creates new rights or duties. Coming at the issue from a different perspective, a legislative rule has actual legal effect in subsequent agency and judicial proceedings. A nonlegislative rule can have no such effect.

   b. Interpretative rule: *Interpretative rules* are rules that interpret existing legal duties.

      i. Definition of interpretative rule: For a rule to be considered an interpretative rule (also called "interpretive rule"), it must not add anything to existing legal rules. Rather, it must merely inform the public of the agency's views of the meaning of existing statutes or regulations.

      Example: In 1988, the Department of Health and Human Services (HHS) promulgated a regulation known as the "gag rule," which prohibited health care professionals (including doctors) receiving federal family planning funds from mentioning abortion to their patients (even if abortion was potentially medically indicated). Violations could result in loss of federal funds. In 1991, the regulation was upheld on judicial review against constitutional and statutory challenges. *See Rust v. Sullivan*, 500 U.S. 173 (1991). At that time, the Supreme Court characterized the regulation as a complete prohibition on abortion counseling by covered professionals, including doctors. After that decision, President Bush directed HHS not to apply the regulations in a manner that restricted the information a woman could receive from a doctor. An HHS undersecretary then issued a directive, characterized as an interpretative rule, instructing enforcement officers not to prevent doctors from discussing abortion with their patients. This directive was challenged as procedurally infirm and the D.C. Circuit held that it should have gone through notice and comment procedures. The court stated that because the directive substantially amended an existing regulation, it was a legislative rule and thus would only be effective after notice and comment rulemaking. A rule amending an existing legislative rule is itself a legislative rule. *See National Family Planning and Reproductive Health Association, Inc. v. Sullivan*, 979 F.2d 227 (D.C. Cir. 1992).

ii. **Impact of interpretative rules:** Interpretative rules can have substantial impact on regulated parties. Although this seems inconsistent with the definition of interpretative rules, courts have allowed interpretative rules to have substantial impact when the rule does not go beyond interpreting the terms of preexisting statutory or regulatory provisions. Further, courts may defer to agency interpretations.

   Example: The Postal Service, based on its interpretation of statutory standards, adopted (without notice and comment) a new method of calculating the retirement annuity benefits of certain substitute postal workers. Although this substantially changed the expected annuity payments for many workers, it was held to be an interpretative rule because the new method was based upon an interpretation of governing law. *See American Postal Workers Union v. United States Postal Service*, 707 F.2d 548 (D.C. Cir. 1983).

iii. **Guidance documents:** Agencies have attempted to avoid rulemaking procedures by issuing "guidance documents" without notice and comment that the agencies claim advise regulated parties of agency policy without legal effects. The problem is that the agencies appear to treat these documents as if they are binding law, promising for example that no enforcement action will be taken against a party following a guidance document or that a party following the guidance document will be granted a permit. *See Appalachian Power Co. v. EPA*, 208 F.3d 1015 (D.C. Cir. 2005) (guidance document "significantly broadened" EPA rule and thus was invalid absent notice and comment); *General Electric Co. v. EPA*, 290 F.3d 377 (D.C. Cir 2002) (guidance document invalid absent notice and comment because applicant following it was assured that it had satisfied certain requirements for a permit).

c. **General statement of policy:** A general statement of policy informs the public of the agency's policy views, but does not purport to add to or alter existing legal rules. As one court has stated, an "agency cannot apply or rely upon a general statement of policy as law because a general statement of policy only announces what the agency seeks to establish as policy." *Pacific Gas & Electric v. Federal Power Comm'n.*, 506 F.2d 33, 38 (D.C. Cir. 1974). When the agency attempts (through enforcement or other administrative action) to realize its policy, it must convince the relevant tribunal of its policy's legality—although a court will show appropriate deference to the views of the agency.

Examples: The Indian Health Service had for many years operated a clinic in Albuquerque, New Mexico, to serve the health care needs of handicapped Indian children. In 1985, the service decided to close the clinic and spend its lump-sum appropriation on a national program to serve such children. This decision was announced in a memorandum, and no notice and comment procedures were used. The court of appeals held that notice and comment procedures should have been used, but the Supreme Court reversed. The Court held that this decision was a general statement of policy because it stated the agency's intention on how it would spend its lump-sum appropriation in the future. *Lincoln v. Vigil*, 508 U.S. 182 (1993).

In another case, the FDA promulgated rules specifying the levels ("action levels") of toxins in food products that would provoke FDA enforcement action against a product as "adulterated." The FDA argued that the action levels were general statements of policy because they described only when the FDA would bring enforcement actions and did not purport to establish binding rules on the permissible level of the toxins. The D.C. Circuit held that the action levels were not policy statements and that therefore notice and comment procedures should have been used. Contrary to the FDA's representation, the court found that in practice the FDA had treated the action levels as binding: for example, by requiring food producers to seek exceptions from action levels if they want to ship food with higher levels of toxins. *See Community Nutrition Institute v. Young*, 818 F.2d 943 (D.C. Cir. 1987). Judge Starr, in dissent, argued that the test for whether a rule is legislative should be whether it has the force of law in future proceedings. In this case, Judge Starr argued that because the FDA would have to prove in court (in an enforcement proceeding) that a product is adulterated, the action levels should not have been considered legislative rules.

d.   **Rules of agency organization:** Rules of agency organization, such as rules establishing the distribution of authority within an agency, are also exempt from the notice and comment procedures of §553. Rules of agency organization may affect the interests of members of the public but are primarily concerned with the internal organization of the agency.

Example: *In Lincoln v. Vigil*, the Supreme Court also suggested that the decision to spend the lump-sum appropriation on a national program, rather than on the clinic in Albuquerque, might qualify as a rule of agency organization. On this analysis, the decision involved the "organization" of the agency's provision of services.

e.   **Rules of agency procedure:** Rules of agency procedure, which inform the public how to proceed when presenting an application or claim to an agency, are also exempt. A rule that appears to be procedural will nonetheless be held substantive if, in operation, it reflects a substantive judgment about particular conduct by substantially altering the rights or interests of certain parties engaging in disfavored conduct.

Example: The Federal Aviation Administration (FAA), in compliance with legislatively mandated changes, and without notice and comment, amended its regulations to increase the maximum civil penalty in safety violation cases. The new rule also created an internal enforcement procedure that covered cases that previously could be prosecuted only in the United States district court. The agency claimed that the new rule was exempt as "procedural." *In Air Transport Association of America v. Department of Transportation*, 900 F.2d

369 (D.C. Cir. 1990), the court of appeals held that although the rule appeared to be procedural, it did not fall within the §553 exemption because it affected the civil violators' rights, including the right to a hearing. Judge Silberman dissented, arguing that, in effect, the majority had mischaracterized the procedural right to a hearing as a substantive right.

3. **Procedural requirements for nonlegislative rules:** Rules that are exempt from §553's notice and comment procedures still must be published in the Federal Register. APA §552(a)(1). If the rule is not properly published, it may not be used against any party not having actual notice of it. *Id.*

B. **Policymaking in formal rulemaking: when are formal procedures required?**

Formal rulemaking is required when the agency's enabling act requires that rules are to be made "on the record after opportunity for an agency hearing." APA §553(c) states that "when rules are required by statute to be made on the record after opportunity for an agency hearing, sections 556 and 557 of this title apply instead of this subsection." Sections 556 and 557 prescribe formal, adjudicatory-type procedures. Rulemaking conducted under these provisions is referred to as "formal," or "on the record" rulemaking.

1. **Presumption against formal rulemaking:** There is a strong presumption against formal rulemaking. Thus, unless it is absolutely clear from the statutory language that formal rulemaking is required (usually through use of the formulation "on the record after agency hearing" or something very similar), courts will conclude that Congress intended that the agency be free to use informal procedures under §553. *See United States v. Florida East Coast Rwy. Co.*, 410 U.S. 224 (1973).

2. **Even statutory language requiring a "hearing" does not, without more, add to §553's informal procedures:** Even if a statute requires a "hearing," informal rulemaking may be sufficient. Absent an unambiguous requirement that the hearing be conducted "on the record," the informal procedures of §553 are sufficient for rulemaking unless the statute clearly contemplates something more.

   Examples: Section l(14)(a) of the Interstate Commerce Act (ICA) gave the Interstate Commerce Commission (ICC) the power to make rules "after hearing." In *United States v. Allegheny-Ludlum Steel Corp.*, 406 U.S. 742 (1972), the Supreme Court held that this language, without a requirement that rules be made "on the record," was not sufficient to require formal rule-making. In *Florida East Coast Rwy. Co.*, a case arising under the same section of the ICA, the railway company made two arguments for procedures in addition to those specified in §553. First, it argued that because the ICA specified the factors that the ICC should take into account, formal rulemaking was required. Relying on *Allegheny-Ludlum*, the Court rejected this argument out of hand. Second, the railway company argued that the "after hearing" language, while not triggering full, formal procedures, required some kind of oral hearing in addition to §553 notice and comment procedures. The Court also rejected this argument, holding that absent evidence to the contrary, when Congress uses the term "hearing," it means the procedures mandated by the applicable APA provision—here §553's notice and comment procedures. Thus, the term "hearing" means the paper procedures of §553.

These decisions illustrate the Supreme Court's strong preference for allowing agencies to proceed with as little procedural formality as statutes and the Constitution will allow, and they are thus of a kind with *Vermont Yankee* discussed in Chapter 6. While the Court in *Allegheny-Ludlum* stated that the words "on the record" were not absolutely necessary to invoke formal rulemaking procedures, without that precise language, pretty strong indications of congressional intent are necessary to require more than §553 procedures.

C. Policymaking by manual or other internal document: *Morton v. Ruiz*

Agencies often make policy internally—in operations manuals and other agency memoranda. Perhaps surprisingly, the requirements of agency manuals are often not supported substantively by any statutory or regulatory provision. Because such manuals and internal memoranda are usually prepared without public input and are often not published, agencies encounter procedural problems when such internal documents are challenged by a member of the public. In *Morton v. Ruiz*, 415 U.S. 199 (1974), the Supreme Court addressed the procedural regularity of "policymaking by manual."

1. **The agency decision in *Morton*:** In *Morton*, the Bureau of Indian Affairs (BIA) denied the Ruizes' (who were members of the Papago Indian Tribe) claim to welfare benefits under a BIA-administered Indian welfare program. The Ruizes lived fifteen miles away from the reservation in a largely Indian community. The BIA relied upon a provision of its manual that stated that only Indians living on a reservation were entitled to benefits under the applicable program. No statute or regulation restricted benefits to Indians living on reservations.

2. **The BIA's argument for the restriction:** The BIA argued that although Congress never wrote the "on reservation" limitation into law, because the BIA requested funds only for Indians "on reservation," Congress intended to restrict benefits to such Indians. The Supreme Court rejected this argument, mainly on the ground that Congress was aware of BIA exceptions to the "on reservation" rule, especially those instances in which the BIA equated Indians living "near" reservations in nonurban areas with Indians living "on" reservations. The Court further noted that Congress had never written the restriction into law.

3. **Procedural problems with policymaking by manual in *Morton*:** The primary procedural problem with the eligibility rule in *Morton* was that it was not published. Rather, it was contained only in an internal agency manual. The *Morton* Court noted that this presented three separate procedural problems. While it is unclear from the opinion which ground is the actual holding of the case, it is clear that the Court disapproved of nonpublic policymaking when the policy arrived at restricts the rights of members of the public.

   a. **The BIA should have published its rule in accordance with the APA:** The *Morton* Court's clearest holding is that the BIA's rule restricting eligibility for benefits to Indians living on the reservation should have been published in the Federal Register as required by APA §552(a)(1). Without such publication, the rule could not be used against the Ruizes since they did not have advance notice of it.

   b. **The BIA must follow its own procedural rule:** Another procedural problem noted by the *Morton* Court is that the BIA should have followed its own procedural rule, which required it to publish any directives that inform the public of eligibility requirements. The Court stated that "where the rights of individuals are affected, it is incumbent upon agencies to follow their own procedures." *Morton*, 415 U.S. at 235.

   c. **The Court hinted that the BIA should have used a rulemaking procedure:** The *Morton* Court also stated that the APA requires that "administrative policies affecting individual rights and obligations be promulgated pursuant to certain stated procedures" and that agencies must "employ procedures that conform to the law." The Court reasoned that proper procedure was necessary to avoid "ad hoc" decisionmaking. *Morton*, 415 U.S. at 232. This has been interpreted by some as a requirement that notice and comment rulemaking should be used in situations like *Morton*. However, the best reading of *Morton* is that the Court was referring to §552's publication requirement, since matters relating to "benefits" are exempt from §553's notice and comment requirements. Nowhere does the Court state that the agency should have used notice and comment rulemaking.

4. **Agencies' obligation to follow their own procedural rules:** Agencies must follow any procedural rules they have formally adopted through notice and comment procedures. If a rule was not formally adopted, courts may invalidate agency action taken in violation of such rules only when there is both detrimental reliance by a member of the public and an agency intent to benefit the public with the informally adopted procedural rule. *See American Farm Lines v. Black Ball Freight Service*, 397 U.S. 532 (1970). Otherwise, agency violation of informally adopted procedural rules does not invalidate the agency's action. *See Schweiker v. Hansen*, 450 U.S. 785 (1981).

D. Informal policymaking more generally: when may an agency act without adjudication or rulemaking?

Agencies often decide policy matters and grant or deny applications or petitions informally, without using either an adjudicatory or rulemaking procedure. For example, in *Overton Park*, the Secretary of Transportation approved a highway design without any particular procedure and without a formal explanation of the decision. The statutory basis for this widespread practice is unclear because the APA appears to divide all agency action between rulemaking and adjudication—with no third, informal, category. *See* APA §551(4)-(7).

1. **Informal agency action is sometimes. referred to as "informal adjudication":** Although the APA's definitions divide all agency action into rulemaking and adjudication, agencies are not required to use a formal adjudicatory procedure for every decision not involving a rule. Because of this definitional dichotomy, informal agency action is often referred to in the cases and literature as informal adjudication. It is more accurate, however, to state that the agency is doing neither rulemaking nor adjudication but is rather deciding a matter informally.

2. **Informal policymaking may be proper when the policy decision is particular and not a rule:** When an agency makes a particular decision that does not result in a rule (and it does not affect an individual in a way that requires formal adjudication) it may be proper for the agency to act without following any APA procedural model. For example, in *Overton Park*, the Secretary's decision to approve the highway route and design was not an order directed at any particular member of the public, and it was not a rule that could be followed in other cases. The Court rejected the plaintiffs' argument that the Secretary was required to make formal findings, and there was no suggestion that the informal procedure used was inappropriate for that type of decision.

3. **APA §555(e) requires a statement of reasons and supports informal decisionmaking: -** When an agency makes a decision informally, the only procedural requirements are notice of the decision and a brief statement of the reasons for the decision. *See* APA §555(e). This provision provides the best support for the agency practice of making some decisions informally because it appears to contemplate decisions without either a rulemaking or an adjudicatory process.

4. **Courts may not add to the requirements in §555:** In *Pension Benefit Guaranty Corp. v. LTV Corp.*, 496 U.S. 633 (1990), the Supreme Court, relying upon *Vermont Yankee*, held that the only APA-mandated procedures for informal adjudication are those specified in APA §555. Courts are not free to impose additional procedures not mandated either by the agency's particular statute or the APA.

Quiz Yourself on
AGENCY CHOICE OF POLICYMAKING MODE

25. A local zoning board decides, at a public legislative meeting, to increase the required side yard requirement for all homes built in the town, from six feet to ten feet. This decision was made based on a perception that, in areas of the town where the homes are closer than ten feet from the side property line, the lots look too crowded and property values might be harmed. The board also decides that in areas of special concern for open space, it will require twenty feet. At the meeting, the board members took a map of the town and designated twelve parcels of the approximately one thousand in the town as "special concern for open space," and thus required a twenty-foot side yard for any new development. Do any of the town's property owners have a due process claim against the changes in the side yard requirements? _____

26. A statute prohibits "unfair practices in the sale or leasing of automobiles." The statute creates an agency and gives the agency the power to enforce the statute through an elaborate adjudicatory process. The statute also gives the agency the power "to make rules to carry out the substantive provisions of the statute." Does this agency have the power to make a regulation specifying that turning back the odometer of an automobile is prohibited by the statute? Can the agency then use the regulation to limit the hearing to the issue of whether the automobile seller turned back the odometer? _____

27. Suppose the agency in the above question announces the odometer rule in an opinion deciding an individual adjudication of an alleged violation of the statute, and then applies the rule in subsequent adjudications under the Act. Should the agency be required to make the rule in a rulemaking as opposed to announcing it while deciding an individual adjudication? _____

28. A federal statute requires that dealers in dangerous wild animals, such as lions and tigers, have fences around the perimeter of their compounds that are "of sufficient structural strength to contain the animals in the event they escape their primary enclosures." For years, the agency in charge had approved fences of heights six feet and higher. Then the agency issued, without notice and comment, an interpretative ruling stating that such fences must be at least eight feet tall. The agency then began revoking the licenses of dealers with fences shorter than eight feet. Is this a proper interpretative rule? _____

29. A statute grants the Secretary of Agriculture the power to move agricultural programs from one Department of Agriculture facility to another. After internal study (with no public process whatsoever) the Secretary decides to move a very large research program about corn growing, from Wisconsin to Iowa. Should the Secretary have conducted a rulemaking or adjudication? _____

Answers

25. Maybe. The legislative process is fine for the owners of most of the parcels in the town since the decision was made to increase the side yard requirement based on general considerations (legislative facts), and it was applied to all property owners across the board. The owners of the twelve parcels that were singled out for special treatment have a good argument that due process requires that they be given notice and a hearing. The relevant facts look like adjudicative facts. Under the *Londoner* case, an adjudicatory hearing may be required as a matter of due process.

26. Probably yes on both questions. Although the legislature may have intended that the definition of unfair practices would be developed in the course of adjudications, the statute grants the agency power to make rules. Even though the statute appears to grant the power to make procedural rules and not substantive rules, courts are usually very willing to recognize rulemaking power because of the policy advantages of rulemaking over case-by-case policymaking in adjudications.

27. No. There are federal agencies, such as the NLRB, that often announce new rules in the course of adjudication. This practice has been justified on two grounds, against the argument that the APA requires that rules be made in rulemaking. First, it is within the traditional adjudicatory process for rules to be announced in opinions and then to be applied as binding precedent in subsequent adjudications. Second, in the subsequent adjudications, the rule will be applied only in the context of an order directed against the subject of that particular adjudication. So long as all the procedural rights of the subject of the subsequent adjudication are followed, the order is proper.

28. No. If the eight-foot requirement is treated by the agency as binding, it is a new legal requirement—not merely a reminder of what the statute itself always required because the statute does not set forth a height requirement. The agency will argue that the eight-foot requirement merely interprets the meaning of "sufficient structural strength to contain the animals," but this is a weak argument especially because the agency had previously approved shorter fences. In any case, because an interpretative rule is not a binding norm, the agency should have to defend its interpretation on judicial review or in enforcement actions. The agency's interpretation would not bind the courts.

29. No. Unless the governing statute indicates otherwise, the Secretary was free to make the decision without a formal procedure because it is not a rule and because the decision does not focus on the conduct or rights of an individual such that adjudication would be required. There is also an argument that §553 would not apply because the decision was about agency organization. There are many situations in which agencies make decisions informally, i.e., without a rulemaking or adjudicatory process. In response to any complaints from Wisconsin, the Secretary is required, by APA §555(e), to provide a statement of the reasons for the decision.

Exam Tips on
AGENCY CHOICE OF POLICYMAKING MODE

☛ As is the case in many areas in administrative law, look for relevant APA sections first, and make sure to apply them to the exam question.

☞ Recall that the APA does not clearly state when agencies must use one process or another, so in a question regarding the choice between rulemaking and adjudication, stress the discretionary nature of the decision.

☞ Consult the definitions in APA §551, but be sure to point out that courts have not found them to be binding.

☛ In questions involving whether due process requires a hearing, be sure to discuss whether the administrative action affects a small number of parties based on their special characteristics.

☞ The discussion here would benefit from pointing out the distinction between legislative and ad-judicative facts. It is often useful to discuss whether the hypothetical is more like *Londoner* or *Bi-Metallic*.

☞ If the agency finding is based on adjudicative facts, perhaps adjudication is required.

☞ If the agency finding is based on legislative facts, a rulemaking process may be sufficient.

☛ In discussing whether an agency has power to use rulemaking, extol the policy virtues of rulemaking, since those virtues seem important when courts broadly construe grants of rulemaking authority.

☛ On the other side, discuss how rulemaking may detract from a party's right to a hearing and how rulemaking may be contrary to Congress's intent for primarily adjudicatory agencies.

☛ For issues regarding agency authority to make policy through adjudication, stress that this is a longstanding practice among agencies and is traditionally part of the common-law adjudicatory process. If *Wyman-Gordon* is relevant, state the views of both opinions in favor of the judgment since no view captured a majority.

☛ If an agency makes a rule without notice and comment, look at the exceptions listed in APA §553 and go down the list to see if the agency's action falls within one of them.

☞ Discuss the question in light of the definition of a legislative rule. Be sure to point out that legislative rules create binding law while non-legislative rules do not.

If an agency makes a decision with no formal process, look to the governing statute to see whether the agency was supposed to use an adjudicatory or legislative process. Also, be sure to point out any agency rules that require procedures in addition to those provided.

☞ If no such requirement appears to exist, mention the APA requirement of providing an answer and a statement of reasons. Also, point out that if an agency does not use a formal process, any norm created cannot be considered binding law.

CHAPTER 6

APA RULEMAKING PROCEDURES

ChapterScope ━━━━━━━━━━━━━━━━━━━━━━━━━━━━━━━━━━━━━━━

This chapter examines the procedures required for rulemaking under the APA. The focus is primarily on informal rulemaking under APA §553, including discussion of the judicial gloss on the most important provisions of §553. The key points in this chapter are:

- The primary process for promulgating rules under the APA is ***notice and comment rulemaking*** under APA §553, which is also referred to as ***informal rulemaking***.

  - The principal requirements of informal rulemaking are ***notice, opportunity to comment***, and ***publication*** of the decision together with a ***concise general statement of basis and purpose*** of any rules adopted.

- Many courts require more notice than specified in the literal words of §553(b).

  - Courts have required that the rule adopted be the ***logical outgrowth*** of the proposal and that the agency not ***materially or substantially depart*** from the proposal.

  - Courts also have required that agencies provide notice of data or studies upon which the agency intends to rely.

  - If notice is inadequate, the cure is a new notice and comment period.

- Interested parties must be afforded a ***meaningful*** opportunity to submit comments. In order for the opportunity to comment to be meaningful, parties must have notice of data or other information upon which the agency is relying.

- ***Exparte comments*** (comments made to administrators outside the normal comment channels) are a problem in informal rulemaking, although it is unclear whether and to what extent they are regulated by the APA.

  - There are several theories under which courts have held that exparte contacts are improper.

  - Some courts have required that if an agency does receive ex parte comments, it should place such comments on the rulemaking record, especially if the ex parte comments turn out to be important to the agency's decision.

- An administrator must have an open mind in rulemaking; an administrator with an ***unalterably closed mind*** may be disqualified from participating in a rulemaking.

- ***The concise general statement of basis and purpose*** must explain the agency's decision on major issues in the rulemaking including providing answers to major concerns raised in the comments.

- ***Hybrid rulemaking*** is rulemaking to which some adjudicatory procedures, such as cross-examination of experts, are added.

  - Some agency statutes require hybrid rulemaking.

  - Courts have required hybrid procedures when they found that notice and comment procedures were inadequate for the particular rulemaking.

- The Supreme Court, in ***Vermont Yankee***, rejected judicial authority to impose procedures in addition to those specified in §553.

- ***Formal rulemaking, or "on the record" rulemaking***, is rulemaking pursuant to trial-type procedures akin to adjudication. Formal rulemaking is required when the agency is statutorily commanded to make rules "on the record after agency hearing."

- ***Negotiated rulemaking*** is a procedure under which a notice of proposed rulemaking is formulated through negotiations among interested parties. These negotiations are presided over by the agency. After negotiation produces a proposal, the proposal is subjected to a normal notice and comment procedure.

I. APA §553 INFORMAL ("NOTICE AND COMMENT") RULEMAKING PROCEDURES

The bulk of agency rulemaking is done under APA §553. This rulemaking is often referred to as "notice and comment" rulemaking or ***informal rulemaking*** and should be distinguished from "formal" rulemaking, which is conducted under the formal adjudicatory procedures of APA §§556-557. Section 553 appears to contemplate a fairly loose legislative procedure, not a highly constrained overproceduralized process.

A. Basic requirements of informal rulemaking

The basic requirements of informal rulemaking are published ***notice*** of the proposed rulemaking, the ***opportunity for public comment***, and (after consideration of the comments) ***publication*** of the final rule, together with a ***concise general statement*** of the rule's basis and purpose.

B. Notice

Section 553 requires that "General notice of proposed rule making shall be published in the Federal Register[.] The notice shall include . . . either the terms or substance of the proposed rule or a description of the subjects and issues involved."

1. **The notice problem:** To have a meaningful opportunity to participate in rulemaking through submission of comments, affected parties need sufficient notice to alert them in advance that their interests are at stake. Sufficient notice is also necessary to ensure that the comments are informative enough to be useful to the agency in the decisionmaking process. However, when an agency relies on comments to alter its proposal before adopting a rule, parties whose interests are affected by changes complain that the original notice did not inform them of the damage that the adopted rule would do to their interests. Despite this unfairness, courts have no explicit statutory authority to require a second comment period whenever the comments convince the agency to promulgate a rule that differs from the proposal. While an agency is certainly free to make significant changes from proposals when promulgating final rules, an agency would violate the notice requirement if it proposed, for example, a rule regulating lawnmowers and then promulgated a final rule about televisions.

2. **APA minimum notice requirements:** The APA itself does not require very detailed notice. While the notice requirement can be fulfilled by publishing the text of the actual proposed

regulation, the terms of §553 are also satisfied with as little as a description of the subjects or issues involved in the rulemaking. As one court has stated:

> the statutory language makes clear that the notice need not identify every precise proposal which the agency may ultimately adopt; notice is adequate if it apprises interested parties of the issues to be addressed in the rule-making proceeding with sufficient clarity and specificity to allow them to participate in the rulemaking in a meaningful and informed manner. *American Medical Association v. United States*, 887 F.2d 760 (7th Cir. 1989).

3. Judicial gloss: The logical outgrowth, material alteration, and substantial departure tests

a. The tests for adequate notice: Courts have required that the rules ultimately adopted be the *logical outgrowth* of the proposal. Courts have also stated that the final rule may not *materially alter* the issues involved in the rulemaking and that the final rule may not *substantially depart* from the proposal. While these courts are motivated by the concern that regulated parties have a meaningful opportunity to participate in the rulemaking, some of the rulings may require greater notice than required under §553. The following examples illustrate differing judicial approaches to the notice problem.

Examples: The IRS was experiencing difficulty accounting for income in taxable activities of tax-exempt organizations. The agency proposed, in a notice and comment rulemaking, a seven-factor accounting test to be employed on a case-by-case basis. Several comments on the proposal claimed that the IRS's proposal was too vague and would leave organizations too uncertain of their potential tax liability. The IRS was convinced by the negative comments and promulgated a rule requiring that organizations use one of three specific accounting methods. The American Medical Association (AMA), whose activities were directly affected by this rule, did not submit comments during the rulemaking but sought judicial review of the rule on the ground that the approach adopted by the agency was such a departure from the agency's proposal that notice of the proposal was not adequate. The Seventh Circuit upheld the adequacy of the notice. The court reasoned that the AMA was on notice that its interests were at stake, and even if it was happy with the initial proposal, it could have submitted comments-in support of that proposal. Thus, notice was adequate. *See American Medical Association v. United States*, 887 F.2d 760 (7th Cir. 1989). While the court quoted the "logical outgrowth" test, its analysis stuck relatively close to the words of the APA notice requirement.

The Department of Agriculture administers the WIC program, which provides food benefits to pregnant women, infants, and children. The benefits are confined to a relatively narrow list of foods. In 1979, after a statutory revision, the agency published a notice of proposed rulemaking that included two elements: a list of all permissible foods and a preamble that stated Congress was concerned about fat, sugar, and salt and that high-sugar cereals and juices were particular problems. Flavored milk, including chocolate milk, was not mentioned in the preamble and was on the list of permissible foods as it had been in the past. (However, seventy-eight commenters urged the agency to remove flavored milk from the list. The agency agreed. In the final rule, flavored milk was not among the foods eligible for purchase under the WIC program. The Chocolate Manufacturers Association (CMA) did not comment. After the rule was promulgated, it sued— claiming inadequate notice. The Fourth Circuit held that because the preamble mentioned specific foods, such as sugared cereals and juices, and did not mention flavored milk, "there was insufficient notice that the deletion of flavored milk from the WIC program would be considered if adverse comments were received." The court thus concluded that the final rule was not the logical outgrowth of the proposal even though the notice asked for comments on all the foods on the list. *Chocolate Manufacturing Association v. Block*, 755 F.2d 1098 (4th Cir. 1985).

While both courts link the notice requirement to the adequacy of the opportunity to participate in the rulemaking, the Seventh Circuit sticks more closely to the APA in the AMA case than the Fourth Circuit does in the CMA case. Given that the APA approves notice even if it only contains "a description of the subjects or issues involved," it is difficult to see how the notice in CMA, which listed all the WIC foods, was deficient. However, the CMA court's approach is the predominate approach to notice among courts of appeals. This model of rulemaking, which requires greater notice than the AMA court, is more akin to an adjudicatory model of rulemaking than the legislative model contemplated by the language of APA §553.

b. Inadequate notice and the second comment period: The cure for inadequate notice is a new notice and a new comment period. If an agency is convinced by the comments it receives to make substantial changes from its original proposal, the agency must issue a new notice and hold a new comment period. The new notice must inform the public of the changes in the agency's views since the initial notice. Even if comments appearing on the public record suggested the changes between the notice and the final rule, substantial changes in an agency's views might render the initial notice inadequate to support the final rule. *See National Black Media Coalition v. FCC*, 791 F.2d 1016 (2d Cir. 1986).

4. Notice of agency studies: Agencies are also required to disclose for public comment any studies, data, or other material that the agency relies upon in formulating the final rule. This requirement is a notice requirement as well as an element of a meaningful opportunity to participate through comments. Participation would not be meaningful if the agency bases its final rule on information not available to the public. *See United States v. Nova Scotia Food Prods. Corp.*, 568 F.2d 240 (2d Cir. 1977); *National Black Media Coalition v. FCC.*

5. The never-ending new notice and comment cycle: Courts have recognized that requiring agencies to reopen the comment period whenever the agency finds comments submitted persuasive presents the potential for a never-ending cycle of repeated notice and comment periods. Thus, in order for new information to require a new comment period, the agency must be contemplating a *substantial or material alteration* of its proposal such that the final rule would not be a *logical outgrowth* of the proposal. Minor changes, or changes within the parameters of the initial proposal, do not justify a new comment period.

C. Opportunity to submit comments: the opportunity to participate must be meaningful

Section 553(c) provides that "the agency shall give interested persons an opportunity to participate in the rulemaking through submission of written data, views or arguments with or without opportunity for oral presentation." Some courts have interpreted §553(c) to require a "meaningful" opportunity to participate, holding that the APA requires more than merely the mechanical right to submit comments. These courts have read into §553 a number of procedural requirements designed to ensure that all interested persons have a meaningful opportunity to participate in rulemaking.

1. **Agencies must give notice of internal studies or data upon which they rely:** Courts have required agencies to provide notice of any data or studies upon which the agency relies, reasoning that it is impossible to participate meaningfully in a rulemaking without sufficient notice of the information the agency is considering. *See United States v. Nova Scotia Food Prods. Corp.; National Black Media Coalition v. FCC.* For example, in *National Black Media Coalition*, the Second Circuit held that the FCC violated the APA by relying on maps and internal studies that were not disclosed to the public for comment when it decided to abandon its minority preference in awarding broadcast licenses.

2. **Agencies should allow interested parties the opportunity to respond to opposing comments:** Although nothing in the APA explicitly requires it, courts have held that for the opportunity to participate to be meaningful, interested persons must be allowed to respond to opposing comments. This right is difficult to implement when comments are received late in the comment period or even after the comment period has ended.

   Example: Each state is required, under provisions of the Clean Air Act, to submit a plan to the EPA for controlling particulate pollution. If the EPA approves, the plan becomes law. If not, penalties apply and a process for formulating a new plan is triggered. The EPA is required to conduct a §553 notice and comment rulemaking on whether to approve the state plan. Arizona submitted a plan for controlling particulate pollution in Phoenix. After the period for comments closed, the EPA requested (and Arizona submitted) additional data amounting to three hundred pages of information which was crucial to the EPA's approval decision. The Ninth Circuit held that the EPA violated the APA by not giving interested persons the opportunity to comment on the postcomment period submissions that were critical to the EPA's decision to approve the plan. *Ober v. EPA*, 84 F.3d 304 (9th Cir. 1996).

D. **The problem of ex parte contacts in rulemaking**

   Exparte contacts consist of communications from interested parties to administrators outside the formalities of the comment process. The prevalence of ex parte contacts in informal rulemaking raises the question whether such contacts violate the APA or some other principle of administrative law.

   1. **What is an ex parte contact?** An ex parte contact is a communication by an interested party to an administrator made outside the normal comment process. For example, an interested party may present information or arguments in person in the administrator's office, place a telephone call to an administrator, or write a letter directly to an administrator without submitting the letter as a comment. Ex parte contacts are made by private parties and, very often, by members of Congress expressing their own interest or the interest of a constituent.

   2. **APA rules on ex parte contacts:** No provision of the APA prohibits, or even explicitly addresses, ex parte contacts with administrators in informal rulemaking. *See Sierra Club v. Costle*, 657 F.2d 298 (D.C. Cir. 1981). By contrast, APA §554(d) prohibits most ex parte contacts in formal adjudication. By negative implication, it would appear that the APA does not prohibit exparte contacts in §553 rulemaking, which would fit with the legislative model of informal rulemaking. Nonetheless, it has been argued (and some courts have been convinced) that ex parte contacts are inconsistent with APA informal rulemaking procedures.

      a. **Ex parte contacts deprive parties of a meaningful opportunity to participate by not giving notice of matters considered by the agency:** Ex parte contacts can threaten the ability of other interested parties to participate in the rulemaking process when the agency considers information or arguments presented outside the comment process. Opposing interests have no opportunity to comment on the content of an ex parte presentation.

b. Consideration of ex parte contacts violates the agency's obligation to make its rules based on the relevant matter presented during the comment period: APA §553(c) provides that the agency shall make and explain its decision "after consideration of the relevant matter presented" in the rulemaking. Based on this provision, it has been argued that the agency should only consider comments presented as part of the comment process and should not consider ex parte comments. Stated more strictly, it has been argued that the agency must base its rule only on matter that was part of the comment process, either received by the agency in comments or put forward by the agency as part of its notice.

c. Receipt of ex parte contacts violates the requirement that judicial review be based on the whole record before the agency: Ex parte contacts (which allow material to be presented to the agency "off the record") arguably violate the requirement (contained in APA §706 and *Overton Park*) that judicial review be based on the whole record, because the exparte comments will not be part of the record before the court on judicial review. *See HBO v. FCC*, 567 F.2d 9 (D.C. Cir.) *cert, denied*, 434 U.S. 829 (1977). At a minimum, courts require that agencies place summaries of all important ex parte communications on the record.

d. Ex parte comments are not part of the record even if they are summarized for the reviewing court: Further, for a comment to be truly part of the record, the *HBO* court stated that the matter presented should have been subjected to "adversarial comment." The *HBO* court held that even if an agency claims it has placed summaries of the substance of all exparte contacts on the record, a court would be justified in doubting the truthfulness of the agency's account once it is known that the agency accepted ex parte comments.

e. When a rulemaking involves a competing claim to a valuable privilege, basic fairness requires a ban on ex parte communications: When rulemaking is the procedure employed to resolve competing private claims to a valuable government privilege, ex parte communications are improper and should not be accepted. In such cases, courts have viewed the rulemaking as in the nature of an adjudication and have held that due process concerns require greater procedural regularity. *See Sangamon Valley Television Corp, v. United States*, 269 F.2d 221 (D.C. Cir. 1959).

Example: In an FCC rulemaking to resolve which of two licensees would receive the license to operate a VHF TV station with a favored channel designation, one licensee had several personal conversations with FCC commissioners, sent each commissioner a substantive letter after the close of the comment period, took commissioners to lunch, and bought them turkeys on Thanksgiving. The D.C. Circuit held that in this context, these ex parte contacts violated "basic fairness" and the rulemaking had to be redone. *Sangamon Valley Television Corp. v. United States*. Later panels of the D.C. Circuit have disagreed over the reach of *Sangamon*. Some panels insist that *Sangamon* has little, if any, relevance in the normal legislative rule-making setting without competing private claims to a valuable privilege. *See Action for Children's Television (ACT) v. FCC*, 564 F.2d 458 (D.C. Cir. 1977).

3. What must agencies do if they receive ex parte communications?

    a. Just say no to ex parte contacts: In *HBO*, the D.C. Circuit stated that once the comment period has begun, an agency should refuse any attempts by interested parties to engage in exparte communications concerning the rulemaking.

    b. If ex parte contacts do occur, they should be placed on the record: Documents and the substance of oral ex parte communications should be placed on the record for other interested parties to comment upon. If the contact occurs after the close of the comment period, the agency may be required to reopen the comment period to allow other interested parties to comment upon the matters in the ex parte contact.

4. Ex parte communications that occur before the notice of proposed rulemaking are allowed: Agencies rely to a great extent on input from the public to identify situations in need of regulation. Agencies must be free to receive communications from the public before a rulemaking has been initiated. Indeed, since there is no proceeding pending, it is a misnomer to characterize prenotice communications as ex parte contacts. However, if a prenotice communication made to an agency is important to the agency's decision, that communication should be placed on the record for other parties to comment upon.

5. Ex parte communications by government officials including the President and members of Congress: Agencies are often contacted by executive branch officials and members of Congress concerning pending rulemakings and other administrative action. Because the agencies are part of the political system, these ex parte contacts have presented courts with special problems.

    a. The President has a right to information and input in the administrative process: The President, as chief executive, has a right to receive information from administrative officials regarding pending rulemakings, and he also has a right to give input on the substance of rulemakings. *See Sierra Club v. Costle*, 657 F.2d 298 (D.C. Cir. 1981). The *Sierra Club* court held that in rulemakings, presidential contact with an agency is allowed unless it violates due process. Nevertheless, Congress may require agencies to place the substance of contacts with the President on the public record. The court also implied that presidential prodding that influences an agency is not a ground for overturning a rule as long as the rule is supported by the record.

    b. Congressional ex parte contacts are also allowed: The *Sierra Club* court also approved congressional contacts with agencies during rulemakings. The court found it appropriate for members of Congress to vigorously represent the interests of their constituents. The court also thought that if it prohibited inquiries and input from Congress during the pendency of rulemaking proposals, the validity of all rules would be questionable. The court did note that congressional input must remain focused on the substantive merits of the rulemaking and must not convince the agency to violate Congress's intent.

    c. The President and members of Congress may not attempt to influence the outcome of adjudications: The President, as chief executive, does not have a right to attempt to influence the outcome of adjudicatory proceedings. In adjudicatory proceedings, the ban on exparte contacts has always been strict and is based on the text of APA §554(d). Likewise, members of Congress have no right to attempt to engage in ex parte contacts with adjudicators. Due process requires that formal adjudications be free of ex parte contacts except in limited, extraordinary circumstances. In general, government officials have no special right to engage in ex parte contacts with adjudicators.

E. Prejudgment in rulemaking: the "unalterably closed mind" standard

Courts have held that decisionmakers in rulemakings must be open to persuasion based on the comments received during the notice and comment process. Being-part of the political system, administrators will naturally have opinions on regulatory matters. However, they may not participate if their mind is so strongly made up that they have an unalterably closed mind. To disqualify an administrator, this showing must be made by clear and convincing evidence. *See Association of National Advertisers, Inc. v. FTC*, 627 F.2d 1151 (D.C. Cir. 1979), *cert. denied*, 447 U.S. 921 (1980). Because the APA does not address this issue, the legal basis for the "unalterably closed mind" standard is unclear.

1. **Rulemaking versus adjudication:** Informal rulemaking, being a legislative process, does not require the same neutrality as an adjudication. In an adjudication, the appearance of a small measure of *prejudgment* may be sufficient to disqualify a decisionmaker from participating. Nonetheless, notice and comment rulemaking presupposes that the decisionmakers at least consider the comments submitted.

2. **Proving an unalterably closed mind:** Proving that a rulemaking decisionmaker has an unalterably closed mind involves showing, from public or private statements made by the decisionmaker, that the decisionmaker is convinced that the proposed rule is necessary without regard to the substance of comments received. This standard is difficult to meet since general statements regarding the need for regulation in an area are not enough to prove an unalterably closed mind. The statements must show that the decisionmaker will not even pay attention to the comments.

Example: In the late 1970s, FTC Chairman Michael Pertschuk made several public and private statements advocating restricting television advertising aimed at children. For example, in a television interview, he stated (in response to a question about "all the garbage that's advertised for the kiddies") that "it's an area of prime concern" and "I have some serious doubt as to whether any television advertising should be directed at a three or four or five year old, a preschooler." In a letter to the FDA Commissioner he stated that "children's advertising is inherently unfair." When the FTC proposed three different possible regulatory regimes regarding television advertising directed at children, opponents of regulation attempted to disqualify Pertschuk from participating in the rulemaking. The case ended up in the Court of Appeals for the D.C. Circuit, where the majority held that Pertschuk should not be disqualified. The court held that discussing and exploring possible regulatory options and expressing opinions is not enough to disqualify an administrator and that based on the totality of Pertschuk's statements, it had not been established that he had an unalterably closed mind. *See Association of National Advertisers, Inc. v. FTC*, 627 F.2d 1151 (D.C. Cir. 1979), *cert. denied*, 447 U.S. 921 (1980).

F. Explanation of the decision: the concise general statement

APA §553 requires the agency to "incorporate in the rules adopted a *concise general statement* of their basis and purpose." The statement must contain a reasoned explanation for the agency's decision. This is viewed as a safeguard against arbitrary agency decisionmaking because it requires the agency to give reasons for rules.

1. **Agencies must respond to substantial issues raised in the comments:** Courts have required that agencies, in their concise general statements, respond to substantial comments

on important issues in the rulemaking. *See United States v. Nova Scotia Food Prods. Corp.*, 568 F.2d 240 (2d Cir. 1977). This ensures that agencies pay attention to the comments received during the comment period. Courts have recognized that requiring detailed comprehensive responses to everything put before the agency is inconsistent with the meaning of "concise general statement." For example, the D.C. Circuit recently approved an agency's concise general statement on the basis that it "demonstrate[d] that the agency considered and rejected petitioners' arguments (and cited support) for adopting [its model.] This is all that the APA requires." *City of Waukesha v. EPA*, 320 F.3d 228, 258 (D.C. Cir. 2003).

2. **Agencies must state their conclusions on major issues of fact and policy:** Agencies are not required to explain every factual, legal, or policy element of the decision. Nevertheless, agencies must inform the public of their views on the major issues that were decided in the rulemaking. The concise general statement should cite support in the record and should identify the policy considerations found to be persuasive. *See Industrial Union Department, AFL-CIO v. Hodgson*, 499 F.2d 467, 475 (D.C. Cir. 1974).

   Example: The rule at issue in *Nova Scotia Food Prods. Corp.* dealt with the method for preparing smoked fish to avoid botulism. The processors of one species of smoked fish, in comments to the agency, stated that the commercial viability of their fish would be destroyed by the agency's proposed (and ultimately adopted) method. The same processors argued that the agency's method was not necessary to prevent botulism in their species of fish. The agency adopted its proposed method and did not address the two concerns raised by the processors regarding their particular species of fish. The court of appeals held that the rule could not be enforced against Nova Scotia Food Products because the concise general statement did not explain the agency's conclusions on these major issues raised in the comments.

G. Publication of final rules and their effective date

Agencies must publish final rules in the Federal Register. APA §552(a)(1)(D). If a rule is not published in the Federal Register, the rule is ineffective as to any party without actual notice of the rule. §552(a)(1). Agencies usually specify a rule's effective date. The effective date may not be sooner than thirty days after publication of the final rule unless the agency finds good cause to specify an earlier date. APA §553(d).

H. Hybrid procedures: judicial decisions requiring more than §553 procedures in informal rulemaking

In the 1970s, federal courts often required agencies to employ procedures in addition to those specified in APA §553 in informal rulemaking. The rulemaking procedures prescribed were referred to as *hybrid procedures* because they combined legislative rulemaking procedures and formal adjudicatory procedures. The most common additional procedures required were cross-examination of adverse experts and additional comment periods so that interested parties could comment on adverse comments submitted.

1. **Additional procedures were required when the agency's organic statute was read to require them. These are referred to as "statutory hybrids":** Congress has often required particular agencies to employ procedures in addition to those specified in §553. These statutory hybrids add procedures such as cross-examination, multiple comment periods, detailed agency explanatory memoranda, and enhanced scrutiny on judicial review to those procedures

specified in §553. So long as the court follows the agency's statute, statutory hybrids do not present a question of legitimacy of judicial action.

2. **Additional procedures were required when the rulemaking had a great impact on a small number of interested parties:** In situations when rulemakings had a great impact on a small number of interested parties, especially when the issues in the rulemaking focused on the behavior or situation of these interested parties, courts required increased procedures out of sensitivity to the due process interests of the affected parties. Judicial action here faces a question of legitimacy since, unless there is an actual statutory or constitutional basis (such as a due process violation) for requiring greater procedures than required by §553, it is difficult to see how courts have the power to add to the APA's procedural requirements.

3. **Additional procedures were required when the rulemaking involved particularly important or complex issues:** Courts also increased the procedures required for informal rulemaking when, in their judgment, §553's procedures were inadequate due to the importance or complexity of the issues involved in the rulemaking. These cases presented the greatest problem for the legitimacy of judicial action, since there is no purported constitutional or strong statutory basis for the addition of procedures. Courts commonly added cross-examination of opposing witnesses, multiple comment periods, and opportunity for oral presentation to the procedures mandated by §553. These courts viewed the APA as setting the procedural floor, but not the ceiling, for informal rulemaking.

I. *Vermont Yankee:* **the rejection of judicial power to require more than §553 procedures in informal rulemaking**

In litigation over the licensing of the Vermont Yankee nuclear power plant, the Supreme Court held that courts may not require procedures in addition to those specified in the APA or other applicable statutes. *Vermont Yankee Nuclear Power Corp. v. NRDC*, 435 U.S. 519 (1978). The Court held that the APA is both the procedural floor and ceiling as far as courts were concerned, although agencies remain free to voluntarily adopt procedures in addition to those specified in the APA.

1. *Vermont Yankee* **in the court of appeals:** In *NRDC v. Nuclear Regulatory Comm'n*, 547 F.2d 633 (D.C Cir. 1976), the court of appeals rejected a Nuclear Regulatory Commission (NRC) rulemaking on how the effects of nuclear waste should be considered in NRC licensing decisions. The court's opinion can be read as holding that the decision was arbitrary and capricious due to lack of evidentiary support in the record. The court also suggested that a better record might be made on remand if the agency employed additional procedures such as discovery, cross-examination, and other forms of more direct interchange.

2. *Vermont Yankee* **in the Supreme Court: Courts may not require procedures in addition to those specified in the APA:** The Supreme Court ruled in *Vermont Yankee* that courts may not require procedures in addition to those specified in the APA (or a statute specific to the agency) unless statutorily prescribed procedures are constitutionally inadequate. The Court noted that if courts had the power to impose procedures in addition to those prescribed by the APA, uncertainty over the correct level of procedure would lead agencies to overproceduralize, thus losing the benefits of §553's relatively streamlined informal rulemaking process. This decision spells the end of judicially imposed hybrids.

3. **What procedural rulings survive** *Vermont Yankee?* After *Vermont Yankee*, the question arises whether decisions like *Chocolate Manufacturers* and other lower court procedural rulings

are still good law. Under the letter of *Vermont Yankee*, any decision that relies on an APA provision is still good law in the sense that it does not violate the terms of the *Vermont Yankee* decision. Thus, because *Chocolate Manufacturers* is about the meaning of §553's notice requirement, it is not necessarily inconsistent with *Vermont Yankee*. Other decisions, such as the D.C. Circuit's effort in the *HBO* case to ban ex parte communications in §553 rulemakings (insofar as they do not rely on a provision of the APA) are cast into doubt by the letter of *Vermont Yankee*. In *District No. 1, Pacific Coast Dist., Marine Engineers' Beneficial Assoc. v. Maritime Administration*, 215 F.3d 37, 42-43 (D.C. Cir. 2000), the D.C. Circuit held that under *Vermont Yankee*, courts may not impose a ban on ex parte contacts without a basis in a statute or rule. However, the spirit of *Vermont Yankee*, which demands certainty and therefore adherence only to explicit statutory requirements, counsels against expansive readings of §553's provisions, and thus may cast doubt even on decisions like *Chocolate Manufacturers* (where a strong argument exists that the agency complied with the explicit terms of §553). Note that statutory hybrids are unaffected by *Vermont Yankee* because courts there are following Congress's instructions and are not imposing additional procedures on their own.

II. FORMAL RULEMAKING PROCEDURES: THE ADDITIONAL REQUIREMENTS OF APA §§556 AND 557

In rare circumstances, agencies are required to employ formal rulemaking procedures. Formal rulemaking means rulemaking done through an adjudicatory process where opposing interests present evidence, arguments, and cross-examine opposing witnesses and where a decision is made under the strict procedural requirements of adjudication.

A. Formal rulemaking is rarely used

The situations in which agencies are required to use formal rulemaking are detailed in Chapter 5. In brief, §553 requires formal rulemaking only in those rare instances when an agency's statute requires that rules be made "on the record after a hearing" or explicity states that formal rulemaking is required.

B. Formal rulemaking procedures resemble adjudicatory procedures

In the rare instance when rules are made formally ("on the record"), APA §§556 and 557 prescribe trial-type procedures with regard to the submission of evidence, the impartiality of the decision-maker, the composition of the record, and the explanation of the decision.

1. **Agency heads or administrative law judges preside at the hearing:** Unless the agency's statute provides otherwise, one or more of the agency heads or one or more administrative law judges preside at the formal rulemaking hearing. §556(b). The official or officials presiding at the hearing have similar powers to those of a judge presiding over an adjudication. §556(c).

2. **Parties to a formal rulemaking are entitled to trial-type procedures regarding the presentation of evidence:** When presenting evidence in a formal rulemaking, parties are entitled to present their cases by oral or documentary evidence, they are entitled to conduct cross-examination when appropriate, and they are entitled to present rebuttal evidence. Nevertheless, an agency may adopt rules requiring written submission of evidence when it is not prejudicial to a party's ability to present the case. *See* APA §556(d).

3. **The record produced at the hearing is the exclusive record for the rulemaking:** The record, including transcripts of oral proceedings and documents admitted into evidence, constitutes the exclusive record for decision in formal rulemaking. This is why formal rulemaking is also referred to as "on the record" rulemaking. §557(e).

4. **Ex parte communications are prohibited in formal rulemaking:** Agency officials presiding at formal rulemaking hearings, and other agency officials expected to be involved.in the decisionmaking process, are prohibited from engaging in ex parte communications regarding the formal rulemaking with any interested person. If such communications nevertheless take place, they must be placed on the public record; the party making such communications may suffer sanctions—including losing the case. §557(d).

5. **The decision must include a detailed statement similar to decisions in adjudicatory matters:** The decision in a formal rulemaking must include findings and conclusions (with record support) on all issues of fact, law, and discretion. When the agency itself did not preside at the hearing, the parties are entitled to present proposed findings and conclusions and to take exception to any tentative or recommended decision. §557(b)-(c).

III. NEGOTIATED RULEMAKING ACT

In 1990 Congress passed the Negotiated Rulemaking Act, which allows agencies to hold formal negotiations among interested parties to formulate rulemaking proposals that have the support of the interested parties.

A. The Negotiated Rulemaking Act

The Negotiated Rulemaking Act allows agencies, under circumstances where negotiations are likely to be fruitful, to form negotiating committees composed of representatives of all interests in the potential rulemaking. The goal of the committee is to reach a consensus among all competing interests on the issues raised by the potential rulemaking. The Act contains detailed requirements for the conduct of negotiated rulemaking. *See* 5 U.S.C. §§561-570.

B. The interaction between §553 and the Negotiated Rulemaking Act

If the negotiation produces an agreement, the proposal still must go through normal notice and comment procedures. 5 U.S.C. §563(a). In other words, the negotiated rulemaking produces a rulemaking proposal for notice and comment, not a final rule.

C. Judicial review of negotiated rulemaking

The fact that a rule was first proposed through negotiated rulemaking should not affect its status on judicial review. The Act precludes review of the conduct of the negotiated rulemaking, and the Act provides that a rule proposed through negotiated rulemaking is not entitled to greater deference in court than any other rule. 5 U.S.C. §570.

D. The judicial response to negotiated rulemaking

In the very few cases in which negotiated rulemaking has arisen as an issue, the fact that a rule was proposed and promulgated after negotiation has not been important to reviewing courts. Any defects in the negotiation process are probably cured by the notice and comment process through which all such rules are ultimately promulgated. Courts have not required agencies to adopt the rule agreed to in negotiation. *See USA Group Loan Services, Inc. v. Riley*, 82 F.3d 708, 715 (7th Cir. 1996).

IV. DIRECT FINAL RULEMAKING

Some agencies have begun to use a procedural innovation called ***direct final rulemaking*** under which an agency publishes a final rule and specifies that it will go into effect on a certain date unless the agency receives adverse comments. This procedure speeds up the process of promulgating rules and collapses the notice and decision steps into one step of promulgation of a final rule (unless adverse comments are received). If the agency does receive adverse comments, the direct final rulemaking is canceled and the agency conducts a normal notice and comment process. While direct final rulemaking has not been tested in court, it will probably be upheld as a method for promulgating legislative rules. As long as the receipt of adverse comments triggers notice and comment procedures, the method is fair—no one is prejudiced by the procedure.

Quiz Yourself on *APA RULEMAKING PROCEDURES*

30. The EPA has evidence that gasoline fumes pose a serious air quality problem. The agency issues a Notice of Proposed Rulemaking (NPRM) that identifies the problem and includes the text of a proposed rule that would require a new gas tank assembly on all automobiles. The new gas tank assembly would reduce the fumes that escape during fueling and whenever the gas cap is taken off. Comments from automobile manufacturers and consumer groups convince the EPA that it would be cheaper to require the addition of a chemical to gasoline that would reduce the fumes emitted. May the EPA promulgate a regulation requiring the reformulation of gasoline without issuing a new NPRM? _____

31. On the same fact situation, assume that officials from General Motors attended a meeting with the Administrator of the EPA during the comment period. At the meeting, the attendees discussed the negative economic effects that would occur if the car makers were required to modify their gas tanks. Does this provide a basis for challenging the final rule? _____

32. Assume that the FDA issues a NPRM that proposes a label on all tobacco products stating "Tobacco is a Deadly Poison; Quit Now and Save Your Life." Suppose that evidence surfaces that, in a personal letter to one of his former medical school classmates, the Administrator of the FDA (who has final decisionmaking authority on the rulemaking) wrote: "I view my mission in life as making business as difficult as possible for tobacco companies so I can save as many people as possible from the effects of tobacco. I will never waver from this mission." Does this provide an argument for disqualifying the Administrator? _____

33. Assume the same rulemaking on tobacco products. The manufacturers of smokeless tobacco submit studies showing that their products are far less dangerous than cigarettes. In fact, the studies show that lives would be saved if people were encouraged to switch from cigarettes to their products. Suppose that the Administrator imposes the requirement on all tobacco products. In his concise general statement he addresses the dangers of tobacco in general terms and does not mention the issues raised by the smokeless tobacco manufacturers. Are there grounds for attacking the result?

_____

34. OSHA is conducting a rulemaking on safety issues regarding employees who work at computer terminals. There are conflicting OSHA studies on the health effects of exposure to radiation from computer monitors. Interests representing employees present reputable studies showing negative health effects and how a relatively inexpensive modification of computer monitors would help. Monitor manufacturers and interests representing employers present studies showing no negative health effects and that monitor modification would be very expensive and would not eliminate the kind of radiation that the opposing experts say is the problem. OSHA imposes the regulation preferred by employees. On judicial review, the court of appeals states that, given the state of the record, the rule is arbitrary and capricious absent an opportunity for each side to cross-examine the other's experts. Is this a proper ruling? _____

35. An agency's organic statute states that the agency, before issuing a rule, "must hold an oral hearing at which interested parties may present argument and evidence." Does this trigger formal rulemaking under APA §§556 and 557? _____

Answers

30. Probably not. Oil companies will argue that the NPRM did not give adequate notice that reformulation of gasoline, instead of redesign of automobile gas tanks, would be considered. For notice to be adequate, the final rule must be the logical outgrowth of the proposal; the final rule must not be a material alteration of the proposal. The purpose of the notice requirement is to ensure that interested parties know when their interests are at stake, and the oil companies would argue that they had no idea that their product would be the subject of the rulemaking. If the NPRM had mentioned the possibility of other solutions, including reformulation of gasoline, then the oil companies' argument would be weaker. Nevertheless, the oil companies could still argue that absent more specific notice, the EPA should be required to issue a new NPRM focusing specifically on gasoline. However, if the reviewing court applies a more literal reading of §553's notice requirement, it might uphold the notice as adequate because it apprised the public of the subject of the rulemaking—gasoline fumes.

31. Possibly. Even though §553 does not address them, ex parte contacts are frowned upon in the rulemaking process. Some courts, on a variety of legal theories, have held that administrators should not willingly receive ex parte contacts; if they do receive them, they should place them on the record for other parties to comment upon. In this case, if the ex parte comments were not part of the record (so that opposing interests had no opportunity to comment upon General Motors' assertion that there would be a negative effect on car makers, and that fact was important to the agency's decision), then there would be a strong argument that the agency should reopen the comment period to allow additional comments on that issue. However, some lower courts have held that ex parte contacts are allowed unless they are statutorily banned, and it violates *Vermont Yankee* to bar them without a statutory basis. Note that the regulation of ex parte contacts is less strict here than in adjudication, where ex parte contacts are strictly forbidden.

32. Maybe. The tobacco companies could argue that the Administrator has an "unalterably closed mind" in his mission against tobacco and that he should thus be disqualified from deciding the rulemaking. Note, however, that there is no mention of bias in informal rulemaking in the APA. *Vermont Yankee*

might thus argue against judicial power to disqualify the Administrator on such grounds, unless the tobacco interests could convince the reviewing court that their due process rights were being violated. In addition, this issue raises the conflict between legal norms (which might counsel against allowing someone with such strong views to make a decision like this) and political norms (which favor strong views and a record of accomplishment with regard to those views).

33. Yes. The concise general statement should address the major issues raised by the comments. This is an important safeguard against arbitrary decisionmaking. Here, the smokeless tobacco manufacturers raised a significant issue distinguishing their product from other tobacco products, and the Administrator should have explained why he rejected their arguments.

34. No. Despite the court of appeals' attempt to link its ruling to the adequacy of the record, the decision violates *Vermont Yankee*, which holds that courts may not impose procedures in addition to those specified by the APA. Here, APA §553 does not provide for cross-examination, and as long as the agency has a rational basis for accepting one side's studies over the other's, the rule should stand.

35. No. Formal rulemaking is triggered when the agency is required to make rules "on the record after opportunity for an agency hearing." The statute here does not appear to require that the decision be made "on the record," so even though the statute might create a statutory hybrid, in that an oral hearing must be held, the agency is not required to use formal rulemaking.

Exam Tips on *APA RULEMAKING PROCEDURES*

☞ The starting place for all discussions of rulemaking procedure should be the APA.

    ☞ For example, if you are asked a notice question, start with the language of §553's notice requirement and then move on to the major cases construing that requirement.

☞ In controversies regarding bias and ex parte contacts, it is useful to point out that the APA does not address these issues with regard to informal rulemaking. Compare and contrast the various courts' approaches to the issues and then return to the APA and discuss whether one approach is more faithful to the APA.

☞ When answering questions regarding potential procedural defects in a rulemaking, in addition to the APA, support your analysis with the policies underlying the rulemaking process.

    ☞ For example, in notice controversies, discuss whether the purpose of notice—providing interested parties a genuine opportunity to participate—is met or not.

    ☞ In controversies regarding ex parte contacts and biased decisionmakers, in addition to discussing the adequacy of the opportunity to participate, discuss the tension between rulemaking on a legal model and rulemaking as part of the political system.

☞ If a party claims that an agency should have used more than §553 procedures in a rulemaking, look to see whether any statute or rule required more. If not, *Vermont Yankee* counsels against requiring more than §553.

☛ *Vermont Yankee* can be raised in all questions regarding procedural issues in rulemaking.

☞ *Vermont Yankee*'s policies of predictability and procedural flexibility are implicated whenever a court is asked to read a provision of §553 broadly. It is thus effective to use *Vermont Yankee* as an argument against any but the most literal reading of the language of §553.

☞ If the question raises an issue regarding whether an agency conducting informal rulemaking might be required to go beyond the procedures specified in §553, *Vermont Yankee* must be addressed.

☛ In a question regarding whether an agency is required to use formal rulemaking procedures, it is important to note that the Supreme Court favors the more streamlined informal rulemaking process.

☞ Be sure to point to the language of §553 and the particular agency's statute and argue that unless the statute clearly requires a hearing and an "on the record" decision, formal rulemaking is not required.

CHAPTER 7

AGENCY ADJUDICATION AND DUE PROCESS

ChapterScope

This chapter examines a variety of questions relating to agency adjudication and due process. The topics include the constitutional limitations on agency authority to adjudicate, due process requirements for agency procedure, and how substantive law affects the scope of an agency hearing. The key points in the chapter are:

- *Article III* restricts Congress's ability to assign adjudication to administrative agencies, especially regarding disputes between two private parties over matters traditionally within Article III jurisdiction.

  - However, even in the private rights area, as long as an agency has limited jurisdiction over matters closely related to a regulatory scheme, agency adjudication is likely to be constitutional unless the independence or constitutional role of Article III courts is threatened.

- *Property interests* protected by the due process clauses are usually created by law external to the Constitution, such as state law.

  - A party has a property interest in a government benefit, license, or job if that law creates an entitlement by prescribing criteria under which the benefit, job, or license will be granted or retained.

- *Liberty interests* protected by the Constitution are often created by the Constitution itself. These include the liberty interest in being free from bodily restraint or bodily harm.

- Once a protected interest is found, federal law determines *what process is due*.

  - Under the *Mathews v. Eldridge* balancing test, this determination is made by balancing the strength of the private interest, the value in accuracy of additional procedure, and the government's interest in proceeding without additional process.

- The traditional model of due process is an *adjudicatory hearing*, usually in advance of the adverse action.

  - In many situations, however, it is constitutionally permissible to hold the hearing after the adverse government action has been taken.

  - Further, in some settings due process may be provided through alternative models such as common-law remedies and informal, consultative processes.

- A basic right under due process is the right to a *neutral decisionmaker*.

  - A decisionmaker is not neutral if he or she has a *pecuniary interest* in the outcome of the case or if he or she has *prejudged* the facts or law of the case.

  - In the administrative setting, bias can be the result of the *capture* of an agency by one segment of an industry which uses its power to harm its competitors.

■ When a statute requires a hearing; the agency must provide a genuine hearing at which the applicant has an opportunity to prevail. However, agencies are free to use rulemaking to narrow the issues decided at a statutorily required hearing as long as the rules made to do so are substantively valid.

I. CONSTITUTIONAL AUTHORITY FOR AGENCY ADJUDICATION

A. Article III

Article III of the Constitution vests the judicial power of the United States in the Supreme Court and in lower federal courts, as established by Congress, that are staffed by judges with life tenure and protected compensation. On its face, the Constitution does not anticipate federal adjudication except in the federal courts. Nevertheless, since the flowering of the administrative state in the New Deal Era, federal agencies have adjudicated disputes. Such adjudication is allowed when it does not threaten the policies and values underlying Article III's assignment of the judicial power to the federal courts.

B. *Crowell v. Benson* and the public rights versus private rights doctrine

The Longshoremen's and Harbor Workers' Compensation Act of 1927 assigned adjudication of worker's compensation claims for covered workers to the United States Employees' Compensation Commission, a non-Article III body. In *Crowell v. Benson*, 285 U.S. 22 (1932), after the Commission made an award to an employee, the employer sued, claiming, inter alia, that the assignment of adjudicatory power to the Commission was unconstitutional. The Supreme Court upheld the Commission's authority to adjudicate the claim, subject to certain restrictions.

1. **Public rights versus private rights:** The *Crowell* Court made a fundamental distinction between *public rights* disputes and *private rights* disputes. Public rights disputes are controversies between a private party and the government over matters such as government benefits, taxation, and immigration. Private rights are disputes between two private parties in which the government's role is primarily adjudicatory. The Court stated that while there is a great deal of discretion over adjudication of public rights, Article III places severe restrictions on Congress's ability to assign adjudication of private rights disputes to non-Article III tribunals such as administrative agencies.

2. **Administrative agencies may conclusively adjudicate facts in public rights disputes:** The *Crowell* Court stated that public rights disputes, while susceptible of judicial resolution, may be assigned to non-Article III adjudicators, such as administrative agencies.

   a. **Public rights and sovereign immunity:** The roots of the public rights doctrine lay in the common-law tradition of sovereign immunity. Because claims against the government were unknown at common law, such claims are not exclusively within the Article III judicial power.

   b. **Congress's power over public rights disputes:** The *Crowell* Court characterized the assignment of adjudication of public rights disputes as "completely within congressional control." Although the analysis was framed in terms of factual issues, the *Crowell* Court may have intended to allow Congress to assign adjudication of both law and fact in public rights disputes to administrative agencies.

3. **Administrative agencies may adjudicate facts in private rights disputes:** In private rights cases (disputes between two private parties such as the workers' compensation claim in *Crowell*), the Court approved agency factfinding on such issues as the "circumstances, nature, extent and consequences of the injuries sustained by the employee." The Court analogized agency factfinding to factfinding in the federal courts by juries, masters, and commissioners and concluded that the Constitution did not bar agency factfinding in private rights disputes.

   a. **Constitutional or jurisdictional facts must be adjudicated in the federal courts:** The primary limits on agency adjudication recognized in *Crowell* were that issues relating to the *jurisdiction of the agency* and issues of *constitutional fact* must be adjudicated de novo in the federal courts. In *Crowell*, jurisdictional fact issues included whether the claimant was actually an employee of the employer and whether the injury occurred on navigable waters (which was necessary for federal jurisdiction over the claim). With regard to constitutional issues, the Court held that the federal judicial power includes the power to make factual determinations necessary for federal regulatory power. The Court held that it was therefore appropriate for the district court to hold a trial de novo on these matters.

   b. **The *Crowell* Court implied that issues of law should be reserved to the courts:** The Court noted that the statute in *Crowell* left the final determination of issues of law to the federal courts, albeit on review of initial determinations by the Commission. The Court implied that an Article III problem might exist if issues of law are reserved to determination by the agency. *Crowell* thus stands for the proposition that Article III requires, in private rights cases, judicial review (and perhaps de novo review) of legal issues. Nevertheless, given the *Chevron* deference doctrine and its early antecedents, while some form of judicial review of questions of law may be required, judicial deference to agency legal determinations is permissible.

   c. **Judicial review of constitutional and jurisdictional facts is required:** The Article III restrictions identified above regarding Congress's power to assign adjudication to non-Article III tribunals mean that in some situations, either exclusive jurisdiction in court, or at least de novo judicial review of agency determinations, is required. The Court stated that with regard to fundamental or jurisdictional facts, ". . . the Federal Court should determine such an issue upon its own record and the facts elicited before it." Because the Court construed the statute in *Crowell* to allow such de novo review, the Court upheld the statute.

C. The current standard for allowing agencies to adjudicate

For several decades after *Crowell*, the Court was largely silent regarding Congress's power to assign adjudicatory functions to non-Article III courts. Over time, the restrictions recognized in *Crowell* receded from legal consciousness until a series of separation of powers decisions (beginning early in the 1980s) revived restrictions on adjudication in non-Article III tribunals. Recently, the Court has retreated to a much more accommodating approach that recognizes broad congressional power to assign adjudication to administrative bodies.

1. ***Northern Pipeline*:** In *Northern Pipeline Constr. Co. v. Marathon Pipe Line Co.*, 458 U.S. 50 (1982), a divided Court struck down a provision of the Bankruptcy Act that gave bankruptcy

courts (created under Article I and not Article III) jurisdiction over common-law claims to which the debtor was a party.

a. **Justice Brennan's plurality opinion:** The lead opinion (by Justice Brennan for himself and three others) applied a categorical approach, holding that Congress may delegate adjudicatory power to non-Article III tribunals in only three situations: (1) *territorial courts* in which complete federal control necessitates the creation of essentially local federal courts; (2) *military courts* or "courts martial"; and (3) *public rights* cases. Common-law civil actions, held Justice Brennan, were not in any of the three exceptions to the vesting of the judicial power in the Article III courts. Thus, the Bankruptcy Act was unconstitutional.

b. **Justice Rehnquist's concurring opinion:** Justice Rehnquist, joined by Justice O'Connor, concluded that the Bankruptcy Act was unconstitutional because it assigned adjudication to a non-Article III tribunal of a claim in the core of traditional Article III judicial power. Justice Rehnquist found it unnecessary to endorse Justice Brennan's categorical approach.

c. **Justice White's dissent:** Justice White (joined by three others) dissented. He insisted that, on balance, the threat to Article III values posed by the bankruptcy court's jurisdiction over common-law claims was outweighed by the policies advanced by the Bankruptcy Act's assignment of adjudicatory authority to those courts. Justice White argued that this balancing test was the proper approach to the problem, not the more categorical approaches adopted by the majority.

d. *Northern Pipeline's* **threat to administrative agencies:** The decision in *Northern Pipeline*, together with the invalidation of the Federal Election Commission in *Buckley v. Valeo*, 424 U.S. 1 (1976) and the invalidation of the legislative veto in *INS v. Chadha*, 462 U.S. 919 (1983), raised fears that the Supreme Court's strict approach regarding separation of powers would ultimately result in severe restrictions on the activities of administrative agencies, including sharp limits on adjudication in agencies. As subsequent developments revealed, those fears were unfounded. In recent years, the Court has settled on a very accommodating approach to the powers of administrative agencies, including adjudication—an approach resembling Justice White's dissenting analysis in *Northern Pipeline*.

2. **The balancing test for the constitutional validity of agency adjudication:** The current test for determining the constitutionality of a delegation of adjudicatory power to an agency is a balancing test that weighs the threat to Article III values against the concerns that led to the assignment of adjudicatory authority to the agency. The primary question is whether the assignment of jurisdiction to a non-Article III adjudicator threatens the institutional integrity of the federal courts.

   a. **Traditional Article III cases:** The Supreme Court has stated that its review will be most exacting when Congress assigns adjudication of a claim to an agency that is of the type traditionally within the jurisdiction of the Article III courts. Thus, in *Commodity Futures Trading Commission (CFTC) v. Schor*, 478 U.S. 833 (1986), the Court stated that "where private, common law rights are at stake, our examination of the congressional attempt to control the manner in which those rights are adjudicated has been searching." *CFTC v. Schor*, 478 U.S. at 851. The Court was also quick to point out, however, that the private, common-law nature of the rights at stake was not determinative. In *CFTC*, the Court approved a statute that assigned adjudication of certain common-law claims to the CFTC.

b. Scope of agency jurisdiction: The broader the scope of the agency's jurisdiction, the more likely there will be a violation of Article III. Conversely, the more an agency's jurisdiction is confined narrowly to a particular area, the less the perceived threat to Article III values.

c. Congressionally created rights: Agency jurisdiction over private rights disputes, where the rights involved are congressionally created, is seen as less threatening to Article III values than when the rights involved arise from another source, such as state law. Even though disputes involving congressionally created rights are technically private rights disputes and thus could be seen as within the core of Article III jurisdiction, the Court analogizes congressionally created rights to public rights. Conversely, where common-law or state statutory rights are involved, agency jurisdiction is less likely to be upheld against Article III challenge.

d. Agency jurisdiction related to an area of extensive federal regulation: Even when the agency's jurisdiction is over matters traditionally within the sphere of Article III adjudication, there is less of a perceived threat to Article III values when such jurisdiction is closely related to an area or dispute subject to extensive federal regulation.

e. Choice of parties to litigate in agency: When the parties have a choice over whether to litigate their dispute in a non-Article III tribunal, there is less of a perceived threat to Article III values than if the parties have no choice over the forum. However, because the structural interests of the Article III courts in preserving their authority cannot be waived by a litigant, the Article III issue remains even when the litigants have chosen the non-Article III forum.

f. Agency power to issue binding orders: When an agency must go to an Article III court to have its order enforced, it is less likely to present an Article III problem than if agency orders are self-enforcing.

> **Example:** *CFTC v. Schor*: The Commodity Exchange Act (CEA) regulates commodity futures transactions. Part of this regulatory scheme creates a reparations procedure under which customers of commodities brokers can seek remedies for brokers' violations of the CEA and regulations promulgated thereunder. The CEA places jurisdiction over reparations actions in the CFTC, an independent agency. The CFTC, in regulations promulgated under the CEA, asserted jurisdiction over counterclaims, including state law contract claims, that brokers might bring in response to their customers' actions.
>
> In *CFTC v. Schor*, 478 U.S. 833 (1986), the CFTC entertained state law counterclaims to a customer's statutory reparations action. After the broker prevailed on both the reparations action and the counterclaims, the Court of Appeals for the D.C. Circuit raised, sua sponte, the issue of whether CFTC jurisdiction over the counterclaims was allowed under the CEA and whether such jurisdiction violated Article III under *Northern Pipeline*. The court of appeals read the CEA as not extending the CFTC's jurisdiction to common-law counterclaims, largely to avoid the constitutional question that would arise if the statute were read differently.
>
> The Supreme Court reversed, holding that agency adjudication of the common-law counterclaims did not violate Article III. The Court stated that the result depends on several factors, including whether the "essential attributes of judicial power" remain in Article III courts versus "the extent to which the [agency] exercises the range of jurisdiction normally vested only in Article III courts, the origins and importance of the right to be adjudicated, and the concerns that drove Congress to depart from the requirements of Article III." *CFTC v.*

Schor, 478 U.S. at 859. The Court relied upon the following factors to conclude that in this case, there was no impermissible intrusion on the jurisdiction of the Article III courts: (1) the CFTC deals only with a particularized area of law; (2) the CFTC's orders are enforceable only by order of the District Court; (3) the factual decisions of the CFTC are judicially reviewable under a relatively nondeferential standard and its legal decisions are reviewed de novo; and (4) the CFTC does not exercise other powers normally reserved to district courts like the power to preside over jury trials or issue writs of habeas corpus. Focusing more specifically on the fact that the CFTC was asserting jurisdiction over common-law counter-claims, a factor weighing against the constitutionality of the statute, the Court stated that the limited nature of the common-law jurisdiction, its connection to the statute's policy of providing an effective remedial scheme, and the fact that the federal courts retain concurrent jurisdiction over the claims all weigh in favor of the statute's constitutionality.

Thomas v. Union Carbide: The Federal Insecticide, Fungicide, and Rodenticide Act (FIFRA) requires manufacturers of covered products to register their products with EPA. Under FIFRA, the EPA has authority to reject applications for registration if the manufacturer cannot establish that the product is safe and effective. The 1978 amendments to FIFRA allowed the EPA to use information submitted by one manufacturer to help evaluate an application for registration of a similar product by a second manufacturer. Because the information often consisted of valuable trade secrets, the second manufacturer was required to offer to compensate the first. If no agreement between the two manufacturers on the amount of compensation was reached, the parties were required to submit the compensation question to binding arbitration. The decision of the arbitrator was subject to judicial review but only for "fraud, misrepresentation or other misconduct." This procedure was challenged as violating Article III by placing jurisdiction over a private dispute in a non-Article III tribunal, here an arbitrator.

In *Thomas v. Union Carbide Agric. Prods. Co.*, 473 U.S. 568 (1985), the Court upheld the FIFRA amendments, relying largely on the ground that because the registration and use of pesticides is subject to heavy regulation, the compensation question was more like a public right than the typical dispute between two private parties. The Court stated that "Congress, acting for a valid legislative purpose pursuant to its constitutional powers under Article I, may create a seemingly 'private' right that is so closely integrated into a public regulatory scheme as to be a matter appropriate for agency resolution with limited involvement by the Article III judiciary." *Thomas*, 473 U.S. at 593. The Court also supported its holding by noting that the arbitrators' narrow jurisdiction did not threaten the judiciary's Article III powers and that limited judicial review was available to ensure that arbitrators did not exceed their authority.

These decisions substantially reorient the doctrines governing Congress's power to assign adjudicatory jurisdiction to non-Article III tribunals. The public rights doctrine has been recast with a focus on whether agency jurisdiction is closely connected to a regulated field in which a narrow set of disputes is subject to non-Article III adjudication. The entire analysis is governed by a balancing-type approach that asks whether the independence and authority of Article III courts is threatened, rather than a potentially more restrictive, categorical approach. While scrutiny is somewhat heightened when matters within the core of traditional judicial powers are assigned to agencies, *CFTC v. Schor and Thomas v. Union Carbide* allow Congress great discretion to assign adjudication to non-Article III tribunals in areas related to federal regulation.

II. DUE PROCESS AND THE ADJUDICATORY HEARING

Due process principles govern whether an agency is required to provide a hearing and, if so, what process is required at the hearing. Once it is determined that a hearing is required, federal due process standards govern the contours of that hearing. That determination is made with sensitivity to the procedures already specified in the governing law.

A. Identifying interests protected by due process: property

Due process hearing rights attach when the government deprives or threatens to deprive a person of *life, liberty*, or *property*. The Fifth and Fourteenth Amendments prohibit government from depriving any person of a protected interest without due process of law. It is sometimes difficult, however, to determine whether government action threatens an interest protected by the Due Process Clauses. At one time, interests such as government benefits, government employment, licenses, and the like were thought of as gratuities that could be withdrawn at any time without due process. More recently, government benefits, licenses, and government employment (referred to below for convenience as "government benefits") have been recognized by the courts as property interests. These are referred to as the *new property* to distinguish them from traditional interests in real and personal property.

1. ***Goldberg v. Kelly* and grievous loss:** *Goldberg v. Kelly*, 397 U.S. 254 (1970), was the first Supreme Court decision to recognize due process rights in new property. In *Goldberg*, the Court held that welfare benefits could not be terminated without first holding a hearing to determine the recipient's continued eligibility. The statute provided that prior to termination, the recipient could object to termination in writing. After termination, a hearing to challenge termination was available. The Court held that in light of the grievous loss likely suffered by a person wrongly terminated from welfare, where eligibility is determined by extreme poverty, due process required some sort of oral hearing before termination.

   Some courts and commentators read *Goldberg* as holding that grievous loss was sufficient to create a property or liberty interest—so that anytime government action could have a severe negative effect on an individual, a predeprivation hearing was required. However, subsequent developments made clear that the grievous loss analysis went to the amount of process that was due, not the existence of a protected interest. Whether due process is required at all is determined by whether the statute or some other source of law created an entitlement to the government benefit. In *Goldberg* the point had been conceded—the government agreed that the welfare statute created an entitlement to benefits.

2. ***Board of Regents v. Roth* and the positive law test:** In *Board of Regents v. Roth*, 408 U.S. 564 (1972), the Supreme Court rejected the grievous loss test for the existence of a property right and instead accepted a test that relies on positive law, usually state common law or state or federal statutes or regulations, for the creation of property interests.

   a. **Legal entitlements create property interests:** In *Roth*, the Court held that property interests are created by sources external to the Constitution, such as state law. If an external source such as state law creates a claim of entitlement to the government benefit, then a property interest exists. Conversely, if state law does not recognize a claim of entitlement, so that the claimant has only a unilateral expectation of receiving the government benefit, then no property interest exists and due process protections do not attach.

b. **Entitlements exist when the interest is governed by criteria, rather than discretion:** A claim of entitlement exists when law, custom, or practice establishes that claims to the government benefit are evaluated under a definite set of criteria. For example, if state law or an employment contract provides that a government employee may not be terminated absent good cause, then the employee has a property interest in continued employment and due process must be followed before termination of employment. Government employees at will, by contrast, have no claim of entitlement and may be terminated without due process. Thus, in *Roth* there was no property interest because nothing in state law or the employment contract constrained the government's decision whether to continue the employment beyond the initial contractual term.

c. **Entitlements are created by substantive, not procedural law:** If a statute provides procedural protections only, no entitlement exists. Procedural constraints on government action are normally insufficient to create an entitlement.

3. **Implicit entitlements. *Perry v. Sindermann*:** Usually, the for-cause standard (if one exists) is explicit in either state law or the contract of employment. In the absence of an explicit entitlement, less formal assurances or state practices may create an entitlement and, therefore, a property interest. For example, in *Perry v. Sindermann*, 408 U.S. 593 (1972), the Court held that a state employee had a property interest in his job even though his contract did not explicitly create an entitlement to continued employment as a teacher at a junior college. In recognizing a property interest, the Court (analogizing to the law of implied contracts) relied upon provisions in a faculty handbook and other assurances that employment would be continued as long as performance was satisfactory.

4. **The rejection of the "bitter with the sweet" argument:** Not all members of the Court were happy with *Roth*—especially with its separation of substance from process. They argued that if the statute that created an entitlement provided claimants with only minimal procedures for securing the entitlement, those procedures should limit the reach of the property interest. In *Arnett v. Kennedy*, 416 U.S. 134 (1974), Justice Rehnquist, joined by two other members of the Court, argued that a civil service employee (with a for-cause termination provision) should receive only the process specified in the statute granting the for-cause entitlement. They stated that claimants should have to take the "bitter with the sweet" and accept the procedural limitations in the statute that created the entitlement. However, a majority of the Court rejected this argument, adhering to *Roth*'s separation of procedure from substance.

Example: The following statute regulates employment within a government agency:

Section A: No employee shall be terminated absent good cause, defined as lack of success in completing assigned tasks, inability to function in the work environment, or misconduct.

Section B: The determination of whether good cause for termination exists shall be made by the personnel manager with no opportunity for input, either written or oral, from the affected employee.

Section A creates a property interest in continued employment. Once such an entitlement is created, federal due process governs what process is due. Section B is, in effect, unconstitutional because it provides for no hearing before the employee is deprived of a property interest. Under Justice Rehnquist's bitter with the sweet argument, Section B would limit any property interest created by Section A. However, this argument was rejected by a majority of the Court in *Arnett* and thus federal standards govern what process is due under the substantive standard contained in Section A.

B. Identifying interests protected by due process: liberty

Some liberty interests are created (like property interests) by external law such as statutes and regulations, while other liberty interests are recognized as part of the constitutional definition of liberty and are thus created by the Due Process Clause itself.

1. **Constitutional liberty:** Traditional liberty interests, such as freedom from bodily restraint and freedom from unwarranted use of force by government officials such as police officers, are part of the Constitution's definition of liberty. These liberty interests exist regardless of the provisions of state law, and due process must be afforded if the state wishes to deprive a person of one of these interests.

   a. **Constitutional liberty interests recognized:** The courts have recognized a variety of constitutionally based liberty interests. For example, in *Ingraham v. Wright*, 430 U.S. 651 (1977), the Court held that corporal punishment deprives paddled students of liberty, regardless of state law. In *Parham v. J.R.*, 442 U.S. 584 (1979), the Court recognized that being confined in a mental institution and labeled "mentally ill" infringes on a liberty interest.

   b. **Rejected claims for constitutional liberty:** The Court has also rejected numerous claims that state action deprives a person of constitutionally based liberty. In *Paul v. Davis*, 424 U.S. 693 (1976), the Court rejected the claim that the plaintiff was deprived of liberty when a police chief included his name on a list of active shoplifters. The Court held that damage to reputation through defamation, without an actual alteration of the person's legal status, did not amount to a deprivation of liberty. Had the defamation altered the plaintiff's legal status, such as making him ineligible for certain employment or unable to shop at stores in the area, the Court said that a liberty deprivation might have been found. In *O'Bannon v. Town Court Nursing Center*, 447 U.S. 773 (1980), the Court held that no liberty interest was affected when nursing home residents were forced to move because their home lost its certification to treat Medicare and Medicaid patients, even if they suffered transfer trauma (which may increase the likelihood of serious illness or death). While the Court relied in part on the fact that the administrative action was aimed at the home and not at the patients, the Court rejected the argument that a liberty interest was involved simply because government action caused potentially great harm.

2. **Statutorily created liberty:** Liberty interests may also be created by positive law in the same way that positive law creates property interests. For example, prisoners have no constitutionally based liberty interest in being considered for parole. However, if state law creates an entitlement to parole, then a liberty interest is created and due process standards govern the procedures employed at parole hearings. *See Board of Pardons v. Allen*, 482 U.S. 369 (1987) (liberty interest exists when state statute specifies that parole board "shall" grant parole under specified conditions). However, in *Town of Castle Rock v. Gonzales*, 125 S. Ct. 2796 (2005), the Court rejected an entitlement-based claim of a liberty interest in the enforcement of a restraining order. The plaintiff brought a claim against the municipality in which she lived, claiming that she was deprived of liberty when town police failed to enforce a restraining order against her ex-husband, who murdered her three children. The Court stated that even though the order

might appear to create an entitlement by stating that the police "shall use every reasonable means to enforce this restraining order . . . [a] well established tradition of police discretion has long coexisted with apparently mandatory arrest statutes." Thus, there was no legitimate claim of entitlement under state law and no liberty interest under federal law.

3. **Prison conditions cases and liberty interests:** Constitutional liberty may be implicated when a change in prison conditions (whether resulting from a disciplinary process or not) such as moving a prisoner into solitary confinement is so harsh as to amount to a change "outside the normal limits or range of custody" implicit in the fact of conviction. Positive law liberty interests may be implicated when the change in prison conditions involves an entitlement, such as state law that governs when a prisoner should be moved into a higher security prison.

   a. **Entitlement liberty in prison:** State or federal law can create a liberty interest if standards govern the treatment of prisoners, such as decisions concerning the nature of confinement, level of security, or placement in punitive conditions. For example, in *Vitek v. Jones*, 445 U.S. 480 (1980), the Supreme Court found a liberty interest when a prisoner was moved to a mental hospital, in part because state law prescribed the conditions under which such a transfer was allowed. However, there is some doubt over whether this aspect of *Vitek* is still good law because, in *Sandin v. Connor*, 515 U.S. 472 (1995), the Supreme Court rejected an entitlement-based constitutional liberty claim brought by a prisoner who had been sentenced to solitary confinement for misconduct under a "substantial evidence" of misconduct standard. The Court, in an opinion by Chief Justice Rehnquist, criticized prior cases for encouraging prisoners to "comb regulations" for entitlement-creating language. The Court appeared to favor confining prisoner liberty cases to the constitutionally based type, recognizing liberty claims only when a prisoner is treated significantly worse than is usual in prison or when the prisoner's sentence is likely to be lengthened.

   b. **Constitutional liberty in prison:** The Court has also recognized constitutionally based liberty interests, and these appear to be more viable after *Sandin*, although it is still difficult to establish a constitutional liberty interest in changed conditions of imprisonment. A prisoner has been deprived of liberty only if a change in conditions is beyond the normal range of the deprivation of liberty inherent in incarceration. Movement from a medium security prison to a higher level of security is not a deprivation of liberty. *See Meachum v. Fano*, 427 U.S. 215 (1976). Further, no liberty interest is implicated when a prisoner is transferred to an out-of-state prison. *See Olim v. Wakinekona*, 461 U.S. 238 (1983) (transfer from Hawaii to California was within the range of permissible incarceration implicit in the conviction). *See also Kentucky Dept. of Corrections v. Thompson*, 490 U.S. 454 (1989) (inmate has no liberty interest in the number and identity of visitors). However, in *Vitek v. Jones*, 445 U.S. 480 (1980), the Court did find that that incarceration in a mental hospital, including being labeled as mentally ill and subjected to mandatory treatment, is qualitatively different from incarceration in a prison, and thus constitutional liberty was implicated. And in *Wilkinson v. Austin*, 125 S. Ct. 2384 (2005), the Court, after *Sandin*, found that assignment of a prisoner to an Ohio "supermax" prison constituted a liberty deprivation, noting that inmates confined to the supermax prison were precluded from almost all human contact, subjected to having a light on in their cell at all times, permitted only one hour of exercise outside the cell per day, and disqualified from parole consideration.

C. Determining what process is due

Once it is determined that a person has been deprived of an interest protected by due process, the next issue is whether the procedures provided are sufficient to satisfy due process. In other words, the issue becomes "what process is due?" The issue of what process is due is determined by applying federal due process standards to the procedures already provided and asking whether those procedures are adequate. If they are not, then federal due process law mandates adding to those procedures to bring them up to constitutional standards.

1. **Due process basics:** When due process applies, it requires a hearing at a meaningful time. Sometimes this hearing must be before adverse government action is taken. Under certain conditions, the hearing may be after government action is taken. The specific requirements of due process vary with the situation, but core due process rights include the following:

   1. *Notice*—advance notice of the issues and the time and place of any hearings;
   2. An *oral hearing* in advance of adverse government action—the oral hearing includes the right to present oral testimony and argument;
   3. The right to *counsel*—the right to be assisted by an attorney or perhaps some other trained aide;
   4. The right to *confront the evidence* against one's position—this includes the right to cross-examine adverse witnesses and the right to present evidence to undercut the government's case; and
   5. The right to a *neutral decisionmaker*—the right to a decisionmaker who is not biased and who has not prejudged the case in advance of hearing it.

   Whether due process requires procedures in addition to those already provided is determined under the three-part *Mathews v. Eldridge* balancing test, described below.

2. **The *Mathews v. Eldridge* balancing test:** In *Mathews v. Eldridge*, 424 U.S. 319 (1976), the Supreme Court established a balancing test for determining what process is due. The Court rejected the argument that *Goldberg v. Kelly* requires a full predeprivation hearing any time adverse government action threatens to cause significant harm. The Court stated that once it is determined that an action will deprive a person of a protected interest, the following three factors must be considered to determine the level of process that must be afforded:

   1. the strength of the *private interest* affected by the government action;
   2. the risk of an *erroneous deprivation* if additional procedure is not afforded; and
   3. the *government's interest* in proceeding with no more process than already afforded.

   a. **The private interest affected:** The stronger the private interest is in being free from the deprivation, the more procedure is required under due process. For example, because *Goldberg v. Kelly* involved welfare benefits that by definition implicate the claimant's very survival, the Court held that due process requires an oral hearing before such benefits are terminated. By contrast, in *Mathews* itself, the Court held that because eligibility for disability benefits is not based on need, they do not implicate subsistence, and an oral pre-termination hearing is not required.

   The Court has found the private interest in continued government employment to be very strong. It has thus held that due process requires that government employees with an entitlement to continued employment be given a pretermination hearing if the government agency wishes to fire them. This was made clear in *Cleveland Board of Education v. Loudermill*, 470 U.S. 532 (1985), when the Court emphatically stated that government employees were entitled at least to a limited pretermination hearing.

b. **Risk of an erroneous deprivation:** The greater the risk of an erroneous deprivation, the stronger the claim is to additional procedures. For example, in *Goldberg v. Kelly*, one reason for requiring an oral hearing was that welfare recipients might be unable to state their claims effectively in writing, thus increasing the risk of an erroneous deprivation. By contrast, in *Mathews v. Eldridge*, the Court reasoned that no advance oral hearing was required, in part because the objective, medical nature of the relevant evidence meant that an erroneous determination was less likely than in *Goldberg*. Thus, the Court approved of a procedure in which the oral, adversary hearing was provided after the benefits had been terminated.

c. **The government's interest in proceeding with no additional process:** The most controversial factor in *Mathews* is the consideration of the government's interest in not increasing process beyond that already afforded. The government's fiscal and administrative interests almost always favor minimizing process. In many circumstances, however, the government has particularly strong arguments for minimizing process. For example, in *Mathews*, the Court noted that if the government were required to continue disability benefits until after an oral hearing, it would be very difficult for the government to recover benefits paid between the determination that disability benefits should be terminated and the hearing. Further, in emergencies such as the discovery of poisonous or rotten food, the Court has allowed for quick action and thus has not required a hearing in advance of adverse government action.

Example: In *Gilbert v. Homar*, 520 U.S. 924 (1997), a state university police officer was arrested and charged with a felony drug crime. Upon learning of the arrest, university officials suspended him immediately. Although the drug charges were subsequently dismissed, he remained suspended after the charges were dismissed. He was first allowed to tell his side of the story weeks after the suspension. Ultimately, he was demoted to groundskeeper. He sued, claiming he should have been afforded a hearing before the suspension. The Supreme Court held that the state's interest in acting quickly justified departing from the classic model of a hearing before an adverse employment action is taken. While reaffirming *Loudermill*'s general rule in favor of pretermination hearings, the Court explained that due process allows flexibility when important state interests favor quick action. In *Gilbert*, the third *Mathews* factor pointed strongly in favor of not requiring a presuspension hearing, since it was important to immediately remove a police officer charged with a drug crime from active duty. The result in *Gilbert* demonstrates how the state's interest can be taken into account without threatening due process generally. The state's interest in *Gilbert* was not simply the general fiscal and administrative preference for less procedure, but was a specific reason that government interests would be threatened if additional procedures were required.

3. **Alternative procedural models:** While due process analysis often focuses on advance notice and adjudicatory hearings, there are other procedural models that can provide due process.

a. **Common-law remedies:** In some situations, common-law postdeprivation remedies provide due process. For example, in *Ingraham v. Wright*, Florida schoolchildren who were subjected to corporal punishment sued, claiming that they had been deprived of liberty without due process since no hearing was held in advance of the punishment. The common law of Florida limited a teacher's privilege to inflict the punishment, and the Court held that them existence of the common-law remedies, coupled with the low incidence of abuse, meant that due process did not require a hearing in advance of inflicting the punishment.

b. Postdeprivation remedies more generally: Where quick action is necessary or predeprivation process is impracticable, due process may be satisfied by postdeprivation remedies. Postdeprivation remedies have been most strongly approved when random and unauthorized tortious conduct by a government official deprives the victim of property or liberty. If the state provides an adequate postdeprivation remedy, that remedy provides due process. *See Parratt v. Taylor*, 451 U.S. 527 (1981), *overruled in part by Daniels v. Williams*, 474 U.S. 327 (1986).

Example: A prison guard allegedly steals property from a prisoner's cell during a routine search. The prisoner sues for damages, claiming that the property was taken without due process of law. Because the prison guard's theft was random and unauthorized, an adequate postdeprivation remedy (such as an administrative claims procedure) satisfies due process. *See Hudson v. Palmer*, 468 U.S. 517 (1984).

c. Process required to impose regulatory penalties: Agencies may not impose legally binding orders on regulated parties without following due process. For example, in *Tennessee Valley Authority [TVA] v. Whitman*, 336 F.3d 1236 (11th Cir. 2003), *cert. denied*, 124 S. Ct. 2096 (2004), the Court held that the TVA must be given a chance to contest the basis of an "administrative compliance order" (ACO) issued by the EPA, because ACO's are issued without affording the alleged violator any right to a hearing. Note that the absence of advance process did not render the ACO invalid, it just meant that the ACO may not be enforced absent some opportunity to contest its basis. Here, the EPA would bring an action in federal district court to enforce the ACO, and the TVA would have a right to contest the alleged violation. In effect, the ACO is treated like a complaint rather than a final determination that a violation has occurred.

d. The consultative model: Due process may also be satisfied in some contexts with an informal, consultative procedure. For example, in *Board of Curators of the University of Missouri v. Horowitz*, 435 U.S.78 (1978), the Court held that due process was not violated when a medical student at a state school was dismissed for academic reasons without a formal, advance hearing. The Court held that the consultative review process employed (which included normal academic monitoring and review by several area physicians) was sufficient.

    i. Disciplinary dismissal distinguished: The Court distinguished dismissal for academic reasons from dismissal for disciplinary reasons. The Court noted that even in the disciplinary setting, a formal, advance hearing was not necessary as long as there was some opportunity for an advance, informal oral discussion of the disciplinary matter. *See Goss v. Lopez*, 419 U.S. 565 (1975).

    ii. Reluctance to intervene in academic affairs: In *Horowitz*, the Court appeared particularly reluctant to judicialize the academic review process at state universities and did not feel that judges should second-guess whether a student's academic performance was up to par.

4. **The right to a neutral decisionmaker:** One of the most important due process rights is the right to a neutral decisionmaker. Neutrality is an acute problem in the modern administrative agency where investigation, prosecution, adjudication, and legislation are often conducted within the same agency. While the courts have not objected in principle to the combination of functions within a single agency, they have developed legal doctrines to safeguard the due process right to neutrality.

   a. **Bias due to pecuniary interest:** Due process is violated if a decisionmaker has a *pecuniary interest* in the outcome of the adjudication. An obvious violation would be a judge presiding over a case involving a corporation in which the judge owns shares of stock. However, less direct pecuniary interests may also violate due process.

      i. *Tumey v. Ohio:* In *Tumey v. Ohio*, 273 US. 510 (1927), the Court held that due process was violated when the official adjudicating certain criminal cases (there the village mayor) was allowed to keep a portion of fines assessed as costs. Because an acquitted defendant paid neither a fine nor costs, the mayor sitting as judge had a direct pecuniary interest in the outcome of the cases within his jurisdiction. The Court stated that it "violates the Fourteenth Amendment, and deprives a defendant in a criminal case of due process of law, to subject his liberty or property to the judgment of a court the judge of which has a direct, personal, substantial, pecuniary interest in reaching a conclusion against him in his case." *Tumey*, 273 U.S. at 523.

      ii. *Ward v. Village of Monroeville:* In *Ward v. Village of Monroeville*, 409 U.S. 57 (1972), the Court extended *Tumey* to cover a case in which the mayor's pecuniary interest in the outcome of cases he was authorized to adjudicate was less direct. In *Ward*, the mayor sat as judge on traffic cases, and fines assessed in such cases accounted for more than a third—sometimes more than half—of the village's total annual revenues. The Court ruled that the mayor could not be viewed as an impartial adjudicator in this situation and that trial de novo before a higher court did not cure the due process violation in the initial tribunal. In contrast with *Ward*, the Court held in *Marshall v. Jerrico, Inc.*, 446 U.S. 238 (1980), that an ALJ is not disqualified from hearing a case when the agency is allowed to retain fines and use the funds to support its enforcement program. The Court noted that the fines accounted for only 1 percent of the agency's budget, and the salary and working conditions of ALJs were not related to the amount of fines collected.

      iii. *Gibson v. Berryhill:* In *Gibson v. Berryhill*, 411 U.S. 564 (1973), the Court held that due to pecuniary interest in the outcome, the Alabama Board of Optometry could not adjudicate whether certain optometrists violated state law-by working in the optical departments of stores instead of engaging in independent practices. All board members were independent optometrists, and the Court held that the independent optometrists' desire to eliminate competition from department store optometrists was a sufficient pecuniary interest to violate due process. The Court noted that *Ward* means that due process is violated by financial interests less direct than that in *Tumey*.

   b. **Bias due to lack of independence:** Due process, or other notions of procedural fairness, may be violated if it appears that the decisionmaker is under pressure to decide cases in a particular way. Administrative law judges are not protected from external pressure, such as political pressure or pressure from supervisors, to the same degree as Article III judges. In *Association of Administrative Law Judges v. Heckler*, 594 F. Supp. 1132 (D.D.C. 1984), the court held it improper to subject the decisions of particular ALJs to closer scrutiny because they ruled in favor of social security claimants more often than other ALJs. The court did not find a due process violation or even a violation of any section of the APA. However, the court disapproved of review based upon allowance rates because of the pressure this would put on ALJs to allow fewer claims.

c. **Bias due to a relationship with a party:** A decisionmaker may also be considered biased if he or she has a relationship, personal or professional, with one of the parties or their attorneys or even a witness. However, judges and other decisionmakers often have professional relationships with government officials named as parties or participating in the presentation of the government's case, and such a decisionmaker has discretion over whether to step aside due to the appearance of impropriety. A recent notorious example is *Cheney v. U.S. Dist. Court for Dist. of Columbia*, 542 U.S. 367 (2004), in which Justice Scalia was asked to recuse himself from hearing a case involving the Vice President of the United States after Justice Scalia accepted a free ride on the Vice President's airplane to a duck hunting trip they went on together with a large group. The case concerned the public's right of access to information concerning President Bush's National Energy Policy Development Group, over which Vice President Cheney presided. Justice Scalia's main reason for refusing to recuse himself was that the case concerned Vice President Cheney's official functions and thus the pair's personal friendship had no bearing on Justice Scalia's ability to participate fairly in deciding the case.

d. **Prejudgment:** Due process is violated if it appears that a decisionmaker in an adjudication has, in some measure, adjudged the facts or law of a particular case prior to hearing it. This must be contrasted with the more lenient standard applied in rulemaking, where officials are expected to have strong views when making legislative decisions and are disqualified only if it is shown that they have an unalterably closed mind and thus will not consider the comments presented in the rulemaking procedure.

  i. *Cinderella:* In *Cinderella Career and Finishing Schools, Inc. v.* FTC, 425 F.2d 583 (D.C. Cir. 1970), the court of appeals held that an FTC commissioner who had publicly criticized certain business practices and referred to them as "deceptive," could not participate in an adjudication over whether those practices violated the FTC Act as "unfair and deceptive" practices. The court stated that the test for disqualification is "whether a disinterested observer may conclude that the agency has in some measure adjudged the facts as well as the law of a particular case in advance of hearing it." *Cinderella*, 425 F.2d at 591. The court held that the commissioner's public reference to the practice at issue as "deceptive" met this test.

  ii. **Prejudgment and combination of functions:** The combination of various functions within a single agency, including investigation, prosecution, adjudication, and legislation, often creates difficult problems concerning possible prejudgment. The APA separates adjudicators from the agency's prosecutorial function by prohibiting the official hearing a case from being responsible to or under the supervision of an agency official involved in the investigation or prosecution of the case. APA §554(d). This prohibition does not apply to agency heads who may participate in the decision to bring a charge and then sit as the adjudicator of the case. This combination has been held not to violate due process. For example, in an earlier ruling in the *Cinderella* case, the court of appeals held that the FTC had the power to issue a press release alerting the public to suspected illegal practices in advance of the hearing. Subsequent FTC adjudication to determine if the practices were illegal did not violate due process. *See FTC v. Cinderella Career and Finishing Schools*, 404 F.2d 1308 (D.C. Cir. 1968).

Example: In *Withrow v. Larkin*, 421 U.S. 35 (1975), a state medical board initiated an investigation of Larkin, a doctor, after he began performing abortions. The board later charged Larkin with licensing violations and set a hearing date at which the board would preside. The board also referred the matter to the local prosecutor after finding probable cause that Larkin had committed criminal acts. Larkin sued to enjoin the board from hearing the case on the ground that, given the board's prejudgment as evidenced by its prior actions, it would violate due process for the board to hear the case.

The Supreme Court held that it would not violate due process for the board to hear the case after its investigation and referral to the prosecutor. The Court held that the combination of these functions did not constitute a per se violation of due process. The Court suggested that a due process violation would be found only when some additional evidence existed that the board had prejudged the ultimate outcome of the case. The Court analogized to judges in criminal cases, when the same judge who issues a warrant or finds probable cause to go forward with a prosecution may ultimately preside over a jury trial or even a bench trial. The *Withrow* decision validates the structure of many administrative agencies under which the agency heads (e.g., FTC commissioners) may take part in deciding which prosecutions to bring and then sit as ultimate adjudicators within the agency.

III. STATUTORY HEARING RIGHTS

In addition to procedural rights required by due process, many statutes grant the right to a hearing to determine matters such as licenses and government benefits. For example, the Social Security Act requires that applicants be given a hearing to determine if they are entitled to benefits. Under some circumstances, the Communications Act requires that applicants for licenses be given a hearing on their applications.

A. The statutorily required hearing must be a genuine hearing—not a sham

When a statute grants an applicant a hearing on an application for a government benefit or license, the hearing must provide the applicant with a genuine opportunity to prevail.

Example: In *Ashbacker Radio Corp. v. FCC*, 326 U.S. 327 (1945), two parties applied for a license to construct radio stations that would operate on the same frequency in nearby communities. The FCC granted one application and set the other (Ashbacker's) for a hearing. Ashbacker sued, claiming that the hearing would not be genuine because its application could not be granted without violating an FCC policy against interference with the signal of the previously granted station in the nearby community. The Court agreed with Ashbacker, holding that granting the competitor's license deprived Ashbacker of the statutorily required hearing. The Court rejected the FCC's argument that it could make adjustments to the previously granted license if it decided to grant Ashbacker's after the hearing. The Court believed that as a practical matter, the grant of the competing application amounted to a denial of Ashbacker's.

B. Substantive standards that limit the right to a hearing

Agencies may employ substantive rules to limit the issues addressed at a hearing.

1. **The argument against rules that narrow issues at hearings:** Agencies often adopt substantive rules to narrow the issues to be decided at statutorily required hearings. When a statute requires that an applicant be given a hearing, applicants often challenge these regulations on the ground that they deprive them of their right to the hearing promised under the statute.

2. **Rules that narrow the scope of hearings are generally allowed:** In general, courts have upheld this widespread practice and allowed agencies to use rulemaking authority to make substantive rules that effectively limit the issues decided at a hearing. The scope of the hearing is tailored to the remaining substantive standards governing the decision to be made.

   Example: A statute allows an agency to deny licenses for "good cause, including matters reflecting on the moral character of the applicant." The agency that administers the licensing program promulgates a regulation specifying several reasons for denying licenses, including a dishonorable discharge from the armed services and conviction of any crime for which the maximum sentence is six months or greater. Smith applies for a license. At the hearing, the agency introduces uncontradicted evidence that Smith received a dishonorable discharge from the Army and was later convicted of misdemeanor assault, a crime with a maximum nine-month sentence. Because of the agency's regulation, this evidence is sufficient to deny the application without more general evidence on Smith's moral character.

3. **The agency must have rulemaking authority and the regulation must be substantively valid:** In order for a rule to limit the scope of a statutory hearing, the agency must have the statutory authority to engage in rulemaking. Otherwise, it would appear that Congress intended that regulated parties receive a hearing on all issues. Further, the rule must be substantively valid under the standards of judicial review of agency rules.

4. **The agency must allow parties to argue that the rule does not apply to the particular case:** Recognizing that the narrowing of rules is in tension with a party's statutory right to a full hearing on all issues, courts have required that agencies provide an opportunity for parties to argue that the rule does not or should not apply to the particular case. If an agency does not respond to an argument against the application of a rule, a reviewing court may remand the case to the agency for an explanation.

5. **FCC hearings:** The Communications Act has long required that applicants be given hearings on their applications for broadcast licenses. Many FCC practices, in addition to the one invalidated in *Ashbacker*, have been challenged as violating the right to a hearing on an application for a broadcast license.

   a. ***Storer*:** In *United States v. Storer Broadcasting Co.*, 351 U.S. 192 (1956), Storer's application for a broadcast license was denied without a hearing because Storer owned more than the maximum allowable number of broadcast licenses under FCC rules. Storer argued that applying the FCC rules without a hearing violated the Communications Act's provision granting applicants a hearing on their applications for broadcast licenses. The Court held that the FCC is free to deny an application when, from the application, it is apparent that the license would be denied under a substantively valid statute or regulation. Here, because it was clear that Storer could not meet the FCC's criteria for an additional license, the FCC could deny the application without holding a hearing. The Court also held that the burden was on the applicant to come forward with reasons not to apply the FCC's rules to the application.

   b. **Comparative hearings and license renewal:** Until very recently, nothing in the Communications Act indicated a preference for incumbent licensees at renewal time. Nonetheless, in a policy statement the FCC attempted to grant a preference to incumbents. The policy statement provided that, in a contest between a renewing incumbent and a new applicant for a frequency, the incumbent would receive a controlling preference if it were shown that the incumbent had rendered "substantial past performance without serious deficiencies." The D.C. Circuit, *in Citizens Communication Center v. FCC*, 447 F.2d 1201 (D.C. Cir. 1971), held this policy unlawful under *Ashbacker* because, in effect, it deprived the challenger of a meaningful hearing on the application. The holding goes beyond *Ashbacker*'s procedural focus because, in order to hold the FCC's action improper, the court necessarily disapproved of the FCC's decision to favor incumbents. If it were proper for the FCC to favor incumbents, then it would be proper to tailor the scope of the hearing to that substantive standard.

6. *Heckler v. Campbell*

a. The "grid" rule: Two principal issues govern eligibility for social security disability benefits: the applicant's medical condition and whether the applicant is employable in the national economy. Rather than relitigate the issue of what jobs exist in each disability hearing, the Social Security Administration conducted a rulemaking to gather information regarding jobs in the national economy for each level of disability and skills. A rule, in the form of a grid, was promulgated that specified whether jobs existed for each level of disability and skills. Entitlement to disability benefits is determined by quantifying the applicant's condition and skills and then plugging that information into the grid. This rule was challenged as depriving applicants of the hearing required by the Act.

b. The decision upholding the grid: In *Heckler v. Campbell*, 461 U.S. 458 (1983), the Supreme Court upheld the grid rule. The Court reasoned that whether jobs existed for each particular skill level and disability presented an issue of legislative fact that could be decided in a rulemaking. Once the rule was promulgated, the hearing could be limited to the remaining issues of the applicant's exact condition and skill level. The Court explicitly stated that this applies "even where an agency's enabling statute expressly requires it to hold a hearing." *Heckler*, 461 US. at 467. The Court also noted that the applicant was free, at the hearing, to attempt to persuade the agency that the guidelines did not fairly reflect the particular applicant's situation and thus should not be applied.

C. The irrebuttable presumption doctrine and the right to a hearing

The irrebuttable presumption doctrine held that where there was a constitutionally protected interest at stake (such as liberty or property), due process required a hearing on all issues. Thus, under the ***irrebuttable presumption*** doctrine, due process was violated when a statute precluded a hearing by deciding a central issue relevant to a claim. This doctrine was abandoned a few years after its genesis; it proved to have massive potential for striking down classifications in statutes and regulations.

1. *Bell v. Burson:* In *Bell v. Burson*, 402 U.S. 535 (1971), the Court struck down a statute that suspended the licenses of uninsured drivers involved in automobile accidents unless they posted security to cover the cost of any damages claimed against them or obtained a judicial ruling that they were not at fault in the accident. The Court held that this statute created an irrebutable presumption that the uninsured driver was at fault or would not pay any damages assessed, and the Court held that a hearing was necessary to reach such conclusions constitutionally.

2. *Stanley v. Illinois:* In *Stanley v. Illinois*, 405 U.S. 645 (1972), the Court struck down a statute that excluded unwed fathers from those parties eligible to take custody of their children upon the death of the other parent. Since married fathers and unwed mothers would be awarded custody unless their unfitness as parents were established at a hearing, the Court ruled that the statute created an unconstitutional irrebuttable presumption that unwed fathers were unfit parents.

3. ***Problems with the irrebuttable presumption doctrine:*** The irrebuttable presumption doctrine threatened the constitutionality of numerous statutory standards drawing somewhat arbitrary substantive lines. Further, the doctrine was substantive constitutional law in a procedural disguise. For example, if it was substantively valid to exclude unwed fathers from those eligible to take custody of the children of a deceased mother, there would be no colorable due process claim to a hearing on fitness.

4. ***The end of the irrebuttable presumption doctrine:*** After the Court recognized the problems with the irrebuttable presumption doctrine, the doctrine died a somewhat sudden death when the Court rejected a challenge to provision of the Social Security Act that excluded widows who were married to deceased workers for shorter than nine months from eligibility for survivors' benefits. *Weinberger v. Salfi,* 422 U.S. 749 (1975). The widow challenging the statute claimed that the nine-month rule was an invalid irrebuttable presumption that marriages lasting less than nine months were shams entered into to procure survivors' benefits. The Court held that the nine-month durational rule was a valid substantive eligibility requirement, and Congress was free to employ such a requirement as a prophylactic, easy-to-administer rule against sham marriages that might be difficult to prove. In its opinion, the Court rejected the irrebuttable presumption doctrine, holding in effect that requirements such as those rejected in Bell and Stanley should be upheld unless the statutory classification is substantively unconstitutional.

Quiz Yourself on
AGENCY ADJUDICATION AND DUE PROCESS

36. Congress decides that NHTSA regulations and state product liability law are not adequate to deal with the problem of defective automobiles contributing to accidents. Therefore, it has passed a statute creating the Automobile Defect Liability Board, an agency within the Department of Transportation. Congress has granted the board authority to adjudicate claims against automobile manufacturers for damages arising out of defective design or manufacture and violations of federal automobile safety regulations. Only a plaintiff may choose to have the case heard by the board. If the plaintiff files a claim to be heard by the board, there is no provision for transferring the case back to a state or federal court, unless the board decides that it lacks jurisdiction over the case. The statute provides that "Board orders are enforceable by application to the District Court" and "judicial review of Board orders shall be had under Chapter 7 of the APA." In its first decision, the board ruled that the seats of a particular car were defectively manufactured and that they did not meet federal safety standards. The board awarded one million dollars in damages to the plaintiff, who was injured when the car seat came loose from the floor of the car in an accident. On judicial review, the automobile manufacturer argues that the board's jurisdiction is unconstitutional. Is it? _____

37. A state statute regulating the employment of guards in a state prison provides that "Guards employed by the Department of Corrections are employees at will, and can be terminated whenever, in the sole discretion and judgment of the Director of the Department or her designate, termination will serve the best interests of the Department." Department regulations provide that "prior to terminating the employment of a Guard, the Director or her designate will, whenever possible, meet with the employee to discuss the reasons for the termination, and to offer suggestions for alternative employment opportunities." Do prison guards have a property interest in continued employment? _____

38. A state statute provides as follows:

Section 1. Teachers in public elementary schools may not be fired without cause, which means substandard performance, misconduct on the job, or illegal or immoral conduct outside the workplace.

Section 2. Whether cause for firing exists shall be determined by the principal of the school in which the teacher teaches, with any hearing or other procedure in the sole discretion of the principal.

    Is this statute consistent with due process? _____

39. A state statute provides that police officers may inflict serious bodily harm to subdue any person acting in a disorderly fashion. Mr. Smith has a reaction to a new prescription medication and begins to behave erratically while walking on a public street. The police inflict serious bodily harm while subduing him. When he brings a constitutional claim for damages, the defense argues that, given the state law, he was not deprived of a protected interest. Is this a good argument? _____

40. A new president pledges to appoint administrators who are willing to be tough and assess large fines against environmental violators. As part of the plan, the EPA (with presidential approval) adopts regulations allowing the EPA to retain 50 percent of all fines collected. The funds must be used to hire more prosecutors and administrative law judges in order to increase enforcement activity. A chemical manufacturer is prosecuted for violations of the Clean Water Act and is assessed a fine higher than any on record, but still within statutory limits. The manufacturer challenges the fairness of the procedure. What result? _____

41. The FTC regulates unfair and deceptive trade practices. The FTC Act provides that the FTC has authority, after an adjudicatory hearing on the record, to order businesses to cease and desist from an "unfair and deceptive practice." The FTC conducts a rulemaking and promulgates a rule declaring that "it is an unfair and deceptive practice to represent through advertising, labeling, or otherwise that a product contains a unit of weight, volume, or other unit of measure that has no fixed meaning." The FTC holds a cease and desist hearing over Bad Cereal Corporation's claim that its raisin bran cereal contains three scoops of raisins, since no scoop size is specified. At the hearing, the only issue is whether Bad Cereal makes the claim in its advertising or labeling. The FTC refuses to reopen the issue of whether the practice is unfair and deceptive. Bad Cereal argues that this violates its right to a hearing. What result? _____

Answers

36. Maybe. This raises a close question under Article III. The Board's jurisdiction is over a private rights dispute, in the core of traditional Article III jurisdiction. On the other hand, the public rights versus private rights divide has been reconceptualized in recent years to be more forgiving of agency

jurisdiction over private disputes that are closely related to an area of comprehensive government regulation. NHTSA regulations may be comprehensive, but the branch of the Board's jurisdiction over defective designs is pure products liability law and is traditionally a matter of state law. In favor of the statute's constitutionality is that Article III courts have concurrent jurisdiction—except that a defendant brought before the board has no choice of forum. Also, the board does not have all the attributes of a district court since its orders are not self-enforcing. The deferential standard of judicial review stands against constitutionality. There is no hard and fast answer to whether this statute is constitutional, and there are good arguments on both sides.

37. No. The statute does not create an entitlement. Further, procedures do not normally create entitlements, and here the right to procedure is qualified anyway. The only hint of a property interest is the "best interests" standard. However, that standard is vague, and the statute makes it a subjective standard of the sort not generally found to create an entitlement. Barring other promises, or a longstanding practice of termination only for cause, there is no property interest in continued employment.

38. No. Section 1 creates an entitlement, i.e., a property interest, to continued employment. A teacher may not be deprived of this interest without due process of law. Section 2 is unconstitutional because, under federal due process law, a hearing is required before the principal may fire a teacher, and the hearing must address whether the standard for cause is met. The amount of process required is determined using the *Mathews v. Eldridge* balancing test, which requires balancing the employee's interest in keeping the job and the accuracy-enhancing value of additional procedure against the government's interest in proceeding without additional procedure. In employment cases, that balance ordinarily requires a hearing in advance of firing. Insofar as section 2 purports to require less than constitutionally adequate procedures, that section is unconstitutional. The argument that claimants should have to take the "bitter" of section 2 with the "sweet" of section 1 was rejected by a majority of the Court in *Arnett v. Kennedy*.

39. No. Not all protected interests are determined using entitlement theory. Some such interests are created by the Constitution itself, including the liberty or Fourth Amendment limitations on the use of force in arrests. Thus, Mr. Smith's constitutional rights may have been violated even though state law does not create an entitlement to be free from excessive force.

40. Based on these facts, it is unlikely that a court would find any procedural problem. There is no allegation that the administrative law judge had any personal pecuniary interest in the outcome of the case, and it is unlikely that the fines collected contribute a high percentage of the EPA's budget. If the ALJ's continued employment depended on large fines, then perhaps a bias claim would succeed. There is also no indication that the ALJ is under explicit pressure to rule against violators or impose large fines, although implicit pressure may be problematic. There is also no direct evidence of prejudgment, and unless the ALJ had made a statement regarding the particular case, it is unlikely that a prejudgment claim would be sustained.

41. As long as the FTC has rulemaking authority, and the rule is not ruled arbitrary and capricious on judicial review, the rule may serve to limit the issues at the hearing. Thus, Bad Cereal's objection should be rejected. However, Bad Cereal must be allowed the opportunity to establish that the rule should be waived (for example, by bringing forward evidence that all advertisements and labels show the actual size of the scoops) or that everyone knows that the claim is meaningless. These arguments are likely to fail.

Exam Tips on
AGENCY ADJUDICATION AND DUE PROCESS

☛ In any problem regarding the constitutionality of administrative adjudication, watch for the private rights issue.

   ☞ Pay attention to whether the right being adjudicated is within the core of Article III or whether it is arguable that the adjudication at issue is in a category normally thought to be appropriate for a non-Article III tribunal.

   ☞ It also may be helpful to contrast Justice Brennan's categorical approach with the majority's approach under which a much looser separation of powers standard applies.

☛ In due process cases, it is important to address first whether there is a protected interest, usually either property or liberty.

   ☞ If the question involves property, clearly identify the source of any protected entitlement. Be creative and go beyond the bare words of state law when there is an argument for an implicit interest under *Perry v. Sindermann.*

   ☞ In liberty cases, distinguish between "entitlement liberty" and "constitutional liberty."

   ☞ In a constitutional liberty case, identify the nature of the protected liberty interest.

   ☞ In an entitlement liberty case, identify the source and nature of the protected liberty interest.

☛ When deciding what process is due, analyze each element of the *Mathews v. Eldridge* test separately.

   ☞ When applying the third element, look for indications that less procedure is desirable for reasons other than the state's pure desire to save time and resources on procedure, e.g., perhaps because an emergency necessitates quick action.

   ☞ In employment cases, note that the Supreme Court has decided categorically that due process requires at least an informal pre-termination oral hearing.

   ☞ In other areas, note that the Court has allowed for paper procedures pretermination except when subsistence benefits are concerned, as in *Goldberg v. Kelly.*

   ☞ Be sure to note that in most situations when a pretermination oral hearing is not required, such a hearing must be provided posttermination.

☛ Be clear about the difference between bias and prejudgment, and discuss explicitly the facts that lead to an argument that one or the other is present.

☛ In cases involving the statutory right to a hearing, identify the source of the right to a hearing. Look explicitly into whether statutes or regulations limit the scope of the hearing.

☞ If there is a due process issue regarding a substantive limitation on the scope of a hearing, the irrebuttable presumption doctrine may be relevant in reinforcing the general rule that the scope of the hearing is tailored to the substantive issues as specified in the statute and regulations. However, it is important to note that the irrebuttable presumption doctrine is no longer good law.

CHAPTER 8

SUBSTANTIVE POLICYMAKING IN AGENCIES

ChapterScope ─────────────────────────────────

This chapter focuses on agency policymaking and explores various important issues concerning the considerations agencies should take into account when making policy decisions. This material should be considered in conjunction with the material on standards of judicial review. The chapter's main points are:

- Agencies should engage in *reasoned decisionmaking*, applying their *expertise* and taking into account only those considerations made *statutorily relevant*.

- *Cost-benefit analysis* has been indentified as a useful tool to improve agency policymaking and reduce the potential for arbitrary agency action.

  - Cost-benefit analysis also has its weaknesses, and courts have not required agencies to apply cost-benefit analysis unless the agency's statute clearly requires it.

- Impact statements are another popular device for improving agency policymaking.

  - The most common type of impact statement is the *environmental impact statement*, but agencies can be required to prepare statements on a wide variety of economic, social, and governmental impacts of their actions.

  - Impact statements require agencies to focus on the *effects of their actions and provide information* that can be used in the political process to influence agency action.

- The *National Environmental Policy Act (NEPA)* requires the preparation of an *environmental impact statement (EIS)* regarding all major federal actions with significant environmental effects.

  - NEPA does not explicitly impose upon agencies any duty beyond preparation of the EIS, and the Supreme Court has held that an agency meets its obligation under NEPA by preparing an adequate EIS and considering it during the decisionmaking process.

  - NEPA does not contain any substantive provision that would require an agency to abandon a project due to excessive environmental costs, but the EIS does provide ammunition in the political process to those opposing agency action on environmental grounds.

- Courts have imposed requirements of *consistency and clarity* on administrative agencies.

  - The clarity requirement holds that agencies may act in some circumstances only under *relatively clear rules*.

  - Related to this requirement is the principle that on judicial review, agency action is evaluated based only on those factors actually relied upon by the agency.

  - The consistency requirement holds that *agencies must treat like cases alike* unless the agency states a new rule and explains the change.

  - A related doctrine holds that *agencies must follow their own rules*, except that courts may not enforce internal agency rules that are not intended to benefit the public.

■ ***Agencies are not estopped*** by the conduct or statements of agency officials.

   ■ If an official gives erroneous advice, the agency may still insist on adherence to the correct rule.

   ■ The rule against estoppel is strongest when the expenditure of federal funds are involved because the Supreme Court has stated that courts have no constitutional power to order the federal government to spend money except as specified by Congress in appropriations legislation.

■ While the federal government may be precluded from relitigating an issue already decided between the government and the same party, ***nonmutual collateral estoppel does not apply against the federal government***. Thus, the federal government remains free to relitigate an issue that it has lost on against a different party.

■ ***Agencies sometimes refuse to acquiesce in court*** decisions that are contrary to the agency's position on a matter.

   ■ Intercircuit nonacquiescence, in which an agency applies its own rule except in the circuit in which its rule has been rejected, is justified by the system of regional courts of appeals under which splits in the circuits are resolved by the Supreme Court.

   ■ Intracircuit nonacquiescence, in which an agency adheres to its rule even in the circuit that rejected the agency's view, is probably unjustifiable and contrary to the rule of law.

I. PERMISSIBLE CONSIDERATIONS IN AGENCY POLICYMAKING

The agency's organic statue, and other generally applicable statutes such as NEPA, determine the range of factors that an agency may take into account in policymaking. Agencies are required to consider the factors made relevant by statute and should not consider extraneous matters not statutorily relevant.

A. Agency policymaking should be the product of agency expertise

Agencies should make policy by applying their expertise to the factors made statutorily relevant. Formally, agencies are required to engage in reasoned decisionmaking and to justify their decisions based upon consideration of the legally relevant factors—not based on the usual give and take among affected interest groups. However, the realities of the political process make it unrealistic to assume that agencies avoid influence from affected interests.

B. Agencies should not consider irrelevant factors

Agencies should not take into account irrelevant factors, i.e., factors that are not within the considerations made relevant by statute or valid regulation. For example, the D.C. Circuit reversed the Secretary of Transportation's decision to build a bridge, in part, because the Secretary apparently was influenced by a congressman's threat to withhold funding for another project if the Secretary did not approve the bridge. *See D.C. Federation of Civic Associations v. Volpe*, 459 F.2d 1231 (D.C. Cir. 1971), *cert. denied*, 405 U.S. 1030 (1972).

II. COST-BENEFIT ANALYSIS

Cost-benefit analysis, under which a policy is evaluated for whether its benefits are greater than its costs, is a powerful tool for evaluating a proposed policy. It has been argued that agencies should be required to conduct cost-benefit analyses regarding their major policy decisions and should not adopt a policy unless the benefits outweigh the costs.

A. Presidential directives to apply cost-benefit analysis

Presidents since Ronald Reagan have, by executive order, required agencies to conduct cost-benefit analyses of their major regulations. The executive orders have given the OMB the authority to review the cost-benefit analysis and reject it if it is not adequate.

B. Statutory cost-benefit requirements

Some organic statutes require agencies to conduct cost-benefit analysis in making regulations. However, the courts have not read more general standards, such as "reasonably necessary or appropriate," as requiring cost-benefit analysis. Rather, cost-benefit analysis is required only when the statute clearly requires it. However, an agency may decide on its own to use cost-benefit analysis unless something in its statute precludes it.

Example: The OSH Act, §3(8), defines an "occupational safety and health standard" as a standard that is ***reasonably necessary or appropriate*** for the health and safety of workers. The Act also provides (in §6(b)(5)) that with regard to toxic substances and harmful physical agents, OSHA should regulate at the level that assures, "to the extent feasible," that no employee will be materially injured by the substance or agent even with regular exposure. After OSHA promulgated standards regulating exposure to cotton dust, the textile industry argued that the agency should have conducted a cost-benefit analysis, under which it would have concluded that the costs of the new standard outweighed its benefits. The Court disagreed, holding that the statute's use of the word "feasible" precluded a cost-benefit analysis requirement and that reading the "reasonably necessary and appropriate" language to require cost-benefit analysis would eviscerate the statute's requirement of regulation to the extent "feasible." The Court also pointed out that other statutes explicitly require cost-benefit analysis: for example, by providing that an agency should act "if the benefits to whomsoever they may accrue are in excess of the estimated costs" or that an agency should not act when "the incremental benefits are clearly insufficient to justify the incremental costs." *See American Textile Manufacturers Institute v. Donovan*, 452 U.S. 490, 510 (1981). This means that general standards like "reasonably necessary" are not likely to be read to require cost-benefit analysis. *See* id. at 512.

C. Reasons favoring cost-benefit analysis

In certain respects, agency decisionmaking might improve under cost-benefit analysis. Cost-benefit analysis would force agencies to consider the **consequences** of their policies in a concrete, rigorous, and material way. It would provide a clear basis for **comparison** with other potential policies. Further, a cost-benefit analysis requirement would limit the potential for arbitrary agency action by specifying, in advance, a set of relevant considerations. Finally, cost-benefit analysis may reveal (in some cases) that when all the costs and benefits are taken into account, the purported beneficiaries of regulation actually stand to lose.

D. Reasons against cost-benefit analysis

Rather than provide increased rigor and certainty, cost-benefit analysis may actually increase the potential for arbitrary agency action by providing a **false veneer** of scientific analysis that hides contestable value choices by the agency.

1. **Valuation problems:** Some costs and benefits are difficult to quantify. For example, it is difficult to place a monetary value on the cost of an illness or the benefit of avoiding an illness. More dramatically, it is even more difficult to place a monetary value on a life lost or saved. In fact, different federal agencies place significantly different valuations on the lives saved or lost under their regulatory programs.

2. **Nonquantifiable factors may be left out:** The difficulty in placing a monetary value on some costs and benefits may lead to leaving them out of a cost-benefit analysis, or it may lead to valuing only those elements of an effect that are easily quantifiable. For example, if the value of a human life is measured only by the wages the person would have earned, other factors such as the emotional and educational effects on the family are not taken into account.

3. **Some programs may be desirable even if the costs outweigh the benefits:** Finally, there may be regulatory programs that are desirable even if the costs outweigh the benefits. Social considerations may favor regulation that does not make economic sense. Thus, courts require cost-benefit analysis only when Congress clearly indicates such a requirement.

III. IMPACT STATEMENTS

A common method for controlling or channeling the exercise of administrative discretion is to require the agency to prepare an impact statement that contains a detailed discussion of the likely effects of the proposed regulation, either comprehensively or focused on a particular type of impact. Impact statements improve decisionmaking by forcing agencies to focus on the effects of their actions and by providing an opportunity for opponents of the agency's plan to put pressure on the agency to change or abandon its plan due to undesirable external effects.

A. Regulatory impact statements

There have been proposals to require agencies, as part of all major regulatory initiatives, to prepare detailed *regulatory impact statements* that would comprehensively address the impact of the proposed regulatory initiative. The impact statement may concern economic effects, social effects, effects on other government programs or institutions, and/or environmental effects. While the idea has merit, several problems with this idea have been identified.

1. **Agencies would be overburdened:** Requiring agencies to prepare detailed, comprehensive regulatory impact statements on every major initiative would add significantly to the substantial legal, political, and technical burdens agencies already face in formulating and implementing policy.

2. **Agencies would be open to attack for inadequate impact statements:** In addition to the time and expense of preparing impact statements, challenges to the adequacy of the statements would place yet another weapon in the hands of parties resisting regulation. This would seriously frustrate agencies' abilities to regulate effectively.

3. **The resources devoted to impact statements would often be wasted:** Because agencies tackle a wide variety of problems and create a wide variety of effects, it would be impossible

to create an impact statement requirement that would not result in a significant amount of waste, as agencies are forced to justify their regulations against imaginary challenges that are unlikely to arise. Based on this concern, it may be better for Congress to specify to each particular agency what factors they should consider rather than attempt to create a global impact statement requirement.

B. Environmental impact statements under NEPA

NEPA requires federal agencies to prepare an EIS regarding "major Federal actions significantly affecting the quality of the human environment" and states that the EIS, "and the comments and views of the appropriate Federal, State and Local [environmental agencies] shall . . . *accompany* the proposal through the existing agency review processes." 42 U.S.C. §4332(C).

1. **Major federal action:** Major federal action includes all significant federal activity, including federal funding of actions carried out by other entities.

2. **"Significantly affecting the quality of the human environment":** NEPA requires consideration of actual and potential effects on the physical environment, such as pollution of air and water.

   a. **Nontraditional environmental effects:** In addition to traditional environmental effects such as air and water pollution, NEPA covers a broad range of effects on the human environment—such as the displacement of social institutions—that a proposed major federal action may have on a community. *See Strycker's Bay Neighborhood Council v. Karlen*, 444 U.S. 223 (1980) (considering the effect that a large concentration of federally funded low-income housing may have on the "social fabric and community structures").

   b. **Nonphysical effects not considered:** Only actual effects on the physical environment must be considered in the EIS. Fear, even psychological harm, generated by a potential effect of a federal action need not be considered. *See Metropolitan Edison Co. v. PANE*, 460 U.S. 766 (1983) (Nuclear Regulatory Commission need not consider psychological damage caused by the fear of a nuclear accident; NRC did consider the risk of physical harm resulting from a nuclear accident).

3. **Within the control of the agency:** Agencies are required to prepare an EIS only when the matter is within the control of the agency. If an environmental effect would occur due to the action of someone else that the agency has no power to control, the agency need not address that effect in an EIS. *See Department of Transportation v. Public Citizen,* 541 U.S. 752 (2004) (agency not required to prepare EIS on the effects of Mexican trucks on the U.S. environment because President, not agency, had power to determine whether Mexican trucks should be allowed to enter U.S.).

4. **Alternatives to the proposed action:** NEPA requires that agencies, in the EIS, consider "alternatives to the proposed action." 42 U.S.C. §4332(C)(iii). The range of alternatives that the EIS must consider is limited to those that are known and feasible at the time that the EIS is prepared. An agency is not required to consider an alternative that is not "reasonably available" at the time the EIS is prepared, and a party raising a novel alternative must provide the agency with sufficient information to allow the agency to evaluate their submissions intelligently. *See Vermont Yankee Nuclear Power Corp. v. NRDC, Inc.*, 435 U.S. 519 (1978) (agency was not required to include "energy conservation" in EIS as alternative to

nuclear power plant because at the time the EIS was prepared energy conservation was not a known, feasible alternative).

5. **NEPA is essentially procedural:** NEPA signifies Congress's adoption of environmental protection as a national goal but contains very little in the way of operative substantive provisions. *See* 42 U.S.C. §4331. The primary requirement of NEPA is the preparation of the EIS. While NEPA does provide that agencies should, to the fullest extent possible, act in accordance with the policies espoused in NEPA, this provision is too general to have any significant substantive effect.

   a. **"Shall accompany":** NEPA provides that the EIS "shall accompany the proposal through the existing agency review processes." 42 U.S.C. §4332(C). This means that the EIS must be part of the record during agency consideration of its action.

   b. **Consideration of the EIS:** Because NEPA does not state explicitly how the agency must consider the EIS or that an agency must abandon a project if the environmental costs are too high, the Supreme Court has stated, with regard to NEPA, that "the only role for a court is to insure that the agency has considered the environmental consequences." *Strycker's Bay Neighborhood Council v. Karlen*, 444 U.S. 223, 227 (1980).

   c. **The value of a procedural NEPA:** While environmentalists might prefer a statute with greater substantive bite, a purely procedural NEPA has value. First, it requires agencies to focus on the environmental impacts of their actions. Second, it results in the expenditure of federal funds on investigating environmental effects that environmental interest groups might not be able to afford to examine. Third, and most important, NEPA creates a vehicle for political activity regarding environmental issues and provides information to fuel the debate.

C. Unfunded mandates

Whenever a federal regulation would impose at least one hundred million dollars of unfunded costs on local governments, the Unfunded Mandate Reform Act of 1995 requires the proposing federal agency to prepare a statement detailing the magnitude and distribution of the regulation's effects on local governments. The Act also requires federal agencies to consider alternatives that would impose less in the way of *unfunded mandates* and to explain why the less burdensome alternatives were not chosen. The Act also contains provisions for alerting members of Congress and the public when a bill in Congress would create an unfunded mandate.

IV. CONSISTENCY AND CLARITY REQUIREMENTS

Courts have, on judicial review, imposed obligations of clarity and consistency upon agencies. Briefly stated, agencies are sometimes required to operate under clearly stated substantive criteria, and they are sometimes required to treat like cases alike unless they explicitly disavow the substantive rule governing prior decisions. These requirements are closely related to APA standards of judicial review and should be understood in conjunction with them.

A. Clarity

Courts have held that certain agency action may be taken only pursuant to clear criteria. This is termed the "clarity" requirement. The clarity cases are in tension with decisions allowing agencies a great deal of discretion under the APA over whether to promulgate rules or decide issues on a case-by-case basis. Three reasons support the clarity requirements: notice to the party of the standards for government action, prevention of arbitrary agency action, and facilitation of review of agency action (both at higher agency levels and in the courts).

1. **Constitutional clarity requirements:** The clarity requirement arises mainly in cases challenging state agency action as inconsistent with federal due process requirements. In light of recent developments in due process norms, including the *Roth* line of cases defining property interests (see Chapter 7), it is unclear whether courts would adhere to these decisions today. It is also unclear whether the APA imposes a similar, nonconstitutional requirement on federal agencies. The following cases are examples of situations in which clarity requirements have been invoked.

   a. **University discipline:** In *Soglin v. Kauffman*, 418 F.2d 163 (7th Cir. 1969), the court held that the use of "misconduct" as the standard for imposing expulsion or prolonged suspension on university students violated the Fourteenth Amendment as too vague.

   b. **Liquor licenses:** In *Hornsby v. Allen*, 326 F.2d 605 (5th Cir. 1964), the court held that the denial of a liquor license to a qualified applicant by the board of aldermen and mayor violated the Fourteenth Amendment, if the aldermen and mayor had not established ascertainable standards governing their decisions.

   c. **Public housing:** In *Holmes v. New York City Housing Authority*, 398 F.2d 262 (2d Cir. 1968), the court held that the agency selecting families for public housing must operate under ascertainable standards, and where many more applicants are equally qualified for the housing available, the agency must adopt a procedure for choosing which applications to grant.

   d. **Immigration status:** In *Fook Hong Mak v. INS*, 435 F.2d 728 (2d Cir. 1970), the court held that the INS was entitled to deny an application for discretionary review of an alien's immigration status on the basis of a rule against aliens in the petitioner's category who applied for discretionary adjustment. Nevertheless, in *Asimokopoulos v. INS*, 445 F.2d 1362 (9th Cir. 1971), the court held that because the governing statute granted the INS "discretion" in deciding whether to adjust an alien's status, the agency could not deny an application based on its own rule limiting discretion. In essence, this latter ruling favors less clarity because it requires the agency to exercise discretion and not rely upon a rule.

2. **Agency decisions are judged on the reasons stated by the agency:** Related to the clarity requirement is the well-established doctrine that agency decisions are evaluated, on judicial review, based on the reasons given by the agency at the time the decision was made. An agency may not, on judicial review, defend its decision on a basis that was not relied upon by the agency at the time it made the decision. However, if the court remands a matter to the agency because its explanation is inadequate, the agency may adhere to its original decision if it constructs an acceptable explanation.

   Example: The Chenery family managed and owned shares in the Federal Water Service Corporation. The corporation was in a reorganization under which holders of preferred stock would ultimately control the corporation. During the reorganization process, the Chenerys purchased a large block of preferred stock on the open market. The Securities and Exchange Commission (SEC) conditioned its approval of the reorganization on the Chenerys' selling their stock back to the corporation. The SEC relied solely upon traditional equity rules governing fiduciary relationships for its finding that the purchase of the preferred stock while the reorganization was pending was improper. On judicial review, the SEC defended its action with traditional equity principles and with arguments based on the policies underlying the securities laws and its expertise in applying those laws. In *SEC v. Chenery Corp.(I)*, 318 U.S. 80 (1943), the Supreme Court held that traditional equity rules did not provide an adequate basis for the SEC's order, and that the SEC could not rely upon its additional securities law justifications because they were not part of the SEC's contemporaneous explanation for its action. On remand to the agency, the SEC reaffirmed its decision but explained itself based upon its expertise in applying the policies underlying the securities law. This time, the Supreme Court upheld the SEC indicating that the SEC "has made what we indicated in our prior opinion would be an informed, expert judgment on the problem." *SEC v. Chenery Corp. (II)*, 332 U.S. 194 (1947). The Court noted that the lack of a preannounced SEC rule against what the Chenerys did was not fatal to the agency proceeding on a case-by-case basis, even if the agency's action had some retroactive effect.

B. Consistency

Agencies are required to be consistent—to treat like cases alike. Agencies must offer an explanation when they treat (apparently) like cases differently. Further, an agency may change its policy. However, the new policy must be within the agency's statutory authority, and the agency must explain the change.

Example: An employer commits an unfair labor practice by threatening reprisals if employees vote to unionize. In a series of cases, the NLRB held that, in the absence of additional factors, such a threat did not inhere in a statement that the employer would "bargain from scratch" with a union (i.e., that the employer would not take into account the current level of wages and benefits but would take the position that all issues were open to negotiation). A management employee of Shaw's Supermarkets told employees, during a representation campaign, that if the employees decided to unionize, Shaw's would start the bargaining with minimum wage and worker's compensation and build from there. At the time, the employees were earning substantially more than the minimum wage. After the employees voted against unionization, the NLRB decided that the statements constituted unfair labor practices as threats of reprisals. The court of appeals refused to enforce the NLRB's order, holding that the NLRB's decision was inconsistent with the NLRB's own precedent. The court noted that if the NLRB wishes to change its rule, it must "focus upon the issue and explain[] why change is reasonable." *Shaw's Supermarkets, Inc. v. NLRB*, 884 F.2d 34,41 (1st Cir. 1989) (Breyer, J.). *See also Brennan v. Gilles & Cotting, Inc.*, 504 F.2d 1255 (4th Cir. 1974) (agencies "must explain departures from agency policies or rules apparently dispositive of a case").

C. Agencies must follow their own rules

Agencies are required to follow their own rules, whether those rules have been adopted in a rulemaking proceeding or announced in the course of agency adjudication. If an agency wishes to change a rule, it must do so in a procedurally valid fashion and must explain the basis for the change.

1. **Rules promulgated formally may be changed in a subsequent rulemaking:** If an agency adopts a rule in a rulemaking or an adjudication, the agency may change that rule in a

subsequent proceeding. The new rule will be reviewed to determine whether it is within the agency's statutory authority and whether the record provides adequate support for it.

a. **Rules formally adopted may not be informally abrogated:** An agency may not informally adopt a policy that contradicts the terms of a formally adopted rule. *See National Family Planning and Reproductive Health Association, Inc. v. Sullivan*, 979 F.2d 227 (D.C. Cir. 1992).

b. **Retroactive changes are disfavored:** Retroactive changes in agency rules are disfavored, especially when the change has material retroactive effects on the regulated party.

   Examples: In *Arizona Grocery Co. v. Atchison, Topeka & Santa Fe Rwy.*, 284 U.S. 370 (1932), the Court held that the ICC could not order a railroad to make refunds to shippers on the ground that the railroad's shipping rates were unreasonable after the ICC had itself established that the very rates at issue were reasonable in a previous proceeding. The Court held that the rates could be changed prospectively but that retroactive reductions were impermissible. In *Bowen v. Georgetown University Hospital*, 488 U.S. 204 (1988), the Court held that the Department of Health and Human Services (HHS) could not retroactively recalculate Medicare reimbursements due to hospitals for 1981 and 1982 based on a regulation promulgated in 1984. The Court held that the Medicare Act did not allow retroactive rulemaking and that such rulemaking would be presumed unlawful absent a specific provision allowing retroactive rules. These cases illustrate that the Court looks upon retroactive agency action that has substantial monetary effects with suspicion because it upsets settled expectations and entails a great potential for arbitrariness.

2. **Agencies must apply their rules as written:** When an agency announces a rule in an adjudicatory process, *it must apply the rule as written*. An agency may not modify a rule sub silentio, in the style of a common-law court, by deciding cases in a manner that is inconsistent with the rule as announced and then defending its decisions on the basis of a practice inconsistent with the written rule. *See Allentown Mack Sales and Service, Inc. v. NLRB*, 522 U.S. 359 (1998).

3. **Agencies should follow their own procedural rules:** It is a general principle of administrative law that agencies should follow their own procedural rules, even when these rules go beyond the rights afforded by any statute or due process. *See United States ex rel. Accardi v. Shaughnessy*, 347 U.S. 260 (1954). Accardi filed for habeas corpus after the Board of Immigration Appeals denied his appeal from the denial of his application for discretionary relief from deportation. He alleged that the Attorney General had, in effect, ordered the Board to deny his appeal before the board heard his case, an alleged violation of regulations that the majority characterized as requiring the Board "to exercise its own judgment when considering appeals." *See also Ballard v. Commissioner of Internal Revenue*, 125 S. Ct. 1270 (2005) (tax court required to disclose recommendation of special trial judges because court's own rules require disclosure).

4. **Agencies may not be required to follow informally promulgated internal rules:** The Supreme Court has stated that an agency's *failure to follow its own informally promulgated rule* might not prejudice the agency's ability to deny relief to the member of the public affected by the violation. *See Schweiker v. Hansen*, 450 U.S. 785 (1981) (retroactive benefits denied to applicant who was erroneously told by social security official that applicant need not file an

immediate application because benefits would be retroactive regardless of when application was filed; agency manual required officials to encourage uncertain applicants to file immediately).

D. Estoppel and administrative agencies

Agencies are normally not estopped by the conduct or statements of agency officials. In some circumstances, principles of collateral estoppel may apply to agencies in judicial proceedings, but nonmutual collateral estoppel normally does not apply to agencies.

1. **Erroneous advice does not estop an agency:** Erroneous advice given by an agency official (for example, by misstating the eligibility requirements for a government program) does not estop an agency from relying upon the program's actual requirements and denying claims based upon the erroneous advice. The reasons relied upon for the lack of estoppel against the government are that government funds should not be spent except as specified by Congress, and the errors of low-level officials should not be allowed to establish government policy.

   Example: In *Federal Crop Insurance Corp. v. Merrill*, 332 U.S. 380 (1947), a local government official, acting on behalf of the Federal Crop Insurance Corporation, told farmers that their reseeded wheat was insurable against crop failure. The farmers paid the premium. After the crop failed, their claim was denied because it turned out that reseeded wheat was not insurable. The Court held that the erroneous statement of the local government official did not estop the government from denying that the crop was insurable.

   a. **The rule against estoppel is strongest when federal government funds are involved:** The rule against government estoppel is strongest when an expenditure of funds is involved because of the constitutional principle that funds should be spent only as specified by Congress acting under the Appropriations Clause. The Court has stated categorically that *principles of estoppel cannot override the limitations placed by Congress on the expenditure of government funds*. See *Office of Personnel Management v. Richmond*, 496 U.S. 414 (1990) (Court cannot order government to pay pension to claimant who was given outdated information by his former government employer on how much outside income he could earn without losing pension benefits). *See also Schweiker v. Hansen* (government not estopped by failure of official to advise eligible benefits applicant to file written application).

   b. **Estoppel may exist in extreme circumstances when government funds are not involved:** In *Moser v. United States*, 341 U.S. 41 (1951), the Court held that an alien who had applied for an exemption from the draft could become a United States citizen despite a statute forbidding persons who had sought draft exemption from becoming citizens. The alien, a Swiss citizen, had been told by the Swiss legation that he could become a United States citizen despite the draft exemption. The Court held that because of this misinformation, the alien had not waived his right to citizenship. While this decision set off a storm of pro-estoppel decisions in lower courts, the Supreme Court has more recently been skeptical of estoppel claims. The Court stated in *Richmond* that if estoppel exists against the government in a nonmonetary claim, it would be only in "extreme circumstances."

2. **Collateral estoppel against the government:** Collateral estoppel, which bars relitigation of a legal or factual issue, may apply against the government—but only if it is mutual, i.e., involves litigation between the same parties.

a. **Mutual collateral estoppel:** Mutual collateral estoppel bars a party from relitigating a point against the very same party in a subsequent proceeding. Mutual collateral estoppel applies against the United States. For example, in *United States v. Stauffer Chemical Co.*, 464 U.S. 165 (1984), the Court held that once a lower federal court held that the EPA could not require Stauffer to open its premises to private inspectors, and the EPA chose not to appeal that decision, collateral estoppel barred the EPA from relitigating the issue against Stauffer in a different federal court.

b. **Nonmutual collateral estoppel:** Nonmutual collateral estoppel bars a party in a subsequent adjudication from relitigating a point that it lost on in a prior adjudication against a different party. Nonmutual collateral estoppel does not apply against the government. *United States v. Mendoza*, 464 U.S. 154 (1984).

Example: A federal district court ruled in 1975 that the United States government had violated the due process rights of Filipinos in its administration of a program allowing noncitizen members of the United States Armed Forces during World War II to apply for citizenship. The United States did not appeal that decision but attempted to relitigate it against Mendoza—who was not one of the plaintiffs in the 1975 case and who applied for citizenship only after the 1975 decision. In *United States v. Mendoza*, 464 U.S. 154 (1984), the Supreme Court held that nonmutual collateral estoppel did not apply against the United States, and thus the government was free to relitigate the issue of whether the administration of the program had violated due process against an applicant who was not one of the 1975 plaintiffs. The Court concluded that nonmutual collateral estoppel would hinder the ability of the government to take numerous factors into account in deciding whether to appeal a particular ruling because nonmutual estoppel would freeze all adverse rulings into law.

3. **Nonacquiescence:** When a lower federal court rejects an agency's position on a legal issue, such as the proper interpretation of a statute or the proper procedures the agency must apply in its decisionmaking process, the agency may decide not to acquiesce in the court's decision and to continue to press its view in other courts. Nonacquiescence is possible because of the inapplicability of nonmutual collateral estoppel. Questions have been raised, however, concerning the propriety of this agency practice.

a. **Intercircuit nonacquiescence:** Intercircuit nonacquiescence, in which an agency refuses to follow a court of appeals decision from another circuit, is justifiable on the ground that the courts of appeals often disagree with each other, and the agency should remain free to press its view in other circuits. Only the Supreme Court can authoritatively resolve a split among the circuits.

b. **Intracircuit nonacquiescence:** Intracircuit nonacquiescence, in which an agency refuses to follow a decision of the court of appeals even within the circuit that rendered the decision, is difficult to defend. In cases of intracircuit nonacquiescence, the agency knows that if a party seeks judicial review of the agency's decision that is contrary to the circuit's prior decision, the party will prevail. The agency's view will prevail only when the party elects not to seek judicial review, which may result from the expense of a court action or ignorance regarding review. The dominant view seems to be that an agency should follow the decisions of the courts of appeals in the circuit within which the decision was rendered.

Example: The Court of Appeals for the Second Circuit had a well-established rule regarding evidentiary standards in social security disability cases that it developed in the course of judicial review of agency benefits denials. The Social Security Administration (SSA) took a different view, which tended to lead to more denials than the Second Circuit's standard. The SSA refused to acquiesce in the Second Circuit's decision. Thus, the agency would determine claims for benefits under its evidentiary rules. If a claim was denied and the party sought judicial review, the SSA would hold a new hearing and use the circuit's evidentiary standard. If the claimant failed to seek judicial review, the denial would stand. The SSA's practice was condemned as illegitimate and a threat to the rule of law (under which agencies should follow the decisions of courts on legal matters within judicial cognizance). *See Stieberger v. Heckler*, 615 F. Supp. 1315 (S.D.N.Y. 1985), *vacated and remanded*, 801 F.2d 29 (2d Cir. 1980). The Second Circuit vacated *Stieberger* because, in another case, it had issued an injunction requiring the SSA to follow circuit precedent. *See Schisler v. Heckler*, 787 F.2d 76 (2d Cir. 1986).

Quiz Yourself on
SUBSTANTIVE POLICYMAKING IN AGENCIES

42. An agency is required to make all regulations "reasonably necessary to accomplish the goal of safety in federally subsidized public housing." After a widely publicized fire in a housing project that killed several people in apartments where the smoke detector batteries had been removed, the agency proposes a regulation requiring that all such housing contain central, hard-wired fire alarm systems. An interest group of owners of subsidized housing presents a study in the comment period, showing that the requirement's costs would be substantially greater than the benefits in terms of total losses from fires. Is this study grounds for a court rejecting the agency's requirement on judicial review? _____

43. An agency proposes to locate a large office building in the midst of a residential neighborhood. The residents are concerned about traffic and other changes in the character of the neighborhood that the office building would cause—including the fact that the government would take several neighborhood stores and a church by eminent domain to make room for the project. Must the agency address these matters in its EIS concerning the project? _____

44. Assume that the government includes the information discussed above in its EIS, and the agency decides to go ahead with the building. In its explanation of the decision; the agency acknowledges the substantial effects on the community but decides that, overall, the benefits justify incurring those costs. The agency also rejects proposals to reduce the size of the building on the ground that it would be less convenient for the agency to have offices in two different places. Do these facts present grounds for a court rejecting the project under NEPA? _____

45. A statute grants the President the power to order the Army Corps of Engineers to make emergency repairs to dams and levees after a disaster. Must the Corps address the environmental effects of the emergency repairs in an Environmental Impact Statement? _____

46. An agency denies an application for welfare benefits on the ground that the applicant earns too much money to qualify. The applicant seeks judicial review, and in his petition he establishes conclusively that the agency erred in calculating his income. The agency responds by pointing out that, under agency regulations, the applicant was ineligible because he had filed prior false applications with the agency. What result? _____

47. Assume that on remand of the above application for benefits, the agency denies the benefits on the ground that the applicant had previously filed false applications. The applicant shows on judicial review that in many prior cases, the agency had granted benefits to people who had previously filed false applications. Is this a reason for reversing the agency? _____

48. A benefits recipient is told by an agency official that his benefits will continue unless he earns more than eight thousand dollars in a year. He earns seven thousand dollars in a year. The agency, relying upon valid statutory standards, terminates his benefits and informs him of the statutory one-year waiting period for reapplying. Is the erroneous advice he received any reason to invalidate the agency's action? _____

Answers

42. No. The agency is not required, by general "reasonableness" language, to regulate only when justified by cost-benefit analysis. Cost-benefit analysis would be required only if the statute clearly required it (for example, by stating that the agency "may impose a requirement only when the benefits achieved by the requirement are greater than the costs of imposing the requirement"). However, under accepted principles, the agency may be required to explain why it chooses to impose the requirement when costs may outweigh benefits and the agency may, if it chooses, reject the requirement on the grounds that it is not cost-effective.

43. Yes. These are actual effects on the human environment that must be addressed in an EIS. The disruption of the social structure of the neighborhood is the sort of impact that must be addressed in the EIS.

44. No. NEPA does not impose a substantive requirement that agencies minimize the environmental effects of their actions. To comply with NEPA, agencies must prepare an adequate EIS and consider the environmental effects in making their decisions. Here, the agency appears to have considered the environmental effects of its proposal. Even though agency convenience may appear to be a rather weak reason to incur substantial environmental damage, the agency has met its NEPA obligations.

45. No, because the matter is in the control of the President, not the agency. An agency is not required to address environmental effects of actions over which it has no control.

46. The court should remand the matter to the agency because in general, on judicial review, the agency may defend its decision only on the grounds relied upon in its initial denial.

47. Yes. The agency may have an obligation to treat like cases alike. If the current case is different from prior cases, or if the agency has decided to change its policy, it must explain either the differences or the reasons for the change.

48. No. Agencies are not estopped by the representations of their officials, especially when the result of estoppel would be to pay money from the treasury in violation of the restrictions placed on such payments by Congress.

Exam Tips on
SUBSTANTIVE POLICYMAKING IN AGENCIES

☞ The material in this chapter can be used to supplement exam discussion of substantive standards on judicial review.

  ☞ For example, on questions regarding substantive standards of review, discussion of reasoned decisionmaking and clarity and consistency requirements could supplement discussion of APA §706's arbitrary and capricious or substantial evidence standards of review.

☞ In questions raising issues regarding cost-benefit analysis, the starting point should be the agency's statute—does it clearly require cost-benefit analysis? If not, then cost-benefit analysis is probably not required.

  ☞ A discussion of the strengths and weaknesses of cost-benefit analysis could supplement an answer raising cost-benefit issues.

☞ If an exam has a question in which an agency conducts a cost-benefit analysis, it might be useful to look at the agency's statute to determine whether the agency is allowed to do cost-benefit analysis or whether a statutory provision precludes it.

☞ The most likely questions regarding NEPA concern the contents of the EIS and what the agency must do with the EIS once it is prepared.

  ☞ In the latter regard, it may be helpful to explain the value of a purely procedural NEPA.

  ☞ Be sure also to explain your answer in light of the text of NEPA, which provides only that the EIS must be prepared and must "accompany" the agency's proposal through all review stages.

☞ Watch for agency arguments in support of agency action on grounds that were not relied upon at the agency level and point out that agency action must stand or fall on the grounds the agency relied upon when it made its decision.

☞ In a question that raises clarity concerns, point out that the cases imposing clarity requirements on due process grounds may be out of date or inconsistent with the *Roth* line of cases regarding property interests.

  ☞ Further, it is unclear whether, as a nonconstitutional matter, the APA imposes a similar requirement on federal agencies. It can be argued, however, that absent a clear standard, agency action is arbitrary.

☞ In a question raising the issue of whether the representations of an official can estop the agency, state the general rule that agencies are not estopped by such conduct. Point out that for constitutional reasons, the rule is even stronger when expenditure of funds is involved.

☞ In a question raising issues of collateral estoppel and agency nonacquiescence, it may be useful to explain why agencies may wish to adhere to their views without necessarily appealing every adverse ruling.

☞ It is clear that nonmutual collateral estoppel does not apply against the government in litigation.

☞ However, within a circuit that has rejected the agency's view, the rule of law may require the agency to acquiesce to the court's ruling.

CHAPTER 9

AGENCY ENFORCEMENT AND LICENSING

ChapterScope _____

This chapter examines methods agencies use to enforce regulatory norms. The chapter examines prosecutorial discretion, discriminatory enforcement, licensing (including broadcast licensing), and ratemaking. The main points of this chapter are:

■ Agencies have a great deal of discretion over whether to regulate and over the choice of targets for enforcement action.

- ■ Clear statutory standards that define when an agency must act and how an agency must choose its enforcement targets can narrow that discretion.

- ■ *Discriminatory enforcement* claims are unlikely to succeed. Agency enforcement targets sometimes argue against enforcement on the ground that their competitors are committing the same violation that they have been found guilty of, and it is unfair for the agency to single them out for enforcement bringing enforcement actions against their competitors also.

- ■ The standard for evaluating such *discriminatory enforcement* claims is *"patent abuse of discretion."*

- ■ Courts are very deferential to agency discretion in this area and accept almost any agency explanation for not prosecuting other violators along with the party raising the challenge.

■ The courts also have been very deferential to agency choices regarding the severity of sanctions in a particular case.

■ Due process is not violated by the combination of investigatory, prosecutorial, legislative, and adjudicative functions that is common in agencies generally and licensing agencies in particular. However, proof of bias in a particular case may violate due process.

■ If members of one segment of a profession dominate an occupational licensing agency, and they take disciplinary action to eliminate competition from another segment of the profession, the bias due to self-interest in the outcome of the disciplinary action may violate due process.

- ■ However, outside the context of a particular disciplinary action, domination of a licensing agency by one segment of a profession does not automatically violate due process.

■ The "public interest, convenience, and necessity" standard for awarding broadcast licenses gives the FCC a great deal of discretion in licensing proceedings.

- ■ The FCC cannot deny a license without offering the applicant a "full hearing" unless it is apparent from the application or other pleadings that the applicant does not meet a statutory or valid regulatory standard.

- ■ When there are competing applications for a new frequency, the *Ashbacker* decision holds that the FCC may not grant one application without holding a hearing on both, because the Court views the grant of one as effectively denying the other.

- The FCC may narrow the scope of its licensing hearings by promulgating regulations that make its general licensing standard more concrete and particular. Under the *Storer* decision, the FCC may deny a hearing to an applicant whose application clearly does not satisfy a requirement of a valid regulation.

- Until 1996, the Communications Act did not distinguish between initial licensing standards and renewal standards.

  - Thus, the FCC was required to hold comparative hearings between the incumbent and a competing applicant when a renewal was challenged.

  - Under the 1996 Act, if the incumbent's past service is sufficient, and there have been no major violations of the Act or regulations, then the FCC should grant renewal without a comparative hearing.

- Ratemaking is the process for establishing prices in a regulated industry.

  - Ratemaking agencies also often manage competition by restricting entry into an industry.

  - Ratemaking agencies normally must offer hearings before finally setting rates. The *Morgan* decisions hold that the official making the decision must review the evidence in the case and not merely consult with other agency officials who have considered the evidence.

I. PROSECUTORIAL DISCRETION

Agencies normally have a great deal of discretion to choose those problems within its jurisdiction on which it will focus. Competitors or victims of alleged violators sometimes attempt to compel an agency to bring an enforcement action against a third party. In most circumstances, as the reviewability discussion in Chapter 3 reveals, *agency decisions not to prosecute are not reviewable*.

A. Reasons for agency prosecutorial discretion

Agencies often have broad regulatory missions and insufficient resources to bring enforcement actions against every alleged violator of regulatory norms. Courts have often concluded that the agency should be left to decide, in its expert judgment, which enforcement actions present the best use of agency resources. Further, like the criminal prosecutor, there may be some violations that the agency believes, in its expert judgment, are better left unremedied because the violations are de minim is or because the agency does not believe that enforcement would serve the goals of the relevant regulatory norm.

B. Potential problems with agency prosecutorial discretion

Agency prosecutorial discretion presents the potential for three serious problems.

1. **Subversion of legislative intent:** An agency can subvert congressional intent by applying different priorities from those that led Congress to pass the agency's enabling act.

2. **Political favoritism:** Agency prosecutorial discretion may allow an agency to play political favorites. The agency may enforce its norms only against businesses or individuals identified with political opponents or without sufficient political power to resist the agency through political channels. The agency may also fail to enforce its program against politically connected

violators. The political power of the regulated party is presumably irrelevant to whether enforcement would advance the policies embodied in the regulatory program.

3. **Easy targets:** Agency prosecutorial discretion may lead the agency to select only easy targets for prosecution—such as small businesses or individuals who may lack the resources to challenge the agency effectively. An agency might justify this strategy as cost-effective, but it may be unfair to the enforcement target and subversive of public policy since the largest violators are left untouched.

C. Reducing discretion through prosecutorial standards

Congress may statutorily reduce or eliminate agency prosecutorial discretion. If an agency's statute requires the agency to prosecute all known violators or if the statute sets a standard that the agency must follow when deciding whether to prosecute, then the agency has less prosecutorial discretion. Courts have held that such standards can overcome the presumption against judicial review of non-enforcement decisions. See the reviewability discussion in Chapter 3.

D. Prosecutorial discretion and discriminatory enforcement

Subjects of agency enforcement sometimes claim that although they may have violated regulatory norms, the agency should not issue an enforcement order against them unless and until the agency issues enforcement orders against others engaged in the same practice. For example, competitors argue that they will suffer a competitive disadvantage if they are ordered to halt a practice while their competitors are free to continue the very same practice. Such claims rarely succeed because courts are loath to upset decisions implicating agencies' prosecutorial discretion.

1. **The discriminatory enforcement claim:** The typical discriminatory enforcement claim has several elements. The regulated party resisting enforcement argues some or all of the following:

    1. the practice that the agency has ordered to be stopped is widespread in the industry;
    2. the agency has not ordered the party's competitors to halt the same practice, and the competitors will continue to engage in it;
    3. requiring the party to halt the practice without ordering competitors to do so as well will place the party at a severe competitive disadvantage;
    4. the party is a minor player in the industry compared with its competitors; and
    5. there is no rational basis for singling out the party ordered to halt the practice from others in the industry who are also engaged in the practice.

2. **The patent abuse of discretion standard for claims of discriminatory enforcement:** The standard for deciding whether a court should preclude an agency from enforcing an order until the agency orders others in the industry to halt the same practice is "patent abuse of discretion." *See Moog Industries, Inc. v. FTC*, 355 U.S. 411 (1958). This standard is intended to make it difficult for a regulated party to prevail on a discriminatory enforcement claim, and the Court has not stated with clarity what facts might lead to a finding of improper discriminatory enforcement. Claims of discriminatory enforcement rarely succeed because courts believe that they should allow agency experts to decide agency enforcement priorities.

    Example: In *FTC v. Universal Rundle Corp.*, 387 U.S. 244 (1967), the Court rejected Universal Rundle's attempt to meet the "patent abuse of discretion" standard. The FTC ordered Universal Rundle to cease and desist from offering its customers truckload discounts on plumbing supplies. The FTC had ordered Universal Rundle to stop offering the discounts because, according to the FTC,. the discounts had an anticompetitive effect since customers receiving the discount were in competition with customers not receiving the discount. Universal Rundle argued that (I) all plumbing manufacturers offered the same truckload discounts; (2) that it had only 5.75 percent of the market while its competitors' market shares ranged from 6 percent to 32 percent; and (3) that it would be forced out of business if it could not offer the truckload discounts while its competitors continued to do so. The Supreme Court rejected this claim, relying primarily on the ground that Universal Rundle's evidence did not show that the discounts offered by competitors had the same anticompetitive effect as those offered by Universal Rundle. However, the Court also stated that even if Universal Rundle had shown that its competitors were engaged in illegal conduct, the FTC might still have discretion to enforce its order against Universal Rundle without also prosecuting the other companies. The patent abuse of discretion standard appears to require only that the agency articulate some rational basis for not proceeding against all competitors simultaneously.

3. **Discriminatory imposition of sanctions:** Agencies may impose any sanctions within their statutory authority. Parties have argued that agencies have imposed overly harsh sanctions for violations—either compared to sanctions imposed on others or under agency policy regarding sanctions. The Supreme Court is not sympathetic to such claims and has held that, absent statutory restrictions, ***an agency is free to impose whatever sanctions are within its statutory power***: "a sanction within the authority of an administrative agency is . . . not rendered invalid . . . because it is more severe than sanctions imposed in other cases." *Butz v. Glover Livestock Commission Co., Inc.*, 411 U.S. 182 (1973). This holding rejects any consistency requirement regarding the severity of sanctions.

4. **Reviewability of discriminatory enforcement and discriminatory sanctions claims:** Because the party raising a discriminatory enforcement or discriminatory sanctions claim is resisting enforcement of an agency order, the claim does not present the same reviewability problems as a claim that an agency has improperly failed to bring an enforcement action against a third party. However, the same principles of agency expertise and discretion in setting enforcement priorities that typically make nonenforcement claims unreviewable lead to the very deferential standards of review applied to discriminatory enforcement and discriminatory sanctions claims.

E. Constitutionally based claims of discriminatory enforcement

Some claims of discriminatory enforcement are based in the Constitution.

1. **Equal protection:** An agency may not base its choice of enforcement subjects on a suspect classification. For example, in *Yick Wo v. Hopkins*, 118 U.S. 356 (1886), the Court held a municipality violated equal protection when it enforced a ban on wooden laundry buildings only against Chinese-owned laundries and not against other laundries.

2. **First Amendment:** When outspoken criticism of an agency or the program the agency administers triggers enforcement, the regulated party may claim that the prosecution punishes or chills speech in violation of the First Amendment. This claim has not been successful.

Example: The Selective Service System adopted a policy of "passive enforcement" under which it would refer for prosecution only the cases of people who openly identified themselves as having failed to register and those who were reported by third parties. Wayte, an outspoken nonregistrant who was prosecuted, claimed that this punished him for speaking out against the draft—in violation of his free speech rights. The Supreme Court, in *Wayte v. United States*, 470 U.S. 598 (1985), rejected this claim, holding that the defendant was not prosecuted because he spoke out against the draft but rather because he identified himself to the Service as a non-registrant. The case does not clarify, however, the circumstances under which a claim based on agency prosecution as retaliation for criticism of the agency would succeed.

II. LICENSING AND RATEMAKING

A great deal of regulation takes the form of *licensing* and *ratemaking*. Licenses are needed to engage in many professions and to operate in many industries. In such cases, licenses are obtained from administrative agencies whose actions are subject to judicial review. Although the volume of rate-making may not be as high as it once was, there are still industries in which administrative agencies set rates or in which companies must file tariffs in an agency with power to disapprove the tariff and require different rates. A great deal of this activity is conducted at the state and local levels, but federal agencies do enough of it that some principles under the APA have developed.

A. Occupational licensing

A common form of licensing is occupational licensing. Doctors, lawyers, optometrists, pharmacists, hair stylists, truck drivers, and many other professionals must obtain licenses from the state in order to practice their professions. While the substance and procedures for licenses vary from state to state, some common factors can be discerned.

1. **Licenses are property protected by due process:** Because legal standards normally govern the grant, denial, renewal, and revocation of professional licenses, such licenses are property under the *Roth* test (see Chapter 7) and are protected by due process. In many situations, licensing boards determine professional licensing issues in formal adjudication governed by the entire range of due process rights. In particular, licensing boards tend to present the following due process problems.

    a. **Combination of functions:** Licensing boards, like many agencies, often combine several functions in one body. For example, the same agency may accept and evaluate applications, investigate allegations of misconduct by licensed professionals, and adjudicate disciplinary cases and challenges to denials of applications. The Supreme Court has found no per se due process violation in this combination of functions. Note that the contrary holding would have invalidated numerous state and federal agencies.

    Example: *Withrow v. Larkin*, 421 U.S. 35 (1975), presented the paradigm case of an agency with multiple roles. The Wisconsin State Medical Examining Board learned that Larkin, a licensed physician, was performing abortions which, at the time, were illegal. The board investigated, ultimately filed formal charges against Larkin, and set a date for a hearing at which it would preside. After a federal court issued a preliminary injunction against the holding of the hearing, the board issued a formal finding of probable cause to believe that Larkin had violated state criminal law. It referred the matter to the state prosecutor. A three judge district court again enjoined the hearing. The board appealed to the Supreme Court. The Court found that the board would not violate due process by holding the hearing, and held that it is not unfair for the same body to investigate, find probable cause, and preside over an adjudication of the charges. The Court noted that this is a common structure in state and federal agencies and that absent specific evidence of bias, the law presumes that administrators act fairly. It was also noted that judges often preside at trials after issuing arrest warrants and finding probable cause at preliminary hearings, in the same case.

b. Bias due to self-interest. The problem of self-regulation: Occupational licensing often presents the potential for bias due to self-interest because the licensing board may be dominated by one segment of a profession seeking to avoid competition from another segment. If the members of the board have an interest in the outcome of a proceeding before it, due process considerations may preclude them from hearing it.

Example: In *Gibson v. Berryhill*, 411 U.S. 564 (1973), the Alabama Board of Optometry (composed solely of independent optometrists) attempted to adjudicate a complaint against optometrists working for a corporation. The complaint set out violations of state law bans on, inter alia, practicing under a trade name and sharing fees with a nonoptometrist employer. These provisions were typical of state law restrictions on professions like optometry and still exist for other professionals, such as lawyers. The Supreme Court held that because board members were in competition with the subjects of the hearing, the board's self-interest in the outcome of the case meant that board adjudication of the disciplinary proceeding violated due process. However, in *Friedman v. Rogers*, 440 U.S. 1 (1979), the Court confined its holding in *Gibson* to disciplinary proceedings, holding that it did not necessarily violate the Constitution for a state to hand over enforcement of a regulatory scheme to one segment of a profession. The Court held that the Texas legislature did not violate the Constitution when it required that two-thirds of the members of the Texas Optometry Board (created to enforce newly legislated restrictions on nonindependent optometrists), be independent optometrists. To invoke *Gibson*'s due process considerations, bias must be shown in the context of a particular disciplinary proceeding, not in terms of the overall administration of the licensing scheme.

B. Broadcast licensing procedures

The federal government has, since World War I, regulated the use of broadcasting frequencies. Although the Telecommunications Act of 1996 significantly altered some aspects of federal broadcast licensing, other elements remain, and broadcast licensing disputes have often helped develop important administrative law principles.

1. **"Public interest" standard for granting licenses:** Regarding applications for broadcast licenses, the Communications Act provides that "if the Commission . . . shall find that public interest, convenience, and necessity would be served by the granting thereof, it shall grant such application." 47 U.S.C. §309(a). This standard gives the FCC a great deal of discretion over the decision whether to grant a broadcast license and, coupled with the procedural requirements attached to the licensing process, has led to a great deal of litigation.

2. **Broadcast licensing hearing requirements:** The process for deciding on an application for a license is a hearing governed by §309 of the Communications Act. Once an application is filed, the Act specifies several steps—the most important of which are detailed below.

   a. **The procedure for opposing an application:** The Act grants "any party in interest" the right to file a petition opposing an application. 47 U.S.C. §309(d). The petition is treated like a pleading and must allege facts, supported by affidavits, to make a prima facie case that granting the license would not be in the "public interest, convenience, and necessity." The applicant has the right to reply to the petition.

   b. **Grants without a hearing:** If an application and the pleadings and other matters before the Commission do not raise any "substantial and material questions of fact," the Commission may grant the application and deny any contrary petitions in a summary judgment-like proceeding without holding a hearing. 47 U.S.C. §309(d)(2).

c. **Hearing required for denials and when material issues are in dispute:** When the Commission does not find, on the pleadings, that the application should be granted (either because it does not find that granting the application would be in the "public interest, convenience, and necessity" or because there are contested material issues), the Commission is required to hold "a full hearing in which the applicant and all other parties in interest shall be permitted to participate. The burden of proceeding with the introduction of evidence and the burden of proof shall be on the applicant, except that with respect to any issue presented by a petition to deny or a petition to enlarge the issues, such burdens shall be as determined by the Commission." 47 U.S.C. §309(e). The "full hearing" specified has been interpreted to mean a formal, adjudicatory hearing.

3. **Mutually exclusive applications.The *Ashbacker* rule:** Under the *Ashbacker* rule, when two applicants file competing applications (both of which cannot be granted because they are either for the same frequency or frequencies too close together to broadcast without interference), the Commission may not grant one of the applications without holding a hearing on the other. *See Ashbacker Radio Corp. v. FCC*, 326 U.S. 327 (1945).

a. **The facts of *Ashbacker*:** In March 1944, the Fetzer Broadcasting Company filed an application to construct a radio station in Grand Rapids, Michigan, to operate at 1230 am, with 250 watts of power. In May of the same year, Ashbacker Radio Corp. filed an application to change the frequency of its Muskegon, Michigan, station to 1230 am, also with 250 watts of power. The FCC determined that the applications were "actually exclusive" because simultaneous operation would result in "intolerable interference" with each other.

b. **The FCC's action on the applications:** The FCC granted the Fetzer application on the pleadings (without a hearing) in June 1944, and on the same day, set Ashbacker's application for a hearing. *Ashbacker*, fearing that the Fetzer grant effectively precluded the FCC from granting its application, petitioned the FCC for a hearing regarding the Fetzer application. The FCC denied this petition, stating that its grant of the Fetzer application "does not preclude the Commission, at a later date, from taking any action which it may find will serve the public interest." *Ashbacker*, 326 U.S. at 331.

c. **Procedural support for the FCC's actions:** The FCC, in granting the Fetzer application and setting the Ashbacker application for a hearing, followed the letter of the Communications Act. The Act, as detailed above, allows the FCC to grant applications on the pleadings. The Commission, in setting Ashbacker's application for a hearing, followed the procedures specified in the Act for when the Commission decides not to grant an application on the pleadings. The FCC's statement (in response to Ashbacker's petition) that it remained free to take any action it found in the public interest, promised Ashbacker that it would change its decision in Fetzer if it was convinced that doing so would serve the public interest. Finally, nothing in the Act states that the Commission may not grant an application on the pleadings while a competing application is still pending.

d. **The Supreme Court's decision in *Ashbacker*:** The Supreme Court held that the Commission violated the Act by granting Fetzer's application without first holding a hearing on Ashbacker's application. The Court held that when two mutually exclusive applications have been filed, "if the grant of one effectively precludes the other, the statutory right to a hearing which Congress has accorded applicants before denial of their applications becomes an empty thing." *Ashbacker*, 326 U.S. at 330. In the Court's view, the hearing that the Commission promised Ashbacker was no longer statutorily adequate once the Commission granted Fetzer's application. As the Court stated, "where two bona fide applications are mutually exclusive the grant of one without a hearing to both deprives the loser of the opportunity which Congress chose to give him." *Ashbacker*, 326 U.S. at 333.

e. **The FCC's reaction to *Ashbacker*. Comparative hearings:** When multiple competing applications are filed, the FCC holds a comparative hearing in which the relative merits of each application are compared so that the license can be awarded to the applicant who, in the eyes of the FCC, will best serve the "public interest, convenience, and necessity."

   i. **Lack of discernible standards:** The FCC's comparative hearing process was criticized as not being governed by any discernible standards. In 1965, in response to this criticism, the FCC issued its Policy Statement on Comparative Broadcast Hearings, which set forth the factors that the FCC would apply to comparative hearings. The factors specified were:

   - **Diversification of ownership of mass media:** The FCC's policy favors diversified ownership of mass media and thus disfavors applicants who already own media outlets including newspapers and other broadcast stations.

   - **Integration of ownership and management:** The FCC's policy favors applicants whose owners intend to participate in the management of the station and to disfavor applicants who have no management role. Local owners and owners who have participated in civic affairs are also favored.

   - **Program service:** The FCC's policy favors owners who propose substantially better programming than the competition. The most important indication of superior service is programming designed to meet local needs arrived at in consultation with local civic groups and other local interests.

   - **Past broadcast record:** The FCC's policy favors an applicant with broadcast experience. Further, the FCC views "unusually good or unusually poor" service as important factors in comparative hearings.

   - **Efficient use of frequency:** The FCC's policy favors efficient uses of frequencies.

   - **Character:** The FCC's policy, and the Act itself, disfavors applicants with past conduct indicating bad character. The FCC will not inquire into character evidence unless the pleadings create an issue of character.

   - **Other factors:** The FCC's policy statement allows it to consider other factors not specified but which it considers relevant to determining which application would best serve "the public interest, convenience, and necessity."

   ii. **Criticism not quelled:** The FCC's critics were not satisfied by the policy statement. They saw the factors as sufficiently pliable to allow the FCC to reach whatever result it would have reached without the policy statement, especially because it reserved the right to consider factors other than those listed.

4. **Restricting the scope of hearings by rule. *Storer*:** A principle of administrative law allows agencies, by substantive rule, to restrict the scope of statutorily required hearings. A related

principle holds that, in such cases, the agency must allow the regulated party to present arguments for waiving or modifying the rule in a particular case to better meet statutory concerns. In *United States v. Storer Broadcasting Co.*, 351 U.S. 192 (1956), the Court held that the FCC may, through rulemaking, make the general "public interest" standard that governs the grant of broadcast licenses more specific by stating particular factors that it will consider important in licensing decisions.

   a. The FCC's multiple ownership rules: Culminating in a rule issued in 1953, the FCC (in its multiple ownership rules) placed restrictions on the number of television and radio licenses that a single licensee could hold. These rules were designed to prevent overconcentration of the ownership of television and radio stations.

   b. The FCC's action in *Storer*: Storer applied for a television station license in Miami. The FCC denied the application without a hearing because another license would have put Storer over the limit for station ownership established in the recently promulgated multiple ownership rules.

   c. Bases for challenge to the multiple ownership rules: Storer challenged the multiple ownership rules on two grounds: one substantive and one procedural. The substantive ground was that the rules violated the Communications Act by precluding the grant of a license to Storer, even if the grant was in the "public interest, convenience and necessity." The procedural ground was that the rules denied Storer its statutorily required hearing by allowing the Commission to deny the application without a hearing whenever granting a new license would violate the rules.

   d. The Court's decision in *Storer*: The Court ruled in favor of the rules and against Storer on both arguments.

      i. Substance: On the substantive argument, the Court held that the Commission is free to enact regulations making the general "public interest," standard more specific. As long as the regulations are valid, they become the definition of the "public interest," and the FCC can judge the application for compliance with them, not with the more general statutory standard.

      ii. Procedure: On the procedural ground, the Court held that if the application reveals that the applicant would exceed the maximum allowed ownership under the rules, the Commission is free to deny the application on the pleadings without holding a full hearing. As the Court stated, "we do not think Congress intended the Commission to waste time on applications that do not state a valid basis for a hearing." *Storer*, 351 U.S. at 250. The Court's only caveat was that if an application presents valid reasons for waiving the rules in a particular case, the Commission must hold a hearing on whether to waive the rules.

      iii. Qualification of *Storer* rule: When an agency has by regulation narrowed a statutory standard, a principle of administrative law holds that the agency must allow affected parties to show that the regulation does not or *should* not apply to them. Thus, even after *Storer*, an applicant must be given the opportunity to show that an FCC rule (like the multiple ownership rules) should not be applied for some reason in the particular case.

5. License renewal: License renewal has long been one of the most controversial elements of broadcast licensing. Although the Act long provided that licensees have no property rights in their licenses and that licenses may be revoked or not renewed whenever such action would be in the public interest, licenses have become very valuable. The FCC has treated licensees as having a presumptive renewal right. (The 1996 Telecommunications Act, as discussed below, created a presumption in favor of renewal.)

a. **The Act made no distinction between initial licenses and renewals:** Until 1996, the Act did not distinguish between an initial license determination and a renewal application. If a competitor sought to displace an incumbent license holder at renewal time, the assumption was that the FCC was required to hold a comparative hearing with the same procedures and standards as comparative hearings for new or vacant licenses. *See Ashbacker*, 326 U.S. at 332 ("licenses . . . are limited to three years, the renewals being subject to the same considerations and practices which affect the granting of initial applications").

b. **FCC practice on renewals:** Despite the lack of statutory support, FCC practice favored incumbent license holders who filed renewal applications.

c. **The FCC's 1970 policy statement on renewals:** In 1970, the FCC issued a policy statement providing that it would grant renewal applications if the incumbent licensee had provided service "substantially attuned to the needs and interests of its area and [whose] operation ha[d] not otherwise been characterized by serious deficiencies." Policy Statement Concerning Comparative Hearings Involving Regular Renewal Applicants, 22 F.C.C.2d 424, 425 (1970).

d. *Citizens Communications Center:* The D.C. Circuit invalidated the 1970 policy statement on renewal applications in *Citizens Communications Center v. FCC*, 447 F.2d 1201 (D.C. Cir. 1971). The court held that the policy statement violated the Act because, by allowing renewal based only upon the incumbent's past service, it deprived competing applicants the "full hearing" required by §309(e) and *Ashbacker*.

e. **The *Cowles* controversy:** Cowles Florida Broadcasting, Inc., operator of a television station in Daytona Beach, Florida, faced a competing application at renewal time from Central Florida Enterprises, Inc.

   i. **The FCC's initial decision:** In *Cowles Florida Broadcasting, Inc.*, 60 F.C.C.2d 372 (1976), the FCC granted Cowles's renewal application even though most of the comparative factors favored a competing applicant—Central Florida Enterprises, Inc. The primary factor relied upon by the FCC was Cowles's past service, which the ALJ had characterized as "thoroughly acceptable" but which the FCC, on review of the ALJ's decision, called "superior, meriting a plus of major significance."

   ii. **Judicial review of *Cowles*:** The D.C. Circuit reversed the FCC's decision on judicial review, concluding that the FCC had, despite the invalidation of the 1970 policy statement, created a de facto presumption in favor of renewal. *See Central Florida Enterprises, Inc. v. FCC*, 598 F.2d 37 (D.C. Cir. 1978), *cert. dismissed*, 441 U.S. 957 (1979). The court observed that Central Florida had a clear advantage on the comparative factors and noted that when the FCC looked at Cowles's past service it shifted into a noncomparative mode, concluding only that Cowles's record was superior without comparing it to Central Florida's proposed service.

   iii. *Cowles* **on remand:** On remand, the FCC reaffirmed the renewal of Cowles's license. It reformulated its renewal policy, discarding any presumption in favor of renewal but making a renewal expectancy one factor to be considered in comparative renewal hearings. The D.C. Circuit affirmed this policy and the result in *Cowles*, but not without expressing reservations regarding the fact that no television licensee had ever lost a license in a comparative renewal hearing.

f. The 1996 Act and renewals: The 1996 Act, for the first time, statutorily recognizes the incumbent license holder's renewal expectation. It provides that the FCC should grant renewal applications if the station has served the public interest and the licensee has neither committed any serious violations of the Act or FCC rules nor engaged in a pattern of less serious violations. 47 U.S.C. §309(1). The FCC is not required to hold a comparative hearing unless the Commission first finds that the incumbent has not satisfied the standards specified above.

6. License revocation: Section 312 of the Communications Act grants the FCC the power to revoke a broadcast license as a sanction for a wide variety of misconduct. The FCC has almost never exercised that power. In one renewal case, involving television stations owned by RKO General, Inc., the FCC decided not to renew licenses because of misconduct by RKO and its parent company, General Tire, Inc. *See RKO General, Inc. (WNAC-TV)*, 78 F.C.C.2d 1 (1980). Although *RKO* was actually a renewal controversy, its focus on misconduct provides insight into the circumstances that might lead to license revocation or other disciplinary action.

a. RKO's misconduct: RKO allegedly filed false financial statements with the FCC. RKO and General Tire used General Tire's market power to increase advertising on RKO stations. General Tire engaged in a pattern of improper conduct involving fraud and payoffs to political candidates and officials of foreign governments. Most important to the Commission, RKO engaged in a persistent lack of candor in the renewal proceedings involving nondisclosure of the misconduct and nondisclosure to the FCC of proceedings against General Tire in another agency.

b. The FCC's criteria regarding misconduct: The Commission stated the following criteria for deciding whether misconduct should lead to nonrenewal:

i. Nature of the misconduct: Nonrenewal is more likely if the misconduct is related to broadcast operations or if the misconduct indicates how the applicant will operate a broadcast station.

ii. Frequency of the misconduct: Nonrenewal is more likely if the misconduct appears to be a pattern and less likely if the misconduct is an isolated incident.

iii. Time of the misconduct: Nonrenewal is more likely for recent misconduct and less likely for misconduct completed long before the proceedings.

c. The FCC's decision in *RKO General*: In proceedings regarding the renewal of RKO's Boston television station, the FCC found against RKO on all three factors. The FCC noted that RKO and its parent engaged in substantial serious misconduct over a long period of time, continuing through the renewal proceedings. The FCC found that RKO withheld material information regarding its misconduct and the misconduct of General Tire from the FCC during the renewal proceedings on the Boston license. The FCC held that both RKO's and General Tire's conduct indicated a lack of trustworthiness and that because General Tire and RKO worked closely together, it was appropriate to attribute General Tire's misconduct to RKO. The FCC disqualified RKO from holding any broadcast licenses.

    d. *RKO General* **on judicial reviewl:** On judicial review, the D.C. Circuit held that only the Boston license was properly subject to nonrenewal because RKO withheld information only in the specific proceeding regarding that license. *RKO General Inc. v. FCC*, 670 F.2d 215 (2d Cir. 1981), *cert. denied*, 456 U.S. 927 (1982). The court found the other grounds for nonrenewal were inadequate for the following reasons.

      i. Antitrust misconduct: The D.C. Circuit found that RKO could not be disqualified for using General Tire's market power to gain advertising because the FCC had, in a prior case, decided that such conduct was irrelevant to fitness to hold a license, and the FCC did not explain the change in policy.

      ii. Financial misrepresentations: The court rejected the FCC's finding that RKO had knowingly falsely certified that certain financial reports were complete and accurate because, although RKO claimed in affidavits that it did not know of any inaccuracies, the FCC did not hold a hearing on the issue.

      iii. General Tire's nonbroadcast misconduct: The court found that General Tire's non-broadcast misconduct could not justify disqualification. The court noted that the Commission itself had held that this misconduct was not an independent ground for nonrenewal of RKO's licenses but merely supported the ultimate decision that was based primarily on other grounds.

7. Alternative methods for allocating licenses—lotteries and auctions: The FCC has recently allocated some non-broadcast frequencies by lottery and by auction. It has used lotteries since 1983 and has had statutory authority to use auctions since 1993. The FCC prefers these procedures to the comparative hearing process when there are large numbers of qualified applicants, and the public interest would be best served by getting the service started quickly. These procedures avoid the delay inherent in comparative hearings and judicial review. The services for which these alternative procedures have been used include low power television and cellular telephony.

C. Ratemaking principles and procedures

One of the earliest forms of regulation is ratemaking, in which an agency sets the rates that may be charged for a product or service. Related to ratemaking is regulation of competition, in which the agency restricts entry into a field and allocates areas of service among regulated businesses. For example, during the later stages of the Civil Aeronautics Board's (CAB) regulation of airline fares and routes, the CAB rejected all applications to provide service from new airlines.

1. Forms of ratemaking procedures: Rate regulation takes many different forms. While the three most common ratemaking procedures are as follows, there are variations on these. Many agencies combine more than one of the models.

    a. Complaints against unreasonable rates: In some industries, like common carriers such as railroads, rates for services such as shipping were subject to challenge as unreasonable. If the agency with jurisdiction found the rates unreasonable, the agency would prescribe a maximum reasonable rate. For example, railroad shipping rates were set by the ICC only after a shipper complained that a carrier was charging an "unreasonable" rate. The ICC would, after a hearing, prescribe the maximum lawful rate.

    b. Comprehensive ratemaking: In traditionally regulated utility monopolies like the electric company, the gas company, and the local telephone company, an agency sets all rates based.

on a comprehensive analysis of the relevant market, costs, and service needs. Agencies often employ formal hearing procedures even though the decision has a legislative character. Usually, the regulated business proposes a rate structure, interested parties participate in the hearing, and the agency issues a comprehensive set of rates.

c. Filed tariffs: In some industries, (e.g., contemporary long-distance telephone services) companies file tariffs with an agency, and those tariffs become effective automatically unless the agency finds unlawful discrimination or some other defect. In many cases, the agency barely looks at the filed tariff, and the principal regulatory requirement is that the company charge its customers only the rates specified in the filed tariff. However, most filed tariff systems allow the agency to reject unreasonable rates and allow customers to challenge filed rates as unreasonable.

2. The ratemaking "hearing" requirement: Typically, agencies conduct ratemaking in a hearing process, and sometimes formal hearing procedures have been prescribed. When formal hearings are required, the regulated party must be given the opportunity to confront the other side's evidence and contentions, and the decisionmaker should not engage in ex parte contacts with other government officials.

Example: The *Morgan* cases involved a lengthy dispute over maximum rates charged by market agencies engaged in the livestock market in Kansas City. The Packers and Stockyards Act allowed the Secretary of Agriculture to set such rates after a "full hearing." The Secretary of Agriculture issued an order setting rates after consolidated hearings regarding conduct by numerous market agencies. The evidence was heard by a trial examiner. The trial examiner issued no tentative report. An acting Secretary of Agriculture heard oral argument in the case, and only the market agencies, not the government, submitted a brief. The market agencies challenged this procedure on several grounds, including: (1) that the Secretary who was planning to make the decision had not heard or read any of the evidence and had not heard the oral argument; (2) that the hearing examiner's findings were not subject to challenge since he did not submit a public report; and (3) that the decision was unlawfully delegated to an acting Secretary. In *Morgan v. United States*, 298 U.S. 468 (1936) (*Morgan I*), the Court held that the statutory "full hearing" requirement meant that the Secretary must act like an adjudicator in a judicial proceeding, i.e., consider only the record evidence, and that the Act required the Secretary, himself, to consider the evidence on the record. On remand, the Secretary admitted that he looked at the record only slightly and that he made his decision based primarily on the briefs, the transcript of oral argument, conferences with other agency officials, and on proposed findings prepared by the agency. The Court found this process unacceptable for several reasons: (1) because the Secretary had not considered the evidence; (2) because the Secretary relied upon the views of agency officials that the regulated parties had no opportunity to rebut; and (3) because the regulated parties were not given an opportunity to rebut the proposed findings since they were not published. On remand, the district court allowed the Secretary to be interrogated about his role in the decision. Although the Supreme Court held that the hearing provided was not adequate, on review the Court stated that "it was not the function of the court to probe the mental processes of the Secretary." *Morgan v. United States*, 304 U.S. 1, 18 (1938) (*Morgan II*). The Court stated this rule more emphatically in a subsequent decision. *United States v. Morgan*, 313 U.S. 409 (1941) (*Morgan IV*). Although the *Morgan* decisions stand for the proposition that when Congress specifies that ratemaking is to be conducted in a "full hearing," the agency must observe proper adjudicatory procedures, they also place limits on the courts' ability to examine whether the proper officials actually examined the record and made the decision independently.

3. **Problems in ratemaking procedure:** There have been significant problems in ratemaking procedures. Often, ratemaking has been used as a device to keep prices artificially high by restricting competition. Other times, the fast pace of changing market conditions has rendered the hearing process too slow, and the complexity of the industry has made it impossible to take into account all relevant factors in any rational way.

4. **Deregulation:** In recent years, the trend has been away from ratemaking and toward deregulation to encourage price competition. Prime examples of deregulated rates include air fares, rates for shipping goods by truck, and legal fees. The advent of competition has also substantially changed the rate structure of long-distance telephone service, which operates under a filed tariff system. However, ratemaking agencies may not deregulate without statutory authority, and when an agency deregulates by rescinding regulations, the rescission decision is subject to judicial review. *See Motor Vehicle Manufacturers Association v. State Farm Mutual Automobile Insurance Co.*, 463 U.S. 29 (1983).

Example: Section 203 of the Communications Act requires long-distance telephone carriers to file tariffs with the FCC, and carriers must charge their customers the rates specified in those tariffs. The Act also allows the FCC to "modify" any requirement of §203. In a series of orders, the FCC eliminated the tariff-filing requirement for all nondominant long-distance carriers, (i.e., all carriers except AT&T). AT&T sought judicial review of this order. In *MCI v. AT&T*, 512 U.S. 218 (1994), the Supreme Court in an opinion by Justice Scalia, held that the word "modify" does not include the authority to eliminate a requirement of the Act. Thus, the FCC lacked legal authority to cease to require tariffs from nondominant carriers. The Court noted that "rate filings are, in fact, the essential characteristic of a rate-regulated industry" and that it would be impossible to enforce the FCC Act's prohibitions of overcharges and unreasonable rates without filed tariffs. *MCI*, 512 U.S. at 230. The Court concluded that the agency could not eliminate the rate regulation without more explicit congressional authorization. However, in *National Cable & Telecommunications Ass'n v. Brand X Internet Services*, 125 S. Ct. 2688 (2005), the Court upheld an FCC rule that regulated cable television-company-supplied internet services more leniently than telephone-company-supplied internet access via telephone lines. Justice Scalia, in dissent, charged that the FCC had once again abused its regulatory authority by radically altering its regulatory scheme in the guise of statutory interpretation.

Quiz Yourself on
 AGENCY ENFORCEMENT AND LICENSING

49. A person living near a large factory is upset that the EPA has not stopped the factory from emitting illegal air pollution. Can the person compel the EPA to bring an enforcement action against the factory owners? _____

50. NHTSA is concerned about minivan safety. It brings a proceeding against one manufacturer to force it to recall its minivans and change the latches on the rear doors, which NHTSA claims may open in relatively low-impact accidents. The manufacturer claims that all minivan latches are the same and that another company's latches open even more easily than its own. Is this a valid defense?

_____

51. A new governor appoints a new state Attorney Disciplinary Board composed exclusively of members of large law firms. One of the board's first actions is to announce that it intends to enforce a long-standing (but rarely enforced) ban on practicing law under a trade name. It then issues an immediate suspension notice to four lawyers practicing under the name "The Legal Clinic" and orders them to appear before the board for a hearing to determine whether the board should revoke or suspend their licenses to practice law, and whether an order should issue prohibiting them from practicing under a trade name. Are.there any procedural problems with the board's actions? _____

52. The FCC announces that a new radio frequency is available in Chicago. Two applications are filed for the frequency—one by Michael Jordan and one by Rupert Murdoch. The FCC, without a hearing, awards the frequency to Michael Jordan and denies Murdoch's application on the ground that he already owns the maximum number of radio stations allowed under FCC rules. Murdoch protests that the FCC should have held a comparative hearing before awarding the license to Michael Jordan. Does Murdoch have a valid complaint? _____

53. The Secretary of Energy is presiding over a ratemaking proceeding regarding natural gas prices. After the close of the hearings, the Secretary asks the head of the agency within the department directly responsible for overseeing natural gas distribution for an analysis of the natural gas market, with recommendations on rates. Only the Secretary and his staff see this memorandum, and the Secretary adopts most of the rate recommendations contained in the memorandum. Does this procedure provide a basis for a challenge to the rates? _____

Answers

49. Not unless there is a clear statutory provision requiring the EPA to act on this type of complaint. Agencies normally have a great deal of discretion in choosing how to use their enforcement resources. If a person petitions the agency and the agency denies the petition, the denial may not be subject to review because courts hold that most enforcement decisions are "committed to agency discretion by law."

50. Probably not. Unless the manufacturer can show that the failure to bring enforcement actions against other makers of minivans has no basis, it is no defense to an enforcement action to claim that enforcement should be brought against a competitor as well. The legal standard is "patent abuse of discretion." Because the manufacturer is unlikely to be significantly injured in its ability to compete with other minivan makers, any discriminatory enforcement claim is likely to be very weak. An agency is normally free to proceed one company at a time. The most successful discriminatory enforcement claims are those that raise equal protection concerns, such as a pattern of enforcing regulations against a particular racial group—but even claims like that are difficult to sustain,

51. A. Yes. First, the immediate suspension without a hearing may have violated due process. Occupational licenses are usually property under the *Roth* line of cases, and due process may require a hearing before an agency may suspend a license unless there is evidence of an immediate threat to public health or safety. Further, the composition of the Board presents a problem under *Gibson* although perhaps not a serious one. If the Board is dominated by lawyers who do not practice under trade names, and they are attempting to destroy competition from another segment of the profession, then there is a problem. They may be biased because of self-interest in the outcome of the hearing. However, it is not clear that the Board is actually in a different market segment from the firms using trade names. This regulation applies to all lawyers, and thus the Board members are limiting their own activities by enforcing this rule. Further, the big firms may not be in competition with this "legal clinic" and thus the members of the Board may have no personal interest in the outcome. There may be no client of The Legal Clinic who could afford to hire a big firm lawyer.

52. No. While Murdoch is correct that in normal circumstances the FCC must hold a comparative hearing to award a new license among competing applicants, the FCC may promulgate substantive licensing standards and deny applications that, on their face, fail the standard. Here, if the limit on the number of stations is part of a valid regulation (and there is no dispute that Murdoch owns more than the maximum), the FCC may deny his application without a hearing and award the frequency to the competing applicant. However, if Murdoch's application raises a potentially valid ground for waiving the rule in the particular case, the FCC must provide Murdoch with a hearing on that argument and must explain why it has rejected the argument. Recall that the 1996 Telecommunications Act eliminates the comparative hearing requirement for contested renewals.

53. Yes. The ratemaking process is normally formal adjudication. Here, the Secretary communicated ex parte with an official and received key information from that official without allowing the sellers of natural gas an opportunity to address that information at the hearing. This violates the sellers' procedural rights.

Exam Tips on
AGENCY ENFORCEMENT AND LICENSING

☞ In questions about prosecutorial discretion, reviewability issues are likely to be very important.

   ☞ Argue that exercises of prosecutorial discretion are presumptively unreviewable.

   ☞ Then, look for any indication that the agency's statute restricts or compels prosecutions under certain circumstances to rebut the presumption of unreviewability.

☞ In questions raising claims of discriminatory enforcement, apply the "patent abuse of discretion" standard to claims of discriminatory enforcement, and discuss how difficult courts have made it to prevail on such claims.

☞ Occupational and business licensing exam questions are most likely to raise due process property interest questions.

   ☞ Analyze the particular scheme under *Roth* and then look for special problems such as capture of the licensing body by a segment of the profession or industry looking to avoid competition from another segment.

   ☞ If capture appears to be present, discuss whether *Gibson v. Berryhill* or *Friedman v. Rogers* should govern. Recall that under *Friedman v. Rogers*, the *Gibson* rule may not extend beyond the context of disciplinary hearings.

☛ In FCC licensing questions, watch for questions raising *Ashbacker* and *Storer* issues.

☞ On *Storer* issues, watch for an argument by the applicant that the FCC's rule should not apply in the particular case.

☞ Note that comparative hearings are now required only on initial licensing decisions and not on renewals.

☛ Ratemaking is not a common area for examination, except perhaps as an example of important issues that apply across the administrative law spectrum.

☞ Due process hearing issues are important since ratemaking is often conducted in a formal hearing.

☞ In ratemaking questions, watch for *Morgan* issues, in which the decisionmaker does not actually hear the evidence or engages in ex parte communications with agency officials before deciding on the proper rate structure. If *Morgan* is relevant, point out that the later *Morgan* decisions make it difficult to police agency conduct in presiding over ratemaking proceedings.

CHAPTER **10**

AGENCY INFORMATION GATHERING

ChapterScope _____

This chapter examines how agencies gather information and the doctrines that restrict agency information gathering. The two methods agencies use most often to gather information are inspections and requests for information or documents. The main points of this chapter are:

- Agencies may *inspect* the premises of regulated businesses only if they have legal authority to do so.

- Under normal circumstances, the Fourth Amendment's warrant clause requires an agency to obtain a search warrant to conduct an inspection without the regulated party's consent.

    - However, *probable cause* that violations are occurring is not necessary to obtain a warrant for an administrative inspection.

    - Rather, agencies may obtain warrants merely by showing that the proposed inspection is *pursuant to normal agency standards* for conducting inspections.

    - *Pervasively regulated businesses* may be inspected *without warrants* as long as the regulatory scheme is supported by a substantial government interest, warrantless searches are necessary to advance the government interest, and the standards governing inspections under the regulatory scheme provide an adequate substitute for the warrant procedure.

- Warrants are required for inspections of homes for compliance with building codes and the like.

    - However, welfare recipients may be required to consent to home inspections as a condition of continued benefits, and convicted criminals on probation and parole may be required to consent to home inspections as a condition of probation or parole.

- Across the board *drug testing* of government employees is not constitutionally permissible.

    - Drug testing of employees engaged in *sensitive functions* such as law enforcement is allowed.

    - Drug testing also is allowed as part of the investigation of an accident, such as testing of the driver of a locomotive involved in an accident.

- Agencies have broad power to require regulated parties to *produce documents and provide information*.

    - The information sought must be related to an area of proper agency concern.

    - However, courts normally do not test the agency's jurisdiction in a proceeding to enforce a subpoena directing a regulated party to provide information or documents.

- It is unclear whether agencies must respect *state-law privileges*, such as the attorney-client privilege, that protect the confidentiality of information or documents.

- If government seeks to *reveal trade secrets or other valuable information*, the takings clause may require it to provide compensation to the party whose information it reveals.

■ **Corporations and other collective-entities** such as labor-unions and partnerships **do not have a Fifth Amendment right** to withhold incriminating information.

   ■ Individual business operators may not use the Fifth Amendment to resist providing documents or information related to a legitimate regulatory program.

   ■ Individual custodians of the information of collective entities do not have a Fifth Amendment right to resist producing entity documents they control.

■ The **Paperwork Reduction Act** requires that agencies seek the approval of the Office of Management and Budget before they may initiate new requirements that parties provide information to the agency.

I. INSPECTIONS

Many agencies monitor compliance with regulatory requirements by inspecting the subjects of regulation. Examples include inspections of food processing facilities and restaurants for proper food handling practices and purity, inspections of workplaces for proper worker safety practices, inspections of pollution-emitting facilities for compliance with environmental requirements, and inspections of residential properties for compliance with fire and building codes. Two legal issues are relevant to inspections. First, the agency must have authority to inspect. Second, inspections are subject to constitutional constraints.

A. Administrative authority to inspect regulated businesses

Agencies may not conduct inspections, or otherwise gather information, without legal authority. APA §555(c) provides that "[p]rocess, requirement of a report, inspection, or other investigative act or demand may not be issued, made, or enforced except as authorized by law."

B. Constitutional constraints on agency inspection

Because they are searches, agency inspections of the premises of regulated businesses (like searches) are subject to constitutional constraints, most notably those imposed by the Fourth Amendment. However, the Supreme Court has recognized exceptions to normal Fourth Amendment requirements for many administrative searches. Probable cause in the criminal law sense is not required for warrants to conduct inspections. Further, in "pervasively regulated businesses" warrants may be unnecessary.

1. **Normally, a warrant is required:** Under normal circumstances, a warrant is required before government agents may enter and inspect a business to monitor compliance with regulatory requirements. *See Camara v. Municipal Court*, 387 U.S. 523 (1967). In *Marshall v. Barlow's Inc.*, 436 U.S. 307 (1978), the Supreme Court held that OSHA inspectors may not search working areas of a business without a warrant. The Court may have feared that OSHA's broad jurisdiction over workplace safety would make almost every business in the United States subject to administrative, warrantless searches.

2. **Warrants for administrative inspections may issue without probable cause:** The Court in *Camara* and *Marshall* stated that **probable cause**, as required for a warrant in a criminal case, **is not required to obtain a warrant for an administrative inspection**. Rather, an agency may

obtain a warrant merely by showing that normal legislative or administrative standards for conducting an inspection are met. Thus, if an agency conducts inspections periodically or when certain circumstances are present, the agency can obtain a warrant merely by showing that the regular time for an inspection has arrived or the circumstances leading to an inspection are present.

3. **Pervasively regulated businesses:** No warrant is required to inspect the premises of a business that is subject to pervasive regulation. This departure from the warrant requirement is justified by the presumed awareness of the operator of a facility under pervasive regulation that inspections are routine and by the fact that the pervasive regulatory scheme provides a substitute for the safeguards provided by the Fourth Amendment's warrant requirement. *See Donovan v. Dewey*, 452 U.S. 594 (1981). The Court has stated three requirements for dispensing with the warrant requirement for inspecting pervasively regulated businesses:

   1. There must be a substantial government interest underlying the regulatory scheme;
   2. Warrantless searches must be necessary to advance the government interest; and
   3. The regulatory scheme must supply standards regarding the occurrence and scope of inspections that provide an adequate substitute for the safeguards of the warrant procedure.

Donovan, 452 U.S. at 602-604.

Example: In *Donovan v. Dewey*, 452 U.S. 594 (1981), the Supreme Court upheld the right of the Department of Labor to inspect a stone quarry without a warrant. The quarry was subject to regulation and periodic inspection under the Federal Mine Safety and Health Act. The Court reasoned that no warrant was required because "the certainty and regularity of [the] application [of the inspection program] provides an adequate substitute for a warrant." *Donovan*, 452 U.S. at 603. The Court found that the Fourth Amendment interest in preventing arbitrary and oppressive searches was satisfied by the Act's specific requirements regarding the timing and scope of inspections.

In *New York v. Burger*, 482 U.S. 691 (1987), the Court upheld a warrantless inspection of an automobile junkyard. A New York statute, designed to combat auto theft, required junkyards to be licensed, required owners of junkyards to maintain a "police book" containing records of the automobiles and parts in the junkyard, and required junkyard owners to permit police to inspect automobiles and parts in the junkyard. This regulatory scheme was designed to combat trade in stolen autos and auto parts. The junkyard involved in *Burger* was not licensed and the owners had not maintained the required "police book." After an inspection turned up stolen autos and auto parts, Burger was convicted of possession of stolen property. Burger argued that this was not a true regulatory scheme but was, in fact, a disguised criminal enforcement effort. The Court rejected this argument, holding that the statutory licensing, recordkeeping, and inspection requirements established that junkyards in New York are closely regulated businesses within the exception to the warrant requirement. The dissent disagreed, arguing that the regulatory scheme was not extensive enough to place junkyards in the category of closely regulated businesses, that the statute lacked criteria under which Burger's junkyard was selected for inspection, and that the regulatory scheme was a pretext for criminal enforcement of the sort that should require a warrant.

C. **Inspections of homes relating to regulatory schemes**

The private home receives a higher degree of protection from government intrusion than businesses and other nonresidential premises. Yet, with regard to regulatory inspections of private homes, requirements for obtaining warrants have been relaxed, and some searches may be conducted without a warrant.

1. **Home inspections for building code and related regulatory compliance:** The Supreme Court has held that homes may not be searched for compliance with building codes and the like, without a warrant. *See Camara v. Municipal Court*, 387 U.S. 523 (1967). However, warrants to conduct such searches do not require probable cause in the criminal sense but may issue if the agency establishes that the inspection is part of its normal regulatory scheme to monitor compliance with the relevant code.

2. **Home inspections of recipients of government benefits:** Recipients of government benefits may be required to allow welfare caseworkers to inspect their homes as a condition of continued benefits. Although private homes normally receive the most Fourth Amendment protection, the Court held in *Wyman v. James*, 400 U.S. 309 (1971), that the state of New York could require that permission for a caseworker to perform quarterly inspections of the home was a condition that had to be met before the state would provide welfare benefits to the child. The only consequence of not consenting to the search was that benefits would be cut off. To the Court, this reinforced the rehabilitative nature of the inspections.

3. **Home inspections of convicted criminals on probation or parole:** Probation officers may, without a warrant or probable cause, search the homes of convicted criminals who have been placed on probation. See *Griffin v. Wisconsin*, 483 U.S. 868 (1987). In *Griffin*, the Court approved searches of probationers' homes when the probation officer had "reasonable grounds" to believe that contraband was present. The Court is likely to extend this reasoning to convicted criminals who have been released from prison on parole.

D. Drug testing

An increasingly common form of governmental information gathering is drug testing, under which individuals are tested for the presence of alcohol and illegal drugs. The Court evaluates drug testing programs according to several factors, including the expectation of privacy of the individual tested, the degree to which the testing program invades that privacy, the importance of the governmental interest underlying the testing program, and the degree to which the testing program's standards ameliorate the potential for arbitrary selection of individuals to be tested. Although several testing programs have been challenged, most have been upheld.

1. **Customs employees:** The government may require warrantless drug testing of applicants for positions in the Customs Service involving drug interdiction, carrying firearms, or access to classified information. *See National Treasury Employees Union v. Von Raab*, 489 U.S. 656 (1989). The Court found a substantial government interest in conducting the testing. The Court relied heavily on the sensitive nature of the duties of the covered employees and the fact that employees knew that they would be drug tested when they applied for employment in the covered positions.

2. **Railroad crew members after accidents:** The government may require warrantless drug testing of railroad crew members after major accidents. *See Skinner v. Railway Labor Executives Association*, 489 U.S. 602 (1989). The Court found a strong government interest in the testing program and relied heavily on the high numbers of drug and alcohol-related accidents in the railroad industry and the need for quick testing after an accident.

3. **Candidates for public office:** The Supreme Court rejected a Georgia statute requiring all candidates for state-wide office to submit to drug testing. *See Chandler v. Miller*, 520 U.S. at 305 (1997). The Court stated that the lack of evidence in the record that Georgia has had problems with drug-abusing state officeholders meant that the invasion of privacy inherent in the drug testing program was not justified by a substantial state interest.

4. **High school athletes:** The Supreme Court has approved mandatory, random drug testing of high school student athletes. The Court reasoned that schoolchildren's expectations of privacy are reduced, that urinalysis is not highly invasive of privacy, and that the government interest in preventing drug abuse among schoolchildren is very strong. *See Vernonia School Dist. 47J v. Acton*, 515 U.S. 646 (1995).

II. PRODUCTION OF INFORMATION AND DOCUMENTS

Agencies monitor compliance with regulatory requirements by requiring parties to provide information and/or documents to the government. A great deal of information reporting is routine, such as the requirement that taxpayers file annual tax returns. In addition to requiring the subjects of regulation to provide information, an agency may subpoena documents. If the custodian of the documents does not comply, the agency may ask a court to enforce the subpoena. In general, agencies may require the provision of information or the production of documents whenever the information or documents relate to a proper subject of agency concern.

A. Agency requests for information or documents

An agency may require regulated parties to provide information or documents as long as the information sought is related to matters within the authority of the agency, the demand is not too indefinite or burdensome, and the information sought is reasonably relevant to a matter of legitimate agency concern. *See United States v. Morton Salt Co.*, 338 U.S. 632 (1950). While at one time courts were reluctant to recognize broad agency power to require regulated parties to provide information or documents, courts today rarely refuse to enforce agency subpoenas.

1. **Within agency authority:** The information sought must be on matters within the regulatory authority of the agency. This should be a very easy test to meet because ordinarily ***the jurisdiction of the agency should not be tested in a subpoena-enforcement proceeding***. However, courts occasionally refuse to enforce agency subpoenas on the ground that the information sought is outside any area of agency authority.

2. **Not too indefinite or burdensome:** Courts have enforced agency requests for information that are extremely broad and where compliance is extremely costly. Nevertheless, courts, including the Supreme Court in *Morton Salt*, have indicated that there are limits to the breadth and scope of agency subpoena power. Courts have been willing to issue protective orders to protect against the burden of disclosure of sensitive or valuable information.

3. **Reasonably relevant:** Agencies may only seek information that is reasonably relevant to a legitimate matter of agency concern. Courts have deferred to agencies' assessments of relevance and have required only that the information be relevant to the general purposes of an agency investigation—a standard that agencies normally find very easy to meet.

B. Disclosure of privileged information or trade secrets

It is unclear whether agencies must respect recognized privileges including (but not limited to) attorney-client privilege, doctor-patient privilege, and husband-wife privilege. The Fifth

Amendment privilege against self-incrimination may apply, although its requirements are relaxed in the business setting. Further, government may be required, under the Takings Clause, to compensate a regulated party whose trade secret information is disclosed to third parties as part of a regulatory scheme.

1. **Privileged information:** It is unclear whether federal agencies must respect recognized privileges, such as the attorney-client privilege, against compelled disclosure of information or production of documents. The Supreme Court unanimously rejected arguments that it recognize privilege based on academic freedom against disclosure of peer review documents in a case alleging discrimination in the denial of tenure to a professor. *See University of Pennsylvania v. EEOC*, 493 U.S. 182 (1990). In its opinion, the Court stated that it was not free to recognize the privilege since Congress had statutorily authorized the EEOC to obtain all relevant evidence. This may imply that federal agencies are free to ignore state law privileges, such as the attorneyclient privilege, when seeking information from regulated parties.

2. **Self-incrimination:** The Fifth Amendment protection against self-incrimination has only limited applicability to agency requests for information or production of documents.

   a. **The collective-entity rule:** Corporations, and other entities such as labor unions and partnerships, have no Fifth Amendment privilege against providing government with information or documents. For example, in *Bellis v. United States*, 417 U.S. 85 (1974), the Court held that the Fifth Amendment did not entitle a partner in a small law firm to refuse to produce partnership records.

   b. **Fifth Amendment rights of custodians of entity records:** Natural persons who have custody of entity records may not assert a Fifth Amendment right against production of such records. *See Braswell v. United States*, 487 U.S. 99 (1988). In Braswell, the custodian of corporate records argued that compulsory production of entity documents would violate his Fifth Amendment right against self-incrimination because the act of producing the records might be incriminatory. The Court (split 5-4) rejected this argument, reasoning that allowing the custodian to assert his or her own Fifth Amendment rights concerning the act of production would effectively recognize an entity privilege against self-incrimination since all entities act only through agents.

   c. **Fifth Amendment rights of sole proprietors:** Sole proprietors of businesses may not assert the Fifth Amendment right against self-incrimination to resist the production of records required to be kept under a legitimate regulatory program. However, the government may not avoid the Fifth Amendment right against self-incrimination by requiring criminals to keep records, subject to government inspection, of their illegal activities.

   Examples: In *Shapiro v. United States*, 335 U.S. 1 (1948), the Court upheld a requirement of the Price Control Act, applied to a sole proprietorship, that sellers of goods keep records of their transactions and make those records available to agency inspection. Shapiro argued that the records would incriminate him, but the Court held that as long as the records were the subject of legitimate regulation (i.e., regulation within the government's constitutional power and within the agency's statutory authority), the Fifth Amendment does not protect against production of records required to be kept by the regulatory program. However, in *Marchetti v. United States*, 390 U.S. 39 (1968), the Court rejected applying this standard to records required to document compliance with a tax imposed on the business of accepting wagers, i.e., illegal bookmaking. Bookies were also required to register with the IRS.

Marchetti argued that these requirements amounted to forced self-incrimination and that the regulatory scheme focused only on people suspected of criminal activities. The Court accepted Marchetti's arguments, distinguishing *Shapiro* on the grounds that registering as a bookie provided information beyond that contained in business records, that the information sought in *Marchetti* was essentially private, and that the records sought in *Shapiro* were created in a noncriminal setting while those sought in *Marchetti* were created in a criminal setting.

3. **Takings Clause:** If an agency requires disclosure of information that is considered a trade secret under state law and then requires that the information be disclosed to third parties (thereby destroying the value of the trade secret), the Takings Clause of the Fifth Amendment may require that the government pay compensation to the party whose information has been disclosed. *See Ruckelshaus v. Monsanto Co.*, 467 U.S. 986 (1984). Note that an injunction against such a taking is not normally available. Rather, the party must disclose the information and then seek compensation for any property taken.

III. THE PAPERWORK REDUCTION ACT

The Paperwork Reduction Act of 1980 (PRA) is a federal statute under which the Office of Information and Regulatory Affairs (OIRA), within the OMB has authority to review agency requests for information from members of the public.

A. The PRA's requirements

Before an agency may promulgate a new request for information, the agency must submit a proposal to OIRA with a justification as to its need for the information. OIRA may reject the agency's proposal if it finds that the agency does not have a legitimate need for the information, and OIRA may also approve the agency's proposal subject to.conditions. Because OMB is an agency subject to direct supervision by the President, this gives the President a great deal of control over information requests.

B. The PRA's limits

The PRA does not apply to information requests pursuant to a rule promulgated under the APA. Further, the PRA applies only to agency requests for information, not requirements that one regulated party disclose information directly to another party. *See Dole v. United Steelworkers*, 494 U.S. 26 (1990) (rule requiring employer to disclose workplace safety information to employees not subject to PRA). In *Dole*, the Court viewed the disclosure requirement as a substantive regulation, not an instance of information gathering.

Quiz Yourself on
AGENCY INFORMATION GATHERING

54. OSHA has regulatory authority over workplace safety. The recent resurgence of cigar smoking has OSHA concerned about the second-hand cigar smoke exposure of people who work in restaurants and bars where cigar smoking is allowed. An OSHA inspector arrives at a Chicago Butt and Brew Pub Restaurant (which is part of a national chain of restaurant-bars that promote themselves as cigar friendly) and informs the manager that he is there to collect air samples in various locations around the restaurant, including "employee-only" areas such as the employee restrooms and employee lounge where employees eat and take breaks. Can the manager refuse entry? _____

55. In the last several years, Los Angeles has seen a substantial increase in the number of illnesses suffered by people who eat raw food in restaurants. The Los Angeles Board of Health decides to inspect, four times per year, all restaurants that serve sushi and all restaurants with salad bars. Any restaurant that is subject to a complaint of food poisoning should be inspected as soon as possible after the Board receives the complaint. The Board's regulations provide that any restaurant that impedes the inspector from carrying out an inspection shall automatically lose its license and be closed until it allows the inspection. A patron of Billy's Salad and Sushi Bar on Melrose Avenue in Los Angeles contracted a severe case of food poisoning after eating at Billy's. Billy refuses to allow the Board's inspector to enter without a warrant. Does Billy have the right to insist that the inspector obtain a warrant? _____

56. As part of welfare reform, the federal government requires that states, in order to monitor eligibility, conduct regular inspections of a randomly selected group of at least 5 percent of the recipients of food stamps and transitional aid to needy families. May state inspectors make consent to such inspections a condition of continued aid? _____

57. May the government require that all prospective government employees undergo drug tests as a condition for securing government employment? _____

58. The president of an insolvent national bank testifies in Congress that he has been unable to locate records regarding a significant number of bad loans, and he blames a former bank employee for the disappearance of the records. Later, the Federal Deposit Insurance Corporation (FDIC), an agency that insures bank deposits, believes that the bank has the records and directs a subpoena to the president of the bank for the bank's records of the transactions. There is a potential for criminal liability of both the bank and the president regarding the transactions and of the president for perjury in his testimony before Congress. Can either the bank or the president resist complying with the subpoena on Fifth Amendment self-incrimination grounds? _____

Answers

54. The first question is whether OSHA has the legal authority to inspect the restaurant, which it probably does as part of its broad workplace safety mission. That mission includes health issues such as the effects of second-hand smoke. The OSHA inspector probably needs a warrant to compel the manager to admit him to the premises since, as to OSHA workplace safety issues, the restaurant is not a pervasively regulated business. However, if OSHA's desire to inspect the restaurant is part of its routine. monitoring of workplace safety, then it can probably obtain a warrant without showing that it has reason to believe that the restaurant is violating OSHA standards.

55. No. Restaurants would probably be regarded as "pervasively regulated businesses" with regard to Board of Health inspections for proper food-handling practices. The government's interest in regulating restaurant food handling is substantial. Warrantless searches may be necessary to ensure that

restaurants don't simply clean up for inspection day. The regulatory scheme's program of regular inspections, and inspections after a complaint, provide the safeguards against arbitrary searches that would otherwise be provided by the warrant procedure. As long as the inspection is part of the normal Board of Health regulatory program, the inspection may take place without a warrant.

56. Probably yes. The Court has allowed such requirements in the past. In the particular case, *Wyman v. James*, the Court relied in part on the rehabilitative nature of the home visits, which involved childcare issues. Here, the only purpose is to monitor eligibility, which puts the inspector in a purely adversarial relationship with the recipient. Nevertheless, if the only consequence of not allowing the inspection would be a benefits cutoff, the Court would likely uphold the requirement.

57. Probably not. The Court has upheld drug-testing programs when there was a special need for the tests, but it struck down a requirement that candidates for statewide office undergo drug testing. For many government positions not involving law enforcement and where drug abuse would not endanger the public or other employees, the Court would likely hold that the need to be certain about drug abuse was not strong enough to outweigh the prospective employees' privacy interests.

58. No. The bank, as a corporation or collective entity of some sort, has no right against self-incrimination. The Fifth Amendment right against self-incrimination protects only natural persons. The bank president, as custodian of corporate records, may not assert his own Fifth Amendment rights even though the act of producing the records amounts to testimony that the records exist, which directly incriminates him of perjury.

Exam Tips on
AGENCY INFORMATION GATHERING

☛ The most likely candidates for examination from the material in this chapter include warrantless inspections and the requirements for obtaining warrants, drug testing of government employees, and the collective entity rule regarding Fifth Amendment rights against self-incrimination.

☛ In a question raising an issue regarding an inspection, discuss first any doubts that the agency has the authority to conduct inspections.

   ☞ Then look to whether the agency had a warrant.

   ☞ If the agency had a warrant, the warrant may be subject to attack if the inspection was not part of the routine operation of a regulatory scheme.

   ☞ If the agency did not have a warrant, look to whether the search meets the requirements for warrantless searches of pervasively regulated businesses.

☛ In a question about drug testing, discuss whether the particular employee or employees that the government wants to test are in sensitive positions or have been involved in an incident justifying special scrutiny. Otherwise, the testing might not be proper.

☛ In a case involving production of documents or provision of information to the government, if it is relevant raise the collective entity rule and the rule that custodians of entity records may not raise Fifth Amendment objections to providing such records.

☞ It also is useful to note that courts do not like issues of agency authority to be litigated in the context of the enforcement of a subpoena.

☞ Finally, if a privilege such as the attorney-client privilege is raised, be sure to note that the applicability of state-law privileges to federal administrative proceedings has not been established.

CHAPTER 11

PRIVATE ENFORCEMENT OF REGULATORY NORMS AND PREEMPTION

ChapterScope

This chapter addresses situations in which private parties may attempt to enforce regulatory norms on their own through a direct action in court against violators or, in some cases, against the government to force the government to regulate. The main points in the chapter are:

- *Citizens' suit provisions* in many regulatory statutes allow injunctive actions against violators (including the government) and mandamus-like actions against the government when the claims involve the government as regulator.

- The citizens' suit cannot be used as a substitute for judicial review of regulations.

  - The government is not considered a "violator" of a regulatory statute if it allegedly fails to regulate properly.

  - Citizens' suit provisions for suing government officials over their regulatory actions normally address only nondiscretionary duties, and there is usually discretion regarding the content of regulations.

  - Agency regulatory failings not involving the failure to perform a nondiscretionary duty are addressed on judicial review, not in the context of a citizens' suit.

- Citizens' suit provisions override prudential standing limitations but cannot override Article 1111 standing requirements such as injury, traceability, and remediability.

- *Private rights of action* under which the victim of a violation of a regulatory statute sues the violator for damages, are sometimes implied from federal regulatory statutes.

  - Under current law, federal courts imply the private right of action only when it appears that Congress intended for the private right of action to be available.

- State law often provides a remedy for conduct that is also addressed by federal regulation.

  - State common law often provides *parallel remedies* that survive the enactment of a federal scheme, but *federal law may preempt state law* expressly or implicitly.

  - *Express preemption* arises from a federal statute identifying the preemptive effect of federal law.

  - *Implicit preemption* exists where federal law *occupies* the field, where state and federal law *conflict*, and where state law presents an *obstacle* to the accomplishment of the purposes of federal law.

- Federal agencies often have primary jurisdiction over disputes arising within their regulatory fields.

■   Primary jurisdiction may not exist where a ***savings clause*** preserves parallel judicial remedies, but agency jurisdiction may overcome a savings clause if the parallel claim is inconsistent with the federal scheme

I. THE CITIZENS' SUIT

Many relatively recent regulatory statutes, especially in the environmental area, include citizens' suit provisions under which private parties are authorized to bring suit against other private parties and government officials for violating statutes and regulations.

A. Statutory requirements for citizens suits

1. **Suits against violators:** Citizens' suit provisions typically authorize "any citizen" or "any person" to seek damages, an injunction, or both against violations of the relevant statute. For example, the Endangered Species Act provides that "any person may commence a civil suit . . . to enjoin any person, including the United States and any other governmental instrumentality or agency . . . who is alleged to be in violation of any provision of this Act or regulation issued under the authority thereof." 16 U.S.C. §1540(g)(1)(A). This type of provision authorizes injunctive suits against government agencies as violators only when their activities violate the substantive provisions of the relevant statute, for example, if a government agency's activities result in harm to an endangered species. However, it is not a "violation" for a government agency to allegedly act improperly as a regulator—for example, by adopting overly harsh or overly lenient regulations. *See Bennett v. Spear*, 520 U.S. 154 (1997).

2. **Suits against government regulators:** Citizens' suit provisions also typically provide for actions in the nature of mandamus against regulators when it is alleged that they have not fulfilled their mandatory, nondiscretionary regulatory duties. For example, another provision of the Endangered Species Act provides that "any person may commence a civil suit on his own behalf . . . against the Secretary [of the Interior] where there is alleged a failure of the Secretary to perform any act or duty under section 1533 which is not discretionary with the Secretary." 16 U.S.C. §1540(g)(1)(C).

B. The distinction between the citizens' suit and judicial review

The citizens' suit cannot be used to attack the substance of regulations. Rather, it allows suit only when the regulator has failed to fulfill a mandatory duty, such as promulgating a regulation by a statutory deadline. It is not a substitute for judicial review because the regulator normally has some discretion over the content of regulations. *See Scott v. City of Hammond*, 741 F.2d 992 (7th Cir. 1984). Thus, in *City of Hammond*, the court of appeals held that an allegation that the Clean Water Act imposes "a nondiscretionary duty to ensure that water quality standards . . . protect the public health and welfare" was in reality a claim for judicial review of the standards adopted and not proper for a citizens' suit. *City of Hammond*, 741 F.2d at 995.

C. The citizens' suit to compel regulation

If an agency fails to meet a statutory deadline, or if an agency fails to act where Congress has statutorily required it to act, then the citizens' suit may be a vehicle for compelling agency action. However, given judicial reluctance to compel agencies to act, it must be clear that the agency had no discretion for the citizens' suit to apply.

D. Standing problems in citizens' suits

Although citizens' suit provisions appear to grant everyone the right to sue over violations of the relevant statute, the Supreme Court has made it clear that normal standing rules apply to citizens' suits.

1. **Article III standing:** Citizens' suit plaintiffs must meet Article III standing requirements, including the requirement that they be among those actually injured by the alleged violation or agency failure that is the subject of the lawsuit. *See Lujan v. Defenders of Wildlife*, 504 U.S. 555 (1992). For citizens' suit plaintiffs to have standing to seek injunctive relief, they must show that they will benefit from the injunction in some concrete way.

2. **Prudential standing limits:** Citizens' suit provisions may overrule prudential limits on standing. For example, the Supreme Court has held that citizens' suit provisions override the zone of interests test by bringing all potential plaintiffs identified by the citizens' suit provisions within the zone of interests. *See Bennett v. Spear*, 520 U.S. 154 (1997). However, if a citizens' suit provision is more narrowly drawn, so that only a particular class of citizens is granted the right to sue, then prudential limitations still apply to those outside the favored class.

II. THE IMPLIED PRIVATE RIGHT OF ACTION

Under some circumstances, even if a federal regulatory statute contains no citizen's suit or other provision authorizing a private claim, a federal court will imply a right of action so that a private party can sue another private party for violating the regulatory statute. The test for whether a federal court should imply the right of action has evolved and now focuses almost exclusively on Congress's intent regarding the private right of action.

A. Understanding the implied private right of action

An implied private right of action under a regulatory statute is a claim brought by an injured private party against another private party based on the defendant's violation of the regulatory statute. The action may be for damages or injunctive relief, depending on normal rules regarding appropriate remedies. The necessity of implying the right of action arises because many regulatory statutes provide for enforcement only by the relevant federal agency or by the Department of Justice through a criminal prosecution.

1. **Relationship to state tort principles:** The *private right of action* is similar to state tort law under which a regulatory statute provides the standard of care in a tort action. However, there are significant differences between state tort law's use of regulatory standards and the implied right of action under federal regulatory norms. In the state law case, the cause of action is established by the relevant branch of state law (usually tort law) and the only issue for which the regulatory statute is relevant is what standard of care should be applied to that cause of action. The issue in the implied right of action cases is ***whether there should be a cause of action at all.*** Without the private right of action, the plaintiff would be left to whatever remedies, if any, exist under state law.

   Example: Section 10(b) of the Securities Exchange Act of 1934, 15 U.S.C. §78j, prohibits, "in connection with the purchase or sale of any [registered] security" the use of "manipulative or deceptive" devices "in contravention of [the] rules and regulations" of the Securities Exchange Commission (SEC). An SEC rule, known as Rule 10b-5, prohibits fraudulent and deceitful devices in connection with the purchase and sale of registered securities. An investor, an insurance company, and others constructed a scheme to purchase the stock of Manhattan Casualty Company without putting up any money except the assets of Manhattan Casualty Company itself. This depleted Manhattan's assets, because all company assets went to the sellers of the stock. After Manhattan Casualty went broke, the state insurance commissioner sued those involved in the scheme in federal court, alleging violations of §10(b) and Rule 10b-5. In *Superintendent of Insurance of New York v. Bankers Life & Casualty Co.*, 404 U.S. 6 (1971), the Supreme Court held that the federal court suit was proper because a private right of action existed under §10(b) and Rule 10b-5. Had the Court not so ruled, the plaintiffs would have had only state law fraud claims, which might not be as easy to prove as the federal claims under §10b and Rule 10b-5.

2. **Federal jurisdiction over implied private rights of action:** If a private right of action is implied under a federal regulatory statute, because the claims are federal, the federal courts have jurisdiction to hear the claims.

B. The early test for private rights of action

When federal courts began implying private rights of action from regulatory statutes, they analogized to state doctrines that used regulatory statutes to supply standards of conduct and held that a private right of action would be implied whenever the private right of action was "necessary to make effective the congressional purpose." *See J.I. Case v. Borak*, 377 U.S. 426, 430 (1964). This test allowed private rights of action under a broad range of federal regulatory statutes that did not explicitly provide a private right of action.

C. The four factors for private rights of action: *Cort v. Ash*

The *J.I. Case* test was criticized for allowing private rights of action in situations that Congress may not have intended and for federalizing claims in areas that had previously been under state control. The Court attempted to tighten up on implied private rights of action in *Cort v. Ash*, 422 U.S. 66 (1975). In *Cort*, the court of appeals had implied a private right of action brought by shareholders on behalf of a corporation against officers who had violated a criminal prohibition against making campaign donations out of corporate funds. (Without a private right of action, the statute would be enforced only if the Department of Justice initiated a criminal prosecution.) The Court stated that henceforth, claims that a private right of action should be implied from a regulatory statute would be judged on four factors.

1. **Membership in a protected class for whose benefit the statute was passed:** The first factor is whether the plaintiff is a member of a class for whose protection or benefit the statute was passed. In *Cort*, the Supreme Court stated that the criminal prohibition on using corporate funds to make campaign contributions was meant primarily to protect voters from corporate influence—not to protect corporations and stockholders from depletion of corporate funds.

2. **Congressional intent:** The second *Cort* factor focuses on Congress's intent regarding whether a private right of action should be recognized. In *Cort*, the Court could find no evidence of congressional intent either way. To the Court, this meant that the expectation probably was that state law would continue to govern the relationship among the corporation, its shareholders, and its officers.

3. **Policy of the statute:** Consistent with *J.I. Case*, the third *Cort* factor is whether implying a private right of action would make the statute achieve Congress's goals more effectively. In

Cort, the Supreme Court observed that forcing the officers of the corporation to repay the funds would not undo the impact those funds had on the election, and thus the private right would not advance the congressional purpose. This conclusion seems wrong. A personal obligation of corporate officers to repay the funds would certainly deter violations, and thus would provide some protection to the electoral process.

4. **Displacement of state law:** The fourth *Cort* factor is that it weighs against recognizing an implied right of action if the federal claim would intrude on an area traditionally regulated under state law. In *Cort*, this factor weighed against recognizing the right of action because corporate law has traditionally been the province of state regulation.

D. **Refocus on congressional intent for private rights of action**

Although *Cort v. Ash* was intended to tighten up on allowing implied private rights of action, it was widely perceived that the four factors still allowed federal courts to imply rights of action when Congress may not have intended them. Thus, *Cort* was followed by a strong movement toward further tightening of the standard for recognizing a private right of action.

1. **Justice Powell's dissent in *Cannon v. University of Chicago*:** In *Cannon v. University of Chicago*, 441 U.S. 677 (1979), the Court implied a private right of action under a statute that prohibits sex discrimination by institutions that receive federal educational subsidies. The only enforcement method provided in the statute itself is that the Department of Education can cut off federal funds to violators. Justice Powell dissented and argued forcefully that federal courts should never allow private rights of action under regulatory or criminal statutes without compelling evidence that Congress intended to recognize private actions. He argued that judicial implication of a private right of action violated separation of powers because it placed the federal courts in a legislative role. He also argued that whenever Congress fails to include a private right of action in the legislation itself, it must mean that any such proposal would have been voted down.

2. ***Karahalios* and the rejection of unintended private rights of action:** In *Karahalios v. National Federation of Federal Employees*, 489 U.S. 527 (1989), the Court apparently accepted Justice Powell's arguments and held that federal courts should not imply a private right of action unless it is clear that, although Congress failed to write the private action into the statute, it intended that the courts recognize it. The Court did not explicitly overrule *Cort v. Ash*, but it recharacterized *Cort*, stating, "Congress was undoubtedly aware from our cases such as *Cort v. Ash* . . . that the Court had departed from its prior standard for resolving a claim urging that an implied statutory cause of action should be recognized, and that such issues were being resolved by a straightforward inquiry into whether Congress intended to provide a private cause of action." *Karahalios*, 489 U.S. at 536. Thus, perhaps the other three *Cort* factors are still relevant but only as aids for determining congressional intent.

III. ALTERNATIVE STATE REMEDIES AND REGULATORY PREEMPTION

Conduct regulated under federal standards may also be regulated under state law and be subject to the general provisions of state common law, such as tort law. A state law claim may exist regardless of whether the conduct also violates federal law. This creates the potential for conflict between state and federal law, and the doctrines of preemption and primary jurisdiction aid in determining whether state and federal standards can coexist. If not, federal law may preempt state law under the Supremacy Clause.

A.   State remedies and the presumption against preemption

While Congress has the power to preempt state law under the Supremacy Clause, Article VI, Clause 2 of the Constitution, there is a presumption, rooted in federalism concerns, that state law is not preempted unless Congress's intent to do so is clear. *See Wisconsin Public Intervenor v. Mortier*, 501 U.S. 597 (1991).

B.   Standards for preemption of state law

While Congress's intent to preempt state law must be clear, it is not always necessary for Congress to announce that it intends to preempt state law. Rather, courts determine whether ***preemption*** has occurred using a variety of standards—all designed to shed light on Congress's intent.

1. **Express preemption:** In the simplest case for preemption, Congress expressly preempts state law by providing in a statute that state law is preempted. For example, the Cigarette Labeling Act (under which warning labels are required to appear on cigarette packages and cigarette advertising) provides that states may not impose any "requirement or prohibition based on smoking or health . . . with respect to the advertising or promotion of any cigarettes the packages of which are labeled in conformity with the provisions of this chapter." 15 U.S.C §1334(b). This provision preempts state law claims based, for example, on failure to warn of the dangers of smoking, even if it is alleged that the cigarette company diluted the warning labels by minimizing health risks in other advertising and promotion. *See Cipollone v. Liggett Group, Inc.*, 505 U.S. 504 (1992).

    a. **Partial preemption:** Often, preemption provisions provide for partial preemption, i.e., preempting certain aspects of state law while preserving other aspects of state law. For example, in *Bates v. Dow Agrosciences LLC*, 125 S. Ct. 1788 (2005), the Court held that the federal statute regulating pesticides may preempt fraud and failure to warn claims if they conflict with federal labeling and marketing requirements, but the federal statute did not preempt state law claims for defective design, defective manufacture, negligent testing, breach of express warranty, and violation of a state deceptive trade practices act. The Court left it to the lower courts to determine whether conflict exists. Partial preemption provisions may also explicitly allow state law to fill gaps in federal law. They may explicitly preserve state law that is more stringent than federal law, so that federal law, in effect, supplies a regulatory floor that state law may exceed.

    b. **Savings clauses:** Many federal statutes contain savings clauses under which parallel remedies, whether state or federal, explicitly survive the enactment of a new federal statute. When a savings clause exists, state tort and other remedies are not preempted. However, it is sometimes necessary to determine the reach of a savings clause. When a state law claim would frustrate Congress's purposes or cause a conflict with a provision of federal law, preemption may occur despite the existence of the savings clause. *See, e.g., Geier v. American Honda Motor Co.*, 529 U.S. 861 (2000).

2. **Implied preemption:** In addition to express preemption, courts sometimes find implied preemption, i.e., courts imply congressional intent to preempt from the circumstances even when no express preemption provision applies. Because there is often little or no evidence of congressional intent to preempt, implied preemption sometimes appears to be created by the

courts rather than based on Congress's intent. There are three main categories of implied preemption.

a. **Field preemption:** Field preemption means that although a federal statute does not expressly preempt state law, the federal law is so comprehensive and the area is of such pressing federal concern that the court concludes that Congress must have intended to displace state law that is within the "field" occupied by Congress. Here, congressional intent to preempt is inferred from the comprehensiveness of federal regulation. Under field preemption, federal law occupies an entire area and state law within the field is displaced.

b. **Actual conflict preemption:** State law in actual conflict with federal law is preempted. If, for example, federal law commands a particular course of conduct and state law prohibits the very same conduct, the state law is preempted because of the actual conflict between the two legal regimes. It is presumed that Congress intends such preemption. Note that if state law is merely somewhat more restrictive than federal law, conflict preemption does not necessarily exist because it would not violate federal law to obey the more stringent state standard.

c. **"Obstacle" preemption:** Federal law also preempts state law when a court concludes that state law poses an obstacle to the accomplishment of Congress's purposes in enacting the federal law. For example, although no actual conflict exists, sometimes when Congress enacts relatively permissive regulation, it means to allow regulated parties to act up to the limits of federal law and thus intends to preempt more stringent state requirements. In such cases, the more stringent state law would pose an obstacle to the accomplishment of Congress's intent, and it would be preempted.

3. **The relationship between express and implied preemption:** At one time, the Supreme Court held that where an express preemption statute is present, implied preemption cannot exist because it is presumed that Congress expressed the limits of its preemptive intent in the statute. However, more recently, the Court has stated that express and implied preemption can coexist. *See Geier.* The strongest argument in favor of this change is that even when an express preemption provision exists but does not apply, Congress must intend to preempt state law that actually conflicts with provisions of federal law.

Example: The requirement that new cars be equipped with passive restraints such as airbags was phased in by NHTSA over a period of years. After Geier was severely injured in an accident involving a 1987 car without an airbag, she sued under state law claiming that the car was negligently and defectively designed because it should have been equipped with a driver's side airbag. The Supreme Court held that this state law claim was preempted by the NHTSA's regulation requiring that only 10 percent of cars from that model year be so equipped. The Court first held that the Federal Motor Vehicle Safety Act's express preemption provision did not apply, mainly because of a savings clause which stated that compliance with a federal standard "does not exempt any person from any liability under common law." However, the Court went on to find implied preemption because the "no airbag" suit brought by Geier would conflict with federal law phasing in the airbags requirement. The Court found that the agency deliberately decided to preserve flexibility so that carmakers might invent cheaper and better alternatives to airbags. *See Geier v. American Honda Motor Co.*, 529 U.S. 861 (2000). This ruling is contrary to the usual understanding that federal law sets a regulatory floor which states are free to exceed, and may signal a greater willingness within the current Court to find implied preemption. *See Sprietsma v. Mercury Marine*, 537 U.S. 51 (2002) (U.S. Coast Guard's rejection of propeller guard requirement did not preempt state tort law claim based on boat manufacturer's failure to include propeller guard in design of boat).

C. Punitive damages and regulatory preemption

Punitive damages present a special case because they are designed to punish and deter. Thus, it was argued that in a field where federal regulation permits particular conduct, punitive damages should not be allowed because, in essence, a state would be deterring conduct permitted under federal law—thus conflicting with or at least frustrating the purpose of federal law. However, in *Silkwood v. Kerr-McGee Corp.*, 464 U.S. 238 (1984), a narrow majority of the Court held that punitive damages should be treated like other common-law remedies; if common-law remedies generally are not preempted, then punitive damages are also not preempted.

D. The primary jurisdiction doctrine

The *primary jurisdiction* doctrine requires that certain claims be heard in an agency either before, or instead of, an action in a court.

1. **Basic primary jurisdiction principles:** At its most basic, the primary jurisdiction doctrine provides that a claim that is within the substantive jurisdiction of an agency must be heard first by that agency, even if the facts give rise to a claim otherwise cognizable in a court. This doctrine is related to preemption since, as applied to a state law claim, primary jurisdiction in a federal agency may preempt a parallel state law claim if it is held that the substantive claim may be litigated only within an agency under federal standards.

   Example: The United States government shipped unfused napalm bombs by rail and refused to pay the tariff rate for "incendiary bombs." The government argued that since the bombs were unfused, the lower rate for "gasoline in steel drums" applied. The railroad sued the government in the court of claims, and the Supreme Court held that the claim should have been presented to the Interstate Commerce Commission (ICC) since the Commission had established the categories at issue and would be in a better position to decide which category applied. *See United States v. Western Pacific Rwy. Co.*, 352 U.S. 59 (1956).

2. **Savings clauses:** *Savings clauses* in federal regulatory statutes (which state that the remedies in the federal statute are in addition to, and do not displace, preexisting remedies) usually mean that the primary jurisdiction doctrine does not bar a claim in court. However, if the judicial remedy would destroy the jurisdiction of the agency, then even a savings clause will not prevent the preemption of alternative remedies.

   Examples: Under state common law, shippers may sue common carriers if they believe the carrier charges "unreasonable" rates. The federal Interstate Commerce Act (ICA) also prohibited carriers from charging unreasonable rates. Congress placed jurisdiction to decide whether rates were reasonable in the now-defunct Interstate Commerce Commission. When a manufacturer of cotton oil sued a railroad over allegedly unreasonable rates, the railroad defended on the basis of the Interstate Commerce Commission's control over rates. The,shipper replied that the Interstate Commerce Act explicitly preserved shippers' common-law remedies. The Supreme Court held for the railroad, ruling that the claim that the rates were unreasonable was within the primary jurisdiction of the Interstate Commerce Commission. To allow the common-law remedy, reasoned the Court, would effectively destroy the jurisdiction of the

Commission since the courts of all the states would be able to declare federally approved rates "unreasonable." *See Texas & Pacific Rwy. Co. v. Abilene Cotton Oil Co.*, 204 U.S. 426 (1907).

Consumer activist Ralph Nader had a speaking engagement in Connecticut. He had a confirmed reservation on a flight from Washington, D.C., to Hartford, but the airline overbooked the flight. Nader, who arrived only five minutes before the scheduled departure, was bumped from the flight. He refused the airline's offer of compensation, and he and the group for whom he was scheduled to speak sued for damages under state tort law. (He was able to get to the engagement by taking a flight to Boston and driving to Connecticut.) The airline claimed that federal regulation of the airline industry under the Federal Aviation Act placed primary jurisdiction over the claim in the Civil Aeronautics Board. The court of appeals agreed with the airline, relying primarily on the heavy regulation of the airline industry, including the Board's close supervision of fares and competition. However, the relevant chapter of the Act contained the following savings clause: "[n]othing contained in this chapter shall in any way abridge or alter the remedies now existing at common law or by statute, but the provisions of this chapter are in addition to such remedies." 49 U.S.C §1506 (repealed). Given this provision, and the fact that Nader did not claim that the airline had violated any provision of the Act or its tariff filed with the Board under the Act, the Supreme Court held that the claim was not within the Board's primary jurisdiction and could be brought directly in a court. *See Nader v. Allegheny Airlines, Inc.*, 426 U.S. 290 (1976).

Quiz Yourself on
PRIVATE ENFORCEMENT OF REGULATORY NORMS AND PREEMPTION

59. A provision of the Clean Air Act grants a citizens' suit for an injunction against any person, including all government entities, who violates any provision of the Act. The statute also grants an action to compel the performance of a mandatory duty against the Administrator of the EPA. The EPA has issued regulations governing second-hand smoke which allow smoking in workplaces as long as sufficient ventilation is in place. The American Lung Association is upset that the EPA did not ban indoor smoking at all workplaces. Can it use the citizens' suit provisions to attempt to compel stronger regulation? _____

60. Assume the same citizens' suit provision and the same set of issues. Does the American Lung Association have standing to sue? _____

61. A federal statute prohibits gender discrimination at high schools receiving federal funds. The statute specifies that the penalty for failing to maintain equality in all programs is a reduction in federal funds, with a total cutoff if the discrimination continues after initial reductions in funding. The school maintains only one hockey team (a boys' team) and a girl tries out for the team. The coach tells her that the hockey program is not open to girls. She brings suit in federal court against the school district for an injunction to allow her to try out for the team and for damages. Her claim is based on a violation of the statute prohibiting discrimination in schools receiving federal funds. Is this a proper claim? _____

62. A farmer complies with all federal regulations regarding the use of pesticides and fertilizer on his fields. However, the runoff from those fields is causing damage to downstream property owners. For example, it is killing the fish in his neighbor's fishing pond. The affected neighbors sue under state law to have the farmer's use of his property declared a nuisance. They ask for damages and an injunction. Does federal law allow this state law claim to be pressed? _____

63. A worker is fired during a union organizing campaign, and she sues her employer in federal court for violating the National Labor Relations Act by firing her in retaliation for pro-union activities. Can the claim go forward in court? _____

Answers

59. No. The provision allowing injunctions against violators applies to the government only when the government itself is polluting, not when the government allegedly is not regulating properly. Unless the statute requires EPA to ban indoor smoking at workplaces, the Administrator does not fail to fulfill a nondiscretionary duty by not banning smoking in indoor workplaces. Only judicial review may be used to attack the substance of regulations.

60. Probably. If a member of the American Lung Association is injured by the failure to ban smoking, e.g., if a member works in an indoor workplace where smoking is allowed, then the Association has standing to assert its member's claim. There should be no zone of interests problem as long as the Association's member is a worker, since it is likely that workers are within the zone of interests of the statute. Further, even if there were a theoretical zone of interests problem, the typical citizens' suit provision places everyone identified as having a claim within the zone of interests.

61. Maybe. The Supreme Court has approved a private right of action under statutes like the one described, largely because the plaintiff is clearly within the class of people who benefit from the statute, and the private action would tend to advance the purposes of the statute. However, in the absence of evidence of congressional intent to allow the private right of action, the courts today would be skeptical of the claim. The Supreme Court now appears to agree with Justice Powell's dissent in *Cannon* that judicial creation of a right of action out of a regulatory statute raises serious separation of powers concerns on the ground that it is for Congress to decide whether to create a federal cause of action.

62. Probably yes. The federal statute probably regulates the safe use of pesticides and fertilizers because of safety and general environmental concerns. Such statutes often have savings clauses and rarely preempt state tort law. The federal statutes that regulate the labeling of pesticides have been held not to preempt state claims based on improper use of pesticides. However, if the federal statute explicitly preempts claims based on the use of pesticides and fertilizers or if the overall context indicates that Congress intended to preempt such claims, then the state claim might not survive.

63. No. A claim that an employer has fired an employee for engaging in pro-union activities states a claim that the employer has committed an unfair labor practice. Such claims are within the primary jurisdiction of the NLRB; it is up to the Board to determine whether the company has committed an unfair labor practice.

 *Exam Tips on*
PRIVATE ENFORCEMENT OF REGULATORY NORMS AND PREEMPTION

☛ The material in this chapter is rarely tested on because it is not central to most administrative law courses. The material on private rights of action may be tested on more often than the remainder of the material.

☛ In any question regarding citizens' suits, the language of the particular citizens' suit provision should be the starting place for analysis.

☛ On a question regarding the relationship between citizens' suit provisions and judicial review, the recent decision in *Bennett v. Spear* provides the framework for understanding.

    ☞ The important point is that citizens' suit provisions are narrow, allowing claims against the government only when the government fails to perform a nondiscretionary duty or violates the relevant statute as a regulated private party might violate it.

☛ Citizens' suits often raise standing issues.

    ☞ You should distinguish between prudential limits on standing, such as the zone of interests test, which citizens' suit provision can affect and constitutional standing requirements, which citizens' suit provisions cannot affect.

☛ In a question about implied private rights of action, it may be useful to compare the current "intent of Congress" standard to the two standards that preceded it, the *J.I. Case* "advance the statutory purposes" standard and the four-factor test of *Cort v. Ash*.

☛ On preemption questions, the starting point for analysis should be statutory language, including preemption provisions, partial preemption provisions, and savings clauses.

    ☞ If there is no express preemption provision, look for implied preemption through "field preemption," "actual conflict preemption," or "obstacle to the legislative purpose" preemption.

☛ In a case involving overlap between judicial remedies and the jurisdiction of a federal agency, apply the primary jurisdiction doctrine.

    ☞ If it appears that the agency has jurisdiction over a dispute, and the dispute is within the expertise of the agency, then there is an argument that a judicial remedy should not be allowed until the agency has had the opportunity to address the case.

LIABILITY OF AGENCIES AND OFFICIALS

ChapterScope ───

This chapter is about government and government official liability in damages for violations of legal and constitutional norms. Damages liability is an alternative to judicial review as a method for controlling administrative and other government officials. The main points of this chapter are:

- *Sovereign immunity* in the United States has traditionally barred government and government officials from liability for misconduct that causes damages to private parties.

    - The federal government, in the *Federal Tort Claims Act (FTCA)* and related statutes, has, to a limited extent, waived its sovereign immunity.

    - Under the FTCA, the government is liable for negligence torts if a private party would be liable in tort under state law.

    - Liability under the FTCA is limited by many exceptions and limiting doctrines, the most important of which is the statutory bar on liability for *discretionary functions*. The discretionary function exception disallows liability for official choices involving the exercise of policy judgment.

    - The **Feres** *doctrine* bars FTCA liability for conduct involving military matters, such as damages claims brought by members of the armed forces for injuries while on duty.

- The **Bivens** action is a judicially created damages action against individual federal government officials for constitutional violations.

    - The *Bivens* action is available for all constitutional violations unless Congress has designated a substitute for the *Bivens* action or special factors counsel hesitation in the absence of congressional recognition of the *Bivens* action.

    - Defendants in *Bivens* actions enjoy immunities from damages awards.

        - Officials performing judicial, legislative, and prosecutorial functions are absolutely immune from damages.

        - Other officials have a qualified immunity under which they may be held liable only if they violate a clearly established constitutional right.

- State officials violating the Constitution or federal statutory law may be sued by parties injured under 42 U.S.C. §1983, which provides a damages action against officials who violate federal constitutional and legal rights under color of state law.

    - State officials enjoy the same immunities as federal officials sued under *Bivens*.

- State governments and state agencies may not be sued under §1983 because of Eleventh Amendment immunity and because the Court has held that Congress did not intend for states to be §1983 defendants.

■ Municipalities may be held liable under §1983, but only when a constitutional violation is caused by a municipal policy or custom.

■ Municipalities may not be held vicariously liable for the constitutional torts of their employees.

I. SOVEREIGN IMMUNITY AND SUITS AGAINST FEDERAL AGENTS AND AGENCIES

When errors, tortious conduct, or other misconduct by administrators cause damage to the property or person of private parties, the victim may attempt to sue for damages rather than merely seek judicial review. Traditionally, sovereign immunity bars suits against the government unless the government consents. Statutory and judicial changes have made suits against the sovereign possible, although the circumstances under which governments and government officials can be held liable for damages are still somewhat limited.

A. Common law sovereign immunity

At common law, sovereign immunity barred damages actions against the government and government officials acting in their official capacities unless the government consented to the suit. In English law, sovereign immunity was actually relatively narrow because consent to suit was granted as a routine manner. In the United States, the formally broad sovereign immunity was adopted from English law without a tradition of routine waiver, so that it was very difficult in the United States to bring a damages action against the government.

B. The Federal Torts Claim Act

The two major waivers of the sovereign immunity of the government of the United States are the Tucker Act (which in 1887 waived the government's immunity in contract, admiralty, and other nontort matters) and the Federal Tort Claims Act (*FTCA*) (which, in 1947, waived the sovereign immunity of the federal government over a large area of tort actions). In administrative law, our focus is on the FTCA because it is often used to pursue damages when the conduct of administrators is allegedly tortious.

1. **The waiver of sovereign immunity:** The FTCA waives the sovereign immunity of the United States for *negligent or otherwise wrongful* acts or omissions by the United States government or its employees.

2. **Liability under the FTCA:** The FTCA creates federal government liability for "tort claims . . . in the same manner and to the same extent as a private individual under like circumstances." 28 U.S.C. §2674. The Act also grants jurisdiction over FTCA claims to the federal district courts, and the jurisdictional provision provides that liability exists "for negligent or wrongful acts or omissions of any employee of the Government . . . in accordance with the law of the place where the act or omission occurred." 28 U.S.C. §1346(b). If the government is liable under the FTCA, the officer or officers involved are individually immune. Government liability is a substitute for individual liability.

   a. **Strict liability not allowed:** Strict liability is not allowed under the FTCA. The statutory specification of liability for "negligent or wrongful" acts has been read to preclude strict liability or other forms of liability without fault. *See Laird v. Nelms*, 406 U.S. 797 (1972).

b. **Liability is determined under state law:** The FTCA's specification that liability exists when "a private person . . . would be liable to the claimant in accordance with the law of the place where the act or omission occurred" means that state law determines when liability exists. 28 U.S.C. §1346(b).

c. **FTCA procedural restrictions:** Procedurally, claims under the FTCA are not as attractive to plaintiffs as traditional tort suits. The FTCA does not provide for jury trial or punitive damages, there are strict requirements that claims be presented to administrative agencies, and administrative remedies must be exhausted before bringing suit. These procedural features of FTCA claims are typical of procedural aspects of state tort claims acts (in which states waive their sovereign immunity in state court) throughout the United States.

d. **No statutory exception exists for "uniquely governmental functions":** The FTCA creates liability even when the government is engaged in a purely regulatory function for which there may be no private analog. Because FTCA liability is tied to state law liability of private persons, the government has often argued in defending FTCA claims that the government is not liable when the conduct giving rise to the claim has no private analog, since in such cases the plaintiff cannot establish that a private person would be liable under state law. The Supreme Court has consistently rejected this argument except with regard to military activities, where the Court has rejected FTCA liability on the ground that there is no private law analog to allowing a soldier to sue his superior officers or the government for damages. *See Feres v. United States*, 340 U.S. 135 (1950). The *Feres* doctrine is discussed below in more detail.

Example: In *Berkovitz v. United States*, 486 U.S. 531 (1988), an FTCA suit was brought alleging that the government negligently approved an oral polio vaccine. An infant who was given the vaccine contracted polio from it, causing serious physical impairments. The government argued that the FTCA's analogy to private liability precluded liability for regulatory conduct. The government's argument is that because private persons cannot engage in regulatory conduct, the plaintiff cannot establish that a private person would be liable for the challenged conduct. The Court, noting that it had twice before rejected a regulatory-function exception to the FTCA, stated firmly that no such exception existed and held that the Berkovitz's claim could go forward.

3. **Exceptions to FTCA liability:** The FTCA contains numerous exceptions and limitations, the most important of which is the discretionary-function exception, which is discussed in detail below. Other exceptions include no liability for negligence in delivering the mail, no liability for negligence in the collection of taxes or customs duties, no liability for intentional torts, no liability for combatant activities of the armed forces, and no liability for claims arising in a foreign country. *Sosa v. Alvarez-Machain*, 124 S. Ct. 2739 (2004) (no liability for tort—kidnapping of Mexican national in Mexico for prosecution in the United States—that occurs in foreign country).

4. **The discretionary-function exception:** The FTCA provides that there is no liability for "the exercise or performance or the failure to exercise or perform a *discretionary function* or duty." 28 U.S.C. §2680(a). In *Berkovitz*, the Court defined the discretionary-function exception as exempting from liability actions where the official has choice and where the action involves the "permissible exercise of policy judgment." There has been a great deal of litigation over the scope of the discretionary-function exception. In addition to law and policymaking functions,

the courts have exempted a great deal of the operations of the government from the coverage of the FTCA.

a. ***Dahelite*:** In *Dahelite v. United States*, 346 U.S. 15 (1953), the government's negligence in manufacturing, labeling, and shipping of fertilizer caused an explosion while the fertilizer was being loaded onto a ship for shipment overseas as part of post-World War II aid to foreign countries. Hundreds of people were killed, thousands injured, and massive property damage resulted. The Court held that the discretionary-function exception barred liability for the negligence that caused the explosion. The Court did not clearly define the discretionary-function exception, but held that there was no liability because the acts involved furthered "governmental functions"; because the acts were initiated by a high-level government official; because the acts involved choices among different methods of production, packing, and shipment; and because the acts followed from planning-level (as opposed to operational-level) decisions.

b. ***Indian Towing*. The planning versus operational test:** Soon after *Dahelite*, a narrow majority of the Court adopted a definition of the discretionary-function exception under which the key distinction was between ***planning-level decisions*** (which were exempt from FTCA liability) and ***operational-level activities*** (which were not exempt). In *Indian Towing Co. v. United States*, 350 U.S. 61 (1955), the owners of a ship that ran aground sued over the Coast Guard's failure to maintain or repair a lighthouse and the failure to warn that the lighthouse was not operating. The Court distinguished between the decision whether to have a light house (which was a planning decision that could not give rise to FTCA liability) and the maintenance of the existing lighthouse (which, being an operational activity, was not a discretionary function within the meaning of the FTCA exemption).

c. **Discretionary function and the government as regulator:** The most difficult questions under the discretionary-function exception arise when government negligence occurs in the course of government regulation. In recent cases, the Court has been skeptical of claims that the government should be held liable for negligence in performing inspections and similar regulatory functions, although, as noted above, the Court has rejected a blanket exception for regulatory functions.

   i. ***Varig Airlines*:** In *United States v. S.A. Empresa De Viacao Aerea Rio Grandense (Varig Airlines)*, 467 U.S. 797 (1984), the Court rejected an FTCA claim which attributed a fire in an airplane to the FAA's negligent certification of the airplane even though the towel disposal area, where the fire started, did not meet FAA fire-resistance standards. The Court stated that the FAA's administration of the certification procedure is within the discretionary-function exception to FTCA liability. The Court held that both the FAA's decision to implement its safety standards through "spot checks" and the application of the spot-check program to the particular airplane involved discretionary decisionmaking regarding the best method for implementing the standards.

   ii. ***Berkovitz*:** In *Berkovitz v. United States*, discussed above, Berkovitz sued the government over alleged negligence in licensing a private company to produce a polio vaccine and in approving the release of the batch of vaccine that contained the dose that gave the Berkovitz child polio.

   ■ Choice and policy judgment. Although the *Berkovitz* Court rejected a blanket exception for regulatory functions and allowed the particular claims to proceed beyond the pleading stage, the Court appeared to approve a rather broad reading of the discretionary-function exception under which all conduct involving "choice" and "policy judgment" within the bounds of legally granted discretion would be exempt from FTCA liability.

■ No discretion to violate mandatory duties. In *Berkovitz* itself, the first claim was not barred by the discretionary-function exception because the plaintiffs alleged that the officials granted the license without receiving statutorily required data from the company (there is no discretion to violate mandatory provisions of governing law). Further allegations regarding this first claim were less clear. The Court left it to the district court to determine whether the plaintiffs were attacking further failures to follow established licensing procedures or whether the plaintiffs were attacking discretionary activity regarding the conduct of regulatory oversight. The second claim survived the government's motion to dismiss because the plaintiffs alleged that the government officials allowed the lot of vaccine to be released without testing it—despite a regulation requiring testing of all lots of vaccine before release. Once again, this conduct would not involve discretion because the testing policy was alleged to be mandatory.

iii. ***Gaubert*:** In *Gaubert v. United States*, 499 U.S. 315 (1991), the Supreme Court held that the discretionary-function exception barred FTCA claims based on negligent government management of the day-to-day operation of a savings and loan. The government became involved in the operation of the savings and loan under federal programs that insure deposits and require institutions to meet certain financial requirements. Insolvent savings and loans cost the government billions of dollars in the 1980s and 1990s. Claims based on negligent bank operation, and claims based on negligent selection of bank officers and directors, were barred because the activities of the regulators involved "choice or judgment" and "the exercise of discretion in furtherance of public policy goals." The *Gaubert* decision may signal a retreat from *Berkovitz* to a broader application of the discretionary-function exception, or it may simply be an application of established principles to a situation in which the government officials had a great deal of choice in how to best pursue their goal of limiting the government's losses when the savings and loan became insolvent.

iv. **The related government contractor defense:** In a series of cases related to the discretionary-function exception, federal courts have accorded government contractors a defense to state tort liability when a government contractor is sued for design defects if the government approved the design specifications. *See Boyle v. United Technologies Corp.*, 487 U.S. 500 (1988). This relates to the discretionary-function test because if the government is shielded from liability because approval of the design specifications is a discretionary function, then the private company that follows the specifications approved by the government should also be shielded from liability or the government will indirectly bear the liability costs in the price of the product. The government contractor defense does not apply if the government was not involved in the design, and it does not apply to manufacturing defect claims.

5. **The *Feres* doctrine and liability for military activities:** The Supreme Court has created a nonstatutory exception to FTCA liability for military activities, basically barring all claims that are "incident to service" in the armed forces.

a. **FTCA exception for military combat:** The FTCA exempts "combatant activities of the military . . . during time of war." Thus, it might be argued that other military claims are implicitly allowed by the FTCA. However, in *Feres v. United States*, 340 U.S. 135 (1950), the Court held that injuries to persons on active military duty were not covered by the FTCA because there is "no liability of a 'private individual' even remotely analogous to . . . permitt[ing] a soldier to recover for negligence, against either his superior officers or the Government he is serving." *Feres*, 340 U.S. at 141.

b. **Scope of the *Feres* doctrine: *The Feres doctrine bars all claims incident to service.*** *Feres*, itself, barred medical malpractice claims by active-duty servicemen against allegedly negligent military doctors and barred a claim for injuries caused by unsafe military barracks. The *Feres* doctrine has been held not to bar a medical malpractice claim brought by a veteran alleging negligent care in a veterans' hospital or a claim by a member of the military arising from negligent driving by a civilian employee. However, the Feres doctrine did bar a claim based on the Navy's decision not to erect lights on a road leading to a naval base. *See Lauer v. United States*, 968 F.2d 1428 (1st Cir.) cert. denied, 506 U.S. 1033 (1992).

II. LIABILITY OF INDIVIDUAL FEDERAL OFFICIALS

Private parties, alleging that they have been injured by the conduct of government officials, often sue the individual officials. Claims against government officials are based on state tort law and also on the Constitution. There are strict limits on the liability of government officials for conduct arising out of their official duties, including immunities and limits on the scope of the causes of action available to seek damages for official conduct.

A. Common-law immunities of government officials

Federal government officials sued for common-law torts allegedly committed while performing official duties have a variety of immunities from liability.

1. **Privilege:** In many situations, government officials are privileged to engage in conduct that, if performed by a private party, would be tortious. For example, police officers have a good-faith defense to false-arrest claims that is not available to private parties.

2. **Scope of duty:** The courts have also recognized immunity from tort liability for federal government officials acting within the scope of their duties. At first this immunity protected only high-ranking officials but was later extended to all officials acting within the "outer perimeter" of their duties. *See Barr v. Matteo*, 360 U.S. 564 (1959).

Example: In *Barr v. Matteo*, 360 U.S. 564 (1959), a federal official issued a press release naming two of his employees as the officials responsible for a questionable practice that had been characterized as a conspiracy to defraud the federal government. The employees brought a defamation action, alleging that their supervisor acted with malice and defamed them. The Supreme Court sustained a plea of "absolute privilege," holding that as long as the action taken is within the "outer perimeter" of the official's duties, the official enjoys an immunity from damages for defamation. The Court further held that it is within an executive official's discretion to publish a press release on a matter of public interest. The Court stated that the immunity is necessary to ensure that officials exercise their discretion free from the fear of damage suits.

B. Immunity under the FTCA

If a claim against a federal government official falls within the scope of the FTCA, the government is substituted as defendant and the official is released from liability. 28 U.S.C §2679(d)(1). How ever, even if the government prevails based on an exception to FTCA liability, the official retains his or her immunity. The plaintiff cannot bring the official back into the case as a defendant simply because government liability is foreclosed.

C. Judicially created constitutional tort liability

Another avenue for seeking damages against government officials is to allege that their conduct violates the Constitution. The Supreme Court, in *Bivens v. Six Unknown Named Agents of Federal Bureau of Narcotics*, 403 U.S. 388 (1971), created a damages action against federal officials for **constitutional torts**, i.e., injury-causing conduct that violates the Constitution.

1. **The FTCA does not create liability for all constitutional violations:** The FTCA does not cover all constitutional claims, and liability under Bivens is assessed against the individual official, not against the government. A federal agency may not be sued under Bivens.

2. ***Bivens* is available for all constitutional claims:** While *Bivens* itself applied only to Fourth Amendment claims, the Supreme Court subsequently made it clear that the ***Bivens*** action presumptively exists whenever a constitutional right is violated and causes injury. *See Carlson v. Green*, 446 U.S. 14 (1980). However, there are several important defenses to *Bivens* actions.

    a. **Special factors counseling hesitation:** In *Bivens* and subsequent cases, the Supreme Court has stated that the Bivens action is not available when there are "***special factors counseling hesitation in the absence of affirmative action by Congress.***" *Bivens*, 403 U.S. at 396. In other words, there are some situations in which a court should not create a damages remedy on its own without some guidance from Congress. For example, in *Chappell v. Wallace*, 462 U.S. 296 (1983), the Court rejected a *Bivens* claim brought by five Navy enlisted men who alleged that their ship's officers racially discriminated against them in work assignments, performance evaluations, and disciplinary penalties. The Court held it should not create a *Bivens* remedy here because of the unique situation and internal disciplinary structure of the military.

    b. **Substitute remedy:** The *Bivens* Court also stated that it would not create a remedy where Congress had provided ***an alternative remedy that Congress viewed as equally effective*** to liability under the Constitution. As reformulated in *Carlson v. Green*, 446 U.S. 14 (1980), this exception bars the *Bivens* remedy when "Congress has provided an alternative remedy which it explicitly declared to be a *substitute* for recovery directly under the Constitution and viewed as equally effective." *Carlson*, 446 U.S. at 18-19 (emphasis in original). This standard is very difficult to meet because it requires an express declaration from Congress that the alternative remedy is a substitute for *Bivens* (which obviously will not apply to statutes that predate *Bivens*).

    Example: In *Carlson v. Green*, the survivor of a federal prisoner (who died in prison) brought an Eighth Amendment claim based on the circumstances of the prisoner's death. The government argued that the FTCA provided an alternative remedy that should preempt the *Bivens* action. The Court rejected this argument because, in the Court's view, the FTCA remedy was not as effective as *Bivens* (because it did not allow, inter alia, jury trials and punitive damages) and because the FTCA did not explicitly preempt the *Bivens* remedy as it did with some other remedies that had been available before passage of the FTCA.

Although it might seem redundant to allow a *Bivens* action when an FTCA remedy is also available, the Court was reluctant to hold that the FTCA is a substitute for *Bivens* because that would eliminate a large number of *Bivens* actions (since many constitutional torts also involve common-law tortious conduct). The Court also viewed the FTCA as insufficiently protective of constitutional rights and thus a poor substitute for *Bivens* liability.

    c. **Alternative remedies as special factors:** Sometimes an alternative remedy can be a "special factor counseling hesitation." For example, in *Bush v. Lucas*, 462 U.S. 367 (1983), Bush, a federal employee, sued his supervisor, Lucas, when Lucas demoted Bush and reduced Bush's pay—allegedly for making statements critical of the operation of the federal agency where both worked. Bush alleged a violation of his First Amendment rights. Bush succeeded in having the demotion reversed through civil service appeals, but he later brought a *Bivens* suit for damages not recoverable in the civil service system. Bush argued that the civil service remedies were not as effective as *Bivens* because punitive damages, attorneys' fees, and jury trials are not available in the civil service system. The Court agreed with the plaintiff that Congress had not explicitly declared the civil service system a substitute for the *Bivens* action. The Court held (even though it was not as attractive to plaintiffs) the existence of the complex system of civil service remedies was a special factor counseling hesitation and thus precluded the assertion of a *Bivens* claim.

It may seem odd that an alternative remedy that does not meet the Court's standard for displacing the *Bivens* remedy as a substitute can qualify as a special factor counseling hesitation. The *Bush* Court appeared trapped by its narrow formulation in earlier cases of the situations in which an alternative remedy can serve to bar the *Bivens* action. Therefore, it held, as it has on a few additional occasions, that the existence of an alternative remedy is a "special factor." It might be simpler for the Court to reformulate its "substitute remedy" test and declare that the *Bivens* remedy is not available when Congress has provided an adequate alternative, even if that alternative is not quite up to *Bivens* standards.

3. **Immunities in *Bivens* actions:** The Supreme Court has recognized *official immunities* in *Bivens* actions. These immunities were developed in civil rights actions against state and local government officials under 42 U.S.C. §1983, but they have been extended to *Bivens* actions against federal officials as well. Under the official immunities, some officials are *absolutely immune* from damages remedies and some have a *qualified immunity*, under which they may be held liable only if they violate a clearly established constitutional right.

    a. **Policy bases for the immunities:** There are two main policy bases for official immunities. The first is to protect the public interest by allowing public officials to make decisions free from personal concerns over potential liability. The fear is that such concerns might lead officials to steer so clear of potential liability for constitutional violations that the public interest in effective government will suffer. The second basis for the immunities is to free officials from the distraction and drain on their time entailed in defending *Bivens* actions.

    b. **Functional approach:** Whether an official is entitled to absolute immunity (or the less-protective qualified immunity) is determined by the function that the official was performing when the alleged constitutional violation occurred. *See Butz v. Economou*, 438 U.S. 478 (1978). This *functional approach* is derived from the common-law background of the immunities as they were developed in §1983 actions. Thus, under *Butz*, even though all officials in administrative agencies are technically in the executive branch of the government, agency officials performing functions that were protected by absolute immunity under the common law receive that immunity, while remaining officials receive a qualified immunity. Because many officials perform more than one function, the immunity any particular official enjoys will vary based on the function being challenged.

c. **Absolute immunity:** Administrative officials performing judicial, legislative, and prosecutorial functions are absolutely immune from damages because at common law, judges, legislators, and prosecutors were absolutely immune from damages. Thus, administrative law judges and other agency officials engaged in adjudication are absolutely immune from damages, as are agency officials engaged in rulemaking (a legislative function) and prosecution.

d. **Qualified immunity:** Officials performing functions not traditionally accorded an absolute immunity are protected by qualified immunity.

Example: A hypothetical federal agency is composed of three commissioners. The commissioners have the power to make rules and regulations, they sit as adjudicators on appeals from decisions of ALJs, and issue reports concerning the practices of the parties they regulate. They also hire, discipline, and fire numerous agency employees. Under the functional approach, they are absolutely immune from damages in *Bivens* actions challenging the constitutionality of rules they promulgated and in *Bivens* actions challenging the constitutionality of their conduct in the course of adjudications. However, in their more purely administrative capacities in the hiring, disciplining, and firing of employees (as well as in their investigative function under which they issue reports), they would only receive a qualified immunity and could be held liable for damages if they violated clearly established constitutional rights.

i. **Original standard:** Originally, plaintiffs could overcome qualified immunity by showing either that the defendant violated a ***clearly established constitutional right*** of which a reasonable official should have known (the objective prong) or by showing that the defendant acted with ***ill will or malice*** against the plaintiff (the subjective prong).

ii. **The current objective standard:** In *Harlow v. Fitzgerald*, 457 U.S. 800 (1982), the Court abolished the subjective prong of qualified immunity because, in the Court's view, the subjective prong was allowing too many insubstantial claims to go to trial and because it was difficult to resolve issues regarding the defendant's state of mind on summary judgment, even though ultimately the defendant would convince the trier of fact that there was no malice or ill will. Thus, under the current purely objective standard for qualified immunity, ***the only way a plaintiff can overcome the immunity is to show that the defendant violated a clearly established constitutional right***. The defendant's state of mind is irrelevant, and proof of malice or ill will does not help overcome the immunity.

Example: An agency official enters a private home without a warrant to search for evidence that a regulated company is engaged in conduct violating regulatory norms. The official tells the homeowner that the search is to get back at her for firing his cousin from the company. Under the old standard for qualified immunity, the official's ill will directed at the homeowner would be relevant in determining whether the qualified immunity defense would protect the official from an award of damages in a *Bivens* action for a warrantless search in violation of the Fourth Amendment. Now, under the purely objective standard, the only issue is whether a reasonable official, based on clearly established law, should have known that the search violated the Fourth Amendment. Thus, it is now more difficult for the plaintiff to overcome the qualified immunity defense.

III. LIABILITY OF STATE AND LOCAL GOVERNMENT OFFICIALS

In addition to the remedies that exist under state law, state and local government officials can be sued in federal court under 42 U.S.C. §1983 for damages and injunctive relief for conduct that violates the federal Constitution and laws. Section 1983 was passed after the Civil War to enforce the Fourteenth Amendment against state and local officials, but it covers violations of all federal constitutional and legal rights committed by state and local officials. There are, however, significant limitations on the availability of the §1983 action.

A. Eleventh Amendment

The *Eleventh Amendment*, as interpreted and applied by the Supreme Court, prohibits the federal courts from awarding damages against states and state government agencies. State officials can be held liable for damages, but the plaintiff must look to the individual defendant, and not the state treasury, for damages. This limitation on federal court jurisdiction cannot be avoided by suing in state court. The Court has held that states and state officials, when damages are sought from the state treasury, are not "persons" subject to suit under §1983.

B. "And laws" actions

While most §1983 actions attack constitutional violations, the statute also provides a cause of action against state officials who violate federal statutory law. Because there are many federal programs that are jointly administered with state agencies, many §1983 actions brought under the "and laws" provision allege that state administrators have failed to follow federal standards in administering such programs. *See, e.g., Maine v. Thiboutot*, 448 U.S. 1 (1980).

1. **Comprehensive remedial scheme:** When the federal regulatory statute contains a *comprehensive remedial scheme* that includes its own private right of action against violations, the Supreme Court has held that plaintiffs must use the particular statutory remedy and not the more general §1983 action. *See, e.g., Middlesex County Sewerage Authority v. National Sea Clammers Association*, 453 U.S. 1 (1981); *City of Rancho Palos Verdes v. Abrams*, 125 S. Ct. 1453 (2005) (no "and laws" claim against local government for violating federal telecommunications law's requirements regarding siting of communications towers because the federal act contains its own remedial scheme).

2. **Federal statute creates no enforceable rights:** The Court has also held that the §1983 remedy for violating a federal statute is not available when the federal statute creates *no enforceable rights*. For example, in *Suter v. Artist M.*, 503 U.S. 347 (1992), the Court held that a §1983 suit was not available to enforce a federal law requiring state officials to make "reasonable efforts" to keep families together and return children placed in foster care to their parents. The Court held that the "reasonable efforts" standard was too vague to create enforceable legal rights.

C. Immunities

Defendants in §1983 actions are protected by the same immunities that the courts have applied in *Bivens* actions. In fact, the immunities were developed in §1983 actions on the theory that, because the immunities were well established under the common law, Congress must have intended to preserve them since it did not expressly overrule them when it passed §1983. *See Pierson v. Ray,* 386 U.S. 547 (1967).

D. Municipal liability

The Supreme Court has held that municipalities are "persons" subject to suit under §1983, but it has also held that municipalities may be held liable only for ***municipal policy or custom*** and may not be held liable on a vicarious liability theory for the constitutional violations of their employees.

1. **Liability for legislative enactments:** The simplest case for municipal liability is when the municipal lawmaking body, such as a city council, has adopted an unconstitutional statute or ordinance. When a city-ordinance is unconstitutional, the municipality is liable under §1983 for damages and other appropriate relief.

2. **Final authority liability:** Municipalities are also liable for policies made by municipal officials with ***final authority*** to make policy in an area even if the policy has not been adopted by the municipality's legislative body. For example, in *Pembaur v. City of Cincinnati*, 475 U.S. 469 (1986), the Court held that a county could be held liable for the decision of the county prosecutor to advise county sheriff's police to execute a warrant in an unconstitutional manner. The Court reasoned that the county prosecutor had, under both state law and county policy, final authority to establish policy over the execution of warrants by sheriff's police. Thus, whatever the prosecutor decided constituted the county's policy.

3. **Failure to train and related cases:** Section 1983 plaintiffs often attempt to avoid the ban on municipal vicarious liability by alleging that a constitutional violation was caused by the municipality's failure to train its employees or the municipality's failure to screen employees for past conduct, such as the commission of crimes. Recognizing that such allegations have the potential to effectively impose vicarious liability, the Court has placed significant burdens on such claims.

   a. **Failure to train:** A municipality may be held liable for grossly inadequate training of its employees, but the training must be so inadequate that the city's failure to train must imply ***deliberate indifference to*** the constitutional rights violated. A single incident of excessive force by a police officer is ordinarily inadequate to infer that the municipality's training is so inadequate as to exhibit deliberate indifference to the safety of citizens injured in such encounters with police. *See Oklahoma City v. Tattle,* 471 U.S. 808 (1985).

      Example: In *Canton v. Harris,* 489 U.S. 378 (1989), the plaintiff alleged that she was injured when the police failed to seek medical attention for her when she became emotionally ill while she was in custody at the police station. She alleged that the municipality was liable because the officers in charge of deciding whether medical care was necessary were not trained to recognize when a person in custody needed treatment for emotional illnesses. The Court held that these allegations were sufficient to raise the possibility that the municipality's training decisions exhibited deliberate indifference to the constitutional rights of detainees to receive adequate medical care.

b. Failure to screen employees: While liability is theoretically possible, the Supreme Court has made it very difficult to hold a municipality liable for failing to screen employees who later commit constitutional violations. The Court has held that inadequate screening can be the basis for municipal liability only if the candidate's background indicates that the failure to screen exhibits deliberate indifference to a high probability that the municipal employee will commit the constitutional violation alleged.

Example: In *Board of Commissioners of Bryant County v. Brown*, 520 U.S. 397 (1997), the county sheriff (with final authority to hire officers) failed to examine the criminal record of his nephew before he hired him as a police officer. His nephew's criminal record included misdemeanor assault convictions and several serious traffic infractions. Later the nephew seriously injured a passenger in a car that had been involved in a police chase; and the injured passenger attempted to hold the county liable. The Court held that the county could be held liable only if the sheriffs failure to adequately screen the candidate entailed a high probability that the candidate would commit the constitutional violation alleged. Only then, the Court held, would it be appropriate to conclude that the county was deliberately indifferent to the plaintiffs constitutional rights. The Court also expressed doubts that the failure to screen the employee actually caused the constitutional violation. This standard is designed to make it very difficult to attribute a constitutional violation to a municipality that is lax in screening job candidates. Further, the Court's analysis appears better suited to a case in which the municipal policymaker was aware of the candidate's background and decided to hire him anyway. Then it might be concluded that the municipality knew of the probability that the candidate would violate constitutional rights and was deliberately indifferent. When the policymaker is unaware of the candidate's background and decides to go ahead and hire the candidate, the policymaker appears to exhibit deliberate indifference. The candidate's actual background is irrelevant to the decision; the decisionmaker is unaware of it since the premise of the allegations is that the background was not investigated.

Quiz Yourself on LIABILITY OF AGENCIES AND OFFICIALS

64. A naval officerz is traveling to his home, which is located off of the naval base, in a vehicle owned by the Navy. The car is part of the Navy's aging fleet of automobiles provided to certain officers. The officer's car is struck head-on by a civilian drunk driver who went through a red light. The officer is seriously injured. He sues the United States Navy under the Federal Torts Claim Act, alleging that the Navy was negligent for not providing him with an automobile equipped with an airbag. Is this a viable FTCA claim? _____

65. NHTSA is charged with developing federal safety standards for automobiles and ensuring that automobiles meet them. Under governing statutes, manufacturers of safety-related automobile parts are required to meet strict standards, and automobiles containing safety-related parts from unapproved manufacturers may not be sold. Global Motors Inc. manufactures a minivan that contains airbags from an unapproved manufacturer. NHTSA knows this but allows the car to be sold anyway. In fact, the manufacturer flunked NHTSA tests and therefore was not certified. May a person, injured when an

airbag fails to deploy in an accident, sue the government under the FTCA for injuries due to the government's failure to enforce the statutory safety requirements? _____

66. A member of the FTC makes a speech in which she criticizes tobacco company executives for pushing deadly drugs on young people. In the speech she argues that tobacco executives should be shunned socially for their contribution to the health problems of the nation. She names the CEOs of the five largest companies, including John Smith. After he became CEO of a tobacco company, Smith ordered the toughest restrictions on company advertising in the industry to keep cigarette advertising away from children. He sues the FTC commissioner under several state law theories, including defamation, tortious interference with contract, and false light. What result? _____

67. USDA inspectors obtained a warrant and inspected an egg farm. The inspection revealed numerous violations of USDA and OSHA regulations, some of which affected the safety of the eggs and some of which affected the safety of workers at the farm. The owner of the farm believes that the information that led to the USDA inspectors obtaining the warrants was gathered in a secret inspection of certain portions of the farm. He believes that USDA inspectors broke in at night and then lied on their warrant applications when they stated that they had been tipped off by an informant. Proceedings on the citations are in preliminary stages, and the USDA has acknowledged that if the evidence was illegally obtained, it could not be used against the egg farmer. The owner wants to sue the individual USDA inspectors for damages for violating his constitutional rights. What result? _____

68. Assume the inspectors in the problem above claim that they learned that the egg farmer was about to destroy evidence of serious violations and that there was no time to seek a warrant. Thus, they justify the search based on a belief that they had exigent circumstances allowing a warrantless search. Further, the first federal court opinion on whether exigent circumstances could justify such a search in similar circumstances was not handed down until after the search was conducted. Does this set of circumstances give rise to a defense? _____

69. Assume the same facts as above except, in addition, the administrative law judge rules that the evidence can be used against the egg farm despite the fact that it was seized in violation of the Fourth Amendment. May the administrative law judge be sued under *Bivens* for damages for violating constitutional rights? _____

70. Assume a city building inspector denies a building permit without providing a hearing for the applicant. Further assume that due process requires a hearing before the permit can be finally denied. Is the city liable for the damages caused by this violation? _____

Answers

64. No, for several reasons. First, under the *Feres* doctrine, members of the military may not sue over decisions of their superior officers even if the FTCA might otherwise provide for liability. Second, because the decision involved discretion and choice, the FTCA's discretionary-functions exception bars liability. Third, under state law, it may not be tortious to provide an employee with an automobile without an airbag. Thus, even if the other obstacles to FTCA liability could be overcome, the predicate for FTCA liability (liability for similar conduct under local law) would not be met.

65. Possibly. The Supreme Court has rejected an exception to the FTCA for all regulatory functions, so even though the government is playing a purely regulatory role, the FTCA might still be available. If NHTSA approved the car in violation of clear statutory directives, then the discretionary-function exception would probably not bar liability. The *Berkovitz* Court held that there is no discretion to violate mandatory provisions of governing law. However, the plaintiff must establish that the approval of the automobile did not involve choice or policy judgment—that there was no discretion regarding observance of the statutory requirement.

66. No. Federal officials have immunity from damages for common-law claims based on conduct within the outer bounds of their official duties. It is within the outer bounds of the duties of FTC commissioners to speak on matters of public interest involving advertising, which is within FTC jurisdiction.

67. He probably has a viable *Bivens* claim against the inspectors. Under *Bivens*, victims of Fourth Amendment and other constitutional violations can sue the perpetrators for damages. Even though the exclusionary rule might prevent the use of the evidence in the agency proceedings, it is not a substitute for a damages remedy against the offending officials. Congress has not declared that the USDA procedures are a substitute for the *Bivens* action, and the fact that the USDA applies the exclusionary rule in its proceedings is not enough to make the existence of those proceedings a "special factor counseling hesitation." While a comprehensive remedial scheme might be a special factor, here the USDA scheme does not really provide a remedy for the Fourth Amendment violation, so it should not displace the *Bivens* action.

68. Yes. They may have a qualified immunity defense. Under qualified immunity, officials are not liable unless they violate clearly established constitutional rights of which a reasonable official should know. If the inspectors establish that no similar case had found a Fourth Amendment violation, they would be immune from a damages award. Note that it is not enough that the general right to be free from an unreasonable search and seizure is clearly established. The cases require that it be clearly established that the particular facts alleged establish a constitutional violation.

69. No. The ALJ has absolute immunity from damages for constitutional violations in performance of her judicial duties. At common law, judges, legislators, and prosecutors had absolute immunity from damages. Under the functional approach, administrative officials are accorded the same immunities as their nonadministrative counterparts. ALJs thus receive judicial immunity, agency prosecuting officials receive prosecutorial immunity, and agency officials making rules receive legislative immunity.

70. Maybe. Municipal liability in this situation depends on many factors. While cities are proper defendants in §1983 cases, they cannot be held liable on a vicarious liability theory. Rather, cities may be held liable only for violations attributable to municipal policy. If the city had an official policy requiring hearings before denials of building permits, then the city cannot be held liable. However, if city policy stated that no hearing was required, or if the building inspector had the final authority under city law to determine whether a hearing would be held, then it would be appropriate to hold the city liable for damages.

Exam Tips on
LIABILITY OF AGENCIES AND OFFICIALS

☛ The issues in this chapter are not often tested on, since they are not at the core of administrative law. However, FTCA issues are sometimes tested on, and some instructors may include minor issues on the liability matters addressed herein.

☛ In answering any FTCA question, look carefully at the statute and ask whether a statutory basis for liability exists and, if so, does an exception bar liability.

☛ In discussing the discretionary function exception, which is the FTCA issue most likely to be tested, it may be helpful to discuss the regulatory functions exception that the Court rejected.

   ☞ Be sure to spell out the governing test for the exception ("choice or judgment" and "the exercise of discretion in furtherance of public policy goals") and compare the official activity in the examination with the official activity in cases such as *Gaubert* and *Berkovitz*.

☛ In a damages action against a government official, if the claim is a constitutional claim, the issue is whether a *Bivens* action is available.

   ☞ Regarding *Bivens* actions, look for remedies that Congress has declared as substitutes for *Bivens* or for special factors counseling hesitation.

   ☞ Be aware that even if Congress has not specified that an alternate remedy is a substitute for *Bivens*, it may displace the *Bivens* remedy as a special factor.

☛ With regard to official liability for damages under either *Bivens* or §1983, apply the functional approach to determine whether the official should receive absolute immunity.

   ☞ For officials entitled only to qualified immunity, remember that the subjective factor is no longer relevant, so that the official is liable only if he or she violated clearly established law.

☛ With regard to municipal liability, watch for attempts to hold cities liable that are actually attempts to get around the ban on vicarious liability through some clever way of alleging a municipal policy or custom.

   ☞ The Court is very strict on requiring a municipal policy, and it thus does not make it easy to hold cities liable for constitutional violations committed by city employees.

   ☞ Thus, while claims for inadequate training or screening of employees exist in theory, you should be clear that such claims are very difficult to win because they are too close to vicarious liability.

CHAPTER 13

FREEDOM OF INFORMATION AND OPEN MEETINGS

ChapterScope

This chapter is about public access to information held by the government and requirements regarding the conduct of government business in public. The main points of the chapter are:

- The *Freedom of Information Act (FOIA)* grants the public access to most *agency records*.

  - In order for the presumption of public access to apply, the material sought must fit FOIA's definition of "agency records."

  - *Agency records* are those records created or obtained by the agency in the course of doing the agency's work and in the control of the agency at the time of the FOIA request.

- There are several *exemptions* to FOIA's disclosure requirement.

  - The exemptions fall roughly into three categories: protection of *proprietary business information*, protection of *personal privacy*, and protection of *internal government functions*.

  - The Supreme Court has stated repeatedly that the exemptions should be narrowly read so as not to frustrate FOIA's pro-disclosure intent.

- FOIA exemptions do not prevent the government from releasing information voluntarily. However, the Trade Secrets Act and the Privacy Act protect suppliers of covered information from government disclosure.

- Government documents also are subject to disclosure through *discovery* in litigation.

  - In addition to the usual doctrines governing discovery, the federal government has two sets of defenses to discovery, the *evidentiary privileges*, which protect sensitive information such as military secrets and foreign affairs information, and *executive immunity*, also known as *executive privilege*, which allows the executive branch, in limited circumstances, to claim immunity to disclosure of information.

- The *Government in the Sunshine Act* requires that agency meetings be open to the public.

  - The Sunshine Act does not apply to agencies with only one person at the top.

  - *"Meeting of an Agency"* means a gathering of agency members where business is conducted.

  - An agency may meet in private if one of the exceptions to the Sunshine Act is met. These exceptions are similar to the FOIA exemptions.

- The *Federal Advisory Committee Act (FACA)* requires that nongovernmental bodies established to provide advice to the President or a federal agency follow the open-meetings requirements of the Sunshine Act and the open-information requirements of FOIA.

■ Serious constitutional questions exist regarding whether FACA unduly interferes with the President's ability to seek advice from private citizens or groups regarding matters within the President's constitutional powers.

I. THE FREEDOM OF INFORMATION ACT

FOIA, adopted by Congress in 1966, opens vast numbers of "agency records" to public inspection and creates a procedure (which was strengthened by amendments passed in 1974) for enforcement of agencies' obligations to make their records public. FOIA, codified as part of the APA at 5 U.S.C. §552, also contains several exceptions to the disclosure requirement. The two main issues arising under FOIA are whether the material sought constitutes an "agency record" within the meaning of FOIA and whether one of FOIA's exceptions authorizes, the agency to withhold the material sought.

A. Public right of access to agency records

FOIA requires that agencies publish certain matters and allow public inspection, upon request, of all other "records" unless the records sought fall within one of FOIA's exceptions. FOIA creates a federal cause of action against an agency that "improperly withhold[s]" requested agency records.

1. **What are agency records?** *Agency records* are those records that are ***created or obtained by the agency in the course of doing the agency's work*** and are in the control of the agency at the time of the FOIA request. *See Department of Justice v. Tax Analysts*, 492 U.S. 136 (1989). The fact that the records are physically located at the agency is not dispositive. Rather, the records must be the product of work on behalf of the agency. Private papers (or papers that were created in a different agency that an official keeps in an agency office) are not agency records merely because they are located on agency premises.

    Example: In *Kissinger v. Reporters Committee for Freedom of the Press*, 445 U.S. 136 (1980), a reporter sought notes of Henry Kissinger's telephone conversations in which either the reporter's name was mentioned or the issue of information leaks was discussed with certain other government officials. The conversations occurred while Kissinger worked in the office of the President, but they were not sought until Kissinger became Secretary of State. Because the notes were stored in Kissinger's State Department office, the reporter sought them as agency records of the State Department. The Court held that these notes were not records of the State Department, and relied on these four factors: (1) the notes were never in the control of the State Department; (2) the notes were not generated in the State Department; (3) the notes were never placed in any State Department files; and (4) the notes were not used in any way by the State Department.

2. **Records "wrongfully withheld":** FOIA creates a legal claim when an agency *"wrongfully withholds" agency records*. *See Kissinger.* An agency does not "wrongfully withhold" records that were not in its possession at the time the FOIA request was made even if the records were improperly removed from agency possession. Agencies are under no obligation to retrieve records wrongfully removed. *See id.*

    Example: In *Department of Justice v. Tax Analysts*, 492 U.S. 136 (1989), Tax Analysts (a nonprofit organization-that publishes *Tax Notes*, a weekly magazine on federal taxation) sought copies from the Department of Justice of the past month's district court decisions in tax cases litigated by the Department. The Department refused to provide the copies, arguing that the decisions were not agency records and that they had not been "wrongfully withheld" since they were publicly available from the district courts that had issued them. The Court held that the decisions were agency records because the Department obtained them from the district courts and had them in Department files at the time the FOIA request was made. The Court also held that the Department, by not turning them over when requested, had "wrongfully withheld" the decisions regardless of whether they were available from another source. Justice Blackmun dissented, mainly on the ground that Congress did not intend, in enacting FOIA, to allow a publisher to impose its research costs on the government. In other words, no FOIA-related purpose was served by ordering the government to turn these decisions over to Tax Analysts.

3. **Government-funded studies:** Only those records actually received and retained by the agency qualify as agency records. For example, data in the possession of a private party are not agency records, even if the data were created in an agency-funded study and even if the agency has, as a term of the grant, the right to receive copies of the documents created in the federally funded study. *See Forsham v. Harris*, 445 U.S. 169 (1980).

4. **Special FOIA definition of "agency":** FOIA defines "agency" as "any executive department, military department, Government corporation, Government controlled corporation, or other establishment in the executive branch of government (including the Executive Office of the President), or any independent agency." 5 U.S.C. §552(f)(1). This definition is broader than the APA's general definition of "agency," which has been held to apply only to agencies with authority to take actions with legal effect. The FOIA definition includes entities that may not be subject to other APA requirements, such as government corporations and executive branch entities that may collect information, but which have no power to take actions having legal effect.

B. Exceptions to FOIA

FOIA contains nine categories of exceptions to the requirement that agencies disclose their records. *See* 5 U.S.C. §552(b)(l)-(9). The exceptions protect several interests including privacy of the subjects of agency records, national security, law enforcement efforts, and internal agency management.

1. **The exemptions should be narrowly construed:** The Supreme Court has stated repeatedly that FOIA exemptions should be narrowly construed so as not to interfere with FOIA's main purpose, which is to allow public access to government records. *See, e.g., Department of the Air Force v. Rose*, 425 U.S. 352 (1976).

2. **National defense and foreign policy:** Exception (1) exempts records from disclosure that the executive branch determines should be kept secret in the interests of ***national defense or foreign policy***. *See* 5 U.S.C. §552(b)(1). The records must be properly classified under the established procedure, set forth in executive orders, for classifying as secret records related to national defense or foreign policy interests. The secrecy determination cannot be made on an adhoc basis in response to a FOIA disclosure request.

3. **Internal agency personnel matters:** Exception (2) exempts records "related solely to the internal personnel rules and practices of an agency." This exception is confined to those internal personnel rules that are unlikely to generate any substantial public interest, including matters cited in the legislative history, such as agency sick leave policies, regulation of lunch breaks, and employee use of parking facilities. This exception does not exempt matters from disclosure that are likely to be of concern to the general public. *See Department of*

the Air Force v. Rose, 425 U.S. 352 (1976) (rejecting an exception (2) argument for withholding case summaries, with names and other identifying facts deleted, of student honor code violations at the Air Force Academy).

4. **Trade secrets and privileged commercial information:** Exemption (4) exempts from disclosure "trade and commercial or financial information obtained from a person and privileged or confidential." 5.U.S.C. §552(b)(4).

   a. **Trade secrets:** A FOIA "trade secret" has been defined as "a secret, commercially valuable plan, formula, process, or device that is used for the making, preparing, compounding, or processing of trade commodities and that can be said to be the end product of either innovation or substantial effort." *Public Citizen Health Research Group v. FDA*, 704 F.2d 1280, 1288 (D.C.Cir. 1983). The *Public Citizen* court rejected applying the general tort law definition of "trade secrets" in favor of this definition, which it found was better suited to the purposes of FOIA.

   b. **Commercial information:** "Commercial information" is information related to activity in commerce of the sort that would affect the submitter's commercial position if it were released. This exception does not protect information from disclosure that is not related to commerce. For example, "a noncommercial scientist's research design is not literally a trade secret or item of commercial information, for it defies common sense to pretend that the scientist is engaged in trade or commerce." *Washington Research Project, Inc. v. Department of Health, Educ. & Welfare*, 504 F.2d 238 (D.C. Cir. 1974).

   c. **Confidential:** Exception (4) applies only to "privileged or confidential" information. Information is confidential under FOIA if its disclosure would impair the government's ability to obtain information in the future or if disclosure would cause substantial harm to the competitive position of the person from whom the information was obtained. *See Worthington Compressors, Inc. v. Costle*, 662 F.2d 45 (D.C. Cir. 1981).

      i. **Commercial information provided under compulsion:** When a private party is required by law to provide information to an agency, the government's ability to obtain information is not threatened by FOIA disclosure. Thus, in such cases, the primary interest weighing against disclosure is the provider's competitive interest in keeping important commercial information confidential. The government also has an interest in the quality of information provided. A party who knows that compulsory information may be disclosed may not provide complete or useful information as would be provided if confidentiality was insured. *See Critical Mass Energy Project v. NRC*, 975 F.2d 871 (D.C. Cir. 1992) (en banc), *cert. denied*, 507 U.S. 984 (1993).

      ii. **Commercial information voluntarily provided:** Because the government has an interest in encouraging people to provide commercial information voluntarily, the D.C. Circuit adopted a broader standard for keeping voluntarily provided information confidential under the fourth exemption. In such cases, "financial or commercial information provided to the Government on a voluntary basis is 'confidential' for the purpose of Exemption 4 if it is of a kind that would customarily not be released to the public by the person from whom it was obtained." *Critical Mass Energy Project*, 975 F.2d at 879.

      Example: The Institute for Nuclear Power Operations (INPO) is an organization of the operators of nuclear power plants in the United States. It studies the construction and operation of nuclear power plants and provides its reports to the NRC on the understanding that the reports will remain confidential. Critical Mass Energy Project (CMEP) filed a FOIA request for the documents, and the NRC claimed that the reports were confidential commercial information within exemption (4). In *Critical Mass Energy Project*, the court held that the INPO reports were confidential and, under exemption (4), not subject to FOIA disclosure. The court reasoned that the reports were provided to the NRC voluntarily, and INPO would probably cease providing them if they were subject to FOIA disclosure. The court thus held that when a party voluntarily provides confidential information to an agency, that information should not be subject to FOIA disclosure if the provider would normally not release such information to the public.

d. FOIA does not prevent voluntary government disclosure of confidential information: Nothing in FOIA itself precludes an agency from voluntarily turning over records that FOIA exceptions would allow the agency to withhold.

i. Trade Secrets Act: However, the *Trade Secrets Act*, 18 U.S.C. §1905, enacted in 1974, makes it a criminal offense for a government official to release information held to be within FOIA exception (4). *See Bartholdi Cable Co., Inc. v. FCC*, 114 F.3d 274 (D.C. Cir. 1997).

ii. "Reverse FOIA": A person whose confidential information is threatened to be released by an agency has a "reverse-FOIA" cause of action under the APA's judicial review provisions (not the Trade Secrets Act itself) to prevent disclosure. *See Chrysler Corp. v. Brown*, 441 U.S. 281 (1979). There is no private right of action under the Trade Secrets Act, but an agency's decision to turn over information in violation of the Privacy Act would violate APA §706(2)(A) as "not in accordance with law." *Id.*

5. Privacy-based exemptions for personnel and law enforcement records: Exception (6) exempts from disclosure "personnel and medical files and similar files the disclosure of which would constitute a clearly unwarranted invasion of personal privacy." 5 U.S.C. §552(b)(6). Additionally, a further exemption is found in exception 7(C) for disclosure of "records or information compiled for law enforcement purposes, but only to the extent that the production of such law enforcement records or information . . . (C) could reasonably be expected to constitute an unwarranted invasion of personal privacy." 5 U.S.C. 552(b)(7)(C). These are the primary FOIA exemptions for which issues of personal privacy are important.

a. Personnel and medical files: Determining whether exemption (6) exempts a particular personnel, medical, or similar file from disclosure "require[s] a balancing of the individual's right of privacy against the preservation of the basic purpose of the Freedom of Information Act 'to open agency action to the light of public scrutiny.'" *Department of the Air Force v. Rose*, 425 U.S. 352, 372 (1976). *In Rose*, the Court rejected the Air Force's argument that exemption (6) applied to summaries of cases of honor code violations by Air Force Academy cadets. The Court held that FOIA policies (including the public's ability to monitor the disciplinary practices of the Air Force Academy) favored disclosure, and that cadets' privacy concerns could be addressed by the elimination of identifying information from the summaries.

b. Law enforcement records and personal privacy: Determining whether exemption (7)(C) exempts law enforcement records from disclosure based on personal privacy concerns involves a balancing test similar to that involving personnel records. *See National Archives v. Favish,* 541 U.S. 157 (2004) (government may withhold death scene photographs of presidential aide on basis of privacy interests of family).

i. Privacy interests in law enforcement records: The subject of law enforcement records (such as a person charged with or convicted of a crime), has a substantial privacy interest against disclosure of the records. This privacy interest exists even though the information was made public at the time of arrest, prosecution, or conviction.

ii. Public interest in disclosure of law enforcement records: The public's interest in disclosure of information that would invade privacy is strongest when the information would reveal important matters concerning the agency's behavior and is weakest when the information would reveal nothing about the agency's conduct.

Example: The Federal Bureau of Investigation (FBI) maintains a database of the records of criminal charges and convictions (rap sheets) of all law enforcement agencies in the United States, including state and local law enforcement agencies. In *Department of Justice v. Reporters Committee for Freedom of the Press,* 489 U.S. 749 (1989), the Department of Justice (DOJ) refused to turn over to CBS news reporters and the Reporters Committee, the rap sheet of a member of a family whose company allegedly procured military contracts "as a result of an improper relationship with a Congressman." Because the rap sheets are in files obtained and maintained by the FBI, they are clearly agency records. However, the Court held that the privacy interest of the subjects of the rap sheets outweighed the public's interest in obtaining them from the FBI. While the fact of conviction was public at one time, the Court recognized that the massive computerized database maintained by the FBI presents a great potential for spreading information regarding the criminal histories of the subjects of the rap sheets. Further, most states place severe restrictions on the public's right to obtain criminal records. The public's interest in disclosing the FBI's records was slight, according to the Court, because they would reveal nothing about the operation of the FBI since the FBI was merely the custodian of records of arrests and convictions in other jurisdictions. Thus, the Court held that the rap sheets maintained by the FBI were exempt from FOIA disclosure under exemption (7).

c. Personal privacy and the Privacy Act of 1974: The Privacy Act of 1974, codified at 5 U.S.C. §552a, is another federal statute that protects individuals' privacy interests in records maintained by the federal government.

i. The provisions of the Privacy Act: The Privacy Act prohibits agencies from disclosing records "except pursuant to a written request by, or with the prior consent of, the individual to whom the record pertains." The Privacy Act also restricts the information agencies are allowed to collect on individuals (only that information necessary to accomplish agency purposes), allows individuals to inspect records pertaining to them, and sets up a procedure for correcting erroneous records.

ii. The Privacy Act and FOIA: The Privacy Act should not affect disclosure under FOIA because the Privacy Act explicitly provides that its nondisclosure provisions do not apply to records required to be disclosed under FOIA. However, in its opinion in *Reporters Committee,* the Supreme Court pointed to the existence of the Privacy Act, and it stressed the privacy implications of computerized databases as a factor weighing in favor of recognizing privacy interests in the records at issue in that case.

6. **Law enforcement records and law enforcement interests:** A large number of law enforcement records are not subject to FOIA.disclosure.

   a. **The law enforcement records exemptions:** Exemptions (7)(A), (B), (D), (E), and (F) exempt law enforcement records from disclosure when disclosure would cause one of several enumerated harms to law enforcement interests. These interests include: (A) protecting against interference with law enforcement proceedings; (B) protecting the right of the accused to a fair trial; (D) protecting the identity of a confidential source of information; (E) protecting the secrecy of law enforcement techniques and enforcement guidelines; and (F) protecting the physical safety of individuals.

   b. **Defining law enforcement records:** Records are law enforcement records if they are used for law enforcement purposes even if they were originally compiled for purposes other than law enforcement. *See John Doe Agency v. John Doe Corp.*, 493 U.S. 146 (1980). Further, records do not lose their law enforcement status even if they are provided by a law enforcement agency to a non-law enforcement agency. *See FBI v. Abramson*, 456 U.S. 615 (1982) (FBI records did not lose their law enforcement status when summaries of the documents were provided to the White House for non-law enforcement purposes). As might be expected, resistance to disclosure of law enforcement records has increased since the terrorist attacks of 2001. For example, in *Center for National Security Studies v. United States Department of Justice*, 331 F.3d 918 (D.C. Cir. 2003), the court held that the government was not required to disclose a list of the names of over 1100 people (and the names of their lawyers) who had been detained in the wake of the attacks. The court found that the list constituted "records or information compiled for law enforcement purposes" that "could reasonably be expected to interfere with enforcement proceedings" under the FOIA exception for law enforcement records.

7. **Inter-agency and intra-agency memoranda:** Exception (5) exempts from FOIA disclosure "inter-agency or intra-agency memorandums or letters which would not be available by law to a party other than an agency in litigation with the agency." 5 U.S.C. §552(b)(5). This exemption protects the agency deliberative processes and other matters that executive privilege and privileges related to the attorney-client relationship would protect. The statutory reference to material that "would not be available by law to a party ... in litigation with the agency" means material protected by the attorney-client and attorney work product privileges.

   a. **Final agency decisions:** Exemption (5) does not apply to agency memoranda that, in effect, constitute final agency decisions on agency matters. For example, exemption (5) does not protect from disclosure a memorandum that explains why an agency decided not to go forward with an enforcement action.

   b. **Agency decisions to pursue enforcement:** Exemption (5) does apply to agency memoranda that result in an agency taking further action in a matter, such as memoranda explaining why an enforcement action should go forward. Such memoranda are considered part of the process of intra-agency deliberation and are kept confidential to protect the deliberative process.

   c. **Protection of the deliberative process:** In general, the exemption for inter- and intra-agency memoranda is designed to protect the process of deliberation. Early drafts of decision memos and other memoranda that are preliminary to actual decisionmaking should not be subject to disclosure. Otherwise, the agency decisionmaking process would be hampered by the fear that tentative views might be subject to public disclosure. However, memoranda containing final decisions are subject to disclosure.

Example: When a party files an unfair labor practice charge with the NLRB, the general counsel has final authority to decide whether to pursue the charge by issuing a complaint. The general counsel operates through regional directors throughout the country. Regional directors often consult with the general counsel regarding whether to pursue a charge. In some cases, as part of the consultation process, a memorandum from the general counsel to the Regional Director (which includes legal and factual reasoning) will order the regional director either to issue a complaint or to dismiss a charge. In *NLRB v. Sears, Roebuck & Co.*, 421 U.S. 132 (1975), Sears made FOIA requests for disclosure of both types of memoranda, and the general counsel denied the requests on the ground that the records were internal agency memoranda under exemption (5). The Supreme Court held that those memoranda that ordered the general counsel to refuse to file an unfair labor practice charge were "final agency decisions" that must be made public under §552(a)(2). However, with regard to the memoranda ordering the regional director to.file a complaint of an unfair labor practice, the Court held that these are not subject to disclosure because they are part of an ongoing process of the general counsel's involvement in the case, since the general counsel may ultimately litigate the case before the NLRB and in court. As to exemption (5), the Court noted that these memoranda include the general counsel's views on the facts and the law of the case, and thus are squarely within the exemption for attorney work product.

8. **Specifically exempted from disclosure by statute:** Exception (3) exempts from disclosure records that are "specifically exempted from disclosure by statute . . . provided that such statute (A) requires that the matters be withheld from the public in such a manner as to leave no discretion on the issue, or (B) establishes particular criteria for withholding or refers to particular types of matters to be withheld." 5 U.S.C. §552(3).

   a. **Three types of exempt records:** Exemption (3) identifies three distinct types of statutes that operate to exempt records from FOIA disclosure. These are:

      i. **Statutes that identify exempt records and leave no discretion regarding non-disclosure:** In such cases, the agency would determine (subject to judicial review under FOIA) whether the agency lacked discretion to make the records public. If the agency had discretion, it might still attempt to withhold the records, and then the question would become whether withholding was statutorily authorized, even though it was not statutorily required.

      ii. **Statutes that establish criteria for withholding:** In such cases, the agency (subject to judicial review under FOIA) would determine whether the criteria for withholding are met.

      iii. **Statutes that refer to particular types of matters to be withheld:** In such cases, the agency would decide (subject to judicial review under FOIA) whether the records contain matters within the types of information referred to in the relevant statute.

      Example: In *CIA v. Sims*, 471 U.S. 159 (1985), the Court upheld the CIA's broad interpretation of its authority to withhold intelligence-related documents from FOIA disclosure. The Court found that §102(d)(3) of the National Security Act of 1947 is a statute that "specifically exempts matters] from disclosure." Section 102(d)(3) states that "the Director of Central Intelligence shall be responsible for protecting intelligence sources and methods from unauthorized disclosure." Sims sought the names of institutions and individuals that had performed research as part of a CIA project to study behavior-control techniques. Sims argued, and the court of appeals agreed, that §102(d)(3) protected only the identity of intelligence sources who would turn over intelligence information only on a guarantee of confidentiality. The Supreme Court disagreed, holding first that §102(d)(3) meets the requirements of exemption (3)'s requirement that the statute refer to "particular types of matters" when it refers to "intelligence sources and methods." Further, the Court held that §102(d)(3) gives the CIA broad discretion to withhold all information within the statutory categories and thus can withhold the identities of all providers of intelligence information, not only those who require confidentiality before providing information. Thus, the identities of the researchers are not subject to FOIA disclosure.

II. DISCOVERY FROM THE GOVERNMENT IN LITIGATION

Another way to obtain information from the government is through the litigation discovery process. The government can resist discovery on the same terms that a private litigant can. In addition, the government has two additional privileges — *evidentiary privilege* and executive immunity (also known as *executive privilege*).

A. Evidentiary privileges

Evidentiary privileges are privileges that protect categories of government matters when release would be contrary to the public interest. These include things like state secrets, military secrets, and sensitive foreign affairs matters.

1. **The privilege must be formally claimed:** Claims of evidentiary privilege must be made formally by the head of the department having control over the material, and that department head must have personally considered the matter. *See United States v. Reynolds*, 345 U.S. 1 (1953).

2. **The claim is evaluated by a court:** Whether the material sought in discovery is protected by a privilege is determined by a court by balancing the litigant's need for the information against the government's interest in secrecy. A court should uphold a privilege claim when there is a reasonable possibility that the material is privileged, without even looking at the actual material. Only if the balance appears to favor the litigant should a court examine the documents to help determine whether the material is privileged.

B. Executive immunity

The executive branch rarely claims immunity from the discovery process. When such a claim is made, a court balances the executive branch's need for confidentiality against the litigant's need for the material. The litigant's interest is held to be strongest in the criminal context where the fairness of the trial may depend on the litigant's ability to discover material relevant to the case.

1. **The claim of privilege is not dispositive:** Executive immunity is not absolute. *See United States v. Nixon*, 418 U.S. 683 (1974) (rejecting President Nixon's argument that once a president claims the privilege, separation of powers requires that courts defer to the claim of privilege). Further, the generalized interest in confidential communication within the executive

branch, while weighty and entitled to respect, is not sufficient to defeat, as a blanket matter, all requests for discovery regarding such communication in a criminal case.

2. **The presumption is in favor of the claim of privilege:** When the President invokes executive privilege, the presumption is that the material sought to be discovered is privileged, and the burden is on the party seeking discovery to demonstrate that the material is essential to justice. This is much more likely in the criminal context because of the potential effects on the fairness of the trial.

III. OPEN MEETINGS REQUIREMENTS

Various provisions of federal law require that agency meetings normally be open to the public. States have similar provisions. We look at two such federal provisions, the *Government in the Sunshine Act* and the *Federal Advisory Committee Act (FACA)*.

A. The Sunshine Act

The Government in the Sunshine Act, passed in 1976 and codified at 5 U.S.C. §552b, was designed to open agency meetings to the public. Three issues are vital to proper understanding of the Sunshine Act: (1) to what agencies does the open meetings requirement apply; (2) what is a "meeting of an agency" for the purposes of the Sunshine Act; and (3) under what circumstances may a covered agency hold a meeting in private?

1. **The open meetings requirement:** The Sunshine Act requires all agencies (using FOIA's definition of "agency") that are headed by a "collegial body composed of two or more individual members" to announce their meetings at least one week in advance and to open the meeting to the public unless a Sunshine Act exception applies.

2. **Agencies with one "member" are not subject to the Sunshine Act:** Agencies headed by a single individual (such as the EPA and the FDA) are not subject to the Sunshine Act even when the head of the agency meets with subordinates to discuss agency business.

3. **What is a meeting of an agency?** A "meeting of an agency" within the Sunshine Act occurs if the members "jointly conduct or dispose of agency business." 5 U.S.C. §552b(b).

   a. **Consultative meetings:** The Sunshine Act does not apply to meetings that are purely consultative in character at which the agency does not purport to conduct business beyond discussing matters of interest to the agency. *See FCC v. ITT World Communications, Inc.*, 466 U.S. 463 (1984).

   b. **Predetermination of later agency action:** The Sunshine Act may be violated if the result of agency decisionmaking was predetermined at a closed meeting characterized by the agency as purely consultative. *See id.* Such a violation is more likely to be found if it is shown that the agency's attention at the closed meeting was focused on discrete proposals rather than an overview of matters of concern. *See id.*

4. **When may an agency meet in private?** The Sunshine Act contains ten categories of exceptions to its open meetings requirement, most of which track the exceptions to FOIA's disclosure requirements. *See* 5 U.S.C. §552b(c)(l)-(8).

   a. **Special Sunshine Act exceptions:** In addition to the exceptions that track FOIA exemptions, an agency may meet in private when an open meeting would have certain effects on financial markets or institutions, when the agency's purposes would be significantly frustrated, or when the meeting concerns certain investigatory or adjudicatory matters. *See* 5 U.S.C. §552b(c)(9)-(10).

   b. **Procedures for closing a meeting:** A meeting may be closed pursuant to the Sunshine Act exceptions only by a public vote of a majority of the members of the agency. Further, for each closed meeting, the chief legal officer of the agency must certify that the meeting meets one of the Sunshine Act exceptions and must designate the applicable exception. A verbatim transcript or recording must be kept of all closed meetings. Agency decisions to close meetings are subject to judicial review.

B. The Federal Advisory Committee Act (FACA)

FACA, enacted in 1972 and amended in 1976, regulates advisory committees "established or utilized" by the President or an agency to give advice to the executive branch. Advisory committees are not agencies but rather are groups with at least one private citizen (usually they are composed largely of private citizens) that advise the President or an agency.

   1. **FACA's requirements:** FACA essentially requires advisory committees to comply with the Sunshine Act with regard to their meetings and to FOIA with regard to their records. The President or agency head may utilize the Sunshine Act's exceptions to close a meeting of an advisory committee.

   2. **Constitutional problems with FACA:** Because it interferes with the President's ability to seek advice from private citizens, it has been argued that FACA violates the separation of powers. For example, in *Public Citizen v. DOJ*, 491 U.S. 440 (1989), Public Citizen argued that FACA applied to meetings of the ABA committee that assessed the qualifications of appointees to federal judgeships because the President utilized those recommendations. The majority of the Court held that FACA did not apply, but three concurring Justices found that FACA did apply but that FACA, as they understood it, unconstitutionally infringed on the President's appointment power. More recently, in *Cheney v. U.S. Dist. Court for Dist. of Columbia*, 542 U.S. 367 (2004), the Supreme Court decided that the Vice President could resist complying with FACA's procedural and disclosure requirements based on separation of powers concerns without asserting executive privilege. On remand, the court held that President Bush's National Energy Policy Development Group—chaired by the Vice President—was not subject to FACA because all of its members were government officials. The Court of Appeals thus issued a writ of mandamus prohibiting the District Court from subjecting the group to FACA. *In re Cheney*, 406 F.3d 723 (D.C. Cir. 2005).

Quiz Yourself on
FREEDOM OF INFORMATION AND OPEN MEETINGS

71. NHTSA pays a private institute to research the driving habits of owners of sport utility vehicles (SUVs). As part of the study, NHTSA instructs the institute to use a control group of drivers of

Ford Taurus and Honda Accord automobiles. An insurance industry group pays the same institute to study seat belt usage in all drivers. The institute, to save money, includes both sets of questions in the same study and uses the same drivers (SUV, Taurus, and Accord) for both the driving habits and seat belt usage studies. The institute turns the data regarding SUV drivers over to NHTSA, the data regarding seat belt usage over to the insurance industry group, but keeps the data regarding the driving habits of Taurus and Accord owners in its files because of methodological problems with that part of the survey. The institute informs the agency that it will redo that part of the study. A consumer protection and government watchdog organization would like to see all of the data and argues that because government funds subsidized the control group and the seat belt research, all the data belong, at least in part, to NHTSA. Further, the consumer group claims that the Taurus and Accord data will show that NHTSA chose the institute because of political favors, not because of the quality of the institute's work. Which, if any, of these data are subject to FOIA disclosure? _____

72. Cost overruns are plaguing the design and manufacture of a new Army boot. A competitor of the boot maker makes a FOIA request for records related to the design and manufacture of the boot. The Secretary of Defense denies the request, claiming that it would reveal secret national defense records. On judicial review, would the Secretary's denial be upheld? _____

73. A drug addiction advocacy group is trying to gather information on how federal agencies treat employees with drug problems. Are personnel records of employees with drug addiction treatment in their files subject to FOIA disclosure? _____

74. A discharged FBI agent seeks judicial review of the agency's decision to fire him. In discovery, he requests files relating to his last ten assignments to show that he performed all assignments competently. He also seeks any communication from the President to the Attorney General and/or to the Director of the FBI. Does the FBI have arguments for withholding this material from discovery? _____

75. A member of the FCC has lunch with a member of the Council of Economic Advisors. At that lunch, they discuss the economics of the marketplace in digital cellular communications and the likely economic effects of various possible regulatory regimes. Did they violate the Sunshine Act? _____

Answers

71. NHTSA is an agency, and any data turned over to it would be considered part of agency records since they would be obtained by the agency for agency purposes. Thus, the data regarding SUV driving habits would be subject to FOIA disclosure unless further information would reveal that some exemption should apply. The remaining data are likely not to be subject to FOIA disclosure because the data are not in government files. Even if NHTSA has a right to obtain the data, courts have held that FOIA does not obligate agencies to obtain files to make them subject to public disclosure. Thus, even though an important FOIA-related purpose would be served by publication of the flawed Taurus and Accord data, because those data are not part of agency records, they are not subject to FOIA disclosure.

72. No, unless the records were properly classified. Records may be withheld as secret national defense records only if the records have been classified as secret pursuant to executive orders creating and regulating the classification system. *See* 5 U.S.C. §552(b)(1). Thus, unless the boot records were

properly classified as secret defense records pursuant to an executive order, the Secretary may not withhold them as secret defense records under FOIA.

73. Maybe. Exemption (6) exempts from disclosure "personnel and medical files and similar files the disclosure of which would constitute a clearly unwarranted invasion of personal privacy." The test for whether an invasion of privacy is "unwarranted" is a balancing test with the interests in monitoring government activity on one side and the individual's privacy interests on the other. Raw data, without names and other identifying factors attached, would pose very little risk of invasion of privacy and thus might be available under FOIA. Any information, however, which might lead to identification of drug-addicted federal employees would not be subject to FOIA disclosure.

74. Yes. The FBI may have an evidentiary privilege if it can show a judge that release of the material would damage important law enforcement interests. Further, the FBI might assert executive immunity to resist revealing the contents of any communication from the President to the Director of the FBI. On the claim of executive immunity or privilege, once the claim is made, the party seeking the material has the burden of establishing that the material is vital to achieving justice in the proceeding. The plaintiff's interest in obtaining the material is substantial but is not as weighty as the interest of a criminal defendant's in obtaining material important to defending a criminal prosecution.

75. No, because the lunch was not a meeting of an agency. A meeting constitutes a meeting of an agency only when there is a possibility that agency business will be conducted. There is no suggestion that a single FCC commissioner or a single member of the Council of Economic Advisors has the power to conduct agency business alone.

Exam Tips on *FREEDOM OF INFORMATION AND OPEN MEETINGS*

☛ The most likely area in this chapter to be tested on is FOIA.

   ☞ Likely questions include those asking about the coverage of FOIA (what are agency records?) and about FOIA exemptions.

☛ The other candidate for examination is the Government in the Sunshine Act, with questions focusing on what constitutes a meeting of an agency and whether an exception to the Sunshine Act allows for a private meeting.

☛ Standing questions also might come up in terms of who has standing to raise a FOIA or Sunshine Act issue in litigation and who has standing to try to prevent an agency from disclosing information in response to a FOIA request.

☛ In a question about FOIA, be sure to cite and quote from the statutory provision at issue.

   ☞ Be prepared to discuss whether particular information is contained in agency records.

   ☞ Watch out for records that are not in the agency's possession and were not in the agency's possession at the time of the FOIA request.

☛ Regarding FOIA exemptions, be sure to quote the statutory provision and keep in mind that courts construe the exemptions narrowly.

☞ Keep in mind that more than one exemption may arguably apply to a particular agency record, and be sure to discuss all exemptions that might apply.

☛ In a case in which a party supplying information to the agency seeks to prevent the agency from providing records in response to a third party's FOIA request, discuss the issue in terms of the requirements for "reverse FOIA" actions.

☞ Point out that the APA provides judicial review of an agency decision to release information, and that other statutes, such as the Trade Secrets Act and the Privacy Act, may provide a legal basis for reversing the agency on judicial review.

☛ Privacy-based FOIA exemptions are likely to be asked about. Be sure to discuss the balancing test used to determine whether the public's need to know is outweighed by a potential invasion of privacy.

☛ On any question regarding discovery from the government in litigation, be sure to point out that the government may not only resist discovery on all the grounds that other parties may employ, but also may raise evidentiary privileges and executive immunity.

☞ In either case, the procedure for raising the objection, including whether the material is presumed to be available in discovery or presumed to be confidential, may be relevant.

☛ In questions about the Sunshine Act, be sure to consider whether an agency meeting is involved and whether the particular agency is covered by the Act.

☞ If an agency meeting is involved, and an agency wishes to hold it in private, look both at the substance of the Sunshine Act's exceptions and whether the agency has followed proper procedures for closing a meeting.

Essay Exam Questions

QUESTION 1: (Note: This is a fictionalized version of an actual case. Parts A and B are not necessarily of equal weight.)

Section 404 of the Clean Water Act (the Act) authorizes the United States Army Corps of Engineers (the Corps) to issue permits "for the discharge of dredged or fill material into the navigable waters." Section 301(a) of the Act provides that the "discharge of any pollutant by any person" is unlawful unless in compliance with the Act's permit requirements. Discharge, in turn, is defined as "any addition of any pollutant to navigable waters from any point source." *Id.*

The statute was prompted because often the least expensive way to dispose of dredged material is to redeposit it at another place in the navigable water. This can disrupt the ecology of the waterway, and may also cause serious pollution if the dredged material contains harmful pollutants. This happens often, for example, when harbor areas or areas suffering from previous industrial discharges are dredged.

In 1977 the Corps promulgated regulations that generally tracked the statutory language, defining "discharge of dredged material" as "any addition of dredged material into the waters of the United States," with a few limited exceptions. 42 Fed. Reg. 37,145 (July 19, 1977). A new regulation, issued in 1986, exempted from the permit requirement "de minimis, incidental soil movement occurring during normal dredging operations." 51 Fed. Reg. 41,232. Although this regulation did not define "normal dredging operations," its preamble gave some guidance as to the exemption's coverage:

> Preamble: Section 404 clearly directs the Corps to regulate the discharge of dredged material, not the dredging itself. Dredging operations cannot be performed without some fallback. However, if we were to define this fallback as a "discharge of dredged material," we would, in effect, be adding the regulation of dredging to section 404 which we do not believe was the intent of Congress. *Id.* at 41,210.

After the regulation was issued, there was some controversy over its coverage. All agree that the 1986 rule did regulate "sidecasting," which involves placing removed soil in the same waterway but at some distance from the point of removal. *See* 58 Fed. Reg. 45,008, 45,013 (Aug. 25, 1993) (noting that sidecasting has "always been regulated under Section 404"). However, there was disagreement over whether the regulation covered "redeposit" and "fallback." Redeposit occurs when material removed from the water is returned to it at the same general location. When redeposit takes place at substantially the same time as the initial removal, for example, when material falls back in while dredging is being done, it is referred to as "fallback." A regulation was promulgated, and it required that once material was removed, a permit should be required to redeposit the material or to allow the material to fall back. In response to an argument that was raised in comments received after the regulation was promulgated, the Corps issued (without notice and comment) an interpretative rule providing that "the permit requirements do not apply to redeposit and fallback." The agency stated, in a statement accompanying the interpretative rule, that redeposit of material dredged from the waterway poses little (if any) threat to the cleanliness or navigability of the waterway.

Part A. In 1992, a developer sought to dredge 700 acres of wetlands in North Carolina. *See* 58 Fed. Reg. at 45,016. Because the developer's efforts involved only minimal incidental releases of soil and other dredged material into the neighboring waterway, the Corps's field office personnel determined that, under the terms of the 1986 regulation, §404's permit requirements did not apply. In response to the developer's query, the field office director issued a statement to that effect. Environmental groups, concerned by what they viewed as the adverse effects of the developer's activities on the wetlands and the neighboring waterway, filed an action seeking enforcement of the §404 permit requirement. *See North Carolina Wildlife Federation v. Tulloch*, Civ. No. C90-713-CIV-5-BO (E.D.N.C. 1992). The environmental groups made the following claims against the Corps's action:

1. The Corps had not included a discussion, in its EIS required under NEPA, of the effects of "redeposit" and "fallback" on the waterway. The EIS stated merely that redeposit and fallback would have no adverse effects since the material was identical to the material already in the waterway and since only a minimal amount of material would be involved. The environmental groups argued that there was no proof that the material would not be dangerous and that the baseline should be the waterway without the material.

2. The de minimis exception to the permit requirement was arbitrary, capricious, and contrary to the statutory language and thus should be declared void.

3. The interpretative rule is void because it should have been promulgated in a notice and comment procedure.

The environmental groups sought an order requiring the Corps to subject the developer to the permit process. The environmental groups also sued the developer in federal court seeking an injunction against the draining and clearing project, claiming violations of the Clean Water Act, NEPA, and state law.

Please identify and analyze potential defenses the Corps and the developer might have to these claims. Please state explicitly any assumptions you need to make if the facts do not provide sufficient information.

Part B.   Assume the portions of the above case against the Corps were settled. As part of the settlement of the case (a settlement to which the developer was not a party), the Corps agreed to propose stiffer rules governing the permit requirements for landclearing and excavation activities. The result (the regulation at issue here) has come to be called the "*Tulloch* Rule." The new rule (rescinding the old regulations) was promulgated after notice and comment, consistent with the settlement agreement. It removed the de minimis exception and expanded the definition of discharge to cover "any addition of dredged material into, including any redeposit of dredged material within, the waters of the United States." 33 CFR §323.2(d)(1). Specifically, the rule defines "discharge of dredged material" to include "*[a]ny addition*, including *any redeposit*, of dredged material, including excavated material, into waters of the United States which is incidental to any activity, including mechanized landclearing, ditching, channelization, or other excavation." 33 CFR §323.2(d)(1)(iii) (emphasis added). The concise general statement provides, inter alia, that the new regulation will minimize the potentially harmful effects of redeposit. The agency also, without notice and comment, rescinded the interpretative rule.

The developer and a trade association (of which the developer is a member) seek immediate judicial review of the rescissions of the former regulation and the interpretative rule and of the issuance of the new regulation. They claim that the Corps lacks power to require a permit for redeposit and fallback under the statutory definition of "discharge."

As part of their investigation, the lawyers for these parties discover that, during the comment period, a manufacturer of dredging equipment demonstrated to Corps officials that new equipment would virtually eliminate fallback. They suspect that this manufacturer has connections to Corps officials and is hoping that the new rule will increase sales of the new equipment because developers will need to eliminate fallback to avoid the permit process. It also appears that the Corps had information that eliminating redeposit, including fallback, would increase jobs in companies specializing in dredging material disposal. Neither the equipment nor the jobs issue was mentioned in the concise general statement.

Please identify and analyze the claims for judicial review and any expected responses from the agency and the environmental groups.

QUESTION 2: (Note: The statutes discussed may have been modified for this problem.)

The federal Food, Drug and Cosmetic Act (the Act) prohibits the use of any "drug" as a food additive without the specific approval of the FDA. The Act contains no definition of a "drug."

The FDA is an agency within the Department of Health and Human Services, which is headed by a single commissioner. The Commissioner has the full power to act on behalf of the agency, including issuing policy statements, regulations (and other such things), and the power to review adjudications conducted under the Act. The Act grants the FDA the power to issue "such rules and regulations necessary to carry out the provisions of the Act." The Act also authorizes the FDA to hold hearings on alleged violations and issue fines and cease and desist orders against violations. The Act provides that the initial hearing is held before an administrative law judge "not under the supervision, direct or indirect, of any employee of the Food and Drug Administration." Appeal is to the Commissioner, who has all the power of the initial decisionmaker, with substantial evidence judicial review "in the court of appeals for the circuit in which the party charged has its main place of business or in which the violation is alleged to have taken place, at the option of the party charged."

Since the passage of the Act, the FDA has interpreted the Act not to cover chemicals found naturally in any food product. Thus it has not regulated the use of caffeine in soft drinks, since caffeine occurs naturally in coffee and chocolate. A 1965 policy statement (issued by its then-commissioner) stated that "[i]t is the policy of the FDA not to require approval for any food additive found naturally in a commonly consumed food product as long as the concentrations of such additive are no greater than concentrations naturally occurring in other food products."

The debate over whether cigarettes should be regulated because of evidence that cigarette manufacturers were carefully setting the amount of nicotine in cigarettes sparked interest in whether soft drink manu-facturers were engaged in similar manipulation of the amount of caffeine in soft drinks. Critics cited the advertising of Jolt Cola that "all the sugar and twice the caffeine" was evidence that soft drinks were being spiked with caffeine to maintain sales of soft drinks. Critics also cited evidence that some drinks, such as Mountain Dew and Mellow Yellow, contained as much caffeine per serving as coffee.

In early 1996, the FDA issued a statement providing: "The FDA will now apply the Food, Drug and Cosmetic Act to require approval as additives for all drugs used as food additives, including those that are found naturally in a commonly consumed food product, even if the concentrations of such additives are no greater than concentrations naturally occurring in other food products: Because this is not a legislative rule, section 553 procedural requirements do not apply." The FDA then conducted research on caffeine in soft drinks: Immediately after the issuance of the 1996 FDA statement, several soft drink manufacturers removed caffeine from their products.

Needless to say, soft drink manufacturers and the manufacturers of caffeine additive powder were not happy with this turn of events. They are seeking advice on what steps they might be able to take now to prevent the FDA from going forward with-its research. They also wonder whether any other of the FDA's actions thus far violate the APA and can be challenged at this time. You have been hired by the soft drink manufacturers and the caffeine additive manufacturers to provide legal advice on what steps they might take at this point. Early in your research, you discover from a disgruntled FDA employee that before the 1996 statement was issued, the Commissioner of the FDA had extensive contacts regarding the effects of caffeine with health care advocates and, at a private research session, he was shown a great deal of evidence regarding the negative effects of caffeine and the prevalence of caffeine addiction among children who drink Mountain Dew and eat chocolate. Also, the FDA Commissioner generally refused to meet with soft drink and caffeine industry lobbyists, citing potential conflicts of interest.

Part A. Please write a memorandum regarding potential challenges at this stage and any issues that might be available on judicial review at a later stage.

(New facts below for Part B)

Assume that the FDA's research continued and ultimately the FDA enforcement bureau brought an enforcement complaint against Jake Cola, Inc., a small Los Angeles-based manufacturer of high-priced organic cola drinks. Jake Cola contains far less caffeine than the leading brands of cola drinks such as Coca-Cola and Pepsi-Cola. Jake Cola's market share is minuscule; it has approximately less than. 1 percent of the market share in the Los Angeles area and only fifty thousand dollars worth of business outside of California, annually. (Assume that this is sufficient to meet any "interstate commerce" requirements for federal regulation.) In fact, Jake Cola advertises that it has less caffeine than the other brands and shows on its label the actual number of milligrams of caffeine per serving, which no other brand does.

In an informal conversation, Jake's lawyer asked the FDA prosecutor why Jake Cola was being singled out at this time. The FDA prosecutor responded that the FDA has an informal policy of prosecuting companies that advertise regarding the additive at issue, and also the FDA usually goes after small companies first to establish a principle that can be applied in later cases against larger companies that, in the words of the prosecutor, "might put up more of a defense." Jake Cola's lawyer then asked whether an enforcement action was being brought against Jolt, which advertises "twice the caffeine." The FDA prosecutor said, "no," and also said he thinks it is related to the fact that Jolt has a lobbyist that used to be general counsel at the FDA.

Part B. Jake Cola's lawyer heard from Jake's caffeine supplier about your earlier work regarding this matter and would like to know whether any of this additional information might either help Jake Cola prevent the hearing from occurring or supply grounds for reversing any adverse decision later on judicial review. Do not address any potential First Amendment issues.

(New facts below for Part C)

Assume that the hearing against Jake Cola went forward. The ALJ, although finding a violation of the Act since Jake Cola admittedly adds caffeine without FDA approval, declined to issue a cease and desist order or impose a fine on the grounds that "Jake Cola is a small player in the soft drink market and uses less caffeine than most. An order should not issue unless other, larger soft drink manufacturers are also prosecuted." The FDA prosecutor then sought review before the Commissioner. The Commissioner, after a full evidentiary hearing, found that Jake Cola was in violation of the Act, that a cease and desist order should issue, and that a fine was not proper at this time. The Commissioner, in the conclusion of his opinion stated the following:

> I hereby find that caffeine is a drug and that as such it may not be added to food products without specific approval from the FDA. Accordingly, allowing for the sale of existing stocks, any manufacturer or distributor of a food product in violation of this ruling thirty days after the date of this order will be assessed substantial fines for violating the Act.

Part C.   At this point, your original clients (soft drink manufacturers and makers of caffeine additives) seek your advice on whether they now have grounds to bring suit against the FDA. They would like your advice on whether there are any procedural or substantive grounds for challenging the Commissioner's apparent order that they stop the use of caffeine in soft drinks and other food products and whether the Commissioner can be prevented from participating in further proceedings on the issue. Please write a memorandum concerning these issues.

QUESTION 3:   Since 1933 prices paid by handlers of milk to producers of milk have been set by the Secretary of Agriculture under what are denominated as Marketing Orders. Handlers, in turn, sell milk to food producers for use in prepared foods and to local dairies for public sale in retail stores. The Secretary's authority to establish Marketing Orders derives from the Agricultural Marketing Agreement Act. A section of this statute provides:

> The price of milk paid by milk handlers to milk producers shall be set by the Secretary, in his discretion, after hearing, to reflect the price of feeds, the available supplies of feeds, and other economic conditions which affect market supply and demand for milk or its products in the marketing area to which the contemplated marketing agreement, order, or amendment relates. Whenever the Secretary in his discretion finds, upon the basis of the evidence adduced at the hearing required by this section that the price of milk is not reasonable in view of the price of feeds, the available supplies of feeds, and other economic conditions which affect market area supply and demand for milk in the marketing area, he shall fix such prices as he finds will reflect such factors, insure a sufficient quantity of pure and wholesome milk to meet current needs and further to assure a level of farm income adequate to maintain productive capacity sufficient to meet anticipated future needs, and be in the public interest. Thereafter, as the Secretary finds necessary on account of changed circumstances, he shall, after due notice and opportunity for hearing, make adjustments in such prices.

The reference to "marketing area" in this provision concerns the Secretary's statutory authority to divide the nation into regions and to issue different Marketing Orders for each. Under this authority the Secretary has delineated 40 marketing areas, and every time he has set a price that handlers must pay milk producers for milk to be sold in a marketing area east of the Rocky Mountains he has added a differential based on the distance of the center of the area from Eau Claire, Wisconsin, the hub of the nation's traditional milk-producing region. This differential was established after a notice and comment rulemaking in 1934. In this rulemaking the Secretary explained that he interpreted the phrase "other economic conditions" to include consideration of distance from the center of the nation's milk-producing region because places distant from this center were not receiving adequate supplies of milk. The Secretary stated that the distance-from-Eau Claire price differential would encourage the transportation of milk into all marketing areas. In 1935 a court of appeals held that the Secretary's rule was supported by substantial evidence and was not arbitrary and capricious.

Since the adoption of this pricing system, milk shortages have not occurred in any regions. During this period milk production also has become more dispersed in the Eastern United States, a dispersal that perhaps has been encouraged by the higher prices that milk handlers must pay for milk that is to be sold in regions more distant from Eau Claire. Nonetheless, the Secretary has not adjusted the pricing system, except periodically, through notice and comment rulemaking, to adjust for changes in the differential due to inflation in shipping costs.

Last year the Secretary issued a notice that he was considering a minor increase in milk prices to adjust for inflation. Consumer groups, milk handlers, dairy farmers in areas relatively close to Eau Claire, food producers in areas distant from Eau Claire, and retail grocery companies from around the country all commented that the entire system of setting milk prices is obsolete and that the reference to Eau Claire, Wisconsin, should be abandoned, because distance from this city has no relation to the actual cost of producing and supplying milk. Milk producers in areas distant from Eau Claire and others commented on other issues, but did not address the Eau Claire-based differential. Both camps of milk producers, however, heavily lobbied the Secretary and his assistants as well as members of Congress, expressing their contrasting views on the retention of the existing milk marketing order price structure.

The Secretary has now promulgated a regulation making the minor adjustments to milk prices he proposed last year. In an accompanying statement, the Secretary explained that the "existing pricing system is maintained with minor adjustments for inflation in shipping and other costs." The Secretary did not make findings on the specific economic factors listed in the statute and did not respond to the comments that argued that the traditional factors used in setting prices were obsolete.

Consumer groups, Wisconsin milk producers, and food producers in areas distant from Eau Claire would like to seek judicial review of the Secretary's failure to alter the system for setting milk prices. Analyze whether each of these groups has standing to seek such review. Then consider the merits of the arguments they might advance against the Secretary. Is the 1935 circuit court decision upholding the system relevant to any of these arguments? What other information would you like to have? (Ignore what you know about the actual regulation of milk pricing and the case on which this problem is based.)

QUESTION 4:   [This question is fictional, and no environmental statutes not referred to in the question should be consulted.]

The Environmental Protection Agency (EPA) is concerned about air pollution resulting from the evaporation of gasoline fumes at gas stations. Under its statutory power to "issue such rules and regulations it finds to be reasonably necessary to protect the human environment," it has issued a notice of proposed rulemaking which states:

> EPA is seeking to reduce or eliminate the evaporation of fumes at gasoline stations. Many options are being considered, including, but not limited to, a recovery device on automobiles and/or a recovery device on gasoline pumps.

In response to this notice, EPA received hundreds of comments. Many comments stated that recovery devices on automobiles would be unsafe and expensive and that recovery devices on pumps would be ineffective and expensive. Several comments, from environmental groups, advocated a reformulation of gasoline that would significantly lower the rate of evaporation and thus would accomplish EPA's goal without any device at all. These comments also argued that gasoline reformulation was the cheapest method of reducing fumes.

After reviewing the comments, EPA issued a regulation requiring, within six months, that all gasoline sold in the United States conform to the reformulation as proposed in the comments.

The Oil Companies were not pleased with this action. They claim they did not have adequate notice or opportunity to comment on this regulation. They have filed petitions for judicial review of the regulation in the appropriate federal court. They also have lobbied Congress for statutory relief and they have lobbied the President to overturn the regulation.

The efforts in Congress failed, but just before the regulation was to go into effect, the President issued an Executive Order suspending the effect of the regulation "until such time as the EPA conducts a thorough reassessment of the regulation in light of the costs the regulation would impose on the oil industry." Environmental groups and automobile manufacturers have sued the EPA seeking an order that the regulation be enforced as written. They argue that the suspension of the regulation is illegal presidential interference with the EPA's rulemaking authority.

You are a law clerk to the judge before whom both cases have been consolidated. Please write a memorandum with your opinion on the cases. He is most interested in whether the APA has been violated and whether the President's action raises constitutional or statutory issues. Do not worry about whether the Oil Company challenge is moot—another clerk is working on that issue.

Essay Exam Answers

SAMPLE ANSWER TO QUESTION 1

Part A. First, the defendants—the Corps and the developer (*D*)—can argue that the environmental group lacks standing to file suit. There are three constitutional requirements for standing: 1) injury, 2) causation, and 3) redressability. There are prudential limitations, including the zone of interests requirement. Because the Clean Water Act allows for citizens' suits and theoretically puts all citizens within the zone of interests, the zone of interests test should not be a problem for anyone who otherwise has standing. The Act allows citizens to sue for violation of the substantive provisions of the Act and for the Administrator's failure to perform a nondiscretionary duty. The Act would also allow the group to sue the developer if he's violating the Act by discharging pollutants without a permit. However, the plaintiff environmental group (*P*) still has to meet the constitutional requirements of injury, causation, and redressability.

To prove injury, *P* will have to show that it is harmed by the redepositing or fallback by showing that it uses the waters at issue and that this use is harmed. Assuming some members use the water, the aesthetic injury of observing dirtier water is probably enough for standing and also any appreciable effect on the cleanliness of the water should be enough. The environmental groups will also have to show that the Corps' regulation that exempts incidental soil movement is causing the injury and that subjecting the developer to the permit process will remedy the injury. This means that the regulation must result in more bad stuff ending up in the water.

The standing cases are wildly inconsistent, so it is difficult to predict how a court would come out on this one. Presumably, the plaintiff read *Sierra Club* and *Lujan* and knows to find some member who uses the waters. Whether a court will find that the injury is fairly traceable to the Corps's failure to subject the developer to the permit process is speculative. Presumably if *P* receives an injunction against the developer, that will at least temporarily stop its project. In ***SCRAP***, the court found a causal connection between an increase in freight rates and a decrease in recycling, resulting in more litter. But in ***EKWRO***, the court didn't find causation in the IRS's grant of charitable status to nonprofits who don't provide emergency medical services to poor people and plaintiffs who were denied the opportunity to receive services there. The trickiest part is whether "harm" to *P* will be stopped by the permit process. If the Corps doesn't think it has authority to regulate fallback, it seems it will likely issue a permit, if required to, to anyone who will only be discharging fallback. The result will be the same—*P* is only trying to add a procedural step. However, some cases would allow standing just based on the chance that the Corps might deny the permit.

Second, assuming standing exists, *D* can try to argue that the suit is not ripe for judicial review. But this is likely to fail. The developer has now acted under the regulations, and the Corps made a final determination that the permit requirements didn't apply in his case. Therefore, in effect, the Corps has enforced the regulation, thus making it final agency action.

Third, the Corps can argue its EIS under NEPA is sufficient. Under *Calvert Cliffs*, an agency must consider the environmental effects as part of its decision in order for the decision not to be arbitrary and capricious. *P* argues the Corps didn't consider the environmental effects of redeposit and fallback and that the EIS merely stated that there would be no adverse effects without any evidence that the matter was considered. The Corps can argue that its statement that the redeposit or fallback of material dredged would not have an adverse effect (since the material was identical to the material already in the waterway) shows that it did consider the effects. It considered it and made a statement about it. Under *Strycker's Bay*, *P* can't challenge an agency's decision just because the agency may have undervalued the environmental effects. *P* claims there is no proof that the material won't be dangerous, but *P* has not offered proof that the material will be dangerous. Under *Strycker's Bay*, it seems the Corps has to only meet a minimum threshold to satisfy the requirements of the EIS.

Next, *P* argues the de minimis exception is arbitrary, capricious, and contrary to the statutory language. When promulgating the 1986 regulation, the Corps exempted incidental soil movement during normal dredging operations, and in the preamble the Corps said it didn't have the power to regulate dredging and, therefore, couldn't regulate fallback material. This raises the question of whether §404 authorized the Corps to regulate dredging operations, and it raises the question of whether fallback should be defined as discharge of dredged material. Both questions involve statutory interpretation, which should be analyzed under the *Chevron* test. Step one of *Chevron* asks whether Congress has directly spoken to the precise question at issue. If so, Congress's intent prevails. If the agency's interpretation is contrary, the court on review should overrule the agency. There are two interpretations of *Chevron* step one. The original *Chevron* looks only at the plain meaning to determine whether Congress has directly spoken to this precise issue. In this case, Congress did define discharge to include *any addition* of *any* pollutant to navigable waters. The Corps can argue that the *addition* of *any* pollutant does not include fallback or redeposit of material that was already there. But *P* may argue that once the material is out of the waterway during dredging, putting it back or allowing it to fall back clearly meets the statutory definition and thus not only is within the Corps's power to regulate, but the Corps must regulate. Additionally, sidecasting has always been regulated and that is not necessarily adding pollutants in the way the Corps interprets it. The agency will argue that to meet the "directly spoken" standard, Congress would have had to be much more specific about fallback and redeposit. But it is not clear whether Congress has directly spoken about whether the Corps has the power to regulate dredging operations.

The court may apply the *Cardoza-Fonseca* version of *Chevron* step one, which uses traditional tools of statutory interpretation, like legislative history, language, and structure, to decide if Congress addressed the specific issue. Under this analysis, the court is more likely to find Congress did address the issue than under the original *Chevron* analysis. It seems as though the court may find that Congress did address the issue and would agree with the agency's interpretation that discharge does not include fallback or redeposit. It seems unlikely that Congress intended the Corps to regulate the dredging process with its pollution-based permit system.

If the court does not find Congress addressed the issue, it will move to step two, which asks whether the agency's interpretation is permissible and within the range of what Congress contemplated. This is very deferential, and a court will likely side with the Corps and determine that the de minimis exemption is not contrary to the statutory language. Even if the court approves the interpretation, it may ask whether the decision here—to not require a permit—is arbitrary and capricious. The arbitrary and capricious test looks at whether the agency considered all the relevant factors, evaluated alternatives, and explained its conclusions on issues raised in the decisionmaking process. In this case, the Corps determined that dredging operations can't be performed without some fallback, and it determined it didn't have the authority to regulate dredging operations. The arbitrary and capricious test is very deferential. There does not appear to be "clear error" here as defined in *Overton Park*. Its conclusion does not seem to be so implausible that it couldn't be ascribed to a difference in view or product of agency expertise, as discussed in *The Airbags Case*. Therefore, the de minimis exception is likely to be held valid.

Finally, *P* argues the interpretative rule is void because it should have been promulgated through notice and comment. APA §553 exempts interpretative rules from its notice and comment provisions. An interpretative rule is one that clarifies a statutory term or reminds parties of existing duties. However, a legislative rule (which is subject to notice and comment) attempts to supplement the statute, adds to the duties or the law, or changes the law. *P* argues the rule is legislative. In support of its argument, it may argue that the interpretative rule is trying to change the 1986 regulation, and agencies can't change legislative rules with interpretative rules. But the Corps can argue that it is not attempting to change the 1986 regulation or add any duties. Instead, it is merely clarifying what it means by incidental soil movement. The interpretative rule merely explains that incidental soil movement includes redeposit and fallback. The 1986 regulation is an existing statutory norm, and the interpretative rule just explains it further. It is unlike *National Family Planning* (which changed the statutory norm), and it's unlike *Hoctor* (which added the duty to build an eight-foot fence). Here, the Corps restated,or clarified what it already said in the 1986 regulation.

Part B. Before the developer and trade association can get judicial review of any claims, they will have to show they have standing. Standing should be fairly easy for the developer. Under the old regulation, he did not need a permit for his dredging operations, but under the new regulation he will need a permit. The permit process itself is probably somewhat costly and time-consuming, which is an injury in itself. And he will likely be injured if he is refused a permit. The trade association is a little more removed, but it should have standing if it meets the normal requirements for associational standing. Because the developer is a member of the association, the association might be able to get standing through him. Additionally, it may have other members directly affected—like the developer.

Next, both will have to show that the suit is ripe for judicial review. In this case, the agency issued a regulation and apparently has not yet enforced it against the developer. Should the developer have to wait for a denial of a permit before seeking review? The first question is whether the agency's act is final. APA §704 provides for judicial review, except where precluded, for final agency action for which there is no adequate remedy in court. The court in *Abbott Labs* said the promulgation of a regulation is final agency action because the process is over. The second question to determine ripeness is whether the issues are fit and whether the party seeking review would suffer hardship if review were delayed until after enforcement. An issue is fit if it is purely legal and does not require additional fact or policy findings. An issue is not fit if it is unclear what its meaning is or when it is likely to be applied. In this case, the issue of whether a permit is required is purely legal and does not require additional findings. Presumably, the regulation applies right away. If the developer wants to begin dredging, he will have to file for a permit. A party will suffer hardship if the regulation is expensive to comply with and if there are substantial impediments to challenging it in an enforcement action. If there is a delay in review, the developer can either apply for a permit (which presumably costs some money) or can go ahead with dredging and risk an enforcement action. The regulation does require a change in the developer's conduct, since he must not dredge until he gets the permit. Depending on the cost of the permit and the delay involved, this may not rise to the same level of hardship as those in *Abbott Labs*. But it is not as little a hardship as in *Toilet Goods*. A court may not find sufficient hardship to determine that the suit is ripe since there is probably not too much money at stake to comply.

Assuming, however, that the suit is ripe, *P* can claim that rescission of the old regulation is arbitrary and capricious and that the issuance of the new regulation in its place is arbitrary and capricious. In *The Airbag Case*, the court reviewed the agency's decision to rescind a regulation under the arbitrary and capricious test. It held that the decision to rescind was arbitrary primarily because the agency didn't consider relevant factors (like the inertia factor), failed to analyze alternatives (like airbags), and failed to explain why it decided the way it did. In this case, there is little information about why the Corps decided the way it did, except that it submitted to pressure from the environmental group that sued it in Part A. There is no new evidence on the record about the harmful effects of redeposit. The general statement just concludes that the regulation will minimize the potentially harmful effects of redeposit. There is absolutely no new evidence to suggest why the Corps switched to this statement after previously concluding that redeposit did not threaten the navigability or cleanliness of the water. And the agency's decision stands or falls based on the rationalizations it made when it promulgated the rule—so it cannot come up with anything new. There are no facts to substantiate the decision to rescind. Therefore, a court should find it arbitrary and capricious. If a court found the decision to rescind was valid, however, then it probably will find this new regulation substantively valid. The arbitrary and capricious standard is deferential and there is nothing wrong per se with a tougher standard, as long as the agency considers all the relevant factors and alternatives. The only problem is that it does not explain how it determined that redeposit is potentially harmful. In other words, it does not explain its conclusions about issues raised in the decisionmaking process. It looks particularly arbitrary because the agency itself may actually agree with the developer but feel legally pressured not to act on its own views. Although we do not know what information it had in the record to substantiate this claim, this might be grounds for finding the regulation arbitrary and capricious.

P can argue there is a problem with rescinding the interpretative rule without notice and comment. Assuming that the interpretative rule is, in fact, an interpretative rule (see discussion Part A), then the agency can change one interpretative rule with another one. The agency could presumably rescind it without notice and comment. *P* might be able to argue that the regulation is void because the agency relied on ex parte information without giving interested parties a chance to comment. Apparently, the Corps had information that eliminating redeposit would increase jobs and that new equipment would virtually eliminate fallback. The agency cannot conceal information that it relied on in making its decision. Interested parties must be afforded a meaningful opportunity to submit comments. In order for the opportunity to be meaningful, parties must have notice of information upon which the agency relies. Also, in the concise general statement, the agency must state the major issues of the policy that were made public in the proceeding, and it must give policy reasons for its decision to choose one course or another. Since the agency did not mention the new equipment or the information about job increases, the court might order a new comment period, when interested parties could reply to this information. It is, however, unclear whether the APA really imposes these obligations.

P can also argue that the agency administrator either prejudged the issue or is biased. The problem is that the standard for showing prejudgment is much tougher for rulemaking than for adjudication. For rulemaking, the standard is clear and convincing evidence that the administrator has an unalterably closed mind on matters critical to the disposition of the proceeding. Proving an unalterably closed mind involves showing, from public or private statements, that the decisionmaker is convinced that the proposed rule is necessary without regard to the substance of the comments received. Apparently, the Corps had ex parte comments with these equipment manufacturers, but it is not apparent that an ex parte contact (in itself) is wrong. *HBO* says, "just say no." *Costle* is not really concerned as long as important contacts be put on the record. Granted, the officials did not put the information on the record, but they could argue it was not important to the decision or the court could order a new comment period. These contacts probably are not sufficient to disqualify the administrator from participating in the proceedings. In fact, based on *Vermont Yankee* (or at least the spirit of *Vermont Yankee*), it is not clear if *Costle* or *HBO* are even valid since the APA does not ban ex parte contacts in rulemaking.

The best evidence of prejudgment is that the Corps settled the case with the environmental group and may have decided to promulgate a stiffer rule regardless of the comments it received. Under the settlement agreement, it said it would propose stiffer rules. This might show an unalterably closed mind—one convinced that a stiffer rule was necessary, regardless of the comments received. However, the key word is "propose." Just as in negotiated rulemaking, the agency was free to adopt a different rule.

Finally, *P* can argue, as the Corps did in Part A, that the agency doesn't have power to regulate dredging operations and interpreting discharge to include redeposit means the Corps will be regulating dredging operations. This may involve using the *Chevron* test again, concerning the meaning of discharge. This time the agency argues it includes redeposit. Assuming Congress didn't address the issue (but see the discussion in Part A), then the agency's interpretation is probably within a permissible range.

SAMPLE ANSWER TO QUESTION 2

Part A.   The first issue is whether there is a dispute that is ripe for review at this time. All the FDA has done is announce that it will take enforcement action in a category of cases in the future. It has not taken action against anyone yet. Assuming that judicial review is available for any enforcement order issued, there may not be any reason to allow judicial review at this time. Further, it is not clear what the FDA will actually do under the new statement, because the statement may be unfit for review. The FDA might be very strict and reject most applications, or it might be very liberal and grant most applications to use additives that occur naturally.

Assuming that review is available now, or perhaps later, there are several grounds for challenging the FDA's new policy. First, the manufacturers may argue that the policy statement is a legislative rule and should have been promulgated with a notice and comment process. This is not a very strong argument. The strongest argument for the challengers is that the FDA will act in the future as if it is bound to take action against caffeine and other similar additives. The new interpretation of the Act also adds to the law since the FDA claims the power to take enforcement action that it previously said it could not take. However, despite these arguments, when an agency announces its enforcement policy, it is considered a policy statement and does not have to use a notice and comment process. Further, this particular statement is arguably interpretative, since it construes the word "drug" and the terms of the agency's power to regulate food additives. A court on judicial review after an enforcement order might reject these interpretations, and the agency's statement is not a binding legal obligation until an enforcement order is actually issued and upheld on judicial review.

Another issue is whether the FDA's view that caffeine is a drug is consistent with the statute. Here,, by not defining "drug," Congress probably left it to the FDA to fill in the gap. Under *Chevron*, Congress has not directly spoken to whether caffeine, or naturally occurring food ingredients generally, can be considered drugs. The question is whether the FDA's interpretation is permissible. Using a looser version of *Chevron* step one, if the legislative history of the statute reveals that Congress would not have wanted the FDA to regulate caffeine, then perhaps a court would overrule the agency. But it is likely that the FDA would be upheld, absent strong evidence of congressional intent to the contrary.

The next issue has to do with the extensive ex parte contacts that occurred prior to the issuance of the statement. Nothing in the APA prohibits these contacts. In fact, without any sort of notice and comment process, it is difficult to imagine any legal doctrine that would prevent the agency from having contacts with anyone it wants to. If there had been an actual rulemaking, then a court might have required the agency to place all the information it had on the record for comment. Insofar as the agency appears to be using the statement plus the threat of prosecution as a substitute for a rulemaking, some courts might be very suspicious of what the agency did. However, it is unclear whether anything could be done at this point. The whole process seems unfair, but there is no apparent remedy.

In sum, it is unlikely that a court would prevent the agency from conducting research and from issuing a policy statement that informs the public that it intends to prosecute certain cases in the future. Perhaps a rule on prosecutions would be unreviewable as committed to agency discretion by law. In any case, judicial review is not likely to be available until the agency brings an enforcement proceeding or promulgates a legislative rule.

Part B.   These facts raise a claim of discriminatory enforcement. Jake Cola would argue that it is a patent abuse of discretion for the FDA to prosecute when Jake Cola has less caffeine than most other sodas and when its market share, even in its local area, is minuscule. The agency would have to articulate some reason for its choice. Courts are so deferential to agency enforcement priorities that the agency might be upheld if it says something as empty as "we chose this company as one of many that we ultimately intend to prosecute." Further, putting First Amendment concerns aside, the agency might rely upon a policy of prosecuting companies that mention caffeine, and could say "we are looking into whether we should bring an action against Jolt." However, if a court took the possibility of a discriminatory-enforcement claim seriously, this should be a good case. There is no question that the other sodas have caffeine—unlike the *Universal-Rundle* case where the agency could say it was an open question whether the other companies were violating the law. However, on the other hand, it is not clear how badly Jake would be hurt if he cannot use caffeine. After all, he uses very little and there are colas without caffeine on the market.

It should be noted that the discriminatory-enforcement issue may not be ripe for review until the agency actually issues an order against Jake. There is no final order and no other obvious basis for immediate judicial review. There is neither fitness nor hardship. We don't really know what order, if any, will be issued; we also do not know what effect the order will have. The cost of defending is not sufficient hardship.

Part C.   First, there is no problem with the agency reversing the ALJ since credibility is not an issue. The basis for the reversal is a matter of policy that the agency should be able to decide itself. The ALJ's discriminatory-enforcement decision is entitled to no deference from the agency. Although a court should take it into account on judicial review, it is purely an issue of policy, and the agency should be free to reverse it.

At this point, there is no ripeness problem since a final order has been issued. The discriminatory enforcement issue is ripe since a cease and desist order has been issued. The analysis in Part B should be applied to the claim.

There is also a question of standing. Do the other soft drink manufacturers or the caffeine producers have standing? It seems clear that the drink makers do have standing in that they are likely to be subjected to an order to change their product in the very near future. They are directly regulated, so the zone of interests is not an issue. The caffeine makers are injured directly by the agency action since the market for their product will shrink (and has already shrunk), but there is a zone of interests question since nothing in the FDA Act is concerned with the interests of ingredient makers. Further, they would be asserting the rights of third parties (the drink manufacturers) who are perfectly able to assert their own rights. Finally, their presence does not really add anything to the case. I would be inclined to allow them to have standing because it does not really hurt anything. They are clearly injured, but a strict court might deny them standing on the ground that they are asserting third party rights and are not within the zone of interests of the law in question.

The main question here is whether it is proper for the commissioner to include what looks like a rule about caffeine in his decision in the case about Jake. He says he will seek large fines in the future even though he has not fined Jake at all. Some members of the Court have thought this is fine since prospective rules are part of the judicial process. Others think it is fine because future subjects will be fined only after a hearing. The dissenters thought that if an agency wants to make a general rule, it should have to use the rulemaking procedure of the APA. In my view, the commissioner will be upheld. The rule announced here is about the particular additive caffeine. The FDA proceeds largely through enforcement actions. It seems appropriate, under *Bell Aerospace*, for it to decide case-by-case which additives will be treated as drugs. As long as future subjects are given hearings, I see nothing wrong with, announcing a strong precedent in the course of an adjudication. Here, a retroactive rule would be worse than the prospective one, since the agency is at least warning people before it issues fines.

The question remains, however, whether the commissioner can announce this rule in an opinion and then rely on it in later prosecutions for levying fines. Here, if the commissioner does not explicitly state "I am assessing a large fine because the Jake Cola rule has been violated," there is not much of a problem. The commissioner should state that the fine is because of the violation found at the hearing. The commissioner will probably argue that he did not issue any rule in Jake Cola, he just stated what he intended to do in future cases. Those cases would still be decided on their own merits, and the violation would be for putting a drug in food, not for violating any aspect of the Jake Cola opinion.

The clients might argue that the Commissioner is biased or has prejudged the law in these cases and should not be allowed to sit on review of ALJ decisions. This argument sounds good, but it would basically destroy the system Congress has established for agency review of ALJ decisions. Agencies often announce rules and then sit as a reviewing tribunal. The agency is no more biased than a court that has announced a precedent and then has a later case on the same issue. Prejudgment raises the same issue. In order to win on this argument, there would have to be a showing that the commissioner is simply unwilling to even look at the evidence in the case. This looks more like the standard for prejudgment in a rulemaking. In effect, on policy decisions, the commissioner should be judged on the rulemaking standard to allow him to carry out the functions Congress has assigned. Just as some judges have clear views on issues, like the death penalty or separation of powers, the commissioner is free to express those views in cases as long as in subsequent cases the commissioner is willing to look at the evidence and weigh the arguments.

In sum, I do not see any basis for reversing the Commissioner or disqualifying him from hearing future cases.

SAMPLE ANSWER TO QUESTION 3

First, the standing of each group of potential plaintiffs should be addressed. The basic requirements for standing should be laid out, including injury traceable to the challenged conduct and redressability. Consumer groups have standing if members pay more for milk than under an alternative regulatory scheme they claim should replace the current scheme for milk pricing. Although many people share in the injury, because the price setting scheme probably increases the price of milk, consumer complaints should not fail based on the generalized grievance doctrine because the consumers of milk are suing over something that affects them directly based on particular market activity, not merely by virtue of being a member of society. There also should be a brief discussion of the requirements for associational standing. Wisconsin milk producers have standing because the system for setting milk prices affects them directly in that it prescribes the price they are paid for their product. Even if deregulation might ultimately hurt them if prices moved lower, they are now not able to compete for business based on price and that restriction is.enough of an injury for standing. Food producers in areas distant from Eau Claire are injured because they pay more for milk than producers closer to Eau Claire which in turn hurts their ability to compete with food producers near Eau Claire. Thus, it appears that all the potential plaintiffs are injured sufficient for standing.

On the merits, this question raises a very interesting issue: If an agency takes an action, and that action has been upheld on judicial review, can changed circumstances render that action arbitrary and capricious or lacking in substantial evidence so that a challenge years after the action was upheld on judicial review could prevail? It appears that the substantial evidence test might apply here if the Secretary held a formal hearing. If not, review could still be had under the arbitrary and capricious test. Since it is not clear whether there really is a difference between the two tests when reviewing policy decisions of the sort at issue here, the specific test will be mentioned only when it might make a difference.

One issue might be reviewability, since the statute says that the Secretary shall make changes "as the Secretary finds necessary." This looks like a deeming clause in that it appears to vest substantial discretion in the Secretary. However, this type of phrasing is not sufficient to overcome the presumption in favor of judicial review. From what the facts indicate, action under this program has been subjected to judicial review since at least 1935. The same phrase also says that under certain circumstances the Secretary "shall" make adjustments to milk prices, indicating a legally enforceable obligation to do so. Further, there is no basis for holding this as unreviewable prosecutorial discretion since the statute states pretty clearly when the Secretary is required to act.

Turning to the merits, the challenge is really not to the failure to act for 60 years, but the latest action which the Secretary took, i.e., making minor adjustments to milk prices when the comments urged the Secretary to make substantial changes based on changed circumstances, which is exactly what the statute appears to tell the Secretary to do. Here, the question is whether, based on everything in the record, a reasonable person could have reached this conclusion (substantial evidence) or whether the Secretary considered the relevant factors, applied the correct legal standard, and made a clear error in judgment (arbitrary and capricious). It would be useful to have more information about what information exactly the record contains. Further, there may be a procedural problem since the Secretary did not address the major issue of the obsolescence of the pricing system in the concise general statement and did not make findings on the issues specified in the statute. While formal findings are not required, courts can insist on a reasoned explanation of major statutory and policy issues in the concise general statement without violating *Vermont Yankee's* prohibition on additional procedural requirements.

The fact that a court, in 1935, upheld this pricing system does not answer whether it is error for the Secretary to issue an order maintaining the 1935 system in light of today's circumstances. While a court might be reluctant to hold that an agency must revise regulations periodically to adjust for changing conditions, here the statute itself, and thus Congress, requires revision, so the 1935 decision should not really matter.

The final issue is ex parte contacts. Although the facts are not very specific, it appears that there was a great deal of lobbying going on from both sides. Some courts have held that ex parte contacts should not occur. If this was a formal adjudicatory hearing or a formal rulemaking, the ex parte contacts would present a reason under the APA to send the matter back to the agency for a new decision. Ex parte contacts are forbidden in such proceedings. If this was informal rulemaking, nothing in the APA prohibits ex parte contacts. Some courts have prohibited them, especially when the rulemaking resolves a competing claim to a valuable privilege, but this may violate *Vermont Yankee* by imposing a procedural requirement not contained in the APA. The court could say that it is merely enforcing §553 by giving everyone an equal, adequate opportunity to participate in the rulemaking, but it is unclear whether the Supreme Court would accept this. More in keeping with *Vermont Yankee*, agencies in informal rulemaking can probably receive ex parte contacts but should place any important information on the record. As long as there is no suggestion that ex parte contacts involved irrelevant factors such as funding of other agency projects, etc., a system that allows ex parte contacts in rulemaking is probably better than one that attempts to prohibit them.

As a last comment, it should be noted that the agency might have run into trouble had it decided in this proceeding to radically alter the milk pricing system. It is not altogether clear that the interests in favor of preserving the system were aware that this was a possibility raised by some of the comments. Perhaps they were since they did support their interests in ex parte contacts. But the notice did not raise the possibility, and if an agency wants to make a substantial change to longstanding practice, it should probably provide better notice than it did in this case, so that any change will not materially alter the proposal, or not be a logical outgrowth of the proposal. Otherwise, interested parties might not realize that they should comment to protect their interests.

SAMPLE ANSWER TO QUESTION 4

The two biggest issues in this problem are notice and presidential power to order an agency to suspend a regulation and do cost-benefit analysis.

The main notice problem is that the notice of proposed rulemaking did not mention the possibility that the agency would require reformulated gasoline. The only possibilities actually mentioned were vapor recovery devices on gasoline pumps or in cars. The oil companies will argue they did not have sufficient notice. They will stress the purposes of the notice requirement (giving parties a meaningful opportunity to comment and ensuring the agency receives useful information) and argue that neither of these purposes were served since the oil companies had no idea that reformulation of gasoline was being considered.

In my view, these notice arguments should fail for several reasons. First, the agency was careful to say that it was considering many options, not limited to the ones mentioned. The oil companies should have realized their product might be affected since it was their product that was causing the environmental problem. Second, the agency complied with the terms of the APA, §553. Section 553 requires notice of the terms of the proposed rule *or* the subjects or issues involved. The notice definitely included the subjects or issues involved in the rulemaking. After *Vermont Yankee*, courts should not add to APA procedural requirements, and since the agency complied with §553, there should be no notice issue. Third, basing the argument on the "opportunity to comment" should not help turn a bad notice argument into one based more firmly on the terms of §553. All notice problems affect the opportunity to comment, and as long as the notice meets the notice requirements of §553, a court should not use a different provision to void the rulemaking.

The EPA may argue that based on the language of the statute, the decision of how much to regulate is committed to agency discretion by law. The statute looks like a "deeming clause" in that it says that the EPA should issue regulations that "it *finds* to be reasonably necessary." While in some contexts this might indicate intent to vest the agency with unreviewable discretion, this kind of language is used all the time and is not sufficient to overcome the presumption in favor of judicial review. The statute is a typical regulatory statute and gives plenty of guidance to facilitate judicial review.

There also is a ripeness issue here because the companies want to challenge a rule before it has been enforced against them. They need to meet the fitness and hardship test to get judicial review before agency enforcement. Here, there probably is hardship. Whatever it costs to reformulate, including potential costs to modify refineries and do all the research and testing to make the new gasoline work properly, cause plenty of hardship. The issue also may be fit for judicial review because there are really no individualized issues, just the question whether the agency had a sufficient basis to require the reformulation based on the facts in the record and also whether the agency observed all required procedures. It is not a purely legal issue like *Abbott Laboratories* but the decision does not vary from company to company based on the situation, so the rule is fit for review at this time.

The second set of issues concerns the President's order suspending the regulation and requiring EPA to reconsider in light of the costs of the regulation. I want to clear away one issue I think is a red herring first, that of ex parte contacts. It could be argued that the oil companies did something wrong by approaching the

President outside the notice and comment process. I think any suggestion that this was improper should be rejected. In a democracy, contact with elected officials is to be expected and in fact valued. Nothing in the APA limits this type of contact, and it might even be unconstitutional to attempt to prevent the President from having contact with members of the public who are interested in a matter before an agency.

The President's order raises a whole set of interesting questions. First, there is the question of the President's inherent power to supervise the executive branch. EPA is an executive agency. The President has the power to fire the administrator of the EPA, and presumably if the President cannot convince an EPA administrator to delay the effective date of a regulation, the President could fire the person and appoint someone more responsive. If you believe the unitary executive theory, the fact that Congress delegated the authority directly to the EPA should not matter, because any effort to prevent presidential influence is unconstitutional. If you take a more moderate view, and hold that the President's power is merely to execute the laws as written by Congress, then you would be more troubled by presidential intervention into the EPA's work. Sure the President could fire the administrator, but he may not want to do so for a variety of reasons, and he should not be able to meddle in authority delegated to the administrator. If Congress has not specifically denied the President the power to suspend regulations, and also has not granted the power, the question falls into Justice Jackson's middle category and raises a difficult, uncertain question. This separation of powers issue is not governed directly by caselaw, so I am not able here to resolve it authoritatively, and leave open the question whether the President has this power.

Coming at the issue from another angle, the question may be whether it violates separation of powers for Congress to delegate power directly to the EPA and not allow the President to directly supervise the EPA's decisions. Unless you believe in the unitary executive theory, this question should be answered under general separation of powers standards which would ask whether the President's ability to carry out his constitutional role or function as an independent branch of government is threatened. Again, unless you believe in the unitary executive, insulation from direct presidential supervision should be upheld. The President has no interest in enforcing the law except as written by Congress, and this law grants the discretion to the EPA.

There is another serious problem with the President's order. The President ordered EPA to reassess its decision in light of the costs to the oil industry. The question is whether cost to the oil industry is a relevant factor that the agency should consider. (I am putting to one side the very uncertain issue of whether the President can order the agency to consider a factor that it would prefer not to consider but which may be within a permissible construction of the statute. That issue is subsumed in the discussion above.) The statute says "reasonably necessary to protect the human environment." The use of the words "reasonably necessary" has been held, in the OSH Act, not to require cost-benefit analysis, and the EPA may interpret this to consider environmental protection only, and not costs. If Congress did not intend for the agency to consider costs, then any rule considering them would be arbitrary and capricious for considering an irrelevant factor. The President does not have the power to amend a statute. If a court finds that Congress did not intend for costs to be considered, then the President would not have the power to order the agency to consider them.

There is an argument that the President should have the rather moderate power to order an agency to rethink a regulation in light of issues that the President finds important. Further, it can be argued that since the regulation had not yet gone into effect, it is not a big step for the President to ask for a delay. However, this ignores the fact that the agency had promulgated the requirement as a final rule. In the *Airbags* case, the Court held that an agency could not just throw out a final rule without good reason, and in that case the rule had not yet gone into effect. By analogy, this rule is entitled to all the respect afforded a rule that has actually gone into effect. The President cannot by fiat suspend the operation of a validly promulgated rule.

Finally, standing should be mentioned. The environmental groups would have to establish injury. They can probably do that just by alleging that some of their members breathe the air that is affected by gasoline vapors. The groups would have to meet the requirements for associational standing: Members must be injured, the claim must be related to the association's purpose, and participation of individuals must be unnecessary to resolution of the case. These factors are likely to be present here.

In sum, the EPA probably gave sufficient notice, and the President's order raises serious questions regarding presidential power to supervise agencies.

Short-Answer Exam Questions

1. **True or false with explanation:** The Line Item Veto Act would have been constitutional had it been incorporated by explicit reference into subsequent appropriations and tax relief bills, but only with regard to the appropriations and limited tax benefits contained in those particular bills. _____

2. **True or false with explanation:** After *Heckler v. Chaney*, a federal court should never delay the enforcement of an otherwise valid order on the ground that a similar order should be issued against another regulated party. _____

3. **True or false with explanation:** A preexpulsion hearing is not required to expel a student from a state university for academic deficiency. _____

4. **True or false with explanation:** As long as an official performs quasi-legislative or quasi-judicial functions, Congress may participate in the appointment of that official and it may restrict the President's removal of that official. _____

5. What are the different meanings of "committed to agency discretion by law"? What evidence should a court look for to determine whether a matter is "committed to agency discretion by law"? _____

6. Does a grocery store owner have standing to challenge the legality of the cutoff of food stamps to her customers? Would your answer change if you learned that an interest group representing shopkeepers lobbied heavily for passage of the food stamp statute and that the legislative history mentions the preservation of food stores in low-income neighborhoods as a positive "side effect" of the food stamp program? _____

7. Assume that the ALJs that decide claims for welfare under the program at issue in *Goldberg v. Kelly* work for the state welfare agency and are subject to yearly performance reviews that the agency head uses to award merit pay raises and promotions. Further, ALJs are subject to discipline by the agency head and may be fired "for good cause including malfeasance in office and neglect of duty." Does this arrangement violate the procedural rights of a welfare recipient in a hearing to terminate benefits? _____

8. Could Congress delegate the authority to establish income tax rates to the Secretary of the Treasury? _____

Short-Answer Exam Answers

1. **True.** The problem with the Line Item Veto Act in *Clinton v. NY* was that the President exercised the line item veto after signing the bill. Signing the bill enacts the entire bill into law. By exercising the line item veto power, the President would be amending or repealing a law that was already in effect, which can only be done through the Constitution's procedure for passing a bill, i.e., bicameralism and presentment. In *Clinton v. NY*, 523 U.S. 1058 (1998), the Court stressed that the Constitution preempts the field; Congress cannot alter constitutionally required procedures. The Constitution does not give the President (whether he signs the bill first or not) the right to participate in the legislative process and make decisions regarding the substance of bills except through the veto power.

   If, however, the procedures in the Act were included in each appropriations or tax relief bill through incorporation by reference, the constitutional objections may be satisfied. In effect, each bill would provide that the President can elect to cancel certain provisions, and the cancellation power would be part of the law (similar to delegated authority regarding tariffs that the Supreme Court upheld long ago). If the bill itself allows the President to knock but spending and tax benefits, perhaps the President would not be amending or repealing the law by exercising the power but, rather, would be exercising the discretion granted in the bill. If the Act is written into the bill itself, then there is never a problem of the President changing the bill. The only question remaining would be whether a nondelegation doctrine problem exists, and the deficit reduction, without harming the national interest goals of the Act, would provide an intelligible principle.

2. **False.** *Heckler* says that there is a presumption against reviewing agency refusals to take enforcement action against a third party. In claims of discriminatory enforcement, the target of enforcement is arguing for a stay of an order against it until similar orders are issued against others engaging in similar behavior—not for an order requiring the agency to prosecute someone else. The *Moog* case held that, in claims of discriminatory enforcement, an agency's discretionary determination to issue an order against one party, without prosecuting competitors, should not be overturned in the absence of a patent abuse of discretion. While this is a very deferential standard, it is still theoretically possible for an agency order to be delayed.

   Heckler does, however, indicate that courts should be reluctant to issue anything that looks like an order for an agency to prosecute. Thus, the argument can be made that after *Heckler*, the enforcement decision is entirely within the agency's discretion, and thus is immune from judicial review. However, in order to find the statement true, one must take a very broad view of *Heckler v. Chaney*. On its face, *Heckler* does not say anything about nonenforcement of an order against a party.

   Further, the "never" in the statement is not true even if one takes the broad view of *Heckler*, because the presumption against review is rebuttable. The court stated that the presumption may be rebutted when the substantive statute has provided guidelines for the agency to follow in exercising its enforcement powers. In *Dunlop v. Bachowski*, the court was willing to review an enforcement decision (although the review was *very* deferential) because the statute used clear language and perhaps set out standards for the exercise of the enforcement power. Therefore, even on a broad view, it does not appear that *Heckler v. Chaney* forbids courts from reviewing *any* agency decision related to enforcement, and it should not absolutely bar federal courts from delaying an order based on a valid discriminatory enforcement claim.

3. **True.**   Determining whether due process requires a preexpulsion hearing involves a two-step inquiry. First, there must be an entitlement that creates a life, liberty, or property interest. If such an interest exists, it is then necessary to determine how much process is due.

In evaluating whether a student has a property interest in remaining at a state university, the question is whether any positive law (*Roth*) or assurances and practices (*Perry*) create an entitlement to the state education. It is very likely that students are evaluated on a specific set of criteria, such as a grade point average. Even if the test is more subjective, like "adequate academic performance," there is an entitlement. Due process would be required before a student could finally be expelled. Contrast a situation in which the school can expel students at will—in which case there would be no entitlement. Once an entitlement is established, the next question is how much process is due in order to determine whether the criteria are met. It is very important to separate the substance from the procedure. In other words, generally the criteria set up an entitlement and a hearing is meant. Thus, in the case of a state law requiring good cause to fire an employee, a state teacher who was assaulting students would still be entitled to a hearing. The performance is relevant to the outcome, but even if the teacher would lose, the entitlement still exists.

However, despite the need to separate the entitlement from the process, due process does not always require *full* process like an adjudicatory hearing before action can be taken. Typically, the determination of what process is due requires a balancing of the three factors set out in *Mathews v. Eldridge*. Here the private interest is important but not as important as the welfare rights in *Goldberg* or perhaps even the disability benefits in *Mathews*. Accuracy is an important issue. If the criteria for expulsion are clear, like a particular grade point average (GPA), then it can be argued that a hearing before expulsion would add very little in terms of accuracy, since the GPA can be determined from the student's academic paper record. The government may not have a very strong interest in removing students immediately when the issue is academic deficiency, but if the criteria are objective, there is no need for a preexpulsion hearing. If the criteria are more subjective, then the student has a stronger claim that expulsion should not occur without the student being allowed to present his or her own side of the story to try to persuade the decisionmakers that he or she is qualified to remain in school.

4. **False.**   While Congress can appoint purely legislative officials, any official that exercises significant authority pursuant to the laws of the United States is an "officer of the United States" and must be appointed according to the Appointments Clause of the Constitution. Principal officers must be appointed by the President, and Congress can vest the appointment of inferior officers in the President, courts of law, or heads of departments. Congress may not ever participate in the appointment of an officer of the United States except through the Senate's confirmation power. While at one time it appeared that the Court accepted the view that an official exercising legislative rulemaking power was an agent of Congress and not of the executive branch, today it is clear that any official exercising legal authority must be appointed pursuant to the Appointments Clause.

Congress can restrict the President's removal of an official if, by doing so, it would not interfere with the President's exercise of the executive power and his constitutionally appointed duty to take care that the laws are faithfully executed. After *Morrison v. Olson*, Congress has broader power to restrict presidential removal powers. If the removal restrictions do not violate general separation of powers norms (and do not expressly violate the Constitution), they are permissible. The old rule in *Humphrey's Executor* and *Myers* may have been that Congress may restrict removal only when the official exercises quasi-legislative or quasi-judicial functions and not when the official was purely executive. However, *Morrison* abolished these rigid distinctions. The question is whether the removal restriction impermissibly interfere with the President's authority and duty.

5. The original meaning is that a statute is so vaguely drafted that there is no law to apply to judge whether the agency has violated the statute. In more recent cases the court has also found an action to be committed to agency discretion by law when the action is in a category traditionally not subject to judicial review. This was a reason given in *Lincoln v. Vigil* for not subjecting the allocation of funds from a lump-sum appropriation to judicial review. Finally, the Court has looked at the language of enabling acts to determine whether the statute appears to assign final, unreviewable discretion to the agency without mentioning judicial review. The Court focused on Congress's use of the word "deem" in the statute granting the director of the CIA power to fire employees to support its conclusion that firing CIA employees is committed to agency discretion by law. These statutory provisions can be called "deeming clauses." The last two meanings appear to be newly created since there is no authority or legislative history to support them before *Webster v. Doe.*

6. Without the second part of the question, it is unlikely that the store owner would have standing to challenge the cutoff. First, the store owner would probably not be within the zone of interests, since Congress's concern would be feeding needy people, not supporting stores. (The fact that the food stamp program is administered by the Department of Agriculture and benefits farmers by keeping a strong market for food products undercuts this argument.) Second, although the shopkeeper may be injured by the cutoff, if it could be shown that sales went down, the shopkeeper would be asserting the rights of third parties, i.e., the food stamp recipients. Presumably, those people would be able to assert their own rights to the food stamps.

    If it were shown that Congress was concerned with food stores when it passed the food stamp program, the zone of interests test might not be a problem. However, the food stamp owners would still be asserting the rights of third parties. The legislative history might make a court more receptive to arguments that the recipients may not assert their own rights, perhaps because finding a lawyer for such small claims might be difficult or because they are very poor and might not understand their rights. The third-party rights issue would not be as serious if the store owner raised a general challenge to the operation of the program as opposed to particular reasons why certain people should continue receiving benefits.

7. This raises the general question of whether an adjudicatory decisionmaker must be completely insulated from agency control. The welfare benefits were considered property in *Goldberg* because the terms of the program created an entitlement to the benefits. Because the benefits are property, recipients must be afforded due process before their benefits can be denied or terminated. One basic due process right is the right to a neutral decisionmaker. Here there is no suggestion of prejudgment. The question boils down to whether a decisionmaker must be considered biased if he or she is subject to the type of agency control here—merit pay, removal for cause, and discipline by the agency head. Nothing in the question suggests that the agency has targeted ALJs based on their decisionmaking record, i.e., based on how often they grant or deny benefits. If it were shown that the agency was giving raises for more denials or punishing ALJs for too many grants of benefits, that would present bias due to a pecuniary interest in the outcome of the cases. If the pattern of discipline and pay raises is based on other factors, such as numbers of cases resolved and numbers of reversals in both directions, then there may not be a problem. In general, the Supreme Court has allowed agencies to combine functions as long as there is not specific evidence of bias. Of course, the agency could not violate any of the particular protections of the APA, such as ex parte contacts or direct supervision of the ALJ by the official presenting the agency's case, but the presence of those particular safeguards actually strengthens the argument that the general structure here does not automatically violate due process.

8. This presents an issue of the nondelegation doctrine. While at first glance it may appear that an agency should not be able to establish something as important as the rates of taxation, as long as the intelligible principle standard is met the Constitution should allow this delegation.

The history of delegations indicates that taxing powers have often been delegated. For example, presidential power over tariffs on imported goods has long been held proper, and such tariffs were the most important source of income for the federal government before the Constitution was amended to allow the income tax. The Court would require that Congress make the basic decision about the form of taxation and guide the Secretary's discretion with an intelligible principle. While it may be argued that the nondelegation doctrine should be more strict when it comes to something as important as establishing income tax rates, the Court has not been receptive to arguments that in particular areas the doctrine should be stricter. For example, the Court held that a heightened standard did not apply to the power delegated to the Attorney General to add substances to the list of controlled substances, which in effect created new categories of crimes.

GLOSSARY

adjudication: The process an agency uses to formulate an order. Adjudication focuses on a particular party or parties and involves facts specific to the parties involved.

adjudicative facts: The type of facts that should be decided in an adjudicatory process, such as historical facts about the parties or facts about the situation of the parties.

administrative law: The field of law concerning the procedures that govern agency action and judicial controls on agency action, including constitutional limits on agency action.

Administrative Procedure Act (APA): The statute passed by Congress in 1948 and amended several times since, which governs agency procedure and judicial review of agency action.

Appointments Clause: The clause of the Constitution that governs the process of appointing officers of the United States.

arbitrary and capricious test: The catchall, most deferential APA standard of judicial review of agency action. Agency action is arbitrary and capricious if the agency fails to consider relevant factors, misconstrues its statutory authority, or makes a clear error of judgment.

Article III court: A court staffed by judges appointed under the provisions of Article III of the Constitution; the judges have life tenure and protected compensation.

bias: A predisposition to decide a matter in a particular way, most often due to pecuniary interest in the outcome or a relationship with a party. To be distinguished from prejudgment.

bicameralism: The requirement of the Constitution that legislation be passed by both the Senate and the House of Representatives.

Bivens action: The damages action against federal of ficials for violations of constitutional rights created by the Supreme Court in the _Bivens_ case.

Chevron doctrine: The doctrine under which federal courts defer to agency statutory constructions unless Congress has directly spoken to the legal issue before the agency.

citizens' suit: A cause of action granted in many recent regulatory statutes in which citizens may sue violators for violations and government for failure to perform a nondiscretionary duty under the statute.

civil service: The system that protects the job security of most government employees. _See also_ patronage.

committed to agency discretion by law: An exemption from reviewability under the APA. Agency action that is committed to agency discretion by law is unreviewable.

comptroller general: An official who works primarily for Congress preparing reports on government action and legislative initiatives. Congress has attempted to grant executive powers to the comptroller general, but these efforts have been held unconstitutional because the comptroller general is subject to removal by Congress.

concise general statement of basis and purpose: The explanation required by APA §553 when an agency promulgates a rule.

conflict preemption: Federal preemption of state law when state law conflicts with federal law.

cost-benefit analysis: Analysis under which agency action is evaluated based upon whether the benefits of agency action outweigh its costs.

de novo review: Review of agency action without deference to the agency. De novo review of facts involves a new trial of the factual issues.

department of government: The departments of the federal government are the largest entities in the executive branch, including the Departments of Defense, Transportation, Justice, and Energy. Departments are headed by cabinet secretaries, except for the Department of Justice, which is headed by the Attorney General.

direct final rulemaking: A rulemaking procedure under which an agency promulgates a final rule without a comment period but promises to withdraw the rule and hold a comment period if adverse comments are received.

due process: The basic constitutional requirement that government action affecting life, liberty; and property be taken with sufficient procedural protections. How much process is due is often decided by applying the _Mathews v. Eldridge_ balancing test.

239

Eleventh Amendment immunity: The immunity that protects unconsenting states from damages awards in federal court.

employee: a low-level official who is employed by the federal government but exercises no discretion or authority to administer federal law and is therefore neither a principal nor inferior officer.

entitlement: An entitlement to a government benefit, job, or license exists if the government's discretion is constrained by criteria under which the government must act. Property interests and some liberty interests exist only if there is an entitlement.

environmental impact statement (EIS): A statement required by NEPA detailing the environmental effects of a proposed government action.

Environmental Protection Agency (EPA): The agency in the federal government with responsibility for environmental protection. The EPA is not within any department, but its administrator is a member of the cabinet.

ex parte contacts: Contacts with a decisionmaker outside of the normal procedural framework and outside the presence of opposing parties. These are strictly forbidden in adjudication but are less clearly a problem in rulemaking.

Executive Branch agency: An agency within the Executive Branch, as contrasted with independent agencies.

executive immunity or executive privilege: A constitutional privilege claimed by presidents to withhold sensitive information or documents from Congress and courts.

executive order: A formal order issued by the President usually directed at officials within the Executive Branch.

exhaustion: The requirement that parties exhaust their remedies within an agency before seeking judicial review.

externalities: Costs imposed on third parties. For example, the health and aesthetic effects of pollution are considered externalities produced by factories. Externalities are often cited as reasons for regulation.

Federal Advisory Committee Act (FACA): A statute that regulates committees that include private individuals and are established to advise the President.

Federal Tort Claims Act (FTCA): A statute waiving sovereign immunity and granting a cause of action against the federal government in certain tort cases.

field preemption: Preemption by federal law of state law when federal regulation is so pervasive that it completely occupies the field.

final agency action: Agency action that is complete; it is a prerequisite for judicial review under APA §702.

formal rulemaking: Rulemaking conducted pursuant to the formal adjudicatory procedures contained in APA §§556 and 557. Formal rulemaking is required only when an agency is required by statute to conduct rulemaking on the record after a statutorily required hearing.

Freedom of Information Act (FOIA): A federal statute, codified largely in APA §552, that requires agencies to make their records available to the public unless one of several exceptions applies.

general statement of policy: An agency rule that informs the public of the agency's view on a matter of policy without purporting to change the law or add legal obligations. *See also* legislative rule.

generalized grievance: A grievance against the government that is widely shared by members of the public and not felt particularly by a party. There is a prudential rule against allowing standing to sue when a party complains of a generalized grievance.

hybrid rulemaking: Rulemaking that adds adjudicatory procedures, such as cross-examination and discovery, to notice and comment rulemaking.

impact statement: A statement detailing the effects of proposed agency action. The most common impact statements are environmental impact statements and more general regulatory impact statements that describe the economic and social effects of proposed agency action.

impeachment: The procedure provided in the Constitution for removing federal government officials including the President, other executive officials, and judges. Impeachment refers specifically to the procedure in the House of Representatives for bringing charges; trial occurs in the Senate with conviction resulting in removal from office.

independent agency: An agency usually headed by one or more commissioners, designated by Congress as independent of the executive branch, and not within any department of government.

inferior officer: An officer of the United States who may, if Congress so provides, be appointed pursuant to the second part of the Appointments Clause, i.e., by the President alone, by a head of a department, or by a court of law. An officer is inferior if he or she is subordinate to executive branch officials who are subordinate to the President.

informal adjudication: Because the APA divides all agency action into rulemaking and adjudication, informal agency action (when no clear procedure is followed) is often referred to as informal adjudication. Courts may require only those procedures specified in APA §555 for informal adjudication.

informal agency action: Agency action, such as the approval of the highway design in the *Overton Park* case, taken without any particular procedure. *See also* informal adjudication.

informal rulemaking: Also referred to as "notice and comment rulemaking." Rulemaking conducted pursuant to the notice and comment procedures contained in APA §553.

intelligible principle: Congress must legislate an intelligible principle governing agency legislative discretion to avoid violating the nondelegation doctrine. The intelligible principle must embody the basic policy choice that governs agency action. *See also* nondelegation doctrine.

interpretative rule: A rule that interprets existing law such as statutes, regulations, or caselaw. Interpretative rules may be issued without notice and comment. *See also* legislative rule.

irrebuttable presumption: Hard and fast statutes or agency rules that do not allow a party to contest their application. The rule that limits the vote to persons eighteen years old, or older, creates an irrebuttable presumption that persons under eighteen lack the maturity to vote. Although such rules were once condemned as violating due process, they are now generally upheld if they make rational distinctions.

judicial review: When a court examines agency action for legal and factual error.

jurisdiction: The requirement that an adjudicatory body, such as a court, have the authority to resolve a particular kind of case. Congress, by statute, prescribes the jurisdiction of the federal courts, and petitions for judicial review may be brought only in a court having jurisdiction.

legislative facts: General facts or predictions concerning the situation of regulated parties and the likely effects of proposed agency action. To be distinguished from adjudicative facts.

legislative rule: A rule made by an agency that changes the law or adds or removes legal obligations. To be distinguished from nonlegislative rules such as interpretative rules and general statements of policy.

legislative veto: A power Congress has reserved in numerous regulatory statutes to veto agency action including regulations and adjudicatory results. A one-house legislative veto was struck down in the *Chadha* case as violating bicameralism and presentment. Two-house vetoes violate presentment alone.

liberty: The constitutional interest in freedom and bodily integrity protected in both Due Process Clauses of the Constitution. Some liberty interests are constitutionally created while others are created by entitlements. *See also* entitlement.

licensing: A form of regulation under which persons wishing to engage in a regulated profession or operate a regulated business must meet certain requirements and obtain a license from the government.

line item veto: The power of the executive to reject particular items in legislation without vetoing the entire bill. While many state governors have this power, the Line Item Veto Act, which granted this power to the President, was held unconstitutional by the Supreme Court as violating the procedures for amending laws.

***Mathews v. Eldridge* balancing test:** The test under which courts decide whether agency procedures meet due process standards. Under the test, the court balances the importance of the interest to the claimant, the accuracy-enhancing value of additional procedure, and the government's interest in proceeding without additional procedures.

241

doctrine specifying when it is too late
nge government action, either because
cy action is over or because the plain-
o longer subject to the agency's action.
Environmental Policy Act (NEPA): A
al statute requiring the preparation of an
environmental impact statement detailing the
environmental effects of major federal action.

National Highway Transportation Safety Administration (NHTSA): The agency that regulates highway safety and the safety of cars, trucks, and buses, including such requirements as safety belts and air bags.

negotiated rulemaking: A process for arriving at rulemaking proposals in which the agency conducts formal negotiation sessions with affected parties. After the negotiation process, the proposed rule is subject to normal rulemaking procedures.

new property: Property interests created by entitlements to things such as government benefits, government employment, and occupational licenses. Called "new property" to distinguish it from traditional real and personal property. *See also* entitlement.

nondelegation doctrine: The prohibition against Congress delegating its legislative power to an agency, the President, or a private group. Congress may grant discretion to the executive branch to make legislative rules as long as Congress, by statute, supplies an intelligible principle guiding the exercise of delegated discretion.

notice: The notification that §553 requires before an agency may promulgate a legislative rule. The final rule must be a logical outgrowth of the notice so that interested parties will be on notice that their interests are at stake. Notice is also a basic due process requirement; parties to an adjudication must receive adequate notice of the time and location of the hearing and the issues involved in the hearing.

obstacle preemption: Federal preemption of state law when state law is an obstacle to the accomplishment of the goals of the federal law.

Occupational Safety and Health Administration (OSHA): The federal agency that regulates the health and safety of workers in the workplace.

officer: *See* officer of the United States.

officer of the United States: An official exercising authority pursuant to the laws of the United States. Officers of the United States must be appointed in a method provided for in the Appointments Clause of the Constitution.

official immunity: The immunities that federal and state officials are granted in suits alleging constitutional damages. Officials performing legislative, judicial, and prosecutorial functions are absolutely immune from damages awards, while other officials have a qualified immunity under which they are liable only if they violate a clearly established constitutional right.

patronage: A system for hiring government workers in which elected officials reward political supporters with jobs. While the patronage system was once prevalent in the federal government, today most employees are hired under the civil service system, and they are protected against losing their jobs for political reasons by civil service rules and the First Amendment.

petition for judicial review: The name for the cause of action brought to challenge agency action. *See also* judicial review.

preclusion of review: The effect of a statute that provides that a particular agency action shall not be subject to judicial review. If a statute specifies that review may be had only in a particular fashion, that statute may preclude other forms of judicial review.

preemption: When federal law displaces or overrules state law. The Supremacy Clause grants the federal government the power to preempt state law.

prejudgment: When an agency official, through public or private statements, appears to have decided a matter prior to hearing it. To be distinguished from bias.

presentment: The constitutional requirement that legislation be presented to the President for his signature or, if he chooses, his veto.

primary jurisdiction: The doctrine under which matters within an agency's jurisdiction must be brought to the agency before they may be the subject of an action in court.

principal or superior officer: Those officers of the United States who must be appointed by the President with the advice and consent of the Senate. These are the highest-level officials in the executive branch.

private right of action: A cause of action in which a party is sued for violating a regulatory statute that explicitly provides only for government enforcement.

private rights: Rights that one private party has against another private party. To be distinguished from public rights. There are serious constitutional questions regarding agency adjudication of private rights.

probable cause: The amount of suspicion normally needed for an arrest or an intrusive search, such as a search of a private home. Probable cause is normally not necessary for regulatory inspections.

property: The interest in ownership of real and personal assets that is protected from government deprivation by both Due Process Clauses and also against uncompensated takings by the Takings Clause. Property interests are created by state law, including property interests in new property created by entitlement theory. *See also* new property; entitlement.

prosecutorial discretion: Broadly refers to the discretion that agencies have in choosing general areas of enforcement and particular enforcement targets.

prudential limitations: Judicially created standing limitations that restrict standing even more than the basic constitutional requirements for standing. Congress may legislatively overrule the prudential limitations.

public choice theory of regulation: A theory that explains regulation by looking at political realities such as which groups have the economic incentive and ability to organize and how such groups use economic and political power to influence legislators and agencies in order to provide them with regulatory benefits.

public goods: Goods or services that, when they are produced, cannot be limited to those who voluntarily pay for their production. A common example is national defense. The fact that something is a public good is a justification for coercing payment through taxes or fees.

public interest theory of regulation: A theory that explains regulation as necessary in order to combat problems (like externalities and market inequalities) or as necessary to ensure production of goods or services that might otherwise be underproduced (such as public goods or utilities that need monopoly protection to be financially viable).

public rights: Rights that private parties have against the government. Agency adjudication of public rights presents few constitutional problems.

quasi-judicial power: Agency adjudicatory power. Agency exercise of judicial power was defended as an adjunct to the judicial power of Article III courts as long as it was subject to judicial review.

quasi-legislative power: Agency legislative power. Agency exercise of legislative power was defended as an exercise of legislative power by the agency on behalf of Congress. This was thought to necessitate insulation from presidential influence.

ratemaking: A form of regulation in which an agency, often in formal hearings, establishes permissible prices for a good or service.

record: The material before the agency when it makes a decision. On judicial review, courts review the record.

redressability: A constitutional standing requirement under which the plaintiff must show that he or she stands to benefit from a favorable ruling in court. Normally, this requirement applies to injunctions when there is a question as to whether an injunction could actually eliminate the harm alleged by the plaintiff.

remand: Sending a matter back to a body that made an earlier decision. Courts, on judicial review, often remand matters to agencies for further proceedings or a better explanation.

reviewability: The doctrine that regulates which agency actions are subject to judicial review.

ripeness: The requirement that a party not seek judicial review too early, i.e., before an agency's action is final or before the issues are sufficiently developed to facilitate judicial review. A common ripeness question is whether review is available when a rule is promulgated or whether review should occur only after the rule has been applied to a regulated party.

rulemaking: The process for making a rule.

separation of powers: The general name for the group of constitutional principles that regulates the distribution of powers among the three branches of government.

_____ clause: A common statutory provision _____ that if part of a statute is held uncon_____ al, Congress intends that the remainder _____ statute continue in effect and if a parti_____ application of a statute is held unconsti_____ al, other applications of the statute are not affected.

sovereign immunity: Government's immunity for damages in court. Both the federal government and state governments enjoy sovereign immunity. The immunity may be waived.

standing: The requirement that a party be among those affected by government action in order to challenge it. The basic constitutional requirement for standing is an injury caused by the challenged conduct that is redressable by a favorable ruling. There are also prudential standing requirements under which a party must be within the zone of interests of the regulatory program, must not assert a third party's rights, and must have more than a generalized grievance.

substantial evidence test: The standard of judicial review that, under APA §706, governs the review of formal adjudication and formal rulemaking. The substantial evidence test requires that agency action be supported by enough evidence that a reasonable person could agree with the agency's decision, considering the evidence both in favor of and against the agency's decision.

Sunshine Act: The statute requiring that agency meetings be open to the public.

tariff: A rate schedule filed with a government agency pursuant to some regulatory schemes.

unfunded mandate: A regulatory requirement imposed by a governmental unit on a lower governmental unit without providing the funds to comply with the requirement.

unitary executive theory: A separation of powers theory under which the first clause of Article II, Section 1 of the Constitution, vesting the executive power in the President, is read to grant the President unlimited constitutional authority to supervise all the activity of the executive branch. Under this theory, all congressional efforts to insulate agencies from presidential control are unconstitutional.

warrant: The paper signifying that a judge has approved a search, seizure, or arrest. In cases of regulatory inspections, warrants are often not required. When they are, they are issued under a lower standard than warrants in the criminal justice system.

zone of interests test: A standing doctrine that applies when a party challenges the government's treatment of someone else (for example, when a party alleges that an agency has been too lenient with a competitor). For the party to have standing, the party's interests must have been considered when Congress constructed the regulatory program.

Table of Cases

Table of Statutes

Index